TARDIS Eruditorum: An Unofficial Critical History of Doctor Who
Volume I: William Hartnell
Second Edition

Elizabeth Sandifer

ERUDITORUM

P R E S S

To Gary Crowley, who randomly bought me a Doctor Who book for my birthday over twenty years ago and ended up causing this entire mess.

Acknowledgments

Shall we do the big block first or last? Last, I think. So first, thanks as ever to Millie Hadziomerovic for her phenomenal work copyediting this book. Thanks also to James Taylor for the cover art. Further thanks to Jill Buratto for putting up with me, and for the community around my blog for, quite inexplicably, seeming to enjoy putting up with me.

Right. Now for the list. This book's production was financed by an appallingly generous Kickstarter campaign. So thank you to all of my backers, presented here in a functionally random order based on the order Kickstarter gives me your names when I browse through it. If I've typoed your name, I apologize profusely – please send me a message on Kickstarter and I'll give you a free copy of something or other.

Thank you very much Tom Dickinson, Jaimie Tarquin Denholm, Huw Buchtmann, Joel Lim, Nicholas Caldwell, James Moss, Matthew Michael, Daniel New, Sean Daugherty, Tim Arding, Chris Combs, James Pearson, Kit Power, Tom Charman, Josh Bernhard, Michel F., "none, anonymous, or however," Will Knott, John Mazzeo, Alan Beirne, Austin "Born between episodes 4 and 5 of *The Silurians*" Loomis, Daniel C Pawlak III, Nancy Novak, Glenn W. Butler, JJ Gauthier, Rob Edwards, Michael Beasley, William McCormick, John G. Wood, Kyle Borcz, Edgardo, Nightsky,

Rachel K. Zall, Andrew Perron, David Dovey, Wm Keith, David Boyer, Phil Vance, L. Ross Raszewski, Simon Booth, David Moreau, Andrew Hickey, Sacha McCormick, Paul Brown, Kevin Jackson, Judith Jackson, Tiffany Korta, Alex, DocGerbil100, Max D, Lee Wells, Daniel Rigby, Dan Abel, A G Dunn, Sean Gaffney, Alexander T. Brown, drjon, Richard Ingram, David Headman, Thomas Hartwell, Ben Knaak, Neil Campbell, Tom Ewing, Jamie Dixon, Aaron Fok, Jacob Wagner, Brian Jacob, Triston Alfaro, Neil Bradbury, Noab "bibulb" Ramon, Ray, Sean Williams, David Ashton, Nick Smale, Nick Lawton – Icewarrior67, Anton Binder, Ken Finlayson, Ozymandias Jones, Will Frazier, Paul Matthew Carr, Steven Moy, Matt Fasham, Nick Bousfield, Jennifer D. Miller, Josiah Rowe, Jonathan L Switzer, Matt Badham, Korshi Dosoo, Patrick Ashforth, Ben Stephens, Michael E. Brown, Richard Walley, Michael Nightingale, Keith Grose, Assad Khaishgi, Jeroen te Strake, Cormac Linde, Jacqui Vriens, Abigail Brady, Dave Stevens, Thomas Keyton, Craig W Lowe, Michael Clark, John Wirenius, Luke Galiazzo, Neil Perryman, Richard Marklew, Michael Leitch, Girvan Burnside, Tim Barnett, David Brain, Sean Cunningham, Wesley Osam, Bob Dillon, John Boettcher, Simon Tolhurst, Anthony D. Perrin, Charles P. Rhoads, S Stevenson, "No need to, you generally thank me anyway," Gary Norton, Allyn Gibson, Patrick Henry Downs, Ray Cole, Andrew D. Simchik, Matthew Searle, Christopher and Shannon Shea, B. Coulstock, Phil Shaw, Peter Tye, Christopher Moore, David Allen, Jerry Snook, William Whyte, Jeremy M. Davies, Jessica Sterling, Neil Scotchmer, Michael Scholtes, Tymothi Loving, David Ainsworth, Brandon Davis-Shannon, Joshua Tasker, James Felder, 5tephe Brewer, Sarah Geerling, Nicholas Whyte, Anonymous Supporter, Patrick Doublethreat Magee, Alasdair Pearce, Chris Ratcliff, Tom Stoodley, Sabrina Purswani, J.D. Dresner, Kevin Clark, Josh Marsfelder, Darren Kramble, Ken Patterson, n/a, Eric Gimlin, Natalie Sydoriak, Adam Riggio, Matt Smith (No, not that one), Rich, Danika Myers, Toby Brown, G.S. Case, Stuart W, Jon Gad, Gordon

Barr, Andrew McLean, Dan Tessier, Nathan Bottomley, Matt Murtagh, Mark Hunter, Rob Newman, Adrian McClure, To be honest, for weird personal reasons I'd rather you didn't. Is that OK?, Karen Ellis, Geoff Bailie, Johanna, Dave Simmons, Joel Phillips, Yonatan Shamgar Bryant, Kyle Strand, Kevin Stafford, Steve Downey, Typhon, Ahania, charles yoakum, Grace Natusch, Ian McDuffie, Andrew Morgan, Paul M. Cray, Thomas Hansen, David R Keely, Brandon Schaefer, Andrew Batty, Nathan Bennett, Andrew Petch, Christopher Schaeffer, Dave Wyman, J Lewallen, Chris Kamp, Robert Rahl, Jasmin Babaie, Yeshe-Phillip Carbo, Gregory A. Wilson, Alex Wilcock, Kyle R. Maddex, Harry Doddema, Stirling Headridge, James Cherry, Lindsey Lee Byrge, Julie Woodgate, John Richards, Danielle Schellens, Colin Brake, Sylvia Orner, James Wylder, Erik Rodkey, Richard Fairweather, Reece Lawrence, Henrik Johansson, Andy Hicks, Ossian Nervefellow, Eric Saylor, Miles Booy, Benjamin, Damian Gordon, Sherri Marx, Jamie Revell, Matt Bracher, Austin Johnson, Travis Dunn, Gavin Schofield, Roderick Thompson, Nathan Voxland, Rachel Rabin, Garrett Aja, Steve Proctor, Dom McIntyre, Mickey Champion, Rachel Corinne Hatton, Travis Butler, Brett Warburton, Alex Antonijevic, Matthew Cadden-Hyde, Sven Andersen, Samuel Erikson, Chris Angelucci, Linda Jeffries-Koontz, Ashley Tuck, The Millennium Squid, Bob Bryden, Graham Muir, Andre Salles, Owain Glyn Jones, Josh McNamee, Yossi W., Jim Hartland, Jesse Matonak, Matthew, Melika Millie Hadziomerovic (again!), Julie Inlenfeldt, John Davies, Glenn Brown, Jacob Solstice, James Leatherbarrow, sam david, Lena Barkin, Ethan Iverson, Woodrow Jarvis "asim" Hill, Keith Martin, Andrew Longhurst, Matt Pedroso, Adam Spielberg, Juliana T. Johnson, Karen Scavarelli, Holly Murdock, Anthony johnson, Dugal McCrow, Amelia Shwartz, Jessica Bay, Gary K. Slinger, Matthias Light, CPT Robert T. Sagris, Saxon Brenton, Cheryl Preyer, Russell Mirabelli, CB, Stefan Mueller, Frank Serafinski, Keith Lane, Greg "schmegs" Schwartz, Kristen Nau, George Lawie, Josh LaLande, Dr

Tigger, The Bats Masterton, Ben Fischer, John Sawyer, Anna Wiggins (you're cute), David Guiot, Jamie Kruser, Stephen A. Shook, Nick Viner, Sammy Yeo, the Encaffeinated ONE, Steve Lord, Bill Silvia, Rob O'Brien, Max Braden, Kit Brash, Zebee, Charles Murray, Charlotte Treadwell, Bruce Rosen, Anonymous, Alex Mobasher, Lu Xin, Curtis Pearson-Peterson, Paul Houlihan, Pranay & Paul, Jonathan K, Louis Mitas, Anne Walek, Adam Musgrave, Geoff A. Cohen, Matt Marshall, John Mairs, Iain Coleman, David Brown, Joshua Spencer, Phil Hayes, Joseph Moyer, David Kalat, Dr. Happypants, P MacD, Chris McGowan, Rod Hedrick, Paul Mason, Erin Farmer, Matt C, Brian Heiar, Chris Munro, Robin Reinert, Jeremy Lindop, Julian Held, Lukasz Bury, David Platt, Jed A. Blue, Matt Wagner, David Stevens, David Mcaleece, Glenn Harrison, and last but most certainly not least, Janna Hochberg.

Seriously – I'm writing these acknowledgments a few days before Christmas, and I remain, months after the Kickstarter, absolutely bowled over by your generosity and kindness. The Kickstarter went from a way of funding a book I wasn't entirely sure about the economics of to something that has made a huge difference in my life. All of you are amazing, and I'm proud to have you as fans. Thank you.

Table of Contents

A Madwoman with a Blog (Introduction)

Why hello there! It looks like you bought a copy of the first volume of *TARDIS Eruditorum*, which I, as the writer, thank you for because that probably means you have given me money. (If you haven't given me money and have downloaded this off the Internet, on the other hand, I hope you enjoy it and will consider not stealing future volumes.)

In the unlikely event that you have no idea what book you're holding, let me explain to you, generally speaking, how this book works. First of all, here's what it isn't: a standard issue guidebook to Doctor Who. Those looking for the nitty-gritty facts of Doctor Who can probably get a decent sense of them by inference, but that's not what this book is for. There are no episode descriptions, cast lists, or lengthy discussions of the behind-the-scenes workings of the show. There are dozens of books that already do that, and a fair number of online sites. Nor is this a book of reviews. For those who want those things, I personally recommend the *Doctor Who Reference Guide*, *Doctor Who Ratings Guide*, and *A Brief History of Time (Travel)* – three superlative websites that were consulted for basically every one of these essays.

What this book *is* is an attempt to tell the story of Doctor Who. Not the story of how it was made, the overall narrative of the Doctor's life, or anything like that, but the story of the idea that is Doctor Who from its beginnings in late 1963 to . . . well, 1966 in the case of this book, but there's more to come. Doctor Who is a rarity in the world – an extremely long-running serialized narrative. Even rarer, it's an extremely long-running serialized narrative that is not in a niche like soap operas or superhero comics – both provinces almost exclusively of die-hard fans. Doctor Who certainly has its die-hard fans (or, as I like to think of you, my target audience), but notably, it's also been, for much of its existence, absolutely mainstream family entertainment for an entire country.

What this means is that the story of Doctor Who is, in one sense, the story of the world from 1963 on. Politics, music, technological and social development, and all manner of other things have crossed paths with Doctor Who over the nearly fifty years of its existence, and by using Doctor Who as a focus, one can tell a story with far wider implications.

The approach I use to do this is one that I've, rather pompously I suppose, dubbed psychochronography. It draws its name from the concept of psychogeography – an artistic movement created by Guy Debord in 1955 and described as "the study of the precise laws and specific effects of the geographical environment, consciously organized or not, on the emotions and behavior of individuals." More contemporarily, the term is associated with writers like Iain Sinclair, who writes books describing lengthy walking tours of London that fuse his experience with the history of the places he walks, weaving them into a narrative that tries to tell the entire story of a place, and Alan Moore, who does the same thing while worshiping a snake.

Psychochronography, then, attempts the same feat by walking through time. Where walking through space involves little more than picking a direction and moving your feet rhythmically, walking through time without the aid of a TARDIS is a dodgier proposition. The easiest way is to take a specific object and trace its development through time, looking, as the psychogeographers do, at history, lived experience, and the odd connections that spring up.

• 2 •

And so this book is the first part of a walk through Doctor Who. The essays within it wear a lot of hats, and switch them rapidly. All involve a measure of critical reading (in the literary theory sense, not in the complaining sense) of Doctor Who stories to figure out what they are about. This generally means trying to peel back the onion skins of fan history that cloud a story with things "everybody knows." But it also involves looking at the legacy of stories, which often means looking at that onion skin and trying to explain how it got there. No effort is made to disguise the fact that the first appearance of the Daleks is massive for instance, but on the other hand, the book still looks carefully at what their initial impact might have been.

This approach also means looking at how a story would (and could) have been understood by a savvy viewer of the time, and at how the story can be read as responding to the concerns of its time. That means that the essays tend to be long on cultural context. And, in the end, it also means looking at how I personally interact with these stories. This book has no pretense of objectivity. It is about my walking tour of Doctor Who. I try to be accurate, but I also try to be me.

To fully grab the scope of the topic, in addition to the meat of the book – entries covering all of the Doctor Who stories produced with William Hartnell as the lead actor – there are four other types of entries. The first are the Time Can Be Rewritten entries. One peculiar feature of Doctor Who is that its past is continually revisited. The bulk of these came in the form of novels written in the '90s and early '00s, but there are other examples. At the time of writing, for instance, Big Finish puts out new stories every year featuring the first eight Doctors. These entries cover occasional highlights from these revisitations, using them as clues to how these earlier eras are widely understood.

The second are the Pop Between Realities, Home in Time for Tea entries, which look at popular media and culture to build context for understanding Doctor Who. These entries usually crop up prior to the bits of Doctor Who they're most relevant for, and provide background and points of comparison for the show as it wrestles with the issues of its many times.

Third, there are the You Were Expecting Someone Else entries, which deal with spinoff material produced concurrently with Doctor Who but that, inevitably, has some significant differences from the approach of the televised material. These entries exist to give a broader sense of Doctor Who as a cultural object and, perhaps more importantly, because they're kind of fun.

Finally, there are some essays just thrown into the book version as bonuses. These mostly consist of me slogging my way through some established fan debate about Doctor Who and trying, no doubt fruitlessly, to provide the last word on the matter.

This book has a particular idiosyncrasy, which is its coda on stories set prior to the first transmitted episode of Doctor Who. In the original version of this book these stories did not pose a huge problem – I squared away the issue with a pair of essays and then went on to *An Unearthly Child*. But the largest single block of added words to this edition is on pre-*Unearthly Child* stories, which necessitated a new approach. I really don't want to spend fifty pages at the start of the book dealing with this sort of material because the story doesn't begin with a bunch of stuff written decades later; it begins with *An Unearthly Child*. Accordingly, what I've done is moved all of the pre-*Unearthly Child* posts to a postscript, which you can opt to flip ahead to, or read as a postscript to the Hartnell era proper.

It's probably clear by this point that all of these entries began as blog entries on my blog, also called *TARDIS Eruditorum*. This book version, however, revises and expands every entry, as well as adding several new ones – mostly Time Can Be Rewritten entries, but there are a few others.

To this end, I should thank the many readers of the blog for their gratifying and edifying comments, which have kept the project going through more than one frustrating stretch. I should also thank the giants upon whose shoulders I stand when analyzing Doctor Who – most obviously Paul Cornell, Martin Day, and Keith Topping for *The Discontinuity Guide*, David J. Howe, Mark Stammers, and Stephen James Walker for the Doctor handbooks, Toby Hadoke and Rob Shearman for *Running Through Corridors*, and Lawrence Miles and Tat Wood for the sublimely brilliant *About Time* series, to which this book is a proud footnote.

A final note – although I have expanded and revised the essays in this book from their original online versions, I have not attempted to smooth out the developing style of the entries. Much like the show it follows, this project has evolved and grown since its beginning, and I did not wish to alter that.

But most of all and most importantly, thank you, all of you. But most of all, thank you, dear reader. I hope you enjoy.

Elizabeth Sandifer

Pop Between Realities, Home in Time for Tea: *It Happened Here*

The relationship between *It Happened Here* and Doctor Who is manifestly non-causal. *It Happened Here* was filmed over the course of eight years, finishing up just as Doctor Who started. It didn't get widespread release until 1966, by which point the Hartnell era was winding down to its end. There's no reasonable argument that one can make that suggests that the two could have meaningfully interacted on a creative level.

Instead what we have here is a film that exists in a sort of cultural parallel to Doctor Who's earliest days. Certainly the similarities are obvious enough – so much of the early days of Doctor Who is bound up in a fear of fascism, not as a political ideology, but as a sort of gravitational tendency to which society succumbs. Stories in Doctor Who's early days aren't just concerned with fascism, but with its ability to creep up into otherwise decent societies.

Terry Nation, of course, is the writer most obviously working in this milieu – each of his first three stories are focused to varying degrees on the notion of tyranny. But we can see it elsewhere as well – the choice of the French Revolution as one of the earliest historicals, for instance, is based firmly on concerns about the line between good people/noble causes and bad people/evil causes. *The Edge of Destruction* is based around the paranoia of subversion and the idea of the normal order of things subtly going wrong. Even something like *The Aztecs* is concerned deeply with the question of how civilization can go wrong.

Which is, of course, the real concern of *It Happened Here*. The obvious clue is in the title. It's not just an alternate history where the Nazis successfully captured Britain, but a bleak piece about how easily Britain adapted to fascism and German control. The point of the exercise is how readily Pauline, the main character, goes from not wanting to join any organization to being a perfectly functioning Nazi, and how even as she asks questions probing Nazi ideology, she never goes beyond asking polite questions to her superiors. It's stressed repeatedly that England is being held not by German occupying forces, but by British collaborators.

More chillingly, the moral line between the good guys and bad guys is consciously obscured. The film opens and closes with the massacre of POWs, but in the opening it's conducted by the Nazis, and in the end by the resistance. In the film's most extended moral discussion of its themes, Dr. Fletcher, the most morally sympathetic character, speaks movingly about how fascism is a tendency all humans suffer from, and of the great irony that fascist measures must be used to fight fascism.

It's important to recognize this as a change in how fascism was thought about. *It Happened Here* is about World War II, but it's a product of the late '50s and early '60s. Hitler had been dead for almost twenty years, and Stalin, the second-choice evil tyrant, had been dead a decade. Totalitarianism was no longer understood as an imminent threat, but as an existential one. The question stopped being "how will we fight those specific fascists?" and rather became a concern about how fascism started in the first place, starting from the observation that it was something that appeared in "civilized" countries like Germany.

This was the era of the Milgram experiments, for instance, and other research into how authoritarianism and control worked. *It Happened Here* fits squarely into that tradition. It's first and foremost a story about how fascism takes root – of how the institutional structures of authority can be subverted and undermined.

These institutional structures of authority were also of immediate concern in Britain at the time. The immediate aftermath of the War had been the Prime Ministership of Clement Attlee, under which the modern welfare state was created, including the NHS, a large housing boom, and the National Insurance Act. Beyond that, there was a boom in technocracy. Scientists, the popular account went, had won World War II, and would lead us into a glorious and rational future.

Certainly that was what was looming on the political horizon, as the clock ticked down towards the 1964 general election, in which over a decade of Conservative rule came to an end. It's easy to overstate this – the election was actually won because a significant portion of the Conservative vote defected to the Liberal party, which had the effect of handing a huge number of seats to Labour. Nevertheless, it would result in Harold Wilson becoming prime minister. Wilson largely existed in the "New Frontier" liberal tradition of John F. Kennedy, who spoke of a new frontier, beyond which were "uncharted areas of science and space, unsolved problems of peace and war, unconquered problems of ignorance and prejudice, unanswered questions of poverty and surplus."

For Wilson's part, this mandate would take the form of massive focus on education, which tied in closely with the view that science and technology would provide some rational way forward. Under Wilson, education spending outstripped defense spending, and he oversaw two major changes. In secondary education, his government made the system more equitable, eliminating the Eleven plus exam and the exclusive grammar schools in favor of comprehensive schools. But his most famous legacy is the Open University, which used television broadcasts and an open admissions policy to offer higher education to a large portion of the population.

The television broadcasts, of course, the BBC – a national broadcaster with a public service remit to serve the entire population. The BBC wasn't a product of either Attlee or Wilson – radio service existed in the 1920s, and television broadcasts began in the 1930s. And the real boom in television came under Churchill's second term as prime minister in the 1950s, with the coronation of Queen Elizabeth, which was watched by an estimated twenty million people. Nevertheless, its ideological origins in this period are firmly entrenched in the sort of populist technocracy that constituted the welfare state. The BBC was there to serve everybody, not just to do reputable, high-culture broadcasts. It was meant to serve everybody in pursuit of a vision of national unity. This idea, though, paralleled other ideas that were increasingly seen to be troublesome. The idea that the people in charge knew better and could help educate and enlighten everybody else wasn't just (as *It Happened Here* points out) chillingly close to the justifications for fascism. It was the moral justification for the rapidly collapsing British Empire, from which the entire notion of the modern "adventure story" arose.

These institutions, while valued, were also figures of some suspicion. There was a fine line to be had between the public good and indoctrination. Especially for a growing youth generation that hadn't seen the War and for whom an anti-authoritarian streak was second nature. So we have, in the culture, two trends that are not so much in opposition as a quiet tension. It's not fascists versus anti-state libertarians, but a complex and nuanced discussion about the line between liberalism (in the classical sense) and authoritarianism.

Into this climate came Hugh Greene, brother of novelist Graham Greene, who became Director-General of the BBC in 1960 and focused the BBC even more explicitly on social concerns and on appealing to the whole of Britain. This is often framed as a turn away from the Reithian values of the "classic" BBC, but this overstates it – Greene's BBC was just as interested in the public good, if not more so. The difference was that Greene took more seriously the mandate that the BBC serve everybody, overseeing the creation of a wealth of populist programming like *Steptoe and Son* and *Z-Cars*, as well as the creation of Radio 1, the BBC's foray into pop music.

For our purposes, though, one of the biggest things Hugh Greene did was poach Sydney Newman from ITV to be the Head of Drama at the BBC. Newman was many things, but one of them was a science fiction fan. Science fiction, conceptually, has been running through all of what we've been talking about so far. *It Happened Here* isn't sci-fi in the spaceships and ray guns sense, but rather in a literary sense, where alternate histories have long been considered a part of the sci-fi tradition. (Indeed, a significant part of *It Happened Here*'s volunteer cast came from sci-fi fandom.)

Because, of course, science fiction is the obvious place to explore all of these themes. It is, in many ways, a genre designed to deal with questions about the shape of society and the role of science within society. It's no surprise that the heyday of science fiction was centered around World War II – it was the perfect genre to address the concerns of that era. And the UK had a bold tradition of science fiction, from populist adventure stories like *Dan Dare* to moody television plays like Nigel Kneale's Quatermass serials, to literary works ripe for dramatic adaptation like John Wyndham's *Day of the Triffids*.

So it was hardly a surprise that shortly after taking over as Head of Drama, Sydney Newman pushed for the creation of a sci-fi serial that would work as a family show, using spectacle and adventure to draw in kids, but engaging in serious-minded explorations of the future to appeal to an adult audience. As part of the BBC's commitment to public service, it was to have a strong educational component as well. So he proposed a time travel show, featuring a core cast that hit all the demographics (mothers, fathers, kids, and grandparents), which would allow both science-minded space adventures and educational trips into history. And after a few months of development and a false start (discussed in the book's appendix) the show was ready for transmission. Which brings us to late November, 1963 . . .

Elizabeth Sandifer

I Was a Dad Once (*An Unearthly Child*)

It is 5:16 p.m., November 23, 1963. Gerry and the Pacemakers' "You'll Never Walk Alone" is the number one single. It will go on to become the anthem of Liverpool FC, one of the most successful English football clubs of all time. Elsewhere in the charts are the Beatles, Roy Orbison, and Chuck Berry. These are classic, innocent days of rock and roll.

Whereas in the news, life has just gotten a lot less innocent. Since 6:30 p.m. the previous day, the BBC has been running news coverage of the assassination of US President John F. Kennedy. There are other news stories, but in terms of the times, this is the only one anyone cares about right now. The Kennedy assassination is, of course, a terribly symbolic event – the end of the innocent portion of the 1960s and the beginning of an altogether rockier period. And so, to shepherd us through that period the BBC unveils one of the most enduring pieces of British popular culture of the twentieth century.

At twenty seconds past the minute, exactly eighty seconds off from its scheduled airtime, normal programming resumes with the first episode of a new children's science fiction serial, Doctor Who. The opening credits are a futuristic psychedelic blur that seems at once miles ahead of its time and oddly quaint as the symbol of youthful revolution has just been gunned down in Texas. The theme music, ostensibly written by Ron Grainer was, for all practical purposes, realized by Delia Derbyshire, who arranged Grainer's score by splicing tape together and speeding/slowing a sample of a single note being plucked on a string, white noise, and some testing oscillators. (Grainer, upon hearing it, is said to have asked Derbyshire if he'd written that. She, rather modestly, replied, "most of it.") Derbyshire would, in her later life, be recognized as an unsung hero – a pioneer of electronic music – but received no on-screen credit because the BBC's policy was that members of the BBC Radiophonic Workshop would remain anonymous. The credits themselves were done by distorting footage of a pen light being moved around using a process called howlaround.

The effect is mysterious and chilling – like nothing that has been seen on television before. The credits give way, although the haunting theme music does not, as we watch a policeman walk through the London fog (a callback to *Dixon of Dock Green,* more about which later) past a junkyard. The camera turns away from him and pushes itself through the gates (which open, despite there seeming to be no person involved in the process) to rest on a police box, on which it lingers. This sequence is hard to comprehend in 1963, as there is nothing particularly strange about a police box save for its apparent location in a junkyard, which, by virtue of being a junkyard is sort of, by definition, a place full of odd things. And yet the camera lingers, stressing the strangeness of this object that does not yet have strangeness, zooming in to the text on the door, but offering no explanation.

With fifty years of history to contend with, Doctor Who has inevitably changed. One must ask, then, when it became Doctor Who. The answer, it seems, is right here, as mysterious, haunting theme music gives way to an iconic shot. Never mind that the shot cannot possibly be read as iconic in this original context – everything about the camerawork and the music tells us it is iconic. Everything tells us this police box is the most important thing about this show. Before we see a single character, before we see the Doctor, before we see a hint of science fiction, we see a police box.

The moment is, in fact, so odd as to stick in the craw for years later. Terrance Dicks, novelizing the encounter in 1981, has the police officer enter the junkyard and stresses the unusual throbbing hum of the police box. He also makes sure to foreshadow the disappearance of Ian and Barbara and the "bigger on the inside" nature of the TARDIS, further ensuring that the moment feels iconic within the context of the larger series. But that's not what is happening in the original episode. It's true that there is an odd sound that accompanies the long shot of the police box, but this fades in from the theme music, making it less than clear that it's intended to signify the alien nature of the police box. Instead we have something that the camera tells us is a mystery, but that doesn't seem all that mysterious.

I should say here that *An Unearthly Child*, the first episode, is usually treated as one story along with the following three episodes. Because Doctor Who had individually titled episodes instead of story arc titles in its first seasons, the name for this story is disputed. The other names all refer to the plot elements of the second through fourth episodes, which are, for all practical purposes, a completely different story from the one in this first episode. The episode titled *An Unearthly Child* was rewritten by Anthony Coburn from an original script by C.E. Webber, and was reshot before transmission. Both of these facts serve to separate it in a meaningful sense from the three episodes that follow, which are pure Coburn. (The pilot episode is one of several covered in the postscript.)

It's thus an open discussion whether this should be treated as one story or two. Oddly the usual consensus within fandom is to treat it as a single story, despite the fact that almost everybody loves the first part and ignores the three episodes of cavemen that follow it. Miles and Wood, in their deeply brilliant *About Time*, argue that the story only makes sense as one four-parter about, as they put it, "making four people who barely know one another learn to trust each other, and turning tribespeople who are at each other's throats into a solid, united clan." There is a lot of merit to this. Equally, however, for the purposes of talking about the episodes here, it makes sense to split them up. And so accordingly, this essay is just on that first episode actually called *An Unearthly Child*, while the next essay will cover the three episodes of cavemen under one of the popular alternate titles for this story, *100,000 BC*.

As an episode, then, *An Unearthly Child* is a simple character piece. Only four characters meaningfully appear – Susan Foreman, a teenage girl, Barbara Wright and Ian Chesterton, a pair of her teachers, and the Doctor, her cranky old grandfather. The story is mostly about Susan – the eponymous child lacking earthiness. Her teachers, Ms. Wright and Mr. Chesterton, are at once enamored with her and scared of her. Enamored because she is a genius, and they know it. Scared because she is the wrong sort of genius. She knows things that people aren't meant to know. She speaks of the future – at times quite rightly. In a moment of inadvertent brilliance that makes this episode sing nearly fifty years later, she predicts the decimalization of British currency with confidence, although this was merely, at the time, a possible future.

So this is where it starts: a mysterious police box, a magical girl, and a mystery that two regular, unimportant people can't quite get over. A mystery that brings them out on a cold London night to 76 Totters Lane to try to find out where this girl came from. There they meet an old man. Smug, superior, and unfriendly, he does not want them there. This is his mysterious girl and his mystery. We are set up for some sort of conflict, but exactly what isn't quite clear. We are, thus far, being pulled along a version of what Tzvetan Todorov calls the fantastic – a sort of tightrope walk between two possibilities. A strange and aberrant event happens, and the story focuses on whether this event is supernatural or the

Elizabeth Sandifer

product of a fractured, insane mind. In a Todorov-style approach to the fantastic, the resolution of this ambiguity is delayed until the end, and that's the primary tension of the story.

That's clearly where we're going – this story is, it seems, about the mystery of Susan, and whether she's unearthly and fantastic, or whether there's a mundane, psychological explanation – perhaps some bit of social realism, a proto-*Cathy Come Home*. And then, suddenly, it goes wrong. The two teachers force themselves past the old man, into the blue box, to try to rescue Susan from whatever awful things he's doing to her.

Instead, they fall out of the world and into another. It is another triumph of design in the show – a stark white of iconic '60s futurism that would age gracefully into retro-futurism. This along with, of course, its being bigger on the inside than it is on the outside – a massive cathedral of lights and switches unlike anything that would be imaginable inside a police box. Suddenly the mystery we thought we were solving is removed, and we see the one we'd almost forgotten in the fuss – the mystery of that strange police box in Totters Lane.

Right here is where the show becomes Doctor Who: a show about a magic box that can take you anywhere and the madman who flies it – a show about running and escape. But the Doctor is not yet the Doctor. He is scared. These two schoolteachers are a threat to him. He is running. He wants to go home and can't – he wants to protect his granddaughter. More than anything, he wants to be free. He'll throw Susan away with Ian and Barbara if that's what it takes. But he is so scared of the idea of anyone having power over him that, even with Susan promising him again and again that they are good people, he will not just let them go and let everything return to normal.

So, in a mad, daft gesture, one that doesn't make any sense at all (but that will, in a sense, characterize every other decision he makes on the show and every decision we imagine him making before this point), he runs. It is the first moment of depth in the cantankerous grandfather. He's scared, and he runs. The mysterious swirls of the credits return while a strange wheezing, groaning noise echoes out, and the TARDIS is suddenly somewhere else. Ian and Barbara, helpless, unconscious on the ground, have fallen out of the world, dragged along by a madman with a box.

In this first episode the questions are obvious. Why is he running? What is he afraid of? Who is he? Already, in the first episode, Doctor Who is about its own mystery. And yet the real mysteries are not the ones about the origins of this strange man who fancies himself, seemingly in response to Ian's suggesting the word, a Doctor. The real question is this – where are we going? Where is this TARDIS thing taking Ian and Barbara?

Or, to put it broadly, what kind of show is this going to be? It doesn't know yet. It doesn't know what it will become. It doesn't know the history and wonder that's coming. Perhaps it's even scared of that history. Running from it. It is, after all, a massive history – unimaginably large even when living it, little yet when imagining it from as small a seed as this.

But that history is here. Right here, in this first episode, with its haunting theme music, impossible knowledge of the future, and obsession with a police box. The episode was clearly made fourty-eight years ago. It is not timeless. Why should it be? Timeless things are things that never happen. Doctor Who happened, and happens still. This is unmistakably 1963 British television drama. And yet it feels, every second of the episode, like Doctor Who. It feels like it was made by people who knew what Doctor Who was.

It's impossible. The fact that a police box would look out of place everywhere in the universe within six years, that the theme and TARDIS console would be iconic, that Britain would go to decimal currency, none of this could have been there in 1963. But watching it, that knowledge does not feel like a secret history, but like a real history, there and unfolding in front of us. And when we stare into it, it is impossibly big.

It is 5:40 p.m. on November the 23, 1963. American President John F. Kennedy has been dead for less than twenty-four hours. And everything in the world has changed. Forever.

All That Counts Is Here and Now, and This Is Me
(*100,000 BC*)

It is 100,000 BC. There is no number one single. There is no music industry. Indeed, there is no industry period. There's not even really a humanity, with the great leap forward of behavioral modernity still lurking 50,000 years in the future. The peak of the ice age currently being enjoyed is about 80,000 years in the future. On a hillside, a blue box appears with a strange wheezing, groaning sound.

More usefully, it is November 30, 1963. The Beatles recapture number one with "She Loves You," the biggest selling single of the 1960s, which is charting for the second time. It will hold that chart position for two weeks before giving way in the final weeks of the year to "I Want to Hold Your Hand." Other artists in the charts include Kathy Kirby, Cliff Richard, and Dusty Springfield.

In practical news, the Kennedy assassination has long since turned to farce with Lee Harvey Oswald himself being murdered two days later, prompting now President Johnson to appoint the Warren Commission to figure everything out. Now the world waits uncomfortably, aware that the progress of history has been diverted but not knowing where or towards what. In British news, both Kenya and Zanzibar attain independence as part of a wave of colonial independences we'll be seeing over the course of this book.

In news of interest, because we are looking at television, instant replay is invented in the United States.

While on UK television, we have . . . well, first of all, we have an odd metaphor for television in the form of the TARDIS itself. In later episodes the disparity between the internal and external sizes of the TARDIS will be explained in terms of the interior being a different dimension. But last week, in the first episode, this was instead explained by analogy, with the Doctor referring to the way in which television allows a much larger world to be contained in a smaller space. It is an odd analogy, in no small part because, in the context of a fictional TV show, it appears to suggest that the interior of the TARDIS is fictional even within Doctor Who. Still, it is an explanation of sorts. We were invited to leave our world via the television. We were, in other words, invited to indulge in escapism. This is a terribly complex word, and one that we'll trace the implications of over this entire project.

To the captured, escape is an end in itself. It is not until you escape that you quite realize that escapes are not merely exits but entries. When last we left them, Ian and Barbara have fallen out of the world. Now we come to see where they have landed, where their escape from reality has brought them. The answer – as the title of the second episode suggests – is "somewhere terrifying." Almost immediately, everything goes wrong. The Doctor is kidnapped by cavemen, sending Susan into a panic such that Ian and Barbara, skeptical and afraid as they are, go to help him.

The rescue is a complete disaster, and the four of them quickly find themselves tied up in the Cave of Skulls, named for its primary decorative feature, a large number of skulls that have been split open by an axe. And here we see something that, to anyone aware of the future legacy of Doctor Who, is bizarre. The Doctor panics and seems to wholly give up hope on escaping. It is, in other words, immediately apparent that he is completely incapable of being the hero of this story.

From here the story is a fairly staid and at times repetitive sequence of escapes and recaptures. But over time, the reality of all of this sinks in. These three episodes' most striking feature, in many ways, is Barbara's nervous breakdown as the four leads wander through a forest following their escape from the Cave of Skulls.

The breakdown is stunning both in how viscerally it is shown and in how much it reminds us that Barbara simply does not belong in this setting. Eventually the show will get to the standard of people being absolutely thrilled by the adventure and excitement that traveling with the Doctor entails. But here, as she collapses, screaming in anguished confusion and wondering what has happened to her, there is none of that wonder. Falling through a hole in the world is not an easy proposition. Travel in the TARDIS is not a gift. It's a nightmare.

Just ask the Doctor. We don't know yet where he came from, or why. In one telling sequence, Ian speculates that if only we knew his name, we might understand him better. Aside from being an excuse to work the words "Doctor who?" into the actual episode, this question is one of the episode's central dramatic tensions. Prior to Barbara's breakdown comes what is, in many ways, an even more interesting moment of breakdown: the Doctor's. As the party sits, tied up and terrified in the Cave of Skulls, he apologizes, saying that this is all his fault. He has not learned to be the Doctor yet. He's just escaped. We first see him having fallen through a hole in his world, and now he, like Barbara, is left to figure out what this means.

It is, of course, a truism that Doctor Who, particularly in the classic series, amounts to little more than the main characters getting locked up and escaping a bunch. Certainly *100,000 BC* demonstrates this tendency in spades. But it's worth thinking, at least briefly, about the way in which this serves as a metaphor for the entire series. From the start the series is about the image of falling out of the world – of tearing apart your entire sense of who you are in favor of the utterly unknown and foreign. The Doctor – indeed the entire series – is defined in no small part by the continual business of escape. The nature of captivity, after all, is about being put into a confined space – a box. When a box can be bigger on the inside and can smash through the walls of any world, this stops being a meaningful condition. Captivity is merely the possibility of escape.

In hindsight, of course, this defines the Doctor. But it's not clear that he, or indeed, even the series actually knows this yet. On one level, nobody knows anything about the Doctor yet. The words "Gallifrey" and "Time Lord" have not been thought of yet. William Hartnell doesn't know that he's playing a Time Lord. He doesn't know why he fled his home world. But most of this is irrelevant. He's escaped. He's not there anymore. What matters more is where he is now, and who he is.

It is telling that the first adventure in which he needs to become the Doctor is set . . . well, that's the funny bit. It's not clear where it's set. The production materials suggest the title of *100,000 BC*. History-wise, the date is tricky. The episode talks as though the major problem facing the tribe of cavemen is the looming ice age. They display behavioral modernity, by and large, with a religious system centered on the sun. That would suggest a later date than 100,000 BC – a date, we should note, that exists on some production documents, not in the story itself. But the main thrust of this isn't the date – it's the era. This is humanity at their dawn – as they are in the process of becoming human.

The question of where, on the other hand, is even trickier, as the range of dates is right along the periods of early human migrations. But the implications are telling. Historically, somewhere around 100,000 BC, a small family of humans crossed the Red Sea, exiting Africa and going on to populate the planet. And the Doctor gave them fire. He aids in their ascension from ape to man. The Doctor will not actually defend present-day Earth from evil threats for almost three years. But here we see, in his first adventure, the Doctor bring us fire. In this regard, we are his creation. This is the story of how the Doctor, in his first adventure, creates humanity, to some extent, it seems, just so he can defend them.

But symbolically, at least, there's an even greater possibility in play here. We recognize the phenomenon of biological evolution. Implicit alongside that is what we might call the idea of cultural evolution – the march of history. History creates new things in much the same way as biology: piece by piece, changing old things into new. A tantalizing implication of this is the possibility of an ur-culture – of some historical civilization from which all contemporary civilizations' cultural ideas evolved. In this regard the premise of *100,000 BC* is one of the cheekiest and most impressively broad in Doctor Who's history, suggesting as it does that the first act of Doctor Who is to write itself into the primordial cultural data of humanity. If, as the suggestion goes, any story can be turned into a Doctor Who story then perhaps it is because of the events in this story. Perhaps every story can be turned into a Doctor Who story because, in the end, Doctor Who is inexorably linked to our very idea of stories. If we are all stories in the end, perhaps it is because that is how the Doctor made us.

Strange, then, how little regard he pays us. He is perfectly willing, at one moment, to bash a man's head in simply because it would make his escape more convenient. As with much in these episodes, it feels wrong. This is not the Doctor, our hero. This is a nasty man every bit as scared as Barbara. Or, perhaps more accurately, despite being played by the oldest actor to take the role, this is a young man in over his head and freaking out over it.

And interestingly, he never becomes the Doctor in this story. Not quite. Much of the story is about the conflict between him and Ian over which of them should be the leader. And it's not quite solved here. In time it will be settled and the show will become Doctor Who as we more or less know it. But for now the conflict is, roughly, between Ian's good nature and the Doctor's actual competence. The Doctor wants to be leader in this story more because he does not want to follow and be imprisoned than out of any actual good-naturedness. This story is paralleled in the conflict between Kal and Za for leadership of the tribe, with each of them being pale and less sympathetic versions of the Doctor and Ian. This story, at a fundamental level, is about forming the show and deciding who the main character is, with this act, in a move of massively mythic proportions, paralleled with the creation of humanity and the establishment of the direction of human development.

And yet the seeds of the Doctor – the real Doctor, the one we know – are there. In the Cave of Skulls he comforts Barbara, saying, in yet another line with resonances of the future, "fear makes companions of us all." Later, it is he who is inventive enough to engineer an escape from the cavemen via some clever manipulation. Already in this story he is learning to be the Doctor.

But he's not there yet. This being, in part, because he does not trust any of his traveling companions save Susan. Crucially, his traveling companions trust Susan and not him, establishing and sustaining Susan's role on the TARDIS. As the show settles and the Doctor and Ian's conflict is resolved, Susan will slowly be squeezed out. The other part of this is that he's still in the state of becoming the Doctor because he's overcome by the drive to escape. He has not realized where he is yet. This is made literal in the closing moments, where the Doctor explains that he can't simply return Ian and Barbara home without first landing in a location he is familiar with. Until he knows his place in the physical space of the story, until he realizes who he is and what role he has in the universe, he can't actually control his ship.

But perhaps most importantly, the Doctor cannot be the Doctor yet because there is something he doesn't know about the universe. Something he won't learn until the next story: monsters are real.

Time Can Be Rewritten: *The Masters of Luxor*

The first few scripts of Doctor Who were, to put it mildly, a slightly chaotic affair. The original first script was supposed to be more or less what became the Season Two premiere, *Planet of Giants*, to be written by C.E. Webber, who was an uncredited cowriter on "An Unearthly Child" (the episode), but the technical capabilities of Lime Grove Studio D, a legendarily awful studio for Doctor Who, meant that the premise had to be abandoned, and Anthony Coburn's cavemen script was moved forward and annexed onto Webber's first episode. Coburn was also to write the second episode, which was to be *The Masters of Luxor*, but script editor David Whitaker, arguably the single most important figure in the development of Doctor Who, was never happy with the script. Instead he hired Terry Nation, who banged out *The Daleks* in a week as a crap throwaway job before he went to work on the more prestigious and interesting job of a comedy special to be made on a Swedish cruise ship.

It's important to frame *The Masters of Luxor* this way, as without that framing you don't quite get the low regard the script was clearly held in. *The Daleks* may have turned out as a massive success that ensured the destiny of the series, but it was in practice a rush job that did the one thing that series creator Sydney Newman had insisted never be done: focus the series on bug-eyed monsters. Clearly *The Masters of Luxor* was a non-starter.

Answering why is at least a little tricky. There are admittedly some obvious problems – the first episode cliffhanger of Susan taking a bite out of a chicken leg was probably not destined to be the enduring classic that the first cliffhanger of *The Daleks* was. Several bits of dialogue can charitably be called "clunky." The opening sequence would be nearly impossible to film without modern CGI, and even still would probably have the Mill weeping openly.

But most of these are things that could have been smoothed out in edits. Whitaker didn't find this script unusable in its current form, he found it unsalvageable. This points to larger problems. Some are probably pacing related – after a few decent opening episodes that, while certainly not high-speed, are at least consistent with the Hartnell era at large the story derails badly. The fourth episode, titled "Tabon of Luxor," involves the Doctor and Ian meeting the eponymous Tabon, creator of the robots that have been the cause of so much trouble in the preceding three episodes. But it takes until the sixth episode to get to the point of having Tabon confront the robots, which is rather a lot of running around. Then again, this is nowhere near the biggest offender in terms of pace and the Hartnell era.

A more fundamental issue is the way in which the script fits into what Whitaker was trying to do with Doctor Who in its first three stories (recognizing that the series had a soft reboot in *Marco Polo*), which was to write a program that was in a large part about the tensions among the TARDIS crew. Here, while Ian and the Doctor may engage in some snarky banter, everyone has basically slotted cleanly into their roles and spends the bulk of the story getting along. Nothing like the Doctor's sabotage of the mercury fluid links is in place.

More broadly, however, *The Masters of Luxor* demonstrates a view of the world that fits uncomfortably with the rest of Doctor Who, or, at least, with David Whitaker, which is, in many ways, the same thing. Coburn positions this story as a tight sequel to *100,000 BC*, with an entire speech about how in this story they're overwhelmed by superior technology, whereas in the previous story they were technologically superior to the cavemen. Given this, it's possible to draw some conclusions about Coburn as a writer and what his interests are.

Tellingly, both *100,000 BC* and *The Masters of Luxor* are focused on God. In *100,000 BC* the tribe is based around Orb, their sun god, whereas *The Masters of Luxor* has the Doctor straightforwardly professing faith in God while Susan and Barbara sing "Land of Hope and Glory," an overtly religious song, to ward off evil robots. Barbara expresses overtly Platonist views suggesting a higher order to the world, and the Doctor talks about how letting science run rampant without religion is a bad thing.

Many commenters suggest that this is the problem – that nobody was entirely comfortable with having the Doctor be explicitly religious. This is certainly possible, but seems a bit overly easy. More likely, I would wager, is that the problem came in the form of religion expressed. The line in which Barbara expresses relatively Platonic views, saying "there is a perfection from which we come and all our lives, we . . . we strive to recreate it . . . as though it was a plan written into our bones" is telling, in that it focuses not only on religion but on the idea of some absolute system or order to the world. This comports well with the Doctor's description of the TARDIS as being beautiful "in the way that scientific principles efficiently translated into machinery are beautiful."

The sense of beauty in question is a fairly classical one, dating back to Kant and other Enlightenment thinkers who suggested that beauty is based on the appearance of an order or purpose to things, generally an unseen one. In this reading the cavemen's worship of Orb is an embryonic form of this – a primitive version of Barbara's suggestion of an innate religious sense. In both of Coburn's scripts there's an endless sense of an external order, and a sense that harmony with that order is a fundamental moral duty. Likewise, the fundamental moral horror of *The Masters of Luxor* is the idea of artificial life, because that's a mockery of the existing order of things.

Where this starts to get problematic is in the line from which the fifth episode of *The Masters of Luxor* takes its title: "we are beings programmed to an infinity of surprises." This line suggests not merely that the world is full of wonder, but that there's a pre-existent desire to take in this wonder. The purpose of travel in the TARDIS becomes the act of experiencing that wonder in all its multitude. But there's a sterility to this. Life's purpose is to go and experience wonder, but this becomes an essentially passive vision that enshrines the series' early tendency to have the Doctor only interested in interacting with a planet and its problems inasmuch as the TARDIS is disabled and he needs to fix it.

Obviously the idea that the Doctor's travels might be motivated in part by a desire to see new things is uncontroversial, but the question of "wonder" is tricky. Wonder is a largely passive experience, defined by looking at something. This is miles from the Doctor's tendency to get involved in things, which is an important concept for Whitaker. Whitaker, in his novelization of *The Crusade*, opens with a discussion of how the TARDIS crew routinely changes and intervenes on worlds other than Earth, but how they can't change human history. This is described in terms of the fact that on Earth the "Time pattern, that is, past, present, and future, is all one – like a long, winding mountain path." This suggests an immutability of Earth's history in one sense, but equally important is its sense of historical progression. What's important about Earth's history is that there is a continual arc of change and development across its entirety.

This is par for the course with Whitaker, who explained to an early viewer that while time cannot be altered, "what we are concerned with is that history, like justice, is not only done but can be seen to be done." That idea of history as a process is, again, crucial. For Whitaker, what matters about time is that it is a process of change. Changing history is a silly idea because history is itself change.

For Whitaker, as we'll see in both this and the next volume of *TARDIS Eruditorum*, a central image of this is mercury – an image that is, fittingly, introduced in the story that replaced *The Masters of Luxor* on the schedule. Coincidentally, the climax of *The Masters of Luxor* centers on a fictional metal that is clearly similar to mercury. The Perfect One, the villainous leader of the robots of Luxor, is said to have his circuits based on a metal called Azzintium, which, in its liquid form, "can store electrical and magnetic impulses almost to infinity." This echoes mercury, a liquid metal symbolically associated with communication. But unlike mercury, Azzintium is only a liquid within a tiny range of temperatures. In other words, it's a liquid metal associated with communication that is defined by the precise and fixed nature of its ability and, unlike mercury, is generally treated as an agent of continual change.

This, more than anything, explains what is "wrong" with *The Masters of Luxor*. It's not that it's an awful script, although it's by no means a great one. But under the hood, its vision is quietly antithetical to Whitaker's own clear and elaborate vision. The introduction to the Titan Books edition of the script rhetorically wonders about a world where this and not *The Daleks* was Doctor Who's second story, and whether Doctor Who would still be on in that world. (The book came out in 1992, so this was a particularly barbed question.) The question is, of course, profoundly silly – it could well have made it just as well with *The Daleks* getting made later in the season, or according to any number of other counterfactuals. But what can be said is this: a show based around the passive acceptance of a fixed world of wonder would never have lasted as long as one about the continual embracing of change. In the end, whatever *The Masters of Luxor*'s virtues, David Whitaker was, on the big issues, right.

Pop Between Realities, Home in Time for Tea: *Dan Dare*

A complete history of pre-Doctor Who British science fiction is terribly worth doing, but it's not this book. That's not to say I ignore it – you'll also find an essay on the *Quatermass* franchise off near *The War Machines* – but rather that it's just too large a topic to cover. That said, to try to understand Terry Nation's contributions to Doctor Who without discussing *Dan Dare* seems fundamentally ridiculous.

First, the top-line summary: *Dan Dare* debuted in *Eagle*, a comics magazine that debuted in 1950 and ran until the end of the 1960s. *Eagle* is one of those collaborations that simply does not make sense in virtually any country other than the UK. Marcus Morris, a vicar in Lancashire, and artist Frank Hampson were dissatisfied with their parish magazine *The Anvil* (despite getting people like C.S. Lewis and Harold Macmillan to contribute), and so they began pitching an adventure comic focusing on Lex Christian, who Morris described as "a tough, fighting parson in the slums of the East End of London." This didn't work out, but Morris was able to sell *The Anvil* in October of 1949 and use the money to fund an adventure comic that would demonstrate what he considered to be good Christian values, though not in an ostentatiously proselytizing way.

Eagle consisted of numerous strips, most of which existed in the basic genre of adventure strips. Many were quasi real-world adventures – sea captain Storm Nelson, righting various wrongs in the West Indies, or *Luck of the Legion*, which follows the French Foreign Legion as they fight the swarthy and villainous tribes of North Africa. As this description perhaps suggests, these strips were heavily indebted to British imperialism. These are stories that still, at their heart, believe in the basic value of British culture and, more to the point, that the rest of the world would be a lot better off if they'd just let some intelligent and competent British people come by and sort everything out for them.

The raft of deeply nasty implications of all of this are matters for another time – we'll watch the empire unravel over the course of this and the next few volumes, and we'll trace that. For now what's more important is the relatively inviolate nature of the Empire as the starting point for adventure fiction. Nothing whatsoever about *Eagle* tries to challenge this. Adventures are the things you have while being British for the rest of the world.

Within this schema, then, *Dan Dare* was something of an outlier. Written and illustrated by Frank Hampton, or, at least, Frank Hampton's studio of artists – a first for a UK comics creator – *Dan Dare* stood out from the rest of *Eagle* by virtue of being a science fiction strip, and, probably more importantly, by being better than everything else in the magazine (which was no mean feat). Nevertheless, it is still, broadly speaking, firmly in the same tradition as the rest of *Eagle*. Dan Dare is a futuristic space hero, yes, but he's defined first and foremost as the "pilot of the future," putting him firmly in the tradition of the RAF and Britain's post-War self-image. His spaceship, the *Anastasia*, is stylized and futuristic (or, at least, '50s-style futuristic), but is still recognizably an airplane.

Similarly, in terms of overall structure, *Dan Dare* is still straightforward adventure fiction in the colonial mould. Dan Dare just goes to other planets to sort things out instead of to the Pacific islands. Being as grounded in World War II iconography as Dan Dare was, it's no surprise that the major thing he sorted out was a race of fascist aliens called the Treens, led by the villainous Mekon, who cruelly oppressed their fellow Venusians, the Therons. The Therons, of course, are a reasonably advanced and well-meaning race, but one that is ideologically unable to help themselves, thus needing the competent Dan Dare to come by and sort them out.

The similarity between this relationship and that of the villainous Daleks to the ideologically pacifist Thals could not actually be more blatant. Both, of course, are World War II images – retellings of the basic parable that appeasement doesn't work, that pacifism is noble but fatally flawed, and that true evil must be fought. This is not, of course, the only way that *Dan Dare* influences Doctor Who, and is especially not the only way it influences Terry Nation. So much of what makes *Dan Dare* work is that it is gorgeous and full of fantastic images. Frank Hampton was a brilliant artist, and he developed a basic look for *Dan Dare* that was absolutely wonderful. It was at once ahead of its time in terms of what 1950s futurism looked like and fundamentally nostalgic, reaching back to World War II, which was already establishing itself as the glory days of Great Britain.

But beyond that, Hampton had a real knack for coming up with cool things. *Dan Dare* was tremendously effective at structuring its plot to do its job, which was basically to, in weekly two-page installments, mix visual spectacle with a reasonable density of thrills and then end with a cliffhanger so people will buy the next issue. The status of *Dan Dare* as the cover strip for *Eagle* only enhanced that – the first page of every strip had to serve as an advertisement for the entire magazine. Whereas one thing *Dan Dare* was manifestly not written for was being read linearly, strip after strip, as though the stories formed what are these days called graphic novels.

This is simply not what *Dan Dare* is. *Dan Dare* is a serial. It's designed to be read over time. Its narrative goal is to provide two pages of condensed thrills per week. These should link into something resembling an overall story, but to treat that overall story as the point is fundamentally misunderstanding how this works. This too is an important structural consideration in Doctor Who, and reflects particularly vividly on Terry Nation. When we get to *The Keys of Marinus* we'll suggest that Nation's plotting oddly anticipates video games, but the simpler explanation, quite frankly, is that Nation is writing pulp serials of the sort that *Dan Dare* was an heir to.

So with *Dan Dare* we find something that is, we must admit, close to the starting point of Doctor Who, which is clearly invested in an imperialist vision of how British people can go through the cosmos and sort other times and places out on a serial structure. Equally, however, Doctor Who cuts against both of those in significant ways. It may be based around a fundamentally Victorian vision in the form of the Doctor, but it augments this with Susan, a vision of youth culture, and two representatives of ordinary Britain. Traveling isn't just entertaining adventure but a source of terror that underlines the fragile nature of our world. The serialization too slowly drops away, with the series' original conceit of being an ongoing serial eventually being revised into a series that does multi-part stories and, eventually, largely switches to single stories. In this regard, the history of Doctor Who can be read as a steady move away from the approach of *Dan Dare*, which also helps explain how Terry Nation goes rather quickly from being the defining writer of the series to being an odd throwback whose stories feel desperately out of pace with the times.

Nevertheless, the influence never entirely goes away. Doctor Who always retains *Dan Dare*'s focus on the visual, and while it eventually, along with Britain at large, grows rather more skeptical about the idea of empire, its roots in the Victorian adventure fiction tradition that *Dan Dare* comes out of never go away. Still, it's important to remember that Doctor Who's starting position wasn't *Dan Dare* – putting this essay before *An Unearthly Child* would have made little sense. Doctor Who announced its ambitions out of the gate to move beyond *Dan Dare*. But in its second story it seems to realize that it's skipped a step, and that it has to start from within a thinly veiled *Dan Dare* clone story and then work its way out. So what we have is *Dan Dare* from the wrong perspective, lingering on things like Ian's horror at his paralysis and Barbara's terror in the face of the Daleks. That's the central alchemy of these earliest Dalek stories – the sense of a popular science fiction icon being surpassed. It's telling that *Eagle* doesn't really last long after the debut of Doctor Who. Terry Nation, for all his influence at the start of Doctor Who, is relevant primarily as a passing of the guard – the writer who best channeled the approach that Doctor Who defined itself as breaking away from.

A Man Who Never Would (The Daleks)

It is December 21, 1963. The Beatles continue to hold the number one chart position with "I Want to Hold Your Hand," with the number two slot still belonging to their earlier single "She Loves You." This, then, is the height of Beatlemania. Its crowning events come during this story: the release of "I Want to Hold Your Hand" in the US, two record companies with dueling releases of the first US Beatles album, the crowds greeting their arrival in New York, and finally, their famous appearance on *The Ed Sullivan Show*. They'll continue to hold the number one slot into 1964, finally losing it in late January to the Dave Clark Five's "Glad All Over." Also around are the Swinging Blue Jeans with "Hippy Hippy Shake," the Hollies with "Stay," and the Searchers with next number one, "Needles and Pins."

In the news, Barry Goldwater begins his doomed challenge to Johnson for the presidency. Johnson declares a war on poverty, John Glenn leaves the space program to become a politician, and we start to figure out that smoking is bad for you. The World Trade Center plans begin. And apparently, nothing interesting happens in the UK ever.

Doctor Who continues apace with another claustrophobic episode featuring the four main characters and nothing else. The show is still feeling its way around, uncertain of what it is. As with the first episode, it is already clear that it is something. This is most notable in Ian's line describing the Doctor as having "a knack for getting himself in trouble," a character trait that will sustain fifty years and counting of stories, but that, notably, Ian has little basis for. It's another wholly forward-looking line.

But in other ways, the show seems lost, following the trends of futuristic design laid out by classic movies like *Forbidden Planet* instead of breaking new ground. The dead world of Skaro is a monument to retro-futurism. The TARDIS is not yet a magical box, with excessive effort being made to actually explain how the thing works. The fact that the change of the Doctor and Susan to aliens instead of futuristic humans was a last-second production decision is still clear, with both acting as though the TARDIS is just future technology that any species would acquire given time.

On top of that, the Doctor is still openly cruel. When his companions – including Susan – beg to leave the planet, he frankly betrays them all, deliberately breaking the TARDIS so that they have to go to the futuristic city and explore. Here we have our first inkling of why the Doctor does what he does – his burning need to explore and see new things. This need, however, it is not yet wedded to any sense of kindness. He is not a hero. He's just about the least sympathetic character on the show.

The show also presents its first aliens. Initially they find a metal creature in the forest, and the Doctor chastises Ian for failing to adequately imagine how much the universe can differ from his experience. Then, in the episode's iconic cliffhanger, Barbara is menaced by an unseen monster with a bizarre arm.

For the third time in a month, everything changes.

And yet it doesn't – not quite. I mean, yes, this is one of the most important stories in Doctor Who's history. The massive success of the Daleks gooses Doctor Who's ratings into the "madly successful" range, spiking from the lower half of the top hundred programs for the week to the top thirty. It also led the Daleks to move from one-off monsters to recurring threats. But none of that applies to this story, which thinks it's creating one-off monsters for a still hazily-defined sci-fi serial. Everything changes, yes, but (and not for the first time) nobody notices it happen.

Even the much-vaunted cliffhanger is misunderstood by audiences and writers alike as the start of Dalekmania – Doctor Who's own parallel to Beatlemania. But the tension of this cliffhanger is not that Barbara is menaced by the Daleks. The Daleks don't exist yet. The cliffhanger is about Barbara's terror at the unseen monster.

It's not until two days after "I Want to Hold Your Hand" reaches the US that anything called Dalekmania might be said to start. It's in the second episode that we get the important shot. While it's not the iconic one, it's the one that had the necessary impact, as the Doctor, Ian, and Susan walk through a door and the camera pulls back to display the unfathomable *things* that we are finally told are Daleks. Certainly the ratings support this, spiking massively for the third episode – after the Daleks are seen, not after the famed cliffhanger. It is not the threat of monsters that matters, but their material reality. (Of course, Raymond Cusick's phenomenally good design work on the Daleks does them all manner of favors.)

But what, exactly, are they? For the second episode, at least, this is held in check. They are devious, and we are certainly not inclined to trust them, especially after the wonderful establishing shot where we pull away from the TARDIS crew to see that they have entered a room full of faceless, anonymous robotic monsters. But they do not seem to be the unquestionably and unambiguously malevolent evil that we will someday know them to be. The Doctor is not helpful here – he does not recognize them, and they do not recognize him. This is their true first meeting, and it is a wary one in which each of them tries to feel out and understand the other. The Daleks seem to warn of a greater threat, namely, the hideously mutated Thals living out in the wilderness.

Meanwhile, the show takes a turn to the crushingly bleak, with the characters slowly dying of radiation poisoning. The

Doctor manages to negotiate for Susan to be allowed to go get the anti-radiation drugs needed to save them. At the end of the second episode, the Doctor lies near death, and his companions, who by now know he sabotaged the TARDIS, seem to want to keep him alive only because they need him to fly the ship to get them home.

(It is here also that Hartnell flubs his first line as the Doctor. This is a problem that will increase over the next three years, eventually being part of why he is forced into retirement. This is an uncanny bit of foreshadowing, given that Hartnell is the only actor to play the Doctor who has no gaps whatsoever in which a large number of additional stories can be added. He has companions the entire time that we can use signs of aging to verify time via, meaning that his eventual regeneration, for the character, comes only a few years after his first appearance. This is secondarily true of Troughton, but with a big asterisk we'll get to later, and actually may not be true of Hartnell, but we're years away from getting to that bizarre retcon. And before some wise-ass fan asks about Davison, there is no reason to assume Nyssa or Turlough age at human rates, and even if they did, Big Finish opens a gap with *Renaissance of the Daleks*, which establishes that the Doctor at one point left Nyssa at an exhibition and traveled on his own.)

It is not until the start of the third episode that we begin to see the Daleks as monsters, though that is accomplished in a scene that is, in hindsight, deeply uncomfortable. Susan, emerging from the TARDIS, encounters a Thal. The camera holds on Susan as she reacts to it, finally saying that she had expected the Thals to be disfigured, but then uttering: "You're perfect." With that, the camera cuts to a strapping blonde Adonis of a Thal, indicating the definition of perfection. The degree to which this definition is Aryan is all the more chilling given that Carole Ann Ford, who plays Susan, is Jewish.

But underneath the flagrant racialism is the beginning of a vital point about Doctor Who – the fact that the show is, at heart, anthropophilic. That is, it loves humans. The Doctor is in the end more human than alien. "Good" species are the ones that look human. The other species of the universe are, by and large, monsters.

In an odd way, this revelation – the fact that the Daleks are contrasted with "perfect" humans – is what creates monsters. After Susan meets the Thals, the Daleks begin talking of extermination, and gun down the Thal leader for no reason other than because they want to kill him. This is where the Daleks become monsters, and Doctor Who acquires one of its fundamental dualisms: people and monsters. But this should make us uncomfortable. Monsters are monsters because they don't look like us. For all the importance monsters have to Doctor Who – and the monsters are a genuinely important part of the show – there is something ugly about the idea of them.

What is interesting is that the fundamental evil of the Daleks is explained by their hatred for things that are not like them. In other words, by the Dalek equivalent of anthropophilia. At the heart of this is a question of race. By and large, the United Kingdom has a much less troubled history of race in the twentieth century than the United States, making the appeal to multiculturalism in this story less pressing in its native cultural context than it would have been in the US some six months before the massive filibuster on the Civil Rights Act of 1964 was broken in the Senate. To give an idea of how entrenched racism was in the US, Senator Robert Byrd, who did not leave the Senate until his death in 2010, joined a filibuster led by President Pro Tempore of the Senate, Richard Russell, who declared that "We will resist to the bitter end any measure or any movement which would have a tendency to bring about social equality."

But here in the early days of 1964, there are still racial troubles in the UK, even if they are overshadowed by the horrific racism in the US. Indeed, the darker side of racism in the UK is its invisibility and its close links with the supposedly proud colonial history of the country. At this point, Doctor Who treats racism in a manner that can only be called uncomfortable. It will be a long time, if ever, before any serious case can be made that this has changed. Indeed, the show quickly hedges against any claims that it might be liberal by painting the Thals as deluded fools for their pacifism. For all that might be made of the Dalek/Nazi parallels in which the Daleks' hatred of the Thals mirrors the Holocaust, that's not the main thrust here. After all, we like the Thals because they're nice Aryan lads. The thing we don't like about the Daleks is that they're not human. The Thals need to buck up and learn to fight bad guys. The idea that racial issues are in play in a positive way in this story is strained at best – the best we can say is that the racial subtext is incidental. The worst we can say is that it's actually deliberate.

The end result is a strange irreducibility to the terrible evil of the Daleks. It is not merely their xenophobia. This becomes clear in their portions of the plot, as they come to realize that the massive radiation levels on Skaro are now necessary to sustain Dalek life (in a bizarrely psychedelic scene) and decide to irradiate the planet and exterminate the Thals. What is interesting at this point is that the Daleks are not wrong. Contrary to the Doctor's insistence that the two races could live in peace, one of them needs radiation to live, and the other needs a lack of radiation to live. It is an unstable, primal state, and the Doctor actively chooses to let the Thals live and the Daleks die. But why?

In the end, the closest thing to a moral difference that can be drawn is that the Thals, perhaps naively, would never try to exterminate the Daleks for their own survival. In fact, it is the Doctor that orchestrates this, planning to drain the Daleks of the static electricity they need to survive. (A quirk of Dalek physiology that will be ignored from this point on, fitting in mostly with the obsession of trying to make the show scientifically plausible that will soon be abandoned.) When this finally comes about, the Doctor says, cruelly, that he does not want to save the Daleks, and anyway, that he can't. There is a moral distinction here that is not yet fully formed. The Daleks are monsters because they recognize nothing that isn't Dalek. This, in the end, is why the Doctor hates them: he is interested in the vast strangeness of the universe, in seeing and learning everything. The issue is not that the Daleks are willing to kill to survive. It is that they don't care about it. It's that they consider killing to be a natural solution to their problems.

The Thals, whatever their flaws, do care. Standing in the wreckage, the Thal leader mourns that there should have been another way – a refrain that the Doctor will someday echo in sorrow. But he has much more to learn about being the Doctor between now and then. As this story ends, the Doctor, with obvious glee, provides the Thals with guidance on how to start a new civilization. He declines to stay – he is too old to be a pioneer, though once, he says, he was. But his love of creating a situation like this is obvious. It is the first time since Ian and Barbara intruded on his life that he appears happy. Here, for the first time, he is truly learning to be the Doctor.

But to learn to be the Doctor, he needed a monster. And those monsters have also learned this episode. Much of their monstrosity is already in place – the Dalek design is sufficiently iconic to be almost wholly unchanged through the show's history. Other parts of them need to be set – although they love exterminating, they have not yet learned the fundamental joy of shouting "Exterminate" a lot. They have also not learned that they really want to avoid lengthy dialogue scenes. But they have learned that they have an enemy. That there is a man with a magic box who will always show up, and will not let their callous destructiveness stand. In hindsight, the Doctor's late revelation to them of the existence of the TARDIS is one of the great throwing downs of the gauntlet in history, the commencement of a fifty-year struggle with no end. Before long, both sides will meet again. And this time, the Daleks will, not for the last time, extract a terrible price from the Doctor.

But for now, having learned from these monsters his role in the universe, the Doctor moves on, seemingly happy. The TARDIS takes off. And then there is an explosion. Something, as usual, goes terribly wrong . . .

Not an Illusion After All (*The Edge of Destruction*)

It is February 8, 1964. In the UK, the number one single is "Needles and Pins" by the Searchers, a Liverpool band. The songwriter, however, is American Sonny Bono, future Republican congressman who will go on to author a massive copyright extension act that is itself a compromise over his own loathsome view that copyright should be perpetual. He will then ski into a tree and die.

Speaking of America, however, the number one single over there is by fellow Liverpool band the Beatles, who have just touched down yesterday at JFK to a throb of fans, offering a strange juxtaposition with Byron de la Beckwith getting away (for at least the next thirty years) with the murder of Medgar Evers.

In the context of Doctor Who, the series' third adventure, a two-part serial hastily cobbled together in order to get the series to fill out its thirteen-episode initial order without requiring the use of any additional sets or characters, is a bit lackluster. As a result of these budgetary crises, both episodes feature only the core cast – something that has, admittedly, happened twice previously in the series, but that will not happen again for more than a decade, and will never again happen for an entire story.

We also have the writing debut of David Whitaker, the show's script editor for its first year, and one of the most influential figures in its development. Whitaker is a significant character in these books, and in future volumes I'll come self-consciously close to suggesting that he's the conscious author of Doctor Who's weird legacy. In particular, Whitaker is responsible for introducing a set of alchemical themes to Doctor Who that actively render the show mystical in its implications. He is easily one of the most important creators of the series. And more to the point, he's easily one of the best – he's a phenomenally good writer who's responsible for some of the best stories of the 1960s. This, however, is miles from his best script. But despite this, it may well be his most important.

Its flaws are largely ones of circumstance. The rush nature of the story is all too clear at points. The opening ten minutes or so are horrendously awkward, with Ian and Barbara alternately acting like children and dementia patients, often changing over mid-word. It's bewildering, and not in a good way. And then, just when it seems like this is going to be a disaster, the episode improbably picks up with an absolutely insane and thoroughly chilling scene in which Susan deliriously stabs a whole lot of things with scissors.

In the early days of Doctor Who, however, even awkward rush jobs can be huge. Doctor Who's canon, you see, is wholly additive, with new things just sort of being grafted on to the knobby bits as time goes on. Basically, it's a giant narrative Katamari. Nothing is ever contradicted or removed. In the event of a contradiction, basically, you've just created a new knobby bit. The only thing likely to happen to a bit of Doctor Who continuity is that it will be smoothed down until it's actually a good story, which, to be fair, it has not always been to start.

But in early Doctor Who, it was all knobby bits. And the knobby bits that survived are now the heart of the thing. So in these first episodes, a lot of things get established. We have the Doctor already. We have monsters. This story gives us two more things – companions and the TARDIS.

We have the TARDIS already, of course. It's where the show started, its incongruous and brilliant central premise. But this is where we are finally allowed to have a look at her. The pronoun, by the way, is not merely homage to naval tradition. The pronoun is there because this story has five characters in it, even if we don't see one of them until the very end. The TARDIS is not just a narrative contrivance. I mean, it is a narrative contrivance, but it is the single best narrative contrivance ever invented. Golden apples, spaceships, evil rings, they have all basically spent their time since November of 1963 sitting around feeling inadequate. The TARDIS has them all beat.

Yeah, there's still the clumsy attempts to make it all make sense. They try to explain why the central column rises and falls, and do a terrible job that is rightly ignored. Most of these clumsy attempts at explaining, actually, get quickly derailed (even in past episodes). An awkward scene in *The Daleks* existed talking about the TARDIS food dispenser and how it makes energy bars that taste just like the real objects. And it made sense, except for being really stupid, pointless and tedious.

But here, the ship, quite frankly, goes a bit mad, starting early in the episode with a long shot in which we can clearly see that the food dispenser has separate buttons for water and ... milk. This is absolutely fantastic. Of course alien species love bovine lactation. Of all the liquids in time and space, they pick water and bovine lactation. Which is clearly about making tea. (Actually, there is a fair case to be made that this sequence is the root of the bit in *The Hitchhiker's Guide to the Galaxy* about trying to get Eddie to make tea.) I mean, that, right there, is the end of any claims that Doctor Who might somehow, if you think about it long enough, make sense. No. Doctor Who might somehow, if you think about it long enough, drive you very productively mad.

From there, the TARDIS's level of "completely and inscrutably insane" ratchets up progressively over the episode, including the first time I, at least, noticed the

TARDIS coatrack, which is so perfectly weird that they eventually get around to writing an episode about it. Then come the TARDIS memory banks, which begin to establish the ship as being alive.

Indeed, the fact that it has memory is intriguing, as it causes the series to firmly cast its lot with one particular view of the universe. One model of time travel, after all, would involve a completely fixed universe. Free will is but an illusion, and all that has ever happened or ever will is already determined. The TARDIS is nothing more than an interactive television that can be flipped on to allow its occupants to view the past. But you can't rewrite history – not one word.

But the existence of memory banks suggests something else – that the TARDIS is in fact subjective. It has memory, which is to say, its own interior history of events. That this is true of a time machine suggests that time is not some fixed and absolute sequence but a collection of memories, experiences, and, in the end, stories.

(The memory banks could, of course, just be a reference to computer memory, which did exist in 1963, but given the overall tone of the story as one in which the TARDIS assaults the main characters with bizarre and surreal imagery, it's tough to argue that the takeaway is meant to be that the TARDIS is just a computer.)

When the memory banks are viewed, one thing that is displayed is the planet Quinnis, in the Fourth Universe. This is a throwaway. The nature of the Fourth Universe, and how it differs from universes one through three, and, for that matter, which universe Doctor Who takes place in, is never explained. All that is known is that the Doctor had an adventure there once with Susan.

We should speak of Susan. I mean, we will need to speak of Susan a lot. She is a scary character – especially in this story, where she's seen stabbing things with scissors and speaking ominously. She is fiercely loyal to the Doctor, even as she at times believes he has gone too far. But she is also not enough, somehow. There is, if you will, the Problem of

Susan, though it's not the first such problem in English fantastic fiction. Here, perhaps, we follow in someone else's archetypes.

The problem can be stated thusly: it is clear that, in order to become the Doctor, he needs companions other than Susan. Barbara snappishly points this out to him, noting that she and Ian have saved the Doctor's life more than once in their adventures thus far. She is not wrong – the Doctor's adventuring would have been disastrous without them. Or, more to the point, since they clearly began his adventuring, it would have been impossible without them. And in this story, his lack of trust in them is nearly catastrophic. Indeed, this story is unusual in that the Doctor takes on the role of villain, behaving so cruelly as to nearly throw Ian and Barbara out of the TARDIS, apparently into deep space, the time vortex, or some similarly inconceivably awful place.

Susan is not sufficient as a companion. What, then, is the role of a companion? This question will recur, but here it is clarified. Not only have the companions saved the Doctor's life, it is Barbara, crucially, who understands that the TARDIS is, to some extent, sentient, and that the bizarre happenings are its version of a warning. This is, notably, something the Doctor does not grasp. He does not understand that the TARDIS is a magical box. He declares that it can't think. But it can, and in this moment, in Barbara's explanation, the TARDIS becomes a character. (Here, again, we get a glimpse of the profound impact of this episode.)

It's her explanation that's wonky. First, all the clocks in the TARDIS melt. Then the fault indicators begin lighting up every fifteen seconds. From these two facts Barbara, in the show's first real piece of completely nonsense technobabble (other than perhaps "Time and Relative Dimensions in Space") proclaims "We had time taken away from us, and now it's been given back to us because it's running out," a declaration that makes no sense whatsoever, but is apparently the key to understanding the problem.

From there the Doctor connects the dots, culminating in a bizarre monologue about the forces of creation and destruction. The problem, as it turns out, is that a spring has busted on a switch (which is labeled conveniently and in Sharpie) and it's stayed on. Which is, in many ways, the full establishment of the TARDIS – on the one hand, it is a magical box that can think and communicate with its inhabitants. On the other hand, it can accidentally have a spring get stuck and proceed to nearly explode. Which is, shall we say, a bit of a design flaw.

But this is indicative of David Whitaker's larger attitude. What's telling is primarily that the TARDIS functions along entirely symbolic and thematic terms. There's not anything resembling a scientific understanding underneath it. Rather there's a patois of cosmic mythology and estranging absurdist weirdness blended together and centered around a glitchy switch. None of it makes sense in a traditionally science fiction sense. Instead it's a symbolic process. The TARDIS communicates by analogy; its danger comes as much from a radical contrast of the forces of creation and destruction as from any sensible concept.

The word "mythic" has been almost systematically devalued these days, but it really is the only word that adequately describes this. There clearly is a logic – even a describable one – to what happens. And yet as presented the logic seems oddly arcane, as though it belongs to an older and rather more terrifying world. And yet equally, everything is caused by the most mundane and pragmatic of concerns: a busted switch.

Inasmuch as the Doctor can be humbled by this, at least, he is. He does not quite apologize to Ian or Barbara for nearly throwing them into deep space. But he does act graciously towards them, accepting that he needs them. The Doctor has his magical box, his friends, and his freedom. With this story, the elements of Doctor Who are, by and large, in place.

The Assembled Hordes of Genghis Khan (*Marco Polo*)

It is February 22, 1964, and the number one single is "Diane" by the Bachelors. Over the next six weeks, Cilla Black and Billy J. Kramer and the Dakotas will both also make it to number one before the Beatles regain the spot on April 2. This feels something like a restoration of order when it happens. Other bands kicking about the charts include Cliff Richard, Manfred Mann, and, perhaps most interestingly, the first single from the Rolling Stones.

In real news, John Glenn, fresh from entering the US Senate race, falls down in his bathroom and injures himself, prompting his withdrawal from that race. Muhammad Ali becomes heavyweight champion of the world, Richard Burton and Elizabeth Taylor get married (round 1), the first pirate radio station in the UK starts up (a major event, by any measure), and Beatlemania continues with the Beatles having slots one–five in the US charts simultaneously.

One of the things that becomes apparent over this book and the next (Troughton-focused) volume is that the zeitgeist, whether through luck or design, throws up concurrences and coincidences. One we will see repeatedly is that the return of the Beatles to the number one slot has a sort of calming effect on things. Thus, after six weeks in which Doctor Who is in a decidedly odd mood, the Beatles show up and we return to normal service.

But that's not actually where we get to start. Due to space-saving measures at the BBC, who inadequately anticipated the eventual demand for home video versions of television shows, the master recordings of numerous Doctor Who episodes, including all seven episodes of *Marco Polo*, were junked between March 9, 1967, and late 1974. This mass junking was further spurred by Equity, the actors' union, which feared that home video and repeats would eventually render the making of new television obsolete. As a result, although rumors endlessly persist, at the precise moment of this book going to press no episodes of *Marco Polo* are known to have survived.

Doctor Who is, as I have said, eternally unfinished. Another way of putting it – as Paul Magrs in fact has – is that it is incomplete. In the case of the missing episodes, this is literally true. Parts of Doctor Who's history are missing. Important parts. Some unimportant parts too – there's (tragically) not a lot of people hugely bent out of shape over *The Space Pirates* going missing. But there are at a minimum a half-dozen stories that have fans who would chew off limbs to recover them, and *Marco Polo* is clearly among them, in no small part because it is the first major gap in the series.

A fundamental premise of this project is that there is such a thing as a story of Doctor Who. But it's the story of a time-traveler, and that shows. It is a story that goes back and revises itself so that early episodes are at times best read in terms of later developments – as evidenced in the incongruous opening shot of the TARDIS in *An Unearthly Child*. Impossibly, the future of Doctor Who causes its past.

There is a sense in which this is only possible because of the missing episodes. Because the past of Doctor Who is incomplete, it is possible – indeed necessary – to rewrite it. As it happens, reasonable reconstructions exist. The audio for every Doctor Who story is preserved, as, for most, are a good number of still images. As a result, fan-made reconstructions that wed the audio to the still images exist, which is how I watched *Marco Polo*. But even still, there is always a sense that one is reconstructing – trying to uncover a past that is lost.

This is doubly true for this episode, as it is a purely historical piece. This is not the first historical we've seen – *100,000 BC* has no sci-fi conceits beyond the TARDIS. But that story shares space with the story of what the TARDIS is in the first place, something *Marco Polo* does not. At its heart, *Marco Polo* is every bit as much of a bottle episode as *The Edge of Destruction* was – it's just that *Marco Polo* bottled everyone on lavish sets with guest stars instead of in the TARDIS.

What I mean by this is that despite spending quite a bit of time making the story look pretty (and the still photographs existing from the episode are gorgeous), the whole story is basically set in Marco Polo's caravan, with minimal intervention from anyone other than Polo; Tegana, the villain of the piece; and Ping-Cho, the token young Asian girl.

I suppose this opens up the question of race in Doctor Who in a thorough fashion, though we touched on it back with *The Daleks*. Then, as now, the issues of race are problematic. We'll start with the good news – only fourteen episodes into the series, in February of 1964, the show cast a minority actress, Zienia Merton, a Burmese-English actress. Less hopeful – despite being Burmese, she is employed to play a Chinese girl. And she is the only minority actress in a serial set in China, with the rest of the parts basically being played in yellowface. Still, when I made a mental note to myself while watching *The Daleks* to remark on the first time a minority actor or actress appeared in Doctor Who, I in no way thought it would happen that quickly.

It's also notable that, thus far, the series is two for two in focusing on non-European cultures in its historical episodes (assuming, as I do, that *100,000 BC* took place during early human migration out of Africa). In the next historical story, *The Aztecs*, it will go three for three. Unfortunately, over the nine other pure historical stories that exist in televised Doctor Who, the score will never advance beyond three. Still, one thing we've already seen is that the approach of these early stories sets the field the later stories will exist in. Even when they are flawed — and if we're being honest, every story thus far has been deeply flawed — their influence is there in that they set the scope of the series up. And so, because concerns about race are embedded (awkwardly) at the start of Doctor Who, the nature of its later treatments of race is set. By being awkwardly pioneering early on, the show gains the license to be less awkward when it smashes down barriers later. (Though Ted Sturgeon's famous observation that the bulk of alien cultures are just Meiji Japan painted green looms ominously over all of these observations.)

To my mind, this is the main way in which *Marco Polo* is interesting in general: in terms of the ways in which it does, and, more importantly, does not anticipate later Doctor Who. I have already said that Doctor Who canon is additive — that nothing is undone, only amended. But there are aspects of the show that have largely been left to lie — the focus in early episodes on ostensibly hard science, for instance. (Which continues here with a scene that spectacularly fails to make condensation exciting.) Historicals are another one of those. The first season of Doctor Who is an almost exact split between historical and science fiction episodes. The second season is only twenty percent historical, the third about thirty percent, the fourth is eighteen percent, and then all remaining series are zero percent save for Season Nineteen, which did a quick two-parter for old time's sake and is thus eight percent historical.

There are two main reasons given as to why historical stories declined. The first, popular among certain segments of fandom, is that they were unfathomably boring stories that existed only to fulfill the original educational remit of Doctor Who. This is not strictly speaking true, although a few were a bit plodding, this one included. But if we're being honest, that view is held mostly by people who believe monsters are the single most important part about Doctor Who, and we can safely ignore them. (The second is that it turned out there was a much better way to do them, but we'll get to that later.)

But there is a grain of truth to this complaint. Given that the show is not huge on completely rewriting history (as we'll see shortly), there are already some heavy limits on a historical plot. In *Marco Polo*, the odds of Tegana murdering Marco Polo before he returns to Italy or of assassinating Kublai Khan are exceedingly low. This is not a matter of lacking suspense – after all, it's also extremely improbable that the Doctor is going to die in a cliffhanger. Doctor Who has always been a show more about the question "how are they going to get out of this one" than "are they going to get out of this one." The problem is that for a purely historical adventure, the answer is pretty limited in scope. They're going to get out of this one . . . much like the history book says they will. (Actually, in this case, very much unlike that, since the story plays fast and loose with history.) All the same, the notion that anything can happen – essential to the mad spectacle of what we tend to consider the best episodes of Doctor Who – just isn't in play here.

As a result, *Marco Polo* amounts to seven episodes of an idiot plot in which the complete inability of the main characters to figure out that Tegana is evil (something that the audience knows almost immediately) and persuade everyone else of this is the only thing that keeps it from being a two-episode story. The contortions necessary to prevent this, however, require the Doctor to basically be absent from most of the story to let Ian carry on proceedings somewhat less competently. In other words, this is six episodes of waiting before what we know will be the real climax in Kublai Khan's court. The only available suspense is what aspect of medieval China we'll see next, which is a bit low stake.

This brings us to the second problem with historicals – their educational and tonal remit can be carried out by pseudo-historicals just as well, and in pseudo-historicals there's considerably more mystery as to what's going to happen. For all the flaws that episodes like *The Shakespeare Code* and *The Curse of the Black Spot* have, the fact that they can mix tropes of their setting with tropes alien to their setting gives them options and power that a pure historical like this can never have. Much of the point of Doctor Who is the juxtaposition of Ian and Barbara – two ordinary people – with places where ordinary 1960s Brits don't belong such as Skaro or medieval China. But if juxtaposition is the point of Doctor Who, doesn't dropping an alien invader into medieval China on top of all of that push it to be just a bit more strange and wonderful?

Instead we get a fairly predictable travel narrative. Which is jarring on its own, but worse is that it interrupts the arc we've been enjoying thus far in which, with each episode, the Doctor becomes more like the Doctor. Here, most of that is discarded, leaving the Doctor's major plot threads to involve being thirsty, being cranky, or both. Instead, inasmuch as the episode advances anything about the characters, it focuses on the companions. Ian and Barbara continue to be odd proto-companions who are defined by their lack of desire to be traveling with the Doctor. In fact, Barbara reiterates in this story her wish to eventually leave the TARDIS forever.

But perhaps the more interesting developments come in the equation of Ping-Cho and Susan, who the story situates as close mirrors of each other. Susan's young age is reiterated – sensible given that the series has yet to make any moves towards establishing the Doctor as functionally immortal. The major contrast between them, then, comes in the form of Ping-Cho's preparation for an arranged marriage and Susan's horror at the concept. Central to this, then, is part of the Problem of Susan – the fact that, as a fifteen-year-old girl, she is sexualized, but the show is unable to give any useful outlet for that sexuality as long as she is familially linked to the Doctor. Later companions will be sexualized in terms of the TARDIS crew, but that option is not available to Susan. This, among many other things, will eventually make Susan untenable as a companion, albeit by far the most interesting failure the show has ever produced.

Marco Polo, then, is in many ways the first dead end we have seen on Doctor Who. It's interesting – well scripted for what it is, lavishly produced, and, perhaps most intriguingly, missing. But it is also, unmistakably, not quite Doctor Who. Of course, little in the first season is quite Doctor Who. But *Marco Polo* manages the odd and slightly unnerving feat of neither feeling like what went before nor what will follow, instead serving as an odd detour into some other show entirely.

Another Self-Aggrandizing Artifact (*The Keys of Marinus*)

It's April 11, 1964. The Beatles have the number one single with "Can't Buy Me Love." In the next six weeks, we will discover why the Beatles are unable to buy love – namely that, as Peter & Gordon observe, this is "A World Without Love," making the Searchers' admonition "Don't Throw Your Love Away" sound advice. Other names in the charts included Doris Day, Gerry and the Pacemakers, and Dionne Warwick.

While in the real world, BBC 2 starts broadcasting and the 1964 New York World's Fair opens. This is the last really major world fair in many regards, in no small part because they rebranded as Expos after that. And the first program written in BASIC is compiled and run.

This last fact is perhaps the most interesting, occurring as it does at the midpoint of *The Keys of Marinus*, a serial which, in hindsight, is plotted like a video game. But there's something of a reason for that. *The Keys of Marinus* went into production in part because every other idea failed. Three separate serials imploded – one about a miniaturized TARDIS crew, one entitled *The Masters of Luxor* by *100,000 BC* writer Anthony Coburn, and one entitled *The Hidden Planet* by Malcolm Hulke, who would go on to write several genuinely classic episodes of the series. As a result, Terry

Nation, who had just written *The Daleks*, was drafted to bang out a script in a hurry.

Due to the compressed timeframe, he opted for an extremely episodic structure in which the serial would go through, essentially, a different adventure each week. The plot structure is extremely bare – the Doctor and his companions must rescue the five microkeys that will power up a machine that can subdue the evil monsters, the Voord. The keys are scattered across the planet Marinus, and the TARDIS crew are given teleporters so they can get from key to key.

The result is a Doctor Who plot that feels like a video game – collect the MacGuffin from each level and move on to the next one before finally confronting the Voord. Except, of course, that *Spacewar!* had only been developed three years prior, and there was nothing resembling a video game industry yet. In fact, the development of BASIC would be integral in the nascent hacking movement of the 1970s that would eventually translate into the video game industry and, in 1975, finally provide *Adventure*, which would begin to codify the video game plot. Doctor Who isn't resembling video games here – video games are resembling Doctor Who.

There are several things to conclude here. First is that video game plotting is not integral to video games, but in fact stems from the highly serialized form of old-time radio and early film which Nation is also using here. But *The Keys of Marinus*, quite honestly, feels more like a video game than radio or film serials do. Doctor Who is always a serial, but this almost level-based structure isn't textbook serial material. It seems, not for the first time, about a decade ahead of itself. Much of this comes from its combination of serialization with infinite flexibility. Ironically, this infinite flexibility is realized in *The Keys of Marinus* not through the mechanism that will provide it through most of the series, the TARDIS, but through a bunch of transporter bracelets that bop the TARDIS crew around an improbably strange planet.

But perhaps the most significant thing to conclude is that Terry Nation is an odd sort of writer. We may praise the video game style of plotting as ahead of its time, and it is, but equally, it's a relatively facile plot structure that is based more on cool concepts than on the actual exploration of them.

Yes, *The Keys of Marinus* is fantastic for the sheer amount of weird stuff it introduces to the show. None of it is major canon or ever returns, but you get a planet with a glass beach and an acid sea, monsters in fantastic rubber gimp suits called the Voord, mind-controlling brains with eyestalks, killer vegetables that psychically scream, snow wolves, robotic knights with plastic capes, and a courtroom drama that out-hams Phoenix Wright. All in just under two and a half hours. It is with this episode, in other words, that Doctor Who becomes completely barmy. This culminates in the final episode, where the audience is treated to the spectacle of a man in awkwardly tight rubber shouting "My power is absolute!"

But none of it is particularly explored or developed. And a lot of this is down to the unpleasant secret of Terry Nation, which is that he's not actually a very good writer. He's got a knack for concepts, but his ability to explore them is muted. Even back in *The Daleks* this is a problem. *The Daleks* is overly long at seven episodes, but the problem with it isn't even the excess of episodes so much as the fact that they're padded with absurd contrivances. The episode anchored by the attack of the mire beast is baleful not just because it's a lame monster, but because it clearly exists only because Nation didn't have any further ideas. Which is actually faintly absurd, given how many subsequent Dalek stories have found things to add to that initial premise. I mean, if there's one idea we know has more than six episodes worth of material in it, it's the Daleks.

This reveals a key truth about Terry Nation, which is that his premises are almost universally better than his execution. Doctor Who fandom necessarily has an odd relationship with Nation, since whatever one might say about him, he is in one sense single-handedly responsible for the show's survival, since it was, in point of fact, the Daleks that made it massively popular. This is, of course, at least somewhat controversial. Nation wrote a robotic monster lurking in a ruined city. Raymond Cusick, the designer of them, created the actual visual Daleks that everybody knows, and later writers, most notably David Whitaker, refined them into legends.

But as with any case where sole credit is given to one person for something that, in practice, was collaboratively created, there's something of an overcorrection. Yes, Raymond Cusick deserves as much credit for creating the Daleks as Terry Nation does, but that often has the odd effect of making people act as though Terry Nation deserves no credit. That's not true. Equally, however, and this is something that a large portion of Doctor Who fandom has figured out, on his own he could not have possibly created anything as significant as he did. And his two non-Dalek stories – this and a Tom Baker story – expose his limitations.

The truth is, as a writer he's beholden to a very serialized action structure that is reasonably fun when applied to shows that are mainly about square-jawed action heroes, but faintly miserable when applied to Doctor Who, a series that is ostensibly about cleverness and creativity. However effective his writing is in some contexts, the fact of the matter is that he's a very weak writer of Doctor Who, and only one of his ten stories can really be described as "working" with a completely straight face.

Still, the action serial format is, at least, often good for mindless fun. Even in this story, where his writing is often at its most banal, there are moments of real charm. At the very least the failure to develop any concept adequately means that, on the other hand, no concept stays around long enough to be greatly annoying. There is, in practice, a sense of giddy excitement to the story that keeps it moving even when it slogs down. It's not enough to make the story hugely fun to watch, but it's enough to give it a sort of endearing charm.

Yes, it's a story that's easier to love than to like, but, well, it is at least lovable in its sheer sense of manic fun.

It's telling, then, that it is this story that first sets in place the idea that the TARDIS crew actually enjoy their adventures. Sure, Ian's grudging trust for the Doctor is still, well, grudging, and Barbara is perhaps a bit tired of all the endless kidnapping, but they enjoy themselves, leading to the first time an episode has started with the crew just milling about the TARDIS and landing – a category of scene that will eventually become not only standard, but arguably the bread and butter of the series.

(Indeed, there are some stories in the Tom Baker era that are fine right up until the Doctor and Romana leave the TARDIS, at which point the whole thing goes to hell in a handbasket, due only half to the facts that the plot is crappy and it has a giant, furry bull monster, and half to the fact that, frankly, when you have Tom Baker and Lalla Ward available for light banter, it's very difficult to come up with a compelling reason for them not to engage in it at great length. And honestly, a similar thing can be said for when you have William Hartnell and Jacqueline Hill, who are equally magnetic.)

This, much more than the aberration of *Marco Polo*, feels like the first episode of Doctor Who we've seen – the first time all the parts of the show are there and working. It's not good, amusingly enough, but it is correct, if you will. And to be fair, many of the problems are structural. The somewhat insane relationship of the show to science is clear here, with a tedious explanation of geothermal energy and Iceland juxtaposing with insane technobabble. Furthermore, the production schedule is just lethal, and it does a number on the cast and crew. The first season of Doctor Who has fourty-two episodes in it, which necessitated giving actors a break. As a result, the Doctor is completely absent from two episodes. This is a bit of a problem, and exacerbated by the fact Susan is in captivity for most of these episodes, at times leaving Ian and Barbara, or, in one case, just Ian to carry the weight of the episode. But from that the show manages to find a silver lining. Handing two episodes to Ian and Barbara requires making them strong enough characters to carry the story for fifty minutes, and increases the role of the companion, which will pay off throughout the rest of the series.

But the other problems of this story spring from it just not having a good enough script. Despite the preposterous number of odd ideas in the story, it drags. Part of this is probably the shuffling of characters – repeatedly reducing your cast to a handful for long stretches means you have little to work with and have to extend scenes – a habit the actors clearly got into. There's a fantastic bit in the final episode where an actor goes on with his exposition about how they're all going to explode a bit too long, and William Russell basically shoves him down a corridor to begin some intense running. Well, walking. We still have Hartnell, after all. I'm also fairly sure the last three minutes of the episode consist solely of every guest character saying goodbye to every main character in a sort of horrifying ode to *The Waltons* eight years too early. "Goodbye, Susan. Goodnight, John-Boy."

But even in the slow bits, there's a sort of manic energy to this story that Doctor Who has not seen before. As though the sheer pluck of vintage '60s sci-fi has found its ultimate expression and final form – a show where mad ideas can be stacked next to each other and swapped about at high speed. Doctor Who is a show that can go from evil snail brains to psychic vegetables in a matter of minutes before sticking all its characters on a deadly snowy mountain.

Why would you ever watch something else?

Elizabeth Sandifer

Does It Need Saying? (*The Aztecs*)

It is May 23, 1964. The number one single is "Juliet" by the (unremarkable) Four Pennies, who will peak at number one for a week before yielding to Cilla Black, another star from the increasingly vital Liverpool. Chuck Berry, Roy Orbison, Cliff Richard, and other such standards fill the remainder of the charts.

In other news, the first stirrings of the antiwar movement begin in the US, along with the announcement that more than fourty hidden microphones were found inside the US Embassy in Moscow. The US Senate brings to an end the filibuster on the Civil Rights Act. And again, nothing much happens in the UK.

Returning to music, then, where the UK is more relevant, it is worth commenting on Liverpool's dominance of the musical scene, since it's one of two major bits in the twentieth century where a city other than London has had such cultural dominance (Manchester in the 1980s being the other). The crucial thing to understand about Liverpool's dominance of the musical scene is that Liverpool was a declining industrial city. The rise of the Merseybeat scene is specifically a rise of an economically depressed youth population.

I highlight this because Doctor Who is unmistakably a product of privilege. An academic and some schoolteachers traveling freely is not something that stems from the working class. In fact, its relationship to the working class is deeply problematic (a fact that will become glaringly obvious in the Pertwee volume). Susan, in the first episode, demonstrates that she is capable of living life without even understanding what money is or how it works. The Doctor, by definition, has no use for money. This tension will not be adequately addressed until very late in the program's history – really not until Russell T Davies takes over. But it will be inadequately addressed repeatedly, and here's a major example of that.

As I said back with *Marco Polo*, one interesting facet of the subgenre of Doctor Who known as the historical is that the first three were centered upon non-European cultures, and then no more ever were. This is the third and final of these, and is furthermore (I believe) the first Doctor Who story set primarily in the New World for over forty years. Set in the fourteenth century, at least a century before Cortés came along, the shadow of European colonialism and its attendant socio-economic issues hangs explicitly over this story. But that doesn't entirely mean that the issues are dealt with well. We have a lot to do with *The Aztecs* in terms of figuring out whether the story deserves a pat on the back and an encouraging thanks for trying, or a whack upside the head for its failures.

In her excellent article "'Sociopathic Abscess' or 'Yawning Chasm'? The Absent Postcolonial Transition in Doctor Who," Lindy A. Orthia (who also compiled the definitive list of homoerotic screencaps in Doctor Who) explicitly calls out *The Aztecs* as one of the explicitly pro-colonial stories of Doctor Who, and thus as one of its most problematic stories. The story features Barbara explicitly trying to change Aztec culture to abandon human sacrifice in the belief that doing so will allow the Aztecs to survive Spanish colonization. This trope may be more familiar to a contemporary reader as the underlying assumption of Mel Gibson's spectacular racist epic *Apocalypto* – that the fundamental problem with pre-Columbian America is human sacrifice, and that this constitutes a sort of original sin that dooms the culture. (That Gibson took such care to depict the culture accurately and with native actors while simultaneously arguing that its extermination at the hands of the Spanish was a sort of inherent justice makes his movie all the more bewilderingly unpleasant. At least Doctor Who has the decency to obliviously cast white British actors who ham their way through the parts, thus giving the racism that smiling liberal face of willful ignorance that continues to protect discrimination so well.)

In terms of the issues of class and social justice, then, *The Aztecs* marks not so much a turning point as an institutional collapse in which the tensions and ambiguities of the first stories give way to unadulterated European colonialism, based, as always, not on overt racism but on the far creepier image of what Rudyard Kipling called "The White Man's Burden." In this poem – one of the most startlingly racist things ever to be written by a major canonical writer – Kipling presents what amounts to a moral defense of the British Empire, concluding that its real purpose and justification is that the British need to help out and elevate the lesser races. Chilling as this is, the Doctor seems quite afflicted with the White Man's Burden, cursed to "hear the truth you've spoken twisted by knaves," as Kipling puts it.

If anything blunts this accusation, it is the fact that thus far the Doctor is not clearly a figure of social justice. The flashes of a desire to help make the world a better place demonstrated against the Daleks have not really been seen since, with the Doctor acting primarily to save his own skin in more recent stories. Once the Doctor embraces the ethos of social justice, his failure to transcend the cultural biases of his writers becomes problematic. This early on, as they say, he's still cooking. In this story, in fact, he is an actively regressive character, upbraiding Barbara for trying to change history in the first place.

Those that find the Doctor's famed quote from this story, "You can't rewrite history! Not one line!" odd given later developments are not alone. Indeed, it's hard even given earlier developments. It's quite a challenge to figure out why the Doctor can actively aid the genocide of the Daleks while not being able to interfere in Aztec society. The best explanation – and certainly the one most compatible with David Whitaker's larger system (and he is script editor here) is that one cannot rewrite one's own history. The problem isn't that Barbara is altering the past, but that she's altering a past of significance to her, the Aztecs having been a formative subject of her own understanding of history. To rewrite this history, in other words, is to rewrite one's self. Which is a lovely theory, but one that is only spottily supported by this specific story, which is altogether more vague on exactly why mucking with Aztec history is bad but Marinusian history is fair game.

But the incoherence of the specifics do not reduce the degree to which the Doctor is expressing the beginnings of a major theme here – one that is, if not the much-needed social justice theme, at least closely intertwined with it. That theme is that the Doctor, despite the freedom of his travels, is held to a higher duty of some sort.

Indeed, given the casual racism of Barbara's position – which amounts to viewing the Aztecs as noble savages – the Doctor's non-interventionalist position of wanting to get back to the TARDIS with minimal fuss is, in many ways, the more liberal position. After all, it is clear that the Doctor is not in favor of human sacrifice – he speaks derisively of Tlotoxl as "the local butcher," and praises Autloc for renouncing the savagery of Aztec society. The Doctor's position, underneath its veneer of arbitrary plot expediency, is actually remarkably subtle, albeit primarily in hindsight, with what is at best ambiguity and at worst sloppy characterization resolving helpfully into nuance with the passage of time.

The story falls well short of what modern tastes would like out of a story about a foreign culture. But there's just enough breathing room that we can convince ourselves otherwise. Whether we should is a tricky matter, and in practice fandom should be harsher to this story than it is and Orthia's critique should be taken more seriously than it is. But to some extent, it can't be. So much of this story is so good, and there's such an incentive to engage in a redemptive reading of these early days and to see a story like this as when the Doctor starts to gel and approach what he will be, as opposed to when the problems with how the Doctor has been being characterized really come to the fore.

(If nothing else, compare the depth of the Doctor's characterization to that of Ian, whose involvement in this story mostly amounts to whacking people in the head and, on occasion, wisecracking about it. Unfortunately, Ian gets the short end of the stick in these early stories. After an interesting role challenging the Doctor's moral authority early on, he is rapidly settling into a bland action-man template. It will work out for him in the end, but it's a bit of a rough road getting there.)

The ambiguity of the Doctor extends to his inadvertent marriage to Cameca in these episodes, giving us the first hint of a romantic side to the character. It is easy to dismiss the brief romance in this story as an aberration, but if it is an aberration, it is a deliberate one. Visual storytelling is used throughout these episodes to cement the fact that the Doctor does genuinely care for Cameca – from his active decision at the end not to abandon the brooch she offers him to the long close-up of his look of happiness, which is held long enough that the audience expects it to fade . . . only to see that it does not, and the Doctor is actually smitten by Cameca.

The problem with romance and the Doctor is that the Doctor, in the end, is defined by his desire to leave. A life defined by escape is not one that enables romantic relationships. Cameca knows this, and at the end begs to go with the Doctor, but is, for reasons that are not made clear at all, refused, and never mentioned again. Fans talk about this as an early exploration of romance for the Doctor, but if we're being honest, it's both an exploration and abandonment of the concept. They try it, embracing it wholeheartedly, and then realize that it doesn't work. The Doctor is always going to escape. He has to.

For all the warmth shown between the Doctor and Cameca, by far the most interesting and nuanced scenes of this episode are the ones shared by Barbara and the Doctor. From the harshness of the Doctor's insistence that she not alter history to his eventual apology for that, Hartnell and Hill light up the screen in this episode. Their chemistry, combined with the fact that this is probably the most tightly paced and plotted Doctor Who story to date, makes it all the more visible that Susan is off in a corner for most of the story (due to Carole Ann Ford getting the two-week break afforded to Hartnell last story) and Ian has nothing to do.

I am not arguing that Doctor/Barbara shipping is the optimal way to read the first two seasons of Doctor Who here. It's not. It's tempting to side with Orthia and suggest that it's Susan/Barbara shipping that makes the world go round, but if we're being honest, as flawed as Ian is in these early stories, it's the triangle of Ian, Barbara, and the Doctor that is driving the show. The Doctor and Ian grudgingly respect each other. Ian views the Doctor as a potential competitor for Barbara. But, crucially, the Doctor does not desire Barbara. He loves and respects her – in many ways, he is more affectionate towards her than he is towards Susan. But there is no evidence of sexual tension on his part. The Doctor, in short, simply opts out of his role in the romantic triangle, which turns out to be by far the most interesting option.

Certainly it's the only one that could possibly generate an interesting relationship between him and Barbara, as if we're being honest, Doctor/Barbara shipping doesn't work. But if we take the early days of the show as a competition between Ian and the Doctor for who is in charge (a competition the Doctor has now won), the obvious proxy for this competition is a love triangle with Barbara. (See Arthur, Lancelot, and Guinevere.) But the show would be deadly dull if it actually went in that direction. Instead, the Doctor displays a complete lack of interest in this even as he displays considerable interest in Barbara as a person. And this story really cements that – the Doctor's romantic interest is clearly situated on Cameca even as he's enormously emotionally invested in Barbara. Which moves the show beyond its very predictable dynamic of two dudes fighting over a woman, and instead to a strange new territory. There's still a triangle, but it's not the one we expect.

The problem with this – and as I said, even with Ian's problems, on the whole the triangle works very well – is that the TARDIS crew, at the moment, is a quadrilateral. Because Carol Ann Ford was on holiday for most of the production of this story, her involvement is minimal, and we have been able to avoid a significant discussion. Next essay, however, we will have to confront the Problem of Susan head-on . . .

You're Not Dealing with Human Beings Here (*The Sensorites*)

It is June 20, 1964. The music charts are about to do some very odd things. Cilla Black still holds the number one, but between now and August 1, Roy Orbison, the Animals, the Rolling Stones, and the Beatles will all reach number one with the Rolling Stones getting their first number one hit. (The songs, respectively, are "You're My World," "It's Over," "House of the Rising Sun," "It's All Over Now," and "A Hard Day's Night.") Chuck Berry, Louis Armstrong, and Dusty Springfield also make the charts in here.

While in the news, the Catholic Church formally condemns the birth control pill, confirming the existence of the sexual revolution. There are some race riots in Harlem, the Civil Rights Act is signed, and Barry Goldwater gets some good lines in about extremism in defense of liberty. In other news, Malawi declares independence from the UK, Manx radio begins on the Isle of Man, and the Beatles return to Liverpool for the premiere of *A Hard Day's Night* (the film), giving the UK something to do in this paragraph for the first time in a few essays.

This generative tumult – a seven-week period in which five artists, four of them solidly major, reach number one, and in which the Beatles make another major advance in their career – is reflected this time in Doctor Who, which airs *The*

Sensorites. While it is unclear that *The Sensorites* is the best Doctor Who story to date (indeed, among fans it's relatively unpopular) it is without doubt the most complex and interesting.

I do not wish to bang the post-colonial gong too many times in a row, but it is worth commenting that this story is cited by Lindy Orthia as one of six stories that are explicitly anti-colonial, especially given that it comes immediately after one of the three stories she cites as being pro-colonial. To some extent, this speaks to a fundamental issue of Doctor Who – its lack of long-term coherence. *The Aztecs* was written by John Lucarotti, who would contribute three historical stories to Doctor Who in the sixties, as well as an uncredited initial script for *The Ark in Space* in 1975. *The Sensorites* was written by Peter R. Newman, for whom it would be his last writing credit for any show.

The thing about the early days of Doctor Who is that little effort was made to provide an overarching vision for the show – mentions to past adventures might be dropped in, a token effort is made to provide a cliffhanger stretching from story to story, and everything gets a rewrite from David Whitaker that makes it a bit shinier and a bit stranger. But the fact of the matter is that continuity from *The Aztecs* to *The Sensorites* exists entirely because of the core concept of Doctor Who, not because of any active effort by Lucarotti and Newman to write complimentary pieces.

In the absence of any guiding vision, then, Doctor Who falls back on what science fiction was in the era. This means its influences are action serials and golden age literary science fiction, the bulk of which was written in a neo-imperialist mode. More broadly, British science fiction dealing with alien cultures is always going to fall back into colonialism just because colonialism is a fundamental part of the British notion of alien cultures. In 1964 there was still an awful lot of British Empire. And a lot of it, just by virtue of being British science fiction in 1964, is fairly pro-empire. Until Doctor Who starts to develop something of its own identity, and it's not there yet, it has to draw on what's around it. But equally, by 1964 there were plenty of anti-imperialist attitudes to draw on as well, and with *The Sensorites* we finally have a story that draws explicitly on those.

As a result of this break with the prevailing attitudes, *The Sensorites* also offers one of the most radical ideas to date in Doctor Who – good aliens. And not good aliens in the creepy Aryan way that the Thals were good. No – the Sensorites are still scary aliens visually. If the show had firmly established the idea of monsters yet – if this were in short, a Patrick Troughton story – they'd be perfect monsters. In fact, the first episode ends with their monstrous visage appearing in the window of the space ship, using their monstrosity (which is at least a usable trope already, if not a cliché) as a cliffhanger in what appears to be the standard mode of "And here's your alien menace for the month!" In truth, it's a red herring for the fact that, for most of the adventure, the Doctor is going to be helping the Sensorites.

The Sensorites, generally speaking, are fabulous. First of all, their costumes are great. Different characters get different masks, which are distinct enough to demonstrate difference, but still similar enough to make them feel alien. The story even lampshades this, having the Sensorites comment on the fact that they all look the same to the humans. The masks are fascinating – stark and alienating, with cat-like hair in odd places. Below the neck the costumes get dodgier – the spandex suits that are apparently supposed to be skin are a bit suspect, and the round feet, though a cool idea, never quite work. But as 1964 aliens go, the Sensorites are quite a nice bit of visual design.

Conceptually, they are also interesting – mildly psychic aliens who are mostly meek, fearful, and vulnerable. Their monstrosity, in other words, is a very careful feint. This is built into the script – we spend the first two episodes assuming the Sensorites to be monsters, only to find out that we've been wrong all along. This is an extremely clever feint – one that adds considerably to the anti-colonialist message of the story because the audience is tricked into making a judgment that is not only shown to be wrong from a plot perspective, but is also ethically wrong. It's an interesting trap to lure the audience into – getting them to make an ethical mistake so that they feel obliged to see it corrected. Which, interestingly, leads to another major development in the Doctor as a character – after the immediate crisis is resolved, he voluntarily sticks around to keep helping. It's the first time that he displays an ethical commitment to helping.

This cleverness, perhaps, is why *The Sensorites* is the earliest Doctor Who story to be explicitly referenced in the new series. The Ood of the new series are explicitly modeled on the Sensorites, both visually (complete with the appendage originating from the head area that is a long cable) and conceptually (a vulnerable psychic species), and it is eventually revealed that their planet, the Ood-Sphere, is in fact spatially near the Sense-Sphere.

Good aliens are not, of course, new to science fiction as of 1964. What is more interesting is that Doctor Who is overtly trying to challenge its audience here. It's not just trying to be a daft serialized adventure story. It's trying to tell stories that matter, and more to the point succeeding – the careful consideration of the nature of colonialism coming, in this case, in the time period during which Nyasaland broke off from the British Empire to form Malawi. This question of vulnerable cultures that want white humans to leave them alone to make their own mistakes is, in other words, immediately relevant. Returning to the "White Man's Burden" theme of earlier, it's not as though the British aren't aware that when they pull out of a colonial territory it leaves some instability behind. On the other hand, they do it and, more to the point, view doing it as the right thing to do. This story literalizes that complaint, putting the Doctor directly into the role of carefully managing the separation of the two cultures and figuring out how much and what kind of aid to offer the Sensorites and to what degree he should just get out of their way. This is the most serious piece of science fiction the show has done – certainly more interesting than the "xenophobia is bad" interpretation that is the best thing that can be said of *The Daleks*, which isn't even that convincing an interpretation.

It is important to note, though, that at this stage, Doctor Who requires stories like *The Sensorites* more than *The Sensorites* requires a setting like Doctor Who. *The Sensorites*, in the end, is a classic bit of vintage sci-fi that could have been an Asimov short story or a decent quality '50s or '60s film. It's an established sort of story. What Doctor Who is doing here is earning its wings as a piece of serious science fiction – something it hasn't actually done despite nearly wrapping up its first season now. But it has to manage that while still being firmly Doctor Who. And thus far, the most defining characteristic of Doctor Who is its ability to juxtapose. Watching the series linearly involves jumping, in a one-week period, from escaping Aztec temples to a claustrophobic spaceship under siege from mysterious psychic invaders. Science fiction tropes take on notably different tones when they are juxtaposed actively with other tropes. And these juxtapositions are eventually what will take Doctor Who to truly mythic form. Specifically, we can see that the Doctor has already become an odd, liminal figure. He belongs neither to the humans nor to the aliens, but is an independent force that is capable of negotiating with both. This comes from the fact that, being a character defined by the juxtapositions he presents, he is always an outsider, and is thus granted a strange power by this.

But that power isn't developed yet. Until then, however, the show is dependent on particularly well-written episodes in its various genres – on inventive stories that steadily add to the nature of what Doctor Who is – that establish this power. The show, like the character, has to earn its identity. Part of this is conceptual – stories like *The Keys of Marinus* embed the idea that Doctor Who is about wild variety, stories like *Marco Polo* embed the idea that Doctor Who is about learning more about strange places, and stories like *The Sensorites* embed the idea that this is a serious science fiction show. But more important than these plot elements, in many ways, are the ways the episodes establish the characters. Where *The Aztecs* was about Barbara and the temptations of time travel, *The Sensorites* is, ultimately, about Susan.

Susan, as you recall, is initially defined by her alienness. Here that is expanded on, with much of the story relying on her previously only hinted at psychic powers. These mean that, initially, she is the person with whom the Sensorites communicate. Unsurprisingly, this quickly brings her into conflict with the Doctor, who is, at this point, still defined in a great part by his protectiveness of Susan.

The main scenes of their arguments are tough to watch, mostly because they make it obvious why Susan is never going to work as a character. The Doctor's response to Susan's taking the initiative is to infantilize her, marginalize her, and declare her input to be worthless. Susan responds to this, basically, by completely caving and renouncing her efforts to be independent. With that scene, basically, she's over as a character. The one major justification for her character is that she occupies a point in between the Doctor and Ian and Barbara, and can thus prove the synthesis of their competing views. But if the Doctor can trump her even when she's clearly right and taking sensible action, she can't fulfill that purpose.

This is especially because, when it comes to their interactions, the Doctor is a complete jerk. Bafflingly, he claims that he and Susan have never had an argument. This is clearly untrue – they argue in all of the first three stories. Given that the Doctor is already established as a bit absent-minded and prone to a bit of obliviousness, this statement can be read less as a lie than as a declaration of the Doctor's absolutism. This can be a positive and a negative trait – and it will get played in both ways as time goes on – but here it seems clearly negative. The Doctor is unable to allow Susan to be an interesting character because, in some sense, this detracts from his own vision of himself. If she is not subservient to him, she is useless to him.

Eventually, Susan's psychic powers provide a key element of the story's resolution, as she uses them to help the Doctor, who is isolated in some tunnels. Thus we can see that Susan is capable of functioning on her own. But as soon as she is back in the TARDIS, it's back to normal – with it being made explicit that her psychic powers will fade. The Doctor makes vague promises to work on the abilities when they return to their homeworld, but it's obvious that this is not going to happen. Susan isn't going to grow up.

And this is the Problem of Susan. I take the name from Neil Gaiman's short story of the same name, which is in turn written in response to C.S. Lewis's Narnia books, and the character of Susan within them. Susan is the lone member of her family not to ascend into Narnia at the end, blocked out of heaven because she is sexualized and, in the argument of her siblings and Aslan, no friend of Narnia due to her shallowness. C.S. Lewis, of course, died the day before Doctor Who premiered, and so it is fitting that the show would inherit this problem from his work.

Put simply, the Problem of Susan is the problem of sexual maturity in children's literature. It is not, I assume, a horrific revelation to you, dear reader, that much of children's literature is about sexual maturity. *Alice in Wonderland* and *Peter Pan* are perhaps the most explicit classic examples. (Hence the existence of Alan Moore's *Lost Girls*, but let's not go there.) Both feature the idea of a character who stares into a fantastic new world and is changed by it. And for children, change is maturity. Susan, at sixteen, is torn between teenage sexuality and being the Doctor's granddaughter. And, crucially, the two are mutually exclusive – one involves asserting herself and pursuing her desires, the other requires that she actively sublimate those desires for a parental figure. She cannot possibly do both.

The Problem of Susan, then, is that these roles are, in addition to being mutually exclusive, also interconnected.

Because we have some pretty messed up ideas of teenage sexuality. Specifically, as a culture, we find the idea of women in danger to be erotic. (This is what feminist media critics describe as rape culture – the fact that in male-dominated after male-dominated story, women are objects to put in peril and rescue – i.e. objects to be threatened with rape, either literal or allegorical.) And so whenever Susan is put in the vulnerable granddaughter position she is sexualized because vulnerable women in peril are considered sexy. And whenever she's put in a position to take charge and do things, she is sexualized because she is made into an adult. Susan, in other words, is caught in a catch-22.

Not only is this tension unsustainable, its resolution furthermore has profound impact on the Doctor. The Doctor, in *The Sensorites*, is still forming. The words "Time Lord" are years away from being spoken or even thought of. Sight of another "Time Lord" besides Susan is over a year out. The nature of the Doctor is still heavily obscured. His motivation for traveling appears to be the pure love of the adventure – the TARDIS crew discusses as much at the start of the story – but on the other hand he was visibly incompetent at adventures in still-recent stories. The Doctor, at this point, is a creature of pure action – in most ways indistinguishable from the TARDIS. (This tension eventually becomes *The Doctor's Wife*.)

And so when Susan, this episode, speaks of her planet, where "the sky is a burnt orange, and the leaves on the trees are bright silver," she fences in the Doctor. When the First Elder of the Sensorites says that Susan wants to return home but also wants to wander, this has grave implications for the Doctor – because right now, the Doctor, endlessly running, and not yet established as himself, cannot return home. He's not ready yet, and it will be a long time before he is. (When he does return, the price will be immeasurable.) Susan, defined by the tension between the desire for home and the desire for escape, is incompatible with the Doctor, who desires only endless escape.

More to the point, Susan is a constraint on the Doctor. As long as the Doctor's primary goal is the protection of Susan, he is unable to be completely free. Susan drags the Doctor back towards home, and away from endless travel. Susan, in other words, is unsustainable. It is unsurprising that, in three stories, she will be the first member of the TARDIS crew to go. But her unsustainability is instructive – the problem of female companions and the tension between putting them in peril and letting them assert themselves, which is essentially a restatement of the budding sexuality of the Problem of Susan – exists for virtually every female companion for the rest of the series.

The results of this, hopefully, will be endings like the ending of *The Sensorites* in which the Doctor, for no visible reason, flips out at Ian and vows to throw him off the TARDIS, seemingly ignoring episodes of characterization. That is the consequence of the Problem of Susan. As long as she is on the TARDIS, the Doctor cannot continue developing as a character. And as we've seen, he isn't quite working as one yet. He develops slightly in this story, yes. But only by steamrolling the supporting cast.

That's Not Me at All (*The Reign of Terror*)

It's August 8, 1964. The Beatles are a week away yielding the number one single to Manfred Mann's "Do Wah Diddy Diddy." It is not that "Do Wah Diddy Diddy" is a bad song – it's not. But it is tough not to feel as though, musically, it's a step backwards, away from the more interesting possibilities that the charts have been exploring. Regardless, it holds number one for two weeks before the Honeycombs take it with "Have I the Right," in turn holding it for two weeks before the Kinks take it with "You Really Got Me." Other artists in the charts include the Beach Boys, Herman's Hermits, and the Four Seasons.

In real news, a Rolling Stones concert in the Netherlands gets wildly out of hand and is stopped after fifteen minutes. Also, the UK conducts its last executions, putting Gwynne Owen Evans and Peter Anthony Allen to death via hanging. Bob Dylan gets the Beatles smoking cannabis, and *Mary Poppins* makes its premiere, launching, in one sense, the dawn of "Swinging London" as a cultural concept.

The sense of things taking a step backwards embodied by Manfred Mann's chart success is mirrored, in a sense, on television as Doctor Who airs *The Reign of Terror*. I generally try to be sympathetic to episodes of Doctor Who – this one, however, is a stretch. It's short on virtues and long on faults, opening the door to a different sort of historical adventure but failing to actually walk through it. The problem isn't anything or anyone in particular. Dennis Spooner will do a better job with this style of historical in the future. But the first draft of history is, if you will, a bit of a misfire.

I have already noted the awkwardness of the cliffhanger at the end of *The Sensorites*, in which the Doctor, for no discernible reason, decides to throw Ian and Barbara off the ship at the next stop. This complete collapse of all characterization of the Doctor is bad enough, but it is followed, at the start of *The Reign of Terror*, with a partial recantation. Now the Doctor believes that he can get Ian and Barbara home to their own time again, and that's why he's sending them off on their way. So we have a lousy cliffhanger that's retconned non-sensibly. Off to a great start, here.

It is worth briefly commenting on the way in which the initial premise of the series has been almost completely discarded by this point. Originally, the reason that the Doctor couldn't get Ian and Barbara home is that he needed precise readings on where he was departing from. This premise is shot through in both of the stories following its establishment – the TARDIS's fast return switch could presumably have brought them back immediately, and the Doctor knew exactly where he was at the end of *Marco Polo*. If one is to try to impose continuity on Doctor Who – never a safe bet – then one has to read his explanation of why he can't bring Ian and Barbara home as a lie, presumably cooked up because he wants Ian and Barbara to keep traveling with him. But that can't be easily reconciled with the start of this episode, where he wants to chuck them off the TARDIS.

We should be clear – this isn't a continuity error. This is the premise of the show. It matters massively the degree to which Ian and Barbara can realistically hope to ever get home. That's what the first episode was about – them being unable to get home. The entire premise of the series hinges on how trapped they are, at least at this point. This isn't a show primarily about the Doctor wandering the universe –

not yet. It's a show about Ian and Barbara having to wander the universe, and will be until their departure.

And when the show can't even remain consistent on who they're traveling with and the nature of their travels, it has a bad effect on the content. Specifically, it means that the premise of this episode doesn't make sense. It feels contrived from the start – it makes no sense why the TARDIS crew is wandering outside at this point, but they're still trying to make excuses for it instead of just trusting their premise to do cool stuff.

Much of this is down to the fact that the Doctor is not yet a hero character. Every story thus far has hinged on the TARDIS being inaccessible or inoperable. Not once has the Doctor shown up in a situation and wanted to fix it for its own sake. Yes, he stuck around in *The Sensorites* for a bit out of something that seemed like moral duty, but that's not the norm, nor why he travels. This is not merely an early stage of Doctor Who – we've already seen repeated evidence that the Doctor wants to be a good guy who shows up and fixes things. But the show doesn't know what it wants to be yet, and this evidence jostles up with stories like this in which the Doctor is selfish, reactive, and not really the character we know him eventually to be, nor, more to the point, the character the show is starting to make him into. It's an odd point after the show has figured out what it will be, but before it's actually gotten to being it yet.

The result is a story that's hard to put a finger on. It's telling that the 2012 animated version of the two missing episodes jarred in a large part because of the animators' decision to go with a fast-cut style that just didn't fit the material. But it's tough to figure out what would have – the degree to which these episodes are static really defies any attempt at a modern presentation. The story wears its age on its sleeve.

This extends to the treatment of the companions. Susan has been reduced to a blubbering capture monkey who can be relied upon to foil any attempt to rescue her. In the first two episodes alone she becomes petrifyingly afraid of rats and then inexplicably too ill to escape the guillotine. (She'll presumably feel better decapitated?) Barbara is no better, generally responding to Susan's freak-outs with a sort of weary sigh of "Oh well, I suppose I'll have to be executed too then." And William Russell gets his two-week break this story, spending a large chunk of the existent episodes in prison doing pre-filmed inserts.

The Doctor, meanwhile, spends the first half of the show walking. Literally. The second and third episodes basically amount to the Doctor walking from a farm house to Paris to catch up with the rest of the plot, wandering through comic set pieces and lengthy shots of a stunt double walking through a forest in the show's first location shooting. There's something to be said for the narrative structure of forcing the audience to wait to see what they're looking forward to and building anticipation, but there's also such a thing as overkill. The Doctor walking with occasional comic interludes as he tries to get to the actual story – which is clearly going on without him – is a bit much.

It's not that this is useless padding though. That's not quite what's going on here. Rather, it's that this story is a very different sort of historical from what we've seen previously. The preceding three historical adventures were about telling specific stories in which the time periods are useful settings for those stories. *100,000 BC* is about paralleling the leadership struggle within the tribe with Ian and the Doctor's conflict. *Marco Polo* is ultimately a story about wonder – having established the sci-fi future of *The Daleks*, the show attempts to establish its historicals in grand style. And *The Aztecs* is about Barbara's desire to fix non-Western cultures. Whereas *The Reign of Terror* is trying to do something else entirely – to play with the expected elements of a French Revolution story, stringing them together into a set of comic set pieces for more or less fun. The problem is they don't quite have it down how best to do this – it's a first attempt at the genre romp, and they miss, instead ending up with lazy comedy in which the jokes are usually some form of "Oh look at the fat and greedy louse" or "hey it's Napoleon."

Which is maddening because it's so easy to imagine a good Doctor Who story in the French Revolution. The Doctor's anarchist tendencies match up well with revolutionary spirit (lending some credence to Susan's claim that the Doctor loves the French Revolution), but his tendency to oppose evil makes him a great opponent of the terror itself. That conflict is a fabulous premise for an episode. Unfortunately, it is an episode that requires Doctor Who to be more advanced than it is at this stage. Maddeningly, what it needs isn't much more advanced. As advanced as it was in *The Sensorites* would be a hair's breadth from what it needs. Except that instead of taking that last step forward, the show unexpectedly regresses before this, leaving an episode that should have been an interesting development of the show's bag of tricks to just stumble around.

Most of what *The Reign of Terror* is trying to do is instead done well a few stories later in *The Romans*, which is largely the real start of the "historical romp" subgenre in Doctor Who. If *The Reign of Terror* introduces a major theme or advances the story of Doctor Who significantly, it is the story that sometimes Doctor Who is . . . a bit of a disappointment. This is simply part of what the show is. There is a reason that it got cancelled in 1989 (though to be fair, that reason had little to do with the show's quality at the time so much as with its quality from 1984–1987). There is a reason the 1996 revival failed. There are reasons why the show spent a lot of its history laughed at as a kind of ridiculous and cheap show. Doctor Who survives because the story is never complete. And part of why it is never complete is that it is always a bit error prone. Indeed, if there were not rubbish episodes that were a waste of everybody's time, there would be no burning desire to tell more Doctor Who stories.

Looking again at what was going on in the news during this story, there is a sense that something is changing. The

Kinks are a harder, angrier band than we've seen at number one before. The Beatles are smoking cannabis now. Things are changing. We've known that since November 22, when a lone madman in Dallas demonstrated the fragility of the world. We've known it since November 23, when a lone TV show in England demonstrated the sturdiness of a magic box. The revolution has started, but it has not reached critical mass, little yet anything that could be called its final form.

In an odd way, this is literalized in *The Reign of Terror* at the end. Being the season finale, with the show going dark for a month and a half, the story is given a coda in which the Doctor talks about how the TARDIS crew's destiny is in the stars. There is no cliffhanger pointing forwards for once, and when it picks up in six weeks, for the first time, an episode will begin without immediate reference to the one before it. In practice, this is the first real gap in the Doctor's adventures – every other story is set up to segue seamlessly into the next. A few later writers have managed to find pseudo-gaps in amongst them, but not many. If you check the Doctor Who Reference Guide, a total of seven stories have been inserted into gaps within the first season. Fifteen stories have been inserted into the gap between *The Reign of Terror* and the next story. What's odd is that the actual next story – *Planet of Giants* – seems to dovetail from this one as much as any of the previous ones do. But on the other hand, this seems to mark a gap – an ambiguity – into which anything can happen, and much of it has.

In other words, it is, ironically, on the way out of a rubbish story that fails to represent what the show can be that the show has its first brush with the infinite. After one season, the show is still not quite Doctor Who. But it could be.

Elizabeth Sandifer

Time Can Be Rewritten: *Campaign*

The thing about the past of Doctor Who is that the show very quickly – two televised episodes from here, actually – started actively engaging with questions of its own mythology and past. And so 1964 is never entirely left behind. Even today, stories are actively produced on CD, under official BBC licenses, set in the William Hartnell era. (We look at several, in fact, in the extra Time Can Be Rewritten entries in this book.) And even beyond that, Doctor Who has, clearly, a long and distinguished history of fandom, which has produced stories, often of dubious value, in the Doctor Who format, often presenting them as parts of eras long past.

These books are a part of Doctor Who, and we're going to cover some of them here. I'm not going to do every Doctor Who audio and novel that has ever been written. I am going to do some of them – ones of particular note or significance. In the Hartnell era, this originally consisted of four novels – this one, Simon Guerrier's *The Time Travellers*, Gareth Roberts's *The Plotters*, and Daniel O'Mahoney's *The Man in the Velvet Mask*, although three more books and an audio CD have been added for this book version of the blog.

Jim Mortimore, when he wrote *Campaign*, was as accomplished a Doctor Who writer as one could find during the fifteen year interregnum of Doctor Who. He'd written or co-written seven previous novels, most of them extremely acclaimed. His reputation was for dense, complex, and ambitious novels. *Campaign* proved to be the climax of that career, however. For complex reasons involving the book being rather a bit weirder and more experimental than the novel Justin Richards thought he was commissioning, the book was rejected, leading Mortimore to self-publish it with proceeds going to charity.

The question of whether it should have been rejected is complex and largely uninteresting. It's a good book, yes, but it's a terribly odd fit for the BBC Books line, which never really went for this level of experimentalism. Doctor Who would certainly be poorer without it, but that doesn't mean that official publication is the forum best suited to this. Some things are better suited to the margins.

In other words, technically, and for what is probably the first and last time, I'm writing up fanfiction here. Though that's a muddy definition. I've gotten yelled at by people in the past for referring to Lawrence Miles's books as "professional fanfiction," for instance, despite the fact that I'd nicked the term from Miles's own *About Time* series of guides. For the most part, there's a gradient from televised Doctor Who to torrid descriptions of the Doctor and Ian getting it on. Across that gradient exist things like the Virgin and BBC Books lines of novels. And then there's something like this that challenges definitions.

On the one hand, the book was commissioned by the BBC and it's by an oft-published Doctor Who author. On the other, sources that accept the books as canon – Lance Parkin's mammoth (and self-admittedly absurd) attempt to provide a universal chronology of the Doctor Who universe, *AHistory*, for instance – often reject *Campaign*. This isn't official Doctor Who – it's fan-published Doctor Who. Fanfic.

Which is fine, if you'll indulge a moment of doctrinal ranting. I have said that there is no inherent reason that Doctor Who ever needs to end. In fact, I've suggested that it never can end. This is almost, but not quite, true. There is one massive problem that could meaningfully bring about the end of Doctor Who, and that is the fact that the major rights to the program are currently held by the BBC, an independent corporation largely under the control of the UK government. Were this corporation to cease production of Doctor Who and not license the property, or simply to go belly up, in effect, Doctor Who stories would cease.

The only long-term solution to this problem is the solution reached around characters like Tarzan, Sherlock Holmes, and Hamlet – that the concept of Doctor Who enters the public domain. Under British law as it stands, that will begin to happen in 2033, but given the zeal with which media corporations lobby for copyright extensions, let's face it, there's reason to be pessimistic. But if Doctor Who does survive the issue of copyright, it will eventually sustain itself not on the canonical efforts of a BBC-appointed set of producers, but rather in the popular consciousness via independent productions. In other words, if Doctor Who is an immortal concept, fanfiction is its future.

Now by that I do not necessarily, or really at all, mean the Teaspoon and an Open Mind crowd. I am not talking about fanfiction in the id-vortex sense of stories written to satisfy bizarre authorial kinks. Sorry to those of you with fifty chapter epic sagas of Fifth Doctor/Turlough BDSM play. I'm talking about unauthorized explorations of the concept of Doctor Who designed to produce art. I'm talking, in other words, about things like *Campaign*. A book that is, quite frankly, too weird for official publication, but still invaluable to Doctor Who by virtue of its strangeness. The unofficial margins of Doctor Who are still a part of what it is.

It's important to stress the context of this novel. The year 2000 was as close to the darkest days of Doctor Who fandom as there were. The show had been off the air for eleven years save the 1996 TV movie, and that TV movie was largely looking like a disaster that had killed the show for good. As we'll eventually discuss, it was not very good at all, and opened a massive schism within fandom on its canonicity. Its only real consequence had been the transition from the

Virgin Books New Adventures novels to the BBC Books Eighth Doctor Adventures novels, which was controversial to say the least. With no serious prospects of the show coming back, Doctor Who gave every appearance of being a dying fandom.

Which makes *Campaign*, a novel that is, in effect, about going back to the earliest days of the show and killing every character over and over again in a spectacular fashion, an interesting choice for the era, to say the least.

Actually, I'm being cheeky there. Defining *Campaign* is a dicey proposition. It may help to reveal its "twist" first, especially since it is easily the lamest part of the exercise. All of the events of the book are in fact part of a virtual reality game being played by the TARDIS crew called the Game of Me. In it, the players, who are not aware that they are playing a game while they play it, are successively reincarnated until they sort out their identity according to Aristotelean principles.

In practice, this plays out with each chapter being set in a visibly different world than the one before it. Character names shift rapidly – Susan goes from being Susan Foreman to Susan English, Ian and Barbara drop out to be replaced with Cliff and Lola, and the TARDIS is likely to become the T.A.R.D.I.S. at any moment. But there's a method to this madness, as we'll see.

But it is still madness. Especially for the era it's set in. Let's be honest: there is absolutely no way that this could ever have been a William Hartnell story. First of all, it actively uses its medium – font changes, page layout, and, at one point, several pages of comic strip are all part of how the novel works, tricks that do not translate well to the television screen. Second of all, its narrative techniques are obviously from the year 2000 – the story is violent, sexualized, and metafictional. Third of all, the story treats Doctor Who's first season as a historical phenomenon. This is where the reality shifts mentioned above come from. For instance, in David Whitaker's novelization of *The Daleks*, Susan is given the surname English instead of the canonical Foreman. Cliff and Lola were the original names of Ian and Barbara in production documents.

In fact, just about every rejected, abandoned, or false path of Doctor Who in its first year is referenced here. Unproduced stories such as *The Masters of Luxor* get extensive coverage, with one of the first major plot twists hinging, in effect, on whether the second adventure experienced by the TARDIS crew was *The Daleks* or, as was originally planned, *The Masters of Luxor*. Ian remembers it one way, Barbara the other, with each of them also remembering the other's death.

Which I suppose I should return to. The characters die. A lot. Barbara is the first to die, and her death largely sets the tone – first of all, she is established as being alive prior to her death. Which I don't mean in the normal sense by which most people are alive prior to death. No, I mean that we learn about Barbara's death when Ian is gobsmacked to see that she is alive. This, along with the apparent deletion of the entire universe, is the initial mystery the novel purports to solve.

Her first death is notable also because it is a further interrogation of the premises of Doctor Who – specifically the farce that the show was to, in its futuristic adventures, be about hard science in some fashion. Barbara dies, in fact, because the Thal anti-radiation drugs from *The Daleks* don't work on humans. Which, once you say it, is actually blindingly obvious. Why would they work on the completely different physiologies of humans and, for that matter, Time Lords? It's a ridiculous pseudo-science plot hack that flies in the face of the supposed scientific realism of the show. It is, in other words, a book about the shadows and edges of what Doctor Who is in its first season.

Or, in other words, it's a book about what Doctor Who could have been. The novel's postscript comes, in fact, from the introduction to the publication of the scripts for *Masters of Luxor*, with John McElroy, the writer of the introduction, musing on whether Doctor Who would still be running in a world where *Masters of Luxor* had been the second story instead of *The Daleks.* Which is a stunning question – would Doctor Who have survived better if the Daleks, as iconic a concept of the show as the TARDIS, had never been a part of it?

Posed in 1992, as it was by McElroy, or in 2000, as it was by Mortimore, this question was fundamentally different than in 2011 for one very simple reason – Doctor Who is not dead right now. In 1992 or 2000, the question is a post-mortem. What is it about Doctor Who that finally gave in after twenty-six seasons and died? Why wasn't this story continuable forever? Why did it have to end? We know now, of course, that the answer is that it didn't. It can run forever. But in 2000, Mortimore was by definition writing a different novel. One that is, necessarily, about why the show died.

But it's a mistake to say that Mortimore is saying the show would have survived if any of these alternate paths had been taken. *Campaign* is not an argument for the superiority of a Doctor Who where *The Masters of Luxor* replaced *The Daleks,* or where *Farewell Great Macedon* got made. Rather, it is an argument that Doctor Who was immortal here, at the end of its first season, in the first narrative gap to really exist, between *The Reign of Terror* and *Planet of Giants.* Already enough concepts, filmed and unfilmed, exist to do anything. Perhaps not properly, under the auspices of the BBC. But for all practical purposes, it is immortal. As long as it has people who want to play with its sandbox. As long as it has . . . well . . . fans.

On television, Doctor Who does not yet know what it is. But here, in the Game of Me, it doesn't need to know what it is. It just needs to be something.

And the fact of the matter is, it's damn near everything.

Elizabeth Sandifer

Time Can Be Rewritten: *The Witch Hunters*

It's March of 1998, nine months into the BBC Books line of Doctor Who novels. This line, which had quite a lot to prove following the somewhat calamitously bad TV Movie they were spinning off of and the fact that they were started by forcibly canceling the much beloved Virgin Books line. Promising less adult books, both in content and in writing style, had not gotten off to a good start, with the Eighth Doctor Adventures running through the torturously bad *The Eight Doctors*. This was followed by, five months later, the even worse *War of the Daleks*, and the Past Doctor Adventures not having put out a hit. Add to this the fact that it was clear the TV Movie had flopped and wasn't going to series (for better or for worse) and you had books that were in a deep hole.

The Eighth Doctor Adventures line began to climb out of that hole in November of 1997 with the much beloved *Alien Bodies*. The Past Doctor Adventures began to prove themselves with a run of three books, beginning with David McIntee's much acclaimed *Face of the Enemy*, then with Jim Mortimore's fiendishly complex *Eye of Heaven*, and then concluding with this book – Steve Lyons's *The Witch Hunters*. *The Witch Hunters* tops multiple polls regarding what the best book in the Past Doctor Adventures line was. So clearly it's an important and well-regarded piece of the First Doctor canon. Unfortunately, it's also a complete mess.

On paper it seems like a lovely idea. The original TARDIS crew are stuck in the Salem Witch Trials. It sounds like a straightforward Hartnell historical – one we might have seen on screen. You can hear the concept and immediately see what trouble everyone will get into. The Doctor will do the "not one line!" speech a bunch while making wise comments on the brutality of the Puritans. Barbara will provide a reasoned and nuanced historical background while arguing fruitlessly with someone to change their ways. Ian will get into some scuffles breaking people out of prison and probably get locked in it himself. And Susan . . . well, Susan is always the tricky one in her stories. She'll probably be helpless and put upon, so you've got to figure she'll be tried as a witch.

Or so it goes on paper. Then we add the two strange things that Steve Lyons throws into the mix. First is that the TARDIS makes multiple arrivals at Salem, generally through the use of the fast return switch from *The Edge of Destruction*. Fair enough, I suppose, though the obvious question of "why the heck wasn't that switch ever used to bring Ian and Barbara home" loomed over it badly enough when it was a sticky switch marked in Sharpie on the TARDIS console, and bringing it back doesn't necessarily make a lot of sense. The stranger thing is that as effectively as these departures and returns are used to make a semi-nonlinear story, the resulting structure feels off for the Hartnell era.

The much larger problem is that the witch trials are established as happening in a large part because of Susan's poorly controlled telepathic abilities. This is jaw-dropping. Aside from making Susan significantly responsible for the deaths of about two-dozen innocent people, it crosses an upsetting line. It's one thing to have the Doctor inadvertently cause Rome to burn – an incident that, while it certainly had a death toll, is removed from contemporary culture and not remembered primarily for its loss of life. It is quite another to have Susan cause the death of people whose names are known in a historical event infamous specifically because of the death of those people.

This is made all the more irritating by the fact that the book is intensely and stridently moralizing. Perhaps the most grating moment, or at least the most emblematic, comes when Ian parts company with John Proctor. The novel gives Ian the following monologue, although, as is characteristic of the novel's style, it is not given as a monologue but is rather dropped into third person narration. "Goodbye, John. Hope you don't mind dying. Never seeing that baby of yours. Becoming a martyr."

Admittedly for a book that owes such an obvious debt to Arthur Miller's *The Crucible*, unsubtle cudgels of moral judgment are a wholly fitting and appropriate trope, but it's tough to get past the degree to which the novel just hammers endlessly on the point that the Puritans were really bad. Barbara mounts a brief (and historically accurate) defense of them early on, but by the end all possible validity for that defense has long since fled the building.

The sheer degree to which the unrelenting badness of the Puritans is hammered home over this book ends up making the fact that Susan is partially responsible for the witch trials all the more problematic. Yes, Lyons hedges in some spots – he spends a lot of time inside Abigail's head, for instance. But none of what he does meaningfully dampens the degree to which he depicts the people of Salem as crazed monsters. And Susan is responsible for it. Which isn't a bad plot arc on its own, except here we run into the problem of what the Past Doctor Adventures are. Susan ostensibly goes from this book to *Planet of Giants*. And it seems nearly impossible to watch that story while pretending that it follows the events of this book.

None of this is as problematic as the book's end take on the nature of history. Much of the book is consumed with a restaging of the argument at the center of *The Aztecs*, with the Doctor insisting that history cannot be changed and his companions trying to change it anyway. And here, as with *The Aztecs*, the implication is that history actually cannot be changed, as opposed to the view taken by later stories (including later in the Hartnell era with *The Time Meddler*) that it merely must not be changed. Which is fine – the idea of history as a force of nature is a valid science fiction trope, if one that, in its stripping away of the idea of human agency, seems to rob most of history of its point. (The obvious follow-up after being told that a time traveler can't change history is whether any of the people of Salem could have done anything else, or if they are beyond judgment because they too are merely caught up in an inevitable and ontological historical force.)

Had the novel stopped there, it would have merely been a bit flat, but still fairly interesting, and this essay would have been mostly about treatments of history in Doctor Who historicals and trying to figure out what the show's take on the inevitability of history is. (The answer to that would have been that it depends entirely on who's writing the story in question, but that generally history can be changed, although it must not be.) Instead, the book has to plow on to the epilogue.

The first thing to note about the epilogue is that it doesn't feature the Doctor. At least, not the same Doctor who's in the rest of the book. We see this Doctor briefly at the start of the book, and learn that he is somewhere towards the end of his first incarnation and that he has gained the right to return to Salem one last time as a result of his service in the Death Zone. This is a reference to *The Five Doctors*, which suggests, perhaps bewilderingly, that the Doctor in these sections is played by Richard Hurndall instead of by William Hartnell. Certainly it is not the post-Season One Doctor seen in the rest of the book. Instead this is some sort of imaginary construction of the First Doctor – the one that fans of a later generation like to pretend was in the first three seasons, as opposed to the one who actually was.

In the epilogue, this Doctor attempts to get Rebecca Nurse to understand the necessity of the witch trials. His argument is essentially based on a progress-centric model of history, in which mankind moves ever forward towards better morality. There is a romanticism to this view that is appealing, but two things about it must be pointed out. First, a view of inevitable progress in history makes messiahs of us all, which is rarely a good thing. Second, and more damningly, it creates the obscene farce that historical travesties are OK because they are for the greater good.

The Doctor's argument is that the slaughter of Salem was OK because it taught future people to behave better. The obscenity of this is galling. And this is presented as the enlightened future – the idea that it's OK if a few people die unjustly for the greater good. This is why we can't rewrite history – because we so fetishize the present as an ideal society that we cannot risk changing it. This Leibnitzian view of the world was pilloried brilliantly by Voltaire, and it's depressing to see it crop up again in the twentieth century. The idea that ours is the best possible present, that all the deaths and wars and assassinations and massacres of history were the best choices, is revolting.

It is tempting to say that this sort of moral equivocation is what ultimately kills the historical – that putting the Doctor in a historical travesty dictates that he act immorally as he must allow the travesty to happen. But that's not quite true. After all, that basic concept is done to chilling effect in *The Waters of Mars*. The idea that the Doctor must stand by while something horrible happens is not in and of itself problematic, although it is by definition an extreme event that should push the character, as in, for instance, *The Massacre* (although by modern standards the ending cops out instead of forcing the Doctor to truly face the consequences of what he did).

The problem is when writers attempt to add any morality for the Doctor's insistence on the course of history beyond the laws of time. It is fine when the Doctor gravely tells us that the consequences of altering a fixed point in history are catastrophic. It is fine also when it simply turns out that one cannot alter history – as is the thrust of most of *The Witch Hunters*. It is quite another when we are told that history is the way it is because it is better that way. And it is something that does not fit with the Hartnell era. What Lyons misses in *The Witch Hunters* is that the era he sets it in is the era of the show with the most moral ambiguity in the characters. To set such an overtly moralizing tale in that era is a mistake. To set one with such a crass morality is a massive one.

Time Can Be Rewritten: *The First Doctor Adventures*

If you're reading *TARDIS Eruditorum* from the start, this is going to be the first essay on Big Finish you read. This is somewhat unfortunate, because it's a late addition to this printing of the book, written in mid-2018, long after all my other attempts at covering Big Finish. And since i first wrote about Big Finish when publishing this book years ago I've grown, shall we say, steadily crankier at them. So if you want essays on their virtues and what's potentially interesting about their approach, well, check out basically any other Big Finish essay in the book. But here I want to talk about their capacity for bizarrely esoteric fanwank with no obvious market in the realm of sanity. The cyberpunk *Invisible Enemy* sequel *Revenge of the Swarm* is probably the most infamously baffling of these, but I mean, there's also a thrilling crossover of Jago & Lightfoot with Strax, a four-disc box set of Jenny's adventures post-*Doctor's Daugher*, and, perhaps most puzzlingly, three whole series of *Vienna*, a spinoff featuring a character that appeared in a Seventh Doctor audio.

Even by their standards, though, this box set is weird. I mean, their *Third Doctor Adventures* line, in which the Third Doctor is played by Tim Treloar, at least has Katy Manning and Richard Franklin in it. This, on the other hand, is the First Doctor era as reinterpreted by actors whose primary claim is that they portrayed William Hartnell, Jacqueline Hill, William Russell, and Carole Ann Ford on TV once. I mean, yes, Bradley also played the actual role once, but the presence of Jamie Glover, Jemma Powell, and Claudia Grant puts the emphasis on *An Adventure in Space and Time* even before you get to the weirdness of trying to fit this in with *Twice Upon a*

Time, which, despite the release being timed to coincide with it, it feels oddly disconnected from. (The set was planned before Bradley was invited back to the show, but recorded after, so its relationship to the episode is complex.)

The crux of the problem is that Bradley does not actually play Hartnell's Doctor in *Twice Upon a Time*. And this isn't just because he says "Time Lord" and "Gallifrey," nor because the Hartnell era never actually had the kind of sexism that Moffat lampoons it for. It's because nothing about *Twice Upon a Time* save for the purely visual elements is trying to match the Hartnell era. Bradley isn't playing the guy who was running around searching for Captain Avery's treasure five episodes ago, he's playing the progenitor of Doctor Who's mythos, which Hartnell never had any opportunity to do. *Twice Upon a Time* is smart about this, largely having Bradley's Doctor be entirely unwitting about that mythos, but it's still that, as opposed to any material recreation of 1960s Doctor Who that Bradley was presenting.

This, however, is Big Finish, which has never looked at something and gone "yeah but it's a bit trad, isn't it?" And so Big Finish's idea of what to do with this cast is overt 60s revivalism. They dust off the original Delia Derbyshire tune, and adopt a number of period conventions; individual episodes have titles, there's a cliffhanger at the end of the first story leading into the second, which is a pure historical. It's overtly retro, in a way that tangibly clashes with the fact that literally all of the parts have been recast.

By far the least interesting way to engage with this tension is through the lens of canon. Unfortunately, Big Finish leaves us no choice by dint of their decision to have the opening story of the set, *The Destination Wars*, be an encounter with the Master. This not only puts the story in tension with various other "origin of the Master" stories (it's nigh impossible to reconcile with David McIntee's work), it raises a perversely fascinating question of canon and continuity: given that the entire TARDIS crew has been recast, was the First Maste, as Big Finish asserts him to be in promotional materials, in fact played by Jamie Dreyfus? Or is this a recasting of a part that had never actually been cast before? (Big Finish apparently have two more Dreyfus Master stories in the can, but that scarcely answers the question.)

But it also complicates the Hartnell homage aspect of it, albeit less than you might think. Big Finish play extremely faithfully with the tonal rules of the Hartnell era. The Master appears, but there's no talk of Gallifrey or Time Lords; Susan and the Doctor remain vague to the point of implausibility about him, describing him entirely in euphemisms even when talking to him. The effect is to render him roughly equivalent to the Monk. But, of course, he's not. He's the Master, a definitive part of Doctor Who's mythology. And so the lack of any acknowledgment of that ends up feeling like a wasted opportunity. The story provides a plausible answer to "what would the Master have been like if he'd debuted in the Hartnell era" (a fairly dull domineering hypnotist, as it happens), but at the expense of actually being reconcilable with basically anything in the new series. It's not just that Jamie Dreyfus's portrayal is shorn of all the things that have been done to make the character more than a comic book cliche or that he's a profoundly reactionary climbdown from the brash queerness of Missy, It's that his interactions with the Doctor simply cannot be interpreted as two old friends who had a falling out meeting for the first time after both of them became renegades from their own people. There's absolutely none of the nuance or emotion that the first post-Gallifrey meeting of these two characters should have in light of what we're repeatedly told about them in the new series.

And so the relationship this has with both the 1960s series and the 2010s one is oddly disjointed. It finds itself retreating from both without actually going anywhere. And the performances of its leads don't actually help it much here. Claudia Grant acquits herself well, playing a Susan much more geared towards competence than the 1960s original was ever allowed to be, although this is fueled in part by the fact that she's being written that way. Glover and Powell's Ian and

Barbara are more in the vein of straight TV impersonations, with Powell being stuck playing a deeply impoverished version of Barbara due mainly to the writers failing to give her much to do. (She's partially resistant to the Master's hypnosis, but that's about all she gets.) But none of them are in a position to *do* anything with the roles. The mandate for fidelity keeps them from moving forward with the parts, while the distance from the original material keeps them from being able to access the sparking magic of the originals.

And then there's David Bradley, who is of course the only one of the cast to have actually played their role before. In most regards this doesn't really help him. In *Twice Upon a Time*, he settled on playing the role as essentially the Doctor before he got any good at it, the unwitting starting point of a vast mythology. But that approach doesn't really work in a 1960s retro script. Hartnell's Doctor wasn't a semi-competent Peter Capaldi; he was a fully formed character that gradually evolved into the modern conception. And so Bradley's approach leaves him sounding perpetually surprised as he comes to the end of a line, as if taken aback to discover that he's the hero in a sci-fi story.

While *The Destination Wars* at least pokes around the edges of being interesting, however, the second story in the set, *The Great White Hurricane*, is an abject disaster that mostly serves to highlight all of Big Finish's worst instincts. As an idea, it's sympathetic: a historical in the classic "the TARDIS crew arrives on the eve of something really bad and has to avoid dying" style. But the choice of the 1888 blizzard in New York City feels like the product of way too much clicking around Wikipedia, and the actual plot is a nothing. The Doctor and Susan get caught up in a war between two absurdly cuddly gangs while Ian and Barbara help a woman reunite with her abusive ex (really). Bewilderingly, in a story about a massive natural disaster no named characters die, with the entire effort to sell the weighty tragedy of historical events being pinned on a random old man found dead in a snowbank. It's cheap, lazy, and on the whole insulting to both the cast and audience.

What makes this uniquely infuriating, howeverm is that there's no reason for it. There's no reason to be doing 1960s revivalism in 2017. The 1960s ended; you can't go back to them. And there are already fifty-one episodes of the Doctor, Ian, Barbara, and Susan (almost as many as there are of Peter Davison in his entirety) that were made in the 1960s and are better at being 1960s Doctor Who than anything Big Finish could do, or indeed that anyone else could. The job of being 1960s Doctor Who is not only already taken, it's already completed. It happened; it's done.

That is not to say, of course, that there's no point in revisiting the characters. There are eras of Doctor Who that case can be made for; I'm not entirely convinced that the bulk of 1980s Doctor Who is capable of bearing any more productive fruit. But that's manifestly not the case for the Hartnell era. There's tons of stuff to do here by exploring the gaps between what the show was in 1964 and what it became. *The Destination Wars* plays at this with an opening sequence that purports to be set in "space year 2003," but it quickly fizzles as it turns out to be an alien world and not Ian and Barbara getting to confront their own cultural future. But there's no reason why this should be. Put the original TARDIS crew in any of the subgenres of science fiction to arise after their time. Use them as a vehicle to explore the lost and abandoned dreams and utopias of the 1960s.

Or hell, just crash them into the future of the program in a way that doesn't involve shearing the future of all its interesting bits. Don't have them meet a regressive version of the Delgado Master; have the First Doctor meet a Master with the bonkers excess of the Simm and Gomez versions. Throw them in with Iris Wildthyme or River Song. Or even just some of the genres of Doctor Who to post-date the era. There are no Ian/Barbara/Susan stories that go for outright scary in the way the new series routinely does. Heck, just throw them up against the Sontarans or the Slitheen or something. (Actually, that last one's a kind of amazing idea…)

And if you must do a historical (which isn't a bad idea), pick something that's more interesting than "here's a natural disaster you may never have heard of." Actually making a serious attempt at a non-European culture that's more politically aware than *The Aztecs* would be nice, but even if we're limiting ourselves to things where the research is easy, go for the Watts Riots or the Russian Revolution or something. Or do a celebrity historical, another subgenre that post-dates the Hartnell era and would thus be actually interesting to explore with those characters.

The same largely goes for the actors, none of whom are served by having to impersonate the original cast on their home turf. All of the characters in these stories have obvious arcs and dimensions that didn't get explored on the television series. Big Finish have a genuinely top rate actor in David Bradley, so why not explore the fears, regrets, and resentments of a renegade Time Lord who's only a few years (or indeed perhaps weeks) past leaving Gallifrey? Why not actually explore Ian and Barbara's relationship in a substantive way in which they have emotions about each other beyond "this person is in peril and I must rescue them?" Why not actually give Susan any character traits whatsoever? Given that the actors are never going to be anything but imitations of the original, you may as well at least have them do stuff it's difficult to imagine the originals doing.

As I said, this is a weird project that fills no obvious demand. What it's not is a project with no obvious potential. About the only way you could screw it up is, well, exactly the way that Big Finish did. Like I said, it's easy to make fun of Big Finish. But that's just because the alternative would be to hate them for how consistently they fuck up the opportunities they have.

Like You're Going to Be Killed by Eggs, or Beef, or Global Warming (*Planet of Giants*)

It's October 31, 1964. Sandie Shaw has the number one single with "(There's) Always Something There to Remind Me," and will hold it for two more weeks before yielding to Roy Orbison's "Oh Pretty Woman." The Searchers, the Supremes, the Kinks, and Manfred Mann also make up the top ten.

Since Doctor Who was last on the air, Martin Luther King has won the Nobel Peace Prize, and thirteen years of Conservative rule in Great Britain have come to an end, with Harold Wilson becoming Prime Minister, a position he will hold until 1970. Wilson's term will be dominated by two trends – significant economic problems (that will eventually result in his being voted out of office) and the rise of British counterculture – a tendency started by the Beatles, who Wilson would ensure received an MBE strategically close to his 1966 re-election.

The wound caused by the Kennedy assassination is festering. The world is not a stable place. The collapse of the British Empire continues, with Rhodesia becoming Zambia. It is easy, in 1964, to be afraid. The year is closer to World War II than it is to Nintendo. It is in no way clear that the defeat of the Nazis was anything other than a postponement of the end of the world.

And now Doctor Who is back. *Planet of Giants*, along with the next story, are odd holdovers – filmed in the first production block and held back a few months, they are the transition from the first season of Doctor Who to the second. In many ways, these will be the nine most important episodes of Doctor Who since *The Daleks* and *Edge of Destruction*, bringing to end one version of what the show is and inaugurating another.

Planet of Giants, on the face of it, may seem like a relatively insignificant episode. Its concept – the TARDIS crew gets shrunk – is one that was attempted twice in the first season, and was actually just about the only idea Sydney Newman, who created Doctor Who, actually had for the series. Now, in its third go-around, this somewhat puzzling idea is actually implemented. The constraints this leaves on the story are significant. Although there is a supporting cast, the TARDIS crew never interacts with them directly, making it an odd juxtaposition of a chamber piece in *The Daleks*-episode-one tradition and, basically, an episode of *The Avengers* (a TV show we deal with in the second volume on Troughton due largely to the fact that, although it exists in 1964, its iconic form and its major influence on Doctor Who comes later).

But there are several vitally important things that happen in this story – three things that make this bit of strange fluff an extremely vital turning point in the series. First of all, this is the first time that Doctor Who has been set in contemporary England since Ian and Barbara fell out of the world. Eventually, contemporary England will become vital to Doctor Who, most obviously in 1970, but Hartnell actually only has two stories primarily set in it, and this is one of them. Still, the return to the present is a key opening of a door that, although it will sit relatively unappreciated for the next few years, will eventually become very important. Note, however, that we also see a fundamental ambivalence in the relationship between the series and contemporary Earth. It can visit contemporary Earth, but only if it makes it as strange and alien as any other place.

But there's a certain ease to making the ordinary strange that the show takes an almost giddy delight in. This is one of several things that leads these episodes to actually be quite well-paced – although the decision to reduce the final two episodes into one episode helps that a lot as well, resulting as it did in things like the exciting sequence where the Doctor and Ian map the molecular structure of a pesticide getting cut.

With the cuts, the bulk of the dramatic weight in this story gets to come from the characters, who, by the nature of the story, are forced to interact with each other instead of splitting into individual subplots. With nothing to do but be interesting, the characters have to provide most of the drama. In practice, the bulk of the task goes to Barbara, who continues to be jaw-droppingly impressive. She and William Hartnell are, by this point, the heart of the show – it positively sings when the two of them are on camera together.

The problem is that it's not clear this chemistry is an unambiguously good thing. I mean, on one level it is, because Hartnell and Hill are magical together. On another, it's not necessarily great that this is the primary character pairing for the show given the nature of the other two characters. The Doctor's concern for Barbara seems to surpass even his concern for Susan, and it is a concern that is characterized primarily by respect for her. The Doctor is actively affectionate and apologetic towards her, and, perhaps more to the point, acts very similarly towards her to how he did with Cameca in *The Aztecs*. It is difficult to argue that this is an overtly sexual relationship – in no small part because that involves the dreadfully unpleasant business of sexualizing the First Doctor – but it is equally difficult to argue that there's not some tension present. Take, for instance, the scene in this story in which Susan attempts to climb up a steep surface, and fails. Barbara goes to try, and the Doctor stops her, saying it's dangerous. At which point Carole Ann Ford – who a glance at *Edge of Destruction* will confirm is actually quite a good actress when someone takes the time to write her a role

– looks immensely irritated that it was OK for her to risk her life, but the Doctor is pampering Barbara. It's solidly subtle and sophisticated storytelling. But it's Carole Ann Ford pushing nobly against the fact that she's all but been written out of the series already, her character functions all being subsumed better by Barbara.

So when Barbara is poisoned by the insecticide that forms the major threat of the plot, it's genuinely gripping. The growing realization that something is wrong with Barbara is one of the creepiest, darkest moments Doctor Who has yet offered, and the show previously gave the entire cast terminal radiation poisoning. Heck, Jacqueline Hill even makes gripping television out of a sequence in which a giant rubber fly is pushed into shot behind her.

The ability of Jacqueline Hill to make Barbara a gripping and dramatic character leads directly to the second major development of this story. In part three, the Doctor knows that escaping to the TARDIS will cure Barbara. Nothing is actually keeping him from the TARDIS. But he insists on staying because Barbara wants to stop the insecticide from being made. Even though Barbara is dying, the Doctor opts to stay and fight for what is right. This switch is crucial – the Doctor is steadily becoming a crusader for good – one who will put himself and the people he loves in danger to do the right thing. Equally importantly, he does so because of his relationship with his companions. And, for that matter, he's becoming a pyromaniac, declaring that he loves a good fire.

Again, all of this is nascent. It is not yet that Doctor Who is Doctor Who. Rather, more and more of the parts of Doctor Who are being moved into place. After all, the basic plot of the story still amounts to a TARDIS crash plot. Admittedly, even in the new series, TARDIS crash plots happen – Season Five had four stories that depended on TARDIS malfunctions as plot points. And if this story were to be restaged in 2011, it would still have to be a TARDIS crash plot because the story needs some excuse to shrink the cast.

But it's still significant that there has yet to be a story where the TARDIS isn't disabled and inaccessible. There are still things like that fact that have to be dealt with. But on the other hand, we can already see that the show is becoming Doctor Who additively. Since taking Ian and Barbara on board, Hartnell's character has steadily been changing from the cranky, dangerous man of *An Unearthly Child* into the Doctor – a name he visibly adopts from Ian's suggestion in the premiere.

There is a third key aspect of Doctor Who, which we've already mentioned, to show up in this story for essentially the first time: domestic horror. Now, this point is arguable – one could claim *The Daleks* as an essentially domestic horror story given the deliberate similarities between the Daleks and domestic appliances. But that was by and large a resemblance of form – the Daleks are not literally an overturned trash can with a plunger and a whisk – it's just that those items can be combined to create a playground-quality Dalek suit. *The Daleks* merely made shapes scary. *Planet of Giants* is all about making domestic objects terrifying.

This is, in Steven Moffat's view, the heart of Doctor Who – he has said many times that Doctor Who is set under your bed. And one of the iconic images of Doctor Who is that of children watching it from "behind the sofa." All of that began here, really with the first episode cliffhanger in which the camera freezes on a still image of a cat that is menacing the TARDIS crew. The cliffhanger works. That's the key thing to stress here – the show succeeds in making a lone cat, or, in the other cliffhanger, a man washing his hands (with the TARDIS crew stuck in the sink) truly terrifying scenes. This isn't just using a familiar form and twisting it – this is making everyday events into objects of horror. It's something that Doctor Who will eventually become very good at, but hasn't yet (and indeed, won't touch all that heavily for a few years to come).

This episode, actually, is also worth remarking on because it's a rare case of Doctor Who attempting a special effects bonanza. This is usually a worrisome move, but in this case, the show actually pulls the effects off reasonably well – there are a few clunkers, in particular a giant phone done by using an old Victorian stage trick involving mirrors that is particularly embarrassing given that a giant phone is one of the famous props from the now decade-old *Dial M for Murder*. But for the most part, due in particular to the work of Raymond Cusick, the show's reach and grasp are relatively in stride here.

Which is one of the odd charms of Doctor Who – one that does not make its debut here (that would be in *The Daleks*, where the eponymous monsters themselves embody this charm), but is well on display here – the way in which its juxtapositions are not just in setting from episode to episode, but in tone and quality within an episode. The aforementioned shot where Barbara is menaced by a giant fly is, as I said, quite good. And is then immediately ruined by Barbara gratuitously fainting. Enormously well-done shots and stagings juxtapose laughable crap on a regular basis.

Crucially, the design team is already aware of this. One of the single worst special effects in Doctor Who is the early model shot of the TARDIS, which frankly looks like a seven year old knocked it up out of modeling clay in about five minutes, possibly while sniffing glue. It looks absolutely horrible, and is obviously a model. Which makes using it as the image of the shrunk-down TARDIS actually very clever, and results in what is possibly the most visually impressive shot thus far in Doctor Who, where the camera pans up from the dinky miniaturized TARDIS model to reveal that it is in fact a dinky miniaturized TARDIS in an ordinary-sized back lawn, making the low quality of the model shot part of the storytelling. What we initially mistake as a tiny model TARDIS masquerading as a real one is in fact . . . a tiny model TARDIS. This is remarkably savvy, and demonstrates a self-awareness on the part of the show – something that will become altogether more important in the next televised adventure . . .

Time Can Be Rewritten: *The Time Travellers*

It is November of 2005. The number one singles for the month are Westlife's "You Raise Me Up" and Madonna's "Hung Up," if you were wondering. If *Campaign*, coming out in 2000, arrived at the absolute low point of Doctor Who, this is more or less the high point. On television, Christopher Eccleston regenerated into David Tennant five months ago, and in this month's mini-episode for Children in Need, the world saw him properly for the first time. Life is grand.

Except, perhaps, at BBC Books, whose line of original novels here winds finally towards its end. This book is a holdover from another era – the second to last book to emerge from BBC Books, which had been carrying the Doctor Who torch since 1997. But we should stress that it is not as though this was a simple transition where the books segued into the series. Even though the main line of the books featured the Eighth Doctor and Davies started with the Ninth, he conspicuously failed to connect them. In fact, he almost went out of his way not to. Russell T Davies's Doctor Who established the Last Great Time War as a major plot thread. For a variety of reasons that we'll deal with when we get to this era, this was a phenomenally massive snub to the BBC Books line, a snub that the series has basically made no effort whatsoever to apologize or make up for. So this book is, in many ways, a ghost – the last breath of an already dead strand of Doctor Who history.

Which is perhaps why, unshackled from any actual responsibilities to be good or carry on the tradition of the series, or break new ground and ensure the series' long-term survival, Simon Guerrier was able to do something that had frankly been lacking in the bulk of the BBC Books output – write a book that is unmistakably about the series' past, but that is still a story worth telling in its own right.

I assume that anyone who is enough of an anorak to be reading this is aware that, in the next televised story, Susan becomes the first regular character to depart Doctor Who. But if for some reason you do not know this, and then, at the end of the third episode of *Planet of Giants*, guess that this is imminent, you are, frankly, psychic, as the story gives no setup whatsoever for that development. So it makes sense to put something in the gap between the two stories – a potentially decent gap, given that the only teaser at the end of *Planet of Giants* is that the Doctor has no idea where they are. Admittedly the next episode also begins with the Doctor having no idea where they are, but let's be fair, that's true of almost every episode of Doctor Who.

(Oddly, *The Time Travellers* is the only story in Doctor Who set in this gap, with other stories preferring a *Reign of Terror/Planet of Giants* gap despite the fact that, that gap is actually a bit dodgy, whereas this gap is pretty solid. Indeed, given that Ian and Barbara are visibly surprised that they might be in London at the start of the next story, moving a few more stories into this gap would not be an unreasonable decision on the part of those who are obsessive enough about Doctor Who chronology to care about this sort of thing. I'm not really, and will thus bring this parenthetical to a close.)

But *The Time Travellers* is more than a novel explaining why Susan departs in the next story. It is also a novel that seeks (as did *The Witch Hunters*) to resolve the unresolved plot threads of *The Aztecs* and explain coherently every single continuity error in the whole of Doctor Who. Which is normally the sort of hubristic overreach that dooms a novel, except to his real credit, Guerrier's book, (unlike the *Witch Hunters*) manages to pull it off.

The novel is set in 2006 – less than one year after its publication. But this is not a 2006 that extends in any way from the experience of 2005. Rather, this is a dystopian 2006 that is designed to feel like it extends from 1964. The UK is locked in a long-term war with South Africa, which appears to be winning, and is, more broadly, concerned with the aftermath of a disastrous incident in 1968 where a computer nearly destroyed the world. In other words, it is a novel that is clearly not set in the right universe. This sets up a wonderfully profound strangeness to the book that gives it a real frisson, reminding us that this is a book both of 2005 and of 1964.

What is most interesting about this decision is that the novel works in two registers. To the sort of obsessive Doctor Who fan who would be reading a First Doctor novel published in the same month that the Tenth Doctor has his first major appearance, the novel makes perfect sense. Those fans immediately recognize that the alluded to computer is WOTAN, the villain of the third season finale *The War Machines*. They'll similarly get the obvious references to *The Tenth Planet* and *Remembrance of the Daleks*. But, just as importantly, the novel also feels like a plausible future of 1964, allowing Ian and Barbara to believe completely that this is not a possible future, but *the* future – a completely immutable fact, as the Doctor told Barbara in *The Aztecs*.

Similarly, the book uses the particulars of the era it is set in to ratchet up tension. In terms of the Doctor's chronology, there are no televised adventures prior to this in which the Doctor involves himself in the plot completely willingly. The closest we've got is last episode where he clearly enjoys involving himself, but seems to do so in part out of fealty to Barbara. Here, however, upon realizing that the British government is experimenting with time travel, the Doctor involves himself completely willingly, actively refusing to run.

This is striking in the context of its season, and is worth looking at. Why does the Doctor suddenly decide to remain?

The answer, in essence, is that he's a Time Lord. This is never said in as many words, but both the Doctor and Susan, as they separately realize what is going on, immediately realize that they have to deal with this. We've seen this once before with the Doctor – with his vicious insistence to Barbara in *The Aztecs* that she not change history. Here the phrase Time Lord makes sense. Indeed, even though it's unmentioned, the term hangs over the entire book. The Doctor, even on the run from his people, sees himself as having a feudal duty to time. He must defend it. Suffering humans, dying planets, these are things the Doctor can walk away from. But the threat of time travel in the wrong hands? That appalls him. That is simply something that, as a Time Lord, he has to deal with. To do otherwise would be an abdication of the Doctor's duty as a nobleman with dominion over time. Even a renegade Time Lord must display some fealty to his vassal.

This requires, then, a revision to *The Aztecs* – sensible enough, given that the Doctor has, in every other story, clearly altered history with some abandon. And so *The Time Travellers* undertakes its most radical conceit – one so blindingly obvious in hindsight that it's a marvel twenty-seven seasons of Doctor Who had to air before anyone thought of it.

In fact, the Doctor finally admits, every time he opens the TARDIS doors, he changes history. After all, the TARDIS was designed to observe history. That's why it has a scanner and chameleon circuit – so it can disguise itself in a given time period and simply watch in silence. The biggest aspect of the Doctor's renegade nature is not that he runs around the universe willy-nilly – it's that he ever leaves the TARDIS. The reasons he lied to Barbara in *The Aztecs* are that he felt this explanation was overly complex and put too much responsibility on her, and that he really doesn't want to muck with time because it would attract the attention of his people.

Furthermore, all changing history does is split the timeline. If you travel back from the future and change the past, what happens is that you're stuck in a past that can never resolve into your own future. In other words, every Doctor Who story is, to some extent, a retcon of previous stories. If a later adventure of the Doctor invalidates a previous adventure, that is resolved simply by deciding that, yes, the Doctor changed history and is no longer in a universe where his own past adventures happened. Which is, cleverly, a key conceit of the novel. The readers know that in two seasons the Doctor will defeat WOTAN and invalidate the entire setting of this novel. But set before the Doctor has met WOTAN, the novel can also be set in a universe where WOTAN won. When *The War Machines* airs, it simply moves this story into an abandoned timeline.

This may seem like an obvious conceit ripped off from, say, *Primer*. But in the context of Doctor Who, it's actually tremendously significant in that it changes the series from being about a wide universe that the Doctor wanders – a concept that makes it mostly the educational program it repeatedly tried to be in the first season – to a series about the Doctor, who is the only consistent figure in the universe. If the entire universe changes at the start of every episode when the TARDIS doors open then it is the Doctor, who remains consistent as he freely alters the timeline in both big and small ways, that becomes the central character of the show. Furthermore, the "lonely wanderer" aspect of the show that is cemented by Russell T Davies in 2005 becomes completely explicable – because the Doctor is, even at the start of *An Unearthly Child*, more profoundly cut off from his home than he lets on. The Doctor has, in fact, already destroyed the timeline he hailed from. In fact, since it's clear that he engaged in mildly disruptive tourism prior to Totters Lane, he has done so several times over. No wonder later in the series he never goes back for a companion. After all, as soon as he's had one adventure without a given companion, that companion is immediately not "his" version of the companion but rather one from an alternate universe. (This interpretation is harder to square away with events from the new series, but this is hardly a major failing.)

Interestingly, *The Time Travellers* refers to a future episode in another key way: the end reveal of how the British attained time travel technology is a reference to 1988's *Remembrance of the Daleks*. This is actually a bit odd – the story seems to simultaneously hinge on the fact that *The War Machines* has not yet happened, but that the twenty-two-years-later story *Remembrance of the Daleks* has. The Doctor in the novel seems utterly unaware of how the Daleks might have made it into 1963, or why they're capable of time travel – both things that will make the next story specifically unusual. But notably, a review of the relevant scenes in the novel shows that the point of view distances itself considerably from the Doctor and Susan. We don't know what the Doctor is thinking here.

What's particularly interesting about all of this is that *Remembrance of the Daleks*, as a story, hinges on the assumption that the Doctor had a reason for being in 1963 in *An Unearthly Child*. The information given to the Doctor about the Daleks' appearance on Earth is sufficient for him to figure out exactly where the Dalek equipment was found and to put two and two together to realize that it's connected to what he did in 1963. Which is another significant addition in this scene – this story is where the Doctor quietly realizes that the Daleks are an arch-nemesis – something that crucially sets up the next story. But more to the point, it ties the monsters in with the Doctor at a fundamental level (which is in part what *Remembrance of the Daleks* is about as well, actually, but more on that in six books).

In other words, what *The Time Travellers* does is fill in a key gap in the series by making it self-reflexive. The book serves to actually make more sense of how the series got from *Planet of Giants* to *Parting of the Ways* over the course of forty-plus years by finding a way to make future developments a subtext of past ones. We've already seen this with *Campaign*, but the elaborate meta-fiction of that via the

Game of Me mostly makes *Campaign* a commentary on the show at large. *The Time Travellers* is still meta-commentary in this sense. Indeed, to some extent, every Doctor Who story after *Planet of Giants* is meta-commentary. But unlike *Campaign*, *The Time Travellers* is not pure meta-commentary, but rather commentary wedded to an actual story.

Alongside this mild apotheosis of the Doctor, see, is a story about Ian and Barbara being scared of the future. The novel opens with Ian reporting Barbara's death. The reader knows this is a feint. And if this were to be televised, the viewer would know it's almost certainly a feint. But as soon as alternate timelines are introduced, an interesting variation of this feint kicks up. We know that Ian and Barbara will both be alive at the end of the story. But we don't actually know which Ian and Barbara. Indeed, early in the novel Ian watches an alternate universe version of himself – one who is, apparently, married to Barbara – get shot.

As in the series itself, it is Barbara who carries the story off. The emotional heart of the novel – a pair of scenes that one reads wishing that Hartnell and Hill had gotten the chance to perform it – are the sequences where the Doctor explains that he lied to her in *The Aztecs*, and where he confides in her that Susan is going to have to leave the TARDIS soon. (Yes, two sequences form the emotional heart. It's a Doctor Who book. It can have two hearts.) I want to actually quote the novel here for these two sequences, because they really are fantastic:

'But Susan,' said the Doctor in his softest voice, 'we change history every time we step out of the doors of the Ship.'

'You said that –' began Barbara.

The Doctor whirled on her. 'Do you really want to know, Miss Wright?' he said. 'Do you really want to know? The TARDIS is built specifically not to change history. We can visit, we can observe, and the Ship can disguise itself so no one need ever know we were there. But only so long as we never step outside. We watch it all on the scanner. My people, you see . . .' He paused, searching for the words.

'Doctor?' Barbara prompted.

'I couldn't do that, could you?' he said. 'It's not travel, it wouldn't be real. We've seen the most incredible things, but without stepping out of those doors, I might as well have stayed in your time, content with your television sets.'

Ian took Barbara's hand, stopping her from responding. He knew what she wanted to say: that the Doctor had lied to them, that time in Mexico.

This sequence – actually the second of the two – is remarkable. For me, it is Barbara's prompting the Doctor to go on as he trails off, unable to continue his explanation. Barbara is clearly furious at the Doctor. She must be. She's a history teacher. Her entire life has been devoted to understanding what the past is. Now she's been given the opportunity to see it and travel through it, and she has found out that the Doctor has been lying to her about what time is. She's furious and betrayed. But on the other hand, that, in this scene, exists side by side with her genuine affection for the Doctor – the fact that when he is clearly having trouble explaining, when he is feeling guilty for having hurt her, she, in the midst of her rage, still steps in to comfort him, prompting him to continue. It's an absolutely note-perfect scene.

Then the other one:

'That's why you don't change history,' she said. 'It's not that
you can't, you just won't. It breaks everything up.'
'And it's easy to get carried away,' he said carefully. She felt like he understood, like he'd wanted all along to spare her this pain and confusion. 'We can't afford to be ostentatious in our travels.'

'But why, Doctor? Who can ever know what you've done, what you've changed?'

He smiled sadly 'There are those who can,' he said. 'And they will find us more easily if we draw attention to ourselves.'

Barbara considered this. 'The experiment here,' she said. 'It's bad news for us, isn't it? I mean for you and me, Ian and Susan.' The Doctor said nothing.

'How bad is it going to be, Doctor?'

His eyes twinkled mischievously at her. 'I haven't any idea at all,' he said. In an instant his mood had changed again. 'But it will be noticed, it will catch up with us, sooner or later. At least, it will catch up with me. I shall have to find a home for Susan. Somewhere safe for her.'

Barbara recoiled from him. 'You're going to abandon her?' She couldn't believe it.

The Doctor rested his chin on his hands. 'If ever I get you and Ian back to your own time, perhaps you would take her with you? Yes, I can see she'd be happy with you.'

Barbara took his hands. 'Of course we'd do anything you asked us,' she told him. 'But you must understand: Susan won't ever leave you. Not voluntarily.'

'No,' said the Doctor, shaking his head. He looked broken. 'I don't believe she would.'

I don't even know what to say here. That's just a phenomenal scene. One that I wish Hartnell and Hill had gotten to act. Or, heck, gotten to read.

It's Jacqueline Hill, in all of this, that I really feel bad for. Her career started in 1953. She was over halfway to her death when she started on Doctor Who. And after Doctor Who, she basically retired, waiting thirteen years to take on her next acting role, instead raising children. From there she had a brief eight-year career in which she made only a handful of appearances. She then retired again, and died of cancer in 1993 at the appallingly young age of 63. And reading what seems to be the one main interview with her on Doctor Who, I'm not sure she was, during her life, entirely aware of how brilliant she was as Barbara. Working on the show, she got grotesquely uneven material – as she points out in the aforementioned interview, she was often reduced to looking scared at the ends of corridors.

But she could do things with those meager scenes that were truly incredible. And more to the point, as I've said, when she is on screen with William Hartnell, the series just sings. Those are the scenes that really, firmly establish what the Doctor/companion relationship is. But more to the point, Barbara is, as a character, uniquely capable of pushing the Doctor into emotionally uncomfortable moments. There really is no other character that the Doctor could have the scene quoted above with – nobody else in whom he would ever be able to confide that he needs to push Susan out of the TARDIS. It's difficult to imagine him having a conversation like that with any future companion. Even Rose Tyler.

Barbara, more than any other character, is the one that pushes the Doctor to become the Doctor. And all of that comes down to the fact that Hill and Hartnell are just jaw-dropping on screen together. Jacqueline Hill, to be frank, deserves as much credit as anyone on the planet for inventing Doctor Who. And I really hope she knew that.

Elizabeth Sandifer

You Were Expecting Someone Else: *Doctor Who In an Exciting Adventure with the Daleks*

It's easy to forget that the first Doctor Who story is not, in fact, *An Unearthly Child*, but *Doctor Who in an Exciting Adventure with the Daleks*. As we'll go over again and again throughout the history of the series, Doctor Who's development has always been inexorably tied to the books produced around the series. The first set of these, published by Frederick Muller Ltd in 1964–65, consisted of novelizations of *The Daleks*, *The Web Planet*, and *The Crusade*, the first and third of these by David Whitaker, and the middle by Bill Strutton. The novelization of *The Daleks*, properly titled *Doctor Who in an Exciting Adventure with the Daleks*, was, unsurprisingly, the most seminal and influential.

It was also (along with the other two) the only take-home version of a Doctor Who story to exist for nearly a decade. Sure, there were comics and annuals and things like that, but what could be defined as "proper" Doctor Who? This book was the crown jewel. Not for nothing did Neil Gaiman write the introduction for the contemporary reissue of it, writing warmly of his childhood memories owning the book – a time period just before he wrote an entire book revisiting that period of his childhood, *The Ocean at the End of the Lane*.

In the course of the introduction Gaiman describes something that, to a modern fan, seems odd – his subsequent surprise at learning that Doctor Who did not actually begin like it does in the book. Whitaker realized that his version of the story's beginning was going to be the definitive one, and so reworked the events of *An Unearthly Child* into the narrative (which he'd do a third time for the first Peter Cushing film). This is significant – remember that on television much of the first season is spent figuring out the relationships among the lead characters and getting Doctor Who to a place where it functions as an adventure plot with the Doctor as the lead character. Removing *100,000 BC* and heavily reworking *An Unearthly Child*, as this book does, fundamentally changes the tone.

In *An Unearthly Child*, Ian and Barbara are in a sense punished for their excessive curiosity – sent off with the Doctor because they couldn't leave well enough alone. But in *Doctor Who in an Exciting Adventure with the Daleks* the sequence of events is more inevitable. Ian and Barbara are well-meaning but have the misfortune of getting caught in a chain of events that leaves them stranded in the TARDIS. There's no sense of fault – Barbara is taking Susan home, and gets in a car crash. Ian stops and helps, Susan disappears, and in searching for what they assume is an injured girl they end up in the TARDIS, or here, simply Tardis, no definite article.

The book, in fact, goes further than the series ever did in making the story about Ian instead of the Doctor by having the novel narrated in the first person from Ian's perspective. Entire plot lines not focused on Ian are thus removed. Arguably the most iconic scene of *The Daleks*, the Dalek-perspective shot of a terrified Barbara at the end of the first episode, is gone because Ian isn't in that scene. On the one hand, at least, this makes the Doctor seem even more mysterious and distant – there's no way for him to become the hero or protagonist in the way he steadily does over the course of the series.

To some extent this is a restoration of the original intent, which clearly was that Ian was the male lead and the Doctor was a more ambiguous and at times scary supporting character – hence the whole rock-crushing scene in *100,000 BC*. But the drift away from that began just three episodes after the end of *The Daleks*, and on Whitaker's watch, so it's difficult to suggest that he's reacting against it as such.

It's worth thinking about why the Doctor didn't last as an amoral or dangerous character. The real problem with having the Doctor be a morally ambiguous character is that it means that the character who knows what the hell is going on and the character who wants to fix things are two different characters, and that's very hard to work with. So unsurprisingly the focus shifts so that the Doctor is a crusading do-gooder, because otherwise you have a very hard time driving the plot forward, since you constantly have to get information from the Doctor (the character who figures things out) to Ian (the character who wants to do something about it).

Notably, after all, the Doctor is not particularly sinister in this. His stunt of draining the mercury fluid links is still in place, but it's the only moment where he really comes off as unsympathetic. Even his kidnapping of Ian and Barbara is made more reasonable by Ian's agreement that he'd have done the same thing if their positions were reversed, and the altered circumstances of their entering Tardis.

Making the Doctor's perspective distant and remote, in other words, is not so much about making him a source of suspicion as it is about making Ian's perspective one of danger and confusion. *Doctor Who in an Exciting Adventure with the Daleks* is ultimately taking the same approach the show eventually did; the Doctor is clearly the hero, but the tension comes from what's going to happen to the ordinary people caught in his wake.

That also helps explain the book's curious fascination with the mechanics of the TARDIS, playing at length with the TARDIS food banks and other such things. The TARDIS isn't just a plot mechanic that's best left unexplored here – it's a strange space unto itself, a sort of training ground for the larger and more dangerous strange space of Skaro. Again, the focus is on taking Ian and putting him in places he doesn't belong that are genuinely scary and unsettling for him.

So in many ways what we see here is Doctor Who re-engineered from scratch, and in light of what Whitaker learned in the early days of actually making it. And, in turn, what we get is very much the Doctor Who of the future. For all the little changes made to the origins of the program, *Doctor Who in an Exciting Adventure with the Daleks* is much closer to what "proper" Doctor Who feels like than the still faltering tone of *The Daleks* itself. The first season of Doctor Who is a lovely, fascinating thing and has some outstanding moments, but it is very much a program still learning what it is, and it's not until the second season that it falls into a regular rhythm of seeming like Doctor Who.

In that regard, *Doctor Who in an Exciting Adventure with the Daleks* is the first Doctor Who story. Certainly it's the first enduring one – the first thing to both feel like Doctor Who seems like it should and to be widely read and picked up for years later. This was, for the first decade of the program, the enduring document of what Doctor Who was. It's entirely arguable that in real and practical terms, this is the single Doctor Who story with the most influence and impact.

Which is fitting. A fair portion of this volume, and even more of the second volume is focused on David Whitaker's conception of Doctor Who. Not to get too far ahead of ourselves, but Whitaker demonstrates an at times strange and always compelling philosophical system that ends up quietly underpinning the entire series. Even without this book he'd easily be a strong candidate for the most influential and important writer of the classic series. With this book, I'm not entirely sure there's still an argument to be had about it.

And tellingly, this book ultimately sets up Whitaker's views on the series. It is, for him, a series about change and danger. Ian spends the entire book in terrifying new situations he does not understand and is ill-prepared for. His entire world has changed, and it's a source of terror. And then, in the end, he decides to stay on the TARDIS. This is, of course, a scene Whitaker adds to the book, and is quite unlike the series, which is about the Doctor trying to get Ian and Barbara home. But here Ian and Barbara become willing, even enthusiastic fellow travellers. They choose the life of strangeness and change, not even in spite of its dangers, but seemingly because of it. (This theme of change, tellingly, is also where he starts in his second novelization, *Doctor Who and the Crusaders*, which begins by talking about how all of the characters change, moving into a discussion about why Earth's history cannot be changed even though the rest of the universe's can be, and into the nature of immutable things. This really is what Whitaker saw the entire series as being about.)

Those readers who have looked at subsequent volumes of *TARDIS Eruditorum* will know that discussions of David Whitaker focus on the theme of alchemy, and particularly on the nature of mercury, which, alchemically, is a symbol of change and transformation. It's fitting that mercury makes its first appearance as a central concept in Doctor Who in *The Daleks* – that we learn there that the TARDIS runs, in part, on mercury. Thematically, symbolically, this is the first time Doctor Who gets all the elements in line. The plot details may be off, but the basic core of what Doctor Who is – the thing it will spend the rest of its life mercurially tinkering with – is here, created immaculately by David Whitaker.

They Always Survive, While I Lose Everything (*The Dalek Invasion of Earth*)

It is November 21, 1964. The Supremes' "Baby Love" is at the top of the charts. It is unseated two weeks later by the Rolling Stones with "Little Red Rooster," which lasts for a week before the Beatles debut at number one with "I Feel Fine" to round out the year. The Kinks, Roy Orbison, and Petula Clark also chart.

In the intersections of real news and music, Wonderful Radio London, one of the offshore radio stations memorialized in Richard Curtis's more or less execrable film *The Boat That Rocked* (aka *Pirate Radio*), debuted. The station would have a huge role to play in the rising New Britain over the next few years. Lenny Bruce is sent to prison for four months for obscenity, capping off a six-month trial. And the Berkeley Free Speech Movement – one of the iconic student protests of 1960s America – continues picking up steam, with Deputy District Attorney Edwin Meese III ordering mass arrests of protesting students. He will go on to be a starring figure in the drama of People's Park in 1969, and then to be attorney general under Ronald Reagan.

And on television, Doctor Who premieres with its eleventh story. Hang on tight. Everything is going to change. Again.

See, there's something about Doctor Who we haven't talked much about yet. And that's the Daleks. Despite having only appeared in six episodes, at this point, about a year into the show and since their debut, they are unequivocally the stars of the show. In June, way back when *The Aztecs* was airing, *The Dalek Book* was published – a collection of stories and comics meant to capitalize on their popularity. (We deal with it along with some other sundry tie-ins in a few chapters.) While this story is airing the Go-Go's (no, not those Go-Go's, the other ones) release the novelty single "I'm Gonna Spend My Christmas with a Dalek." In other words, the Daleks were the show's best claim to pop culture relevance. This craze, called Dalekmania in a mirroring of the more famous Beatlemania, was the biggest success the show had.

Their return, then, was inevitable, and gives us what is basically the most important Doctor Who story to air yet with the possible exception of the first episode. Certainly it was the most hyped: the return of the Daleks was a known and promoted factor before the first episode of this story aired, making this Doctor Who's first real dalliance with event television.

Which makes the pacing of the first episode somewhat odd. The entire episode is structured around its final scene – a Dalek emerging from the Thames to menace the Doctor and Ian. And rightly so – it's an absolutely phenomenal cliffhanger. But to work, it has to be the first appearance of the Daleks in the story. The cliffhanger hinges on being a spectacular reveal and a culmination of deferred desire. It's exciting not because you suspect the Doctor and Ian are in real danger – if you've watched the show before you know they're going to be fine. The thrill of this cliffhanger has nothing to do with them. The thrill is purely because the Daleks are finally here, and this is the moment that pays off the desire that had been building over the previous twenty-two and a half minutes.

Unfortunately, it means that those twenty-two and a half minutes are horrifically dragged-out attempts to hold off starting the story. Which requires such unfortunate set pieces as Ian being surprised to find out that a man who tumbled out of a cardboard box is dead.

But there are some key things in the first episode to look at. The first is the starkness of the setting – ruined landmarks and a silent London. For the second story in a row, the story hinges on making the familiar seem foreign and scary. In this context, its opening shot – a helmeted man staggering down towards the river with a sign reading "It is forbidden to dump bodies in the river" visible in the backdrop, then screaming and throwing himself in the river to drown – is an absolutely stunning way of efficiently communicating that something is *wrong* with this world. (Interestingly, the story also ends away from the TARDIS, making this the first Doctor Who story that is portrayed from the world's perspective through and through instead of from the Doctor's.)

Much of the effect of this horror-London is historically dependent – the Daleks are visibly invading a ruined 1960s London. The iconic shot that shows that London is ruined is the Battersea Power Station, which was abandoned within twenty years of the episode airing, and comes off as a bizarre choice of ruined landmarks in 2011. But the end effect of this – bolstered by the handful of location sequences a few episodes in – is that the familiar images of London become scenes of potential horror. When you see Daleks milling around Trafalgar Square, the effect is not to have Daleks become scarier by making them more real; it's to make Trafalgar Square scarier by making it less real.

Also interesting in the first episode is the use of the Robomen, who are basically a placeholder monster so that there can be some good running around before the Daleks show up. This is not a hugely sophisticated narrative technique, but it is sufficiently sophisticated to tell us something important about the show, namely that it has, by this point, established monsters as part of its paradigm. You can only have a fake-out placeholder monster if the expectation is that there will be a monster. In other words, you need to have a sufficiently developed sense of what the monster should be so that you can create an imitation of that role. Of course, the show doesn't quite have that yet. It has a sense that monsters are good things to have around, but if we're being honest, it's not until Season Four that it's going to actually come up with a second monster design that works well and recurs. Which is, again, a case of the show being somewhat better at knowing what it's doing than it is at actually doing it.

But it's at the start of the second episode that the story really takes off. Because as soon as the Dalek emerges from the Thames, the Doctor is a completely different person. Many pixels have been illuminated on the subject of where the Doctor changes from a guy who would smash a man's brain out because it's convenient to the character we recognize as The Doctor. In truth it's a gradual process – the Doctor was, after all, still prone to deciding to chuck Ian and Barbara out a mere two stories ago. But it seems to me that the final stage in that process clearly takes place here.

And it appears that it is the image of a Dalek emerging from the Thames that finally completes that process. Once the Dalek shows up, all the Doctor really wants to do is have a proper chinwag with it, which is really the moment where you know the show you have is Doctor Who. If the Doctor and his companions escaped and fell out of the world in the first story, here is where we really see the infinite extensibility of the premise.

See, I've said that every decent story is a Doctor Who story. And I stand by that. But it's not the TARDIS that makes the show what it is. The show is the fusion of four distinct elements that add up to make the greatest concept in television ever. The TARDIS is the first of these to be introduced – literally, with that first shot, it is the magic box that makes the world strange.

From there we have seen two more elements clearly emerge. First, monsters, of which the Daleks are the archetypes. There are better occasions to talk about monsters than this, so for now let's simply note that they serve to make the world scary.

Next are the companions, introduced mostly in the stories from *The Aztecs* through *Planet of Giants*. Traditionally the companion is described as the audience identification figure. For a variety of reasons, this is deeply wrong-headed, although it's such a key piece of received wisdom that even people who are frankly smarter than that – Steven Moffat, for instance – are forced to repeat it. In fact there are hardly any companions in the history of the show who are actually audience identification figures, and even they are only audience identification figures in a handful of stories. Their role may be to occasionally have things the audience needs explained told to them instead, which is sort of close to audience identification, but even there, not really.

No – the role of the companions is to serve as a check on the Doctor. The companions are, both literally and metaphorically, what makes the Doctor confront the monsters. This is the major takeaway of all those exquisite Doctor/Barbara scenes – especially in *Planet of Giants*, and really in *The Time Travellers*. The Doctor fights because his companions want him to, and he loves his companions. And inasmuch as the companion is the audience identification figure, this is how – because they stand in for his broader love of humans, and thus stand in for the audience's desire that he fight.

Which leaves us with the fourth part, which makes its appearance here in something approximating its full and final form. That, of course, is the Doctor himself. It's not enough to have people in peril from scary things in a strange universe. You also need a man who genuinely loves exploring the universe and getting into trouble. You need, in other words, a sense of fun. And that's what the Doctor injects. He takes the danger his companions are in and turns it into fun. And this is why he has to chinwag with the Daleks. For no other reason than that it is more fun. Every Doctor Who confrontation, in the end, is built around the expectation that the Doctor will enjoy it, and thus that it will be fun to watch. The Doctor talks his way out of trouble because it's more exciting. You don't want to see the Doctor just blow up the Daleks from afar. You want to see him mock them first, then go defeat them.

And you get that here. The Daleks emerge from the Thames, and within a few minutes, even though the Daleks do not recognize the Doctor as The Doctor and thus as their arch-nemesis, they're terrified of him. As the Doctor is led off to prison, the Dalek neurotically repeats "We are the masters of Earth," making it sound less like a triumphant Dalek boast than like a small child rocking itself back and forth and trying to convince itself that it will all be OK. Paul Cornell's great line that the Doctor is what monsters have nightmares about starts here. The Daleks take one look at the Doctor and are terrified of him. Meanwhile, the Doctor is having the time of his life – giggling like a schoolboy as he breaks out of prison, mocking Daleks, insisting that he is the Doctor, not simply "Doc," etc. And it's made him a better person – far from head-smashing Doctor, here the Doctor scolds other characters for being overly violent. All due, it seems, to the Daleks.

So let's talk about the Daleks in their second appearance. In their first appearance, they were simply generic monsters. It's not entirely clear, in fact, that the story has any particularly high expectations for them or has the slightest clue how special what it's got is. In this story, however, because they're the first monster ever to return, the story implicitly treats them as the Doctor's arch-nemesis – as something truly extraordinary.

Which makes it strange that, in this story, they are almost, but not quite, totally incoherent as a concept. The Daleks' plan in this episode is easily one of the most insane in the series' long and storied history. They want to, and I want to stress here that I am not making this up or exaggerating at all, remove the Earth's magnetic core so they can install an engine and drive the planet around as a spaceship.

It is very much unclear why an un-aerodynamic planet is the ideal place to do this, or why England is the perfect place to do the drilling. Clearly, if the Daleks have a fully functional invasion fleet, there's not a huge need for spaceships. They're in pretty good shape on that front. So presumably the Earth is to be a sort of prestige vehicle. A sort of Porsche for the mid-life crisis of a Dalek. I picture Daleks pulling along upside another planet and saying "Hey baby, I drive a planet." It's like the original Zaphod Beeblebrox.

But there's actually something strangely brilliant about the arbitrariness of this plot. Because it makes it clear that the plot doesn't matter. The plot is literally nothing more than an excuse to bring the Daleks around again. The Daleks don't need a good reason to invade a planet or be evil. They're just Daleks. They're the bad guys. They are, at this point, designed to be the things that, when they show up, you go "Oh no, it's the Daleks!"

Adding to this sense of the Daleks being pure plot devices is the fact that their history is insane. The Doctor claims that this must be the "middle period" of Dalek history, at an earlier point in their history. Except that the Daleks in this story are more advanced than the late-period Daleks, who were unable to move around except on their metal floors. Furthermore, the conceit in this story as to why they can move off of their special floors – the circular dishes installed on their backs – vanishes without comment after this story. And the last story was ostensibly the Daleks' origin, making it an open question when, exactly, in the course of their hiding from the fallout of their war with the Thals they built an intergalactic empire.

Pages have been spent trying to sort all of this out, but the fact of the matter is, all of them are trying to fit together two things that obviously don't fit together and were never meant to. Which is usually the case with Doctor Who continuity, but rarely do we end up with this problem when two stories come out in a one-year period and have the same writer, producer, and script editor.

In raw continuity terms, *The Time Travellers* comes in real handy with this story. Thanks to that book, the Doctor knows the Daleks have time travel technology. Thus their chronology is not entirely at issue – as that book makes it clear that time can be rewritten. Why the Doctor declines to own up to this is the sort of unanswered question that is necessarily going to come up when you try to reconcile two stories written by two totally different people forty-one years apart, but to *The Time Travellers'* credit, it does file off some of the rough edges of this story.

But more to the point, the book files them off with only one reference to a story outside of the Hartnell era, and that one is itself drenched in references to the Hartnell era. The episode knows full well that the Daleks are the Doctor's arch-nemesis. It has the paradigm of Doctor vs. Daleks down. But right now, the phenomenon is purely a pop phenomenon. The reason this story exists is because it's the Doctor vs. his most popular enemies in the capital of the country the show airs in. This could be dismissed as a pander to the fans, but that misunderstands what's going on here. It's not a pander to the fans – it's Doctor Who as pop spectacle. (An idea heightened by the fact that the idea of Daleks in different colors appears here for the first time.) That's at the heart of the Doctor's character – his contribution to the four tent poles holding the series up. The Doctor has fun doing what he's doing, and so of course he has a big pop spectacle of an adventure here and there.

Terry Nation is the writer who understood this first. *The Daleks* was an invitation to over the top spectacle. *The Keys of Marinus* was based around the show's ability to create madcap spectacle. In his next contribution for the show, he'll take this to its logical end, and then basically retire from Doctor Who for eight years. But by that point – indeed, by this point, he's already been responsible for large amounts of the paradigm of Doctor Who.

But if Nation understands here that the Daleks are a pop spectacle, he doesn't quite get why. Hence the ridiculous plot and incoherent history on their second appearance. I mean, with nearly fifty years of Dalek stories, it's no surprise that the repeated efforts to destroy them all have gotten a bit wonky, but screwing up Dalek history irretrievably in the short span of only two stories is a sort of rare art of ignoring continuity that most writers can only aspire to. It works here, but only because the pop spectacle is audacious enough to carry you through the nonsense.

But if you add in *The Time Travellers*, you get one key detail, which is that the Doctor has a reason to know that the Daleks are his arch-nemesis. He knows they travel in time. He knows that eventually he'll have to face them down over what he did in Coal Hill School in 1963. When the Dalek rises from the Thames, in other words, the Doctor has a reason to recognize the Doctor-Dalek relationship. And in recognizing the Daleks as his arch-nemeses, he implicitly fixes them into their role in the binary. This is, perhaps, what they are scared of – because they, for the first time, realize they are facing their arch-nemesis.

This is key. With all four tent poles clearly in place and the Doctor running around having the time of his life, the show can finally begin the frankly quite important process of what I would describe as making the Doctor an ontological force in the narrative. Here, I should admit, I'm staking a major position in Doctor Who fandom – one that is specifically and categorically opposed to that of Lawrence Miles, who, along with Tat Wood, wrote a six-volume set of books analyzing every Doctor Who story, and thus owns a frightening amount of the territory *TARDIS Eruditorum* is working in. Lawrence Miles is adamantly opposed to treating the Doctor as a fetish object. Which, I'll admit, is exactly the same thing I'm talking about, albeit in different terms.

See, in this episode, we start to get characters talking about how fundamentally special and wonderful the Doctor is. He's treated, by the story, as the big hero of a character. Miles describes this sort of thing as "removing any possible dramatic tension." I describe it as Doctor Who fully embracing its own potential. You say potato . . .

See, to my mind, there is no dramatic tension as such in Doctor Who, because you know exactly when in the story the Doctor is going to make it all work, namely about ten minutes from the end of the final episode. Cliffhangers are a bit of a joke, and when they work – as they do when the Daleks rise from the Thames – it's not because you fear for the characters, but because you're desperate to see what happens next. The tension of Doctor Who is not whether the characters are going to survive or win. It's not even when they're going to win. It's how. And it's specifically a writerly sort of how. That is, you tune into Doctor Who next week having spent a week trying to guess where the story is going to go so as to check your answer. It's a game of whether you can come up with something as good as the writers to get the Doctor to the next part of the story. Crucially, the audience knows what the next part is full well. What makes a Doctor Who episode great is when every episode is a better solution than what the audience can come up with for what to do next.

And so reveling in the Doctor as a mythic figure and openly accepting that around twenty minutes into the last episode he's going to save the day is not a matter of destroying dramatic tension. It's a matter of actively engaging with your audience. Because anyone who sticks around for the long haul of Doctor Who is doing it because they want to see what's next, not out of concern that it might be all the characters dying. Miles objects that this is pandering only to long-term viewers, but I think this mistakes an investment in the mythos with an investment in the continuity. Fanwank stories that are all about making allusions to past stories are pandering to long-term viewers. But if your show positions the Doctor as a mythic character continually, then writing explicitly around that fact isn't pandering to long-term viewers, it's doing what you said you were going to do.

And that's part of the genius of Doctor Who in this episode. Exactly a year on the air, and it's figured out that if you just have William Hartnell walk around acting like he's totally confident that he's got everything under control and like he's having the time of his life, the rest of the show will click into place behind it. You don't need to spend years or decades establishing the Doctor as a mythic character. You can just have him go out there and be mythic, and the audience will go "Oh, he's a mythic character, gotcha." To my mind, understanding how to use the mythic like that is one of the show's primary geniuses – not a horrid wrong turn.

For why it's great, one need look no further than the end of the episode, where the Daleks are defeated because Barbara tells the Robomen to attack them. This scene is beautiful. First, it's a follow-up to an earlier scene where Barbara has her own glorious chinwag with the Daleks by spinning an extended story about the threats they face that is (quite flagrantly) stitched-together bits of American history. This is so she can get to the panel that controls the Robomen, but she's stopped at the last second. So when the Doctor finally shows up and they try the plan again, it's a lovely moment of vindication for Barbara, the useful companion.

But more to the point, Barbara orders the Robomen to attack the Daleks with an absolutely hilarious imitation of Dalek voices produced by moving her hand back and forth in front of her face to stutter her voice. Then the Robomen riot against the Daleks, including what is probably the single most barmily wonderful shot of Doctor Who thus far: a bunch of Robomen with a Dalek basically crowd-surfing on top of them. This entire sequence is pop-spectacle payoff. The episode is ending not with a careful and logical sense of narrative teleology, but with the fact that the Dalek voices are fun to do and it's funny to watch a Dalek crowd surf. And that works here, on the Daleks' second appearance. And it's why you watch Doctor Who. Because *Star Trek* is never going to have a crowd-surfing Klingon.

But there's another huge aspect of this story to deal with. The Doctor, at the end of it, is fully the Doctor for, really, the first time in the series. But that, in turn, means that it is necessary to return to the Problem of Susan. We can see the problem in starker relief now. If the role of the companion is to push the Doctor into having fun as a hero, then Susan is an abject failure, as the Doctor's primary motivation with her is to shelter and protect her.

This becomes somewhat clear in this episode. In a restaging of their feud in *The Sensorites*, the Doctor and Susan differ on whether they should head north or try to get back to the TARDIS. In this case, as before, it's Susan who wants to go get into danger and the Doctor that wants to retreat. In other words, because the Doctor is the parent figure to child-Susan, he is unable to adventure. Susan, then, needs to grow up. Which is a sexualized process.

Accordingly, the Doctor hits on a very sensible solution – dump Susan off with the first man she's attracted to and tell her to make babies. In fact, when the Doctor does lock her out of the TARDIS, his stated reason is that she's a woman now. In other words, it's because she's had a sexual awakening – and earlier in the story she and David have, in the words of Amy Pond, a snog in the shrubbery.

What I want to stress, though, is that this remains enormously problematic. Not just in that the Doctor is basically forcing Susan to marry the first guy she kisses, but in the staggeringly creepy moment where David tells Susan that staying on Earth with him is finally her chance to have an identity. Yes, this is a callback to a scene a few episodes earlier, but still, it highlights how appallingly powerless Susan is made.

None of this is helped by the staging of the farewell scene. Carole Ann Ford hits it out of the park, showing the producers quite clearly how much they wasted her talents. But William Hartnell, doing his part of the scene on the

TARDIS set, feels like he's reading off a teleprompter (or, if one wants to be proper, a TelePrompTer brand cueing device). Which, to be fair, he probably was, since fusing two scenes together like this was actually a bit of a technical challenge, but it ends up looking like the Doctor really is eager to get rid of Susan. Which, to be fair, he has seemed to be much of the episode, but it does suck the drama out pretty quickly.

The Doctor promises that some day he will return. He never does. One can try to fill in some missing story for this – a couple exist from the Eighth Doctor era – but the fact of the matter is, here Susan is treated like any other companion. Which is to say, she's abandoned. Looking at the Doctor and Susan together, it's tough to explain why. The Doctor so clearly cares deeply about Susan. And he has family reasons to be with her. But he abandons her forever.

Why?

There's not really an answer to that. The Problem of Susan proves here to be more resilient than we might have hoped. Initially, it appeared to be the problem of sexual awakening. But the Doctor's promise to return eliminates that – he clearly means years down the road, after she is more comfortable as an adult. So why does he lie? Why is an adult Susan such an anathema to the Doctor that he abandons her? This is, in hindsight, a huge problem. Admittedly at the time we expect Susan will grow old and die normally, but later developments in the series make it clear that Susan, as a Time Lord, will regenerate and live for ages, stuck, apparently, on Earth with no TARDIS and a lover who grew old and died as she stayed young forever. This is really, really, intensely not nice of the Doctor. (Yes, there are retcons that explain this.)

There is not a resolution here. The Problem of Susan endures stubbornly across the series. It has, perhaps, been so long now that it cannot be resolved. And so the Doctor's final promise hangs in the air, unfulfilled and unfulfillable. Much of becoming Doctor Who is the process of casting off the odd decisions that didn't quite work over the course of the first season. And ultimately, Susan is one of them. The Doctor says one day he'll return. But how? In the end, that's the Problem of Susan – the most important character in the first episode is the one who turns out to be a bit of a bad idea.

A Rather Special Model (*The Rescue*)

It's 1965. January 2, 1965, to be precise. Life is good. The Beatles are at number one on both the album and singles charts with *Beatles For Sale* and "Day Tripper." Lower on the charts it is somewhat stranger. Probably some of these artists are noteworthy and some reader is going to laugh at me for saying otherwise, but this is the book version and I don't have to read your comments after you complain at me, so let's just go with this list: Twinkle, Val Doonican, and P.J. Proby.

In real news, Lyndon Johnson proclaims the Great Society, a term with obvious echoes to anyone following the coalition government in the UK circa 2011. And . . . um . . . look, this is a two-parter, it's not like there's time for a lot of news to happen, OK?

While on TV, Doctor Who, having plowed through Christmas with its epic of Daleks in London, settles in for a two-parter that, while lacking somewhat in raw glamour, is at least of significant historical merit in that it is the first time since the show appeared that a new regular cast member is debuted. Plus it's the second full writing credit of David Whitaker, who is steadily going to become visible as the best writer Doctor Who had in the 1960s.

The Rescue is not Whitaker's most acclaimed script, nor should it be. But it is a script that is, particularly when watched in sequence, visibly a massive progression in storytelling for Doctor Who. Watching, it is clear from the start that this is a different sort of story – fully ten percent of the story has already passed when the TARDIS crew makes its first appearance. Instead, it starts by focusing on Vicki – the new girl, and by making the story about her. The result is arguably the first modern Doctor Who story.

See, in 2005, Doctor Who changed to be predominantly fourty-five minute, single-episode stories with occasional two-parters. But the original, classic approach was twenty-five-minute stories of varying episode counts. For most of the series, however, the norm was four-part stories with occasional two, three, or six-parters. Of these, the two-parter is in some ways the most interesting now because its end length, when you cut out the cliffhanger reprise and a full set of credit sequences, comes out right around the length of the modern single-episode stories. And yet there are only seven of them in the history of the series. The first was *The Edge of Destruction*, which was an early story that was made under such a massive pile of constraints as to be difficult to compare it to anything at all.

But here we get something that is, actually, shaped more or less like modern Doctor Who. Not just in terms of being the right length either. The story has surprisingly modern pacing – certainly compared to the rest of the era, where stories are often structured with excruciating tedium and delaying tactics, whereas this rolls right along.

On top of that, because the story consciously situates Vicki at its center, it is the first time since the very beginning of the series where we see the TARDIS heavily from the perspective of someone unused to it. This, keep in mind, is also the hallmark of the new series, with Rose, Martha, Donna (on her return), and to a lesser extent Amy all being introduced in that fashion. But more to the point, this story's approach of having a central character who serves as the primary focus of the story – someone the story is about, if you will – is much more in line with things like *The Big Bang*,

Vincent and the Doctor, *Turn Left*, or *Father's Day* than it is with things like *The Dalek Invasion of Earth* and *The Sensorites*.

One thing that's been very clear in the stories already watched is that Doctor Who quickly became a show with real aspirations. *The Aztecs*, *The Sensorites*, and *The Dalek Invasion of Earth* are all stories that, conceptually, could be made today. Their basic ideas are still genuinely daring. Hell, plot-wise *The Sensorites* basically is the plot to *The Doctor's Daughter*. It's just that it's stretched to three times the length and doesn't have Jenny in it to provide a unified emotional through line to the entire plot. Which is the thing – all of these past stories, however good their ideas, would need massive replotting and reconceptualizing to actually work in modern times, due largely to the fact that they are not structured with the kind of intense, focused, and character-based unity we expect from modern drama. *The Rescue*, while it would still need a good rewrite, would not necessarily need any drastic changes to its structure.

This is not, I admit, the consensus view of *The Rescue*. The major critique of the story is that its central mystery is obvious, and thus there's no suspense. This is hard to evaluate when you know what the central twist is, but I will point out two things in the twist's defense. First, even if you do somehow decide that Koquillion is a human in disguise and thus has to be Bennett, this assumes that the viewer isn't supposed to get ahead of the Doctor. Which is an arbitrary decision. If we do take this as a mystery, plenty of mysteries are based on the idea that the audience is ahead of the detective. *Cracker*, one of the great British police series of all times, usually starts by showing you the crime, criminal and all, and then spends hours watching Robbie Coltrane catch up. The reveal of Koquillion's identity hardly ends the dramatic tension and removes all problems the characters face on Dido, and so is hardly a blow to the story's overall suspense. Indeed, the scenes of the Doctor following Bennett's trail are probably even more suspenseful if you've made the leap all the way to figuring out that Bennett is the monster rather than merely in league with the monster. Much of *The Rescue* works precisely because we realize that the characters are in more trouble than they do.

Secondly, the fact that there is only one possible solution to the mystery is only a problem if the viewer realizes there's a mystery. *The Rescue* avoids making this obvious. This is perhaps the more important point, because it reflects a real cleverness on Whitaker's part. Instead of sustaining the plot by diverting suspicion from the suspect, Whitaker diverts suspicion from the mystery itself.

Yes, if anyone is secretly Koquillion the evil monster guy it is Bennett, the lone character who is neither a regular nor recently announced as a new regular. But all of this presumes that the audience assumes that Koquillion is not an alien, when almost everything suggests that he is an alien. Even once the audience firmly knows that something is up with Bennett, the idea that he actually is Koquillion is in no way the obvious conclusion to draw. It makes much more sense for him to be in some way in league with Koquillion, and it seems to me obvious that this is the assumption Whitaker expects the audience to make.

Why? Simply put, because Koquillion is visibly a monster. This is, in fact, a brilliant joke on Whitaker's part – probably the funniest one in the series thus far, and arguably one of the funniest in the entire run of the series. See, when we find out that Koquillion is really Bennett in disguise, the Doctor notes that the clothes worn by Koquillion are ceremonial garb that a native of this planet would not normally wear. Koquillion then removes his mask and we realize that he's just Bennett in a rubber suit. Furthermore, the real aliens on the planet, when we see them a few minutes later, are actually humanoid.

This is a great reversal of expectations, and, as I said, a hilarious joke. Because the whole reason we assumed that Koquillion was a monster was that he looked like a man in a rubber suit. In the context of Doctor Who, looking like a man in a rubber suit is extremely convincing evidence that you are an alien and possibly a monster. Watching Doctor

Who, in fact, requires that we rarely assume a man in a rubber suit to actually be a man in a rubber suit. And so Whitaker pulls off the absolutely brilliant trick of hiding the villain in the most obvious place ever. Nobody will ever think that the man in a rubber suit is secretly a man in a rubber suit.

Indeed, the idea of unexpected monsters is in many ways the primary theme of *The Rescue*. Everything that looks like it should be a monster – Koquillion and Vicki's pet sand creature – turns out not to be a monster. None of the things that are signified by the effects are, in fact, what they appear. To read the story by assuming that anything that looks like a special effect is supposed to be taken as though it were a plausible space alien is exactly the wrong way to read it. This is also gleefully meta, in that it makes it clear that the show has known from the start that its effects were wobbly, and thus that the effects have never been about being persuasive illusions, but rather have been tools in a particular sort of storytelling. The limitations of the effects are part of the narrative structure of Doctor Who.

Which basically sums up where people go wrong with *The Rescue*, and to some extent with the Hartnell stories in general. They expect too little of the stories. To be fair, low expectations can often be rewarded in any period of Doctor Who. But the fact of the matter is that there's some genuinely elegant visual storytelling going on here. Consider, for instance, the early scene in which Vicki gives most of the exposition about the nature of the planet and the crashed ship. Exposition scenes are essential to Doctor Who, but brutal to stage well. This one is, frankly, the series' best yet – a long close-up of Vicki as she describes the situation, holding close to her face and her expressions in a way that makes the scene not about the recitation of technobabble but about her desperation and fear.

If the story has one major failing it is that Ian and Barbara are a few characters too many. Their presence helps explain why Bennett is the only other human around – a short story like this suffers if it has too many characters – but the fact of the matter is, they're taking up space in this story. This is not their fault — after all, a four-lead-character structure is an awful lot for Doctor Who in forty-five minutes, which is why the new series has stuck to two leads for most of its time. This story is about Vicki and the Doctor, and that's about all, in forty-five minutes, it can afford to be about.

But still, Ian contributes literally nothing to the plot, while Barbara gets some good scenes opposite Vicki. But looking at the story, it's clear that Barbara is paired up with Vicki not because it makes sense (Vicki stumbling upon Barbara, who is conveniently unconscious but mostly unhurt after being shoved off a cliff, is a bit of a stretch). It's because someone has to give Vicki some characterization scenes. Barbara is really just filling a role that would normally be filled by another stranded human if the story had room for one. (All the same, Jacqueline Hill turns in a typically sublime performance.)

But for the most part, this is a two-character drama of Vicki and the Doctor. Vicki is the girl who is scared and trapped on an alien planet, and the Doctor is the man who drops out of the sky and rescues her. That's what this story is.

Interestingly, when we do cut to the TARDIS for the first time, steps are taken to increase doubt about the Doctor. He appears out of sorts, apparently because Susan is gone (there's a lovely scene where he calls for Susan to open the doors, then stops, clearly pained and embarrassed at his lapse, and Barbara steps up and asks him to show her how to open the doors). Ian suggests that he's gone nuts, opting to nap inside the TARDIS instead of explore.

This is something we haven't seen of the Doctor on television since the early days of the show, and there he is more spiteful than vulnerable. Here he is wounded and clearly not firing on all cylinders. It's not until he meets Vicki and feels compelled to try to help her.

This entire dynamic is interesting, because it's also the first time the show has really asked the question of whether the TARDIS did more harm than good in arriving. At one point, Barbara mistakes a friendly alien for a monster and brutally guns down Vicki's pet sand monster. Which is an absolutely horrifying scene. (Or a hilarious moment of camp, as with most great scenes in Doctor Who.) But the really key scene comes in response to it, when Vicki makes the quite reasonable point that a rescue ship will be along in a few days, she's alive, she can deal with Koquillion's threats and menacing, and thus far all the Doctor and his friends have managed is murdering her pet.

This – not the Doctor confronting Koquillion later in the episode – is the story's actual climax. The Doctor is confronted with the accusation that he's doing harm, not good, and his response is, basically, to fall head over heels for the young girl, turn on the charm offensive, win her over, and save the day, all of which he accomplishes in a few minutes once he puts his mind to it. Indeed, from Ian and Barbara's perspective, he wanders off into the other room of the ship, disappears somewhere, and when he reappears a bit later he's solved everything and they're ready to go. His showing up to a concerned Ian and Barbara and basically saying "Oh, yes, I got that all taken care of" is hilarious – almost as funny as a monster that actually turns out to be a man in a rubber suit.

It is probably worth a side trip to briefly observe that this is the third story in a row to be directly connected to the UK. The last two were set there, and here the spaceship is explicitly a British ship. There's a rush of nationalism here – particularly in this story and the one before. The Daleks invade Earth, yes, but what they really want is Britain, and it's the Brits (helped by the Doctor, our honorary Englishman) who drive them off. This story is expressly set a few hundred years after the Dalek invasion, and Britain is flourishing. Given that the show just sent a major character off to rebuild Britain, it's non-trivial that it immediately goes and shows the viewers that Britain does rebuild. But, equally crucially, it does not rebuild into the old Britain of empire.

Rather, it is vibrant youth like Vicki who are the visible symbol of post-Dalek Britain. Given the parallels between

Daleks and the Nazis and the fact that World War II is now firmly in the past, this message is striking, suggesting as it does a profound desire for broad social reform. And it is worth remembering specifically that the first time the Doctor really lit up and engaged with the world around him was at the prospect of the Thals rebuilding Skaro.

The show, then, has quietly but explicitly allied itself with the burgeoning New Britain. Doctor Who is not only a show for kids (although it's clear that it was designed with them in mind) but for youth. Compare the ethos of a youthful, rebuilt Britain of the future with the liner notes of *Beatles for Sale*:

There's priceless history between these covers. When, in a generation or so, a radioactive, cigar-smoking child, picnicking on Saturn, asks you what the Beatle affair was all about, don't try to explain all about the long hair and the screams! Just play them a few tracks from this album and he'll probably understand. The kids of AD2000 will draw from the music much the same sense of well being and warmth as we do today.

The implications of this shift are completed when Vicki, our starchild (complete with Scouse accent), is invited by the Doctor to join them. It is very, very clear that the Doctor is a bit smitten with her (in the way that he often is with his companions). In the growing cultural divide of Britain, there is no real ambiguity as to what side the Doctor is on now. This story and the last one are the first time the show has re-invented itself, going from adventure serial to cultural icon. To a real extent, they are as important a pair as the *Tenth Planet/The Power of the Daleks*, in that they firmly establish the show's capacity for reinvention and unlimited length.

And so we get, at the end of the episode, one of the series' most iconic shots – one we'll see repeated over and over again in the forty-six years following this episode. Vicki walks into the TARDIS for the first time, and we see her awe at its mysteries. When Ian and Barbara fell into the TARDIS, it was a place of menace. Now it is a place of wonder, and the sequence here is the baseline that every other first-TARDIS-entrance scene is responding to.

And with that completed, the Doctor takes off again, new companion in tow. What a surprise. Everything has changed forever. Again.

Like You Do When You're Young (*The Romans*)

It's January 16, 1965. It's Georgie Fame, the Moody Blues, and the Righteous Brothers on the charts for the next four weeks, while at the tail end of the four weeks the Rolling Stones take over the album sales with their imaginatively titled *The Rolling Stones No. 2*. The Beatles also remain in the charts, along with Gerry and the Pacemakers, Sandie Shaw, Cilla Black, the Kinks, and Manfred Mann.

The most significant thing to happen in these four weeks, however, occurred on January 24, when Sir Winston Churchill, twice former Prime Minister, dies. His state funeral on January 30 coincides with the third episode of *The Romans*, the Doctor Who story du jour for the month.

Production-wise, *The Romans* sees the return of Dennis Spooner, who did not particularly impress on his last outing with *The Reign of Terror*. In addition to writing the story, Spooner has also just assumed the position of script editor for the series. The script editor, for the original run of Doctor Who, was the closest position to the current role of head writer/executive producer. The biggest difference is that rules prohibited script editors from commissioning themselves to write scripts in most circumstances. Instead, generally speaking, they did revisions and rewrites to other scripts. But with some frequency the situation got complicated and various pen names and other schemes arose to cover the fact that the script editor had written a script.

In this case, David Whitaker, the outgoing script editor, hired Dennis Spooner to write *The Romans*, then quit, and his replacement, Dennis Spooner, hired him to write *The Rescue*. Oh, and for accounting purposes, *The Romans* is actually *The Rescue* Parts Three through Six.

It's fitting, given the tortured logic of its creation, that *The Romans* is the first Doctor Who story to be explicitly devised as a comedic farce. (Indeed, it's also basically the last one until *Partners in Crime* in 2008.) So, a comedic historical tale. Exactly what one imagines the nation wanted as their great wartime hero of a former prime minister is buried. This is, of course, not Spooner's fault – he obviously wrote the thing while Churchill was still alive. But it does mess up the reception of the story considerably.

Of course, Churchill's legacy in the UK is somewhat more complex than one might assume. In the election immediately following the war, the Tories were hammered and he was replaced by Clement Atlee, who, in historical hindsight, is actually about as much of a lion as Churchill. Then, in 1951, an aging Churchill was returned to power for a frankly lackluster second spell that did no favors for his reputation. Churchill, in his second term, fought hard to keep the British Empire together. By 1965, the Empire was not so much on life support as in hospice care.

In other words, Churchill, though unmistakably a national hero and national treasure, was also part of the fading old Britain. Watched through that lens, *The Romans* seems an even worse match for the national mood. After all, the occasion of Churchill's death is hardly the ideal time to begin a long, self-reflective jag about the passing of his era so much as it is to celebrate that era's high points, of which, let's be perfectly clear, there were many. But the fact that Churchill was, at the time of his death, a figure of the past does make this somewhat more interesting.

On the one hand, *The Romans*, despite being a comedy, is fundamentally a conservative story, miles from the oddly post-anarchistic youth revolution of the last two stories. The Doctor's adventuring spirit that blossomed in the last two episodes has mostly vanished, he's back to abusing Ian and Barbara, and all sense of ambition towards challenging storytelling is out the window. This is increasingly seeming like a hallmark of Spooner, which is a slight problem, but it's also oddly apropos for a period of mourning for the old Britain.

On the other hand, there are ways in which the show seems to resist the over-simplification. The storytelling as a whole may be unambitious, but it does open with one of the most unusual starts of an episode: the TARDIS falls off a cliff, then we cut to a month later with the TARDIS crew vacationing in a Roman villa. This is a jarring but enormously clever start, poking clever fun at the fact that Doctor Who stories generally start with something bad happening to the TARDIS and the crew trying to get it back/back to working order.

The story also pushes the characters subtly. I've spoken in past entries about the lack of significant support in the show thus far for the theory that Ian and Barbara are lovers. That goes out the window with their scenes at the Roman villa, where they have a visible intimacy and closeness that we've just never seen before. One gets the sense that a month of relaxation in Rome has . . . nudged things forward in their relationship, shall we say. (Or we can just go with Lawrence Miles and Tat Woods's description of their interactions as "post-coital.")

If the Doctor has regressed in his general behavior and treatment of Ian and Barbara, he's helped by the fact that Susan, who gave Spooner no end of trouble in *The Reign in Terror*, is gone. Instead we have Vicki, and the Doctor has a whole new relationship to set up. And it's one that Spooner actually does enormously well with.

A brief word here about Maureen O'Brien. Much has been made of the scope of the task Patrick Troughton faced in Season Four in reinventing the role of the Doctor. But Maureen O'Brien's Vicki is mostly overlooked as a major companion despite the fact that her job was identical to Troughton's – revamp the role of the companion, and in particular the young girl companion role originated by Carole Ann Ford. That is, on the one hand, she's clearly meant to be basically the same character. On the other, she's clearly hired to fix some problems people were having with the original version. Yes, in practice her character suffers continually at the hands of writers who view the young girl companion as someone to be kidnapped. But she gives the role some real effort, and is easily the most charismatic person in the cast. The result is that huge swaths of the modern female companion get codified by O'Brien, who doesn't get nearly the credit she deserves for that.

Thankfully, this story is structured in order to give her some real chances to shine. Ian and Barbara are sent off on a separate plot so that Vicki gets to be the main companion to the Doctor. The Doctor, for his part, seems primarily interested in impressing Vicki this episode. He ditches Ian and Barbara to take her to Rome and spends almost the whole time showing off, including one of his most memorable name-drops as he claims to have trained the Mountain Mauler of Montana.

It's worth commenting on the Doctor's tendency to name-drop his involvement in various historical figures' lives. He begins this behavior with Ian and Barbara, which implies a lot of adventures before he met them. But for a variety of reasons, I'm not fond of putting much of anything before *An Unearthly Child*. (For more on that, however, see the first essay in the book.)

But this really poses no problem in terms of his name-dropping. It just means he's lying. Which makes total sense after seeing this episode, given that he simultaneously claims to have inspired "The Emperor's New Clothes" and claims he wouldn't do something like inspire the Great Fire of Rome. Of course he makes up encounters with famous historical figures to impress the girls. It's completely consistent with his character – especially when you take into account the fact that lying is about the only way to account for the disparities in claims about his age. (Again, see the next essay, although I'm sure some future volume will have a Doctor's age essay.)

For instance, it's clear the writers intend the Doctor to be the old man that he appears to be. But in this story, he, for lack of a better phrase, does not act his age. He enjoys getting into fights, tries to impress the ladies, and is extensively vigorous. Which makes sense in the context of later developments – the Doctor is, in fact, a young man here. This is especially stressed by the fact that his primary allegiance in this story appears to be towards Vicki, who we've already established is a utopian image of the youth culture of 1965. Here the Doctor, old man that he appears to be, seems also to be a symbol of youth.

What's funny is that this interpretation works pretty well in most Hartnell stories. Most of them work well with it, and it's certainly a reliably entertaining approach. But more to the point, in *The Romans*, it's hard to identify any other working approach, particularly when the Doctor is giddy at the notion that he helped cause the Great Fire of Rome. The Doctor as giddy pyromaniac anarchist is an easier sell if one imagines the guy as being about equivalent to a seventeen-year-old human in terms of development.

Ah, yes. The pyromaniacal anarchy bit. Because here's the thing – the story ends with Vicki and the Doctor helping to torch Rome, and both of them seeming downright delighted with it. Suddenly the character that, visually, is the most old Britain character on the show is allied with the New Britain youngster in wanting to burn it all down. It's an iconic moment for the series – the point where the Doctor's moral code really clarifies. He has a sense of moral duty and will help people who need it. But he'll *delight* in upsetting the apple cart.

What's most interesting is that this seems almost accidental in the story. The story's lone solidly funny gag is the idea of the professional poisoner. There is nothing ambitious in this story, little yet pyromaniacally anarchistic. The story is a lowbrow runaround of a farce that even Jacqueline Hill seems tired of by the end, in no small part because her entire plot involves being sleazily hit on by Nero. Spooner did basically the same thing to her in *The Reign of Terror*, which, actually, borders on being a bit of a thing – certainly the plot here is uncomfortable in its rapey overtones and is something that's hard to feel good about in the modern day. It's alleged that the next story contains the moment when William Russell decides he's done with Doctor Who. If so, then this one equally clearly contains the moment where Jacqueline Hill decides that she just doesn't want to do stories like this any more. And given the tone and nature of her plot line, it's very difficult to argue with the decision.

Which is the crux of the problem with *The Romans* – it's a comedy without an era. It missed its own time by being a farce that went out alongside Winston Churchill's death and misses contemporary taste by being a 1965-style farce, which is to say, by being badly dated. Neither is a deal-breaker, but the combination poses an odd sort of problem.

But despite that somewhat unsatisfying fact, somehow, the story works. It's worth contrasting this with *The Reign of Terror*, which is, after all, only five months previous. There a similar combination of factors made the story stumble unsatisfyingly. But in just five months and three stories the show has seemingly transformed itself, such that even with uneven material it can spin gold. The strong implication is that we've gotten to where there's such a thing as Doctor Who, as a coherent idea unto itself, that is capable of transcending its source material when needed. The show has become self-sustaining.

Pop Between Realities, Home in Time for Tea: *Z-Cars* and *Dixon of Dock Green*

The thing you have to understand is that in the mid-'60s, Doctor Who was one of three extremely important shows on the BBC to feature police prominently. The other two being *Dixon of Dock Green*, which aired on the same days as Doctor Who, and *Z-Cars*, which aired on Tuesdays. (A quick sidenote for unfortunate Americans. There is nothing more embarrassing in life than making an erudite, informed point about mid-century British television only to be corrected on the fact that the show is pronounced *Zed-Cars*, not *Zee-Cars*. Trust me.) Admittedly, Doctor Who is the only one of these three shows to be a science fiction show. The other two were good old-fashioned cop shows.

Still, the fact of the matter is that if you talk about early Doctor Who for long enough with people, one or both of these shows will come up. Usually as follows – *Dixon of Dock Green* is, typically, cited in terms of the prominence of the police box, being as it's the other show to feature them at all regularly. *Z-Cars* is cited more broadly – often in terms of how badly other shows fared in the Old Episode Demolition Derby years of the BBC, though occasionally more esoterically. (Steven Moffat has a hilarious bit on the commentary track for *Forest of the Dead* in which he notes that anybody complaining about the effects on Doctor Who should look at *Z-Cars*, where they couldn't even get cars to look realistic despite driving them to work every day.) Certainly the opening of *An Unearthly Child* quietly evoked them, particularly *Dixon of Dock Green*, with its image of a policeman walking through the fog. For our purposes, however, I want to talk about the two shows in terms of realism.

Let me back up and say that I have serious issues with realism. Passionately. I consider it to be ethically bankrupt as an aesthetic and think that texts that claim to be realist are perpetuating active fraud upon the reader. Now, to be fair, there are a lot of things called realism, and only some of them should be shooting offenses. I'm not saying that all fiction should be sci-fi or anything. There is such a thing as realistic sci-fi, and there is such a thing as a non-realistic cop show. So let's make some distinctions. In fact, let's ask this – what's more realistic? *Dixon of Dock Green*, or *Z-Cars*?

On paper, you'd say *Z-Cars*. After all, *Dixon of Dock Green* is a bizarrely slow-paced drama that presents a ridiculous and idyllic view of what London police officers do. It exists purely to reinforce the social order and teach people that police officers are kind, good people who should be respected, adored, and trusted. Episodes begin with the whistling George Dixon strolling up to the camera, delivering a rambling monologue, and then treating us to half an hour of characters standing in various rooms talking before George Dixon sums up the moral of the story and sends us on our way. The show is overtly theatrical – huge stretches consist of characters arranged at a 30-degree line of sight so they half face the audience as they talk to each other. The show also flagrantly telegraphs character motivation – no effort is made to conceal when a character is lying so as to build dramatic tension or anything. The show would lose no subtlety whatsoever if a giant blinking light came on whenever someone lied and said "Oi! He's lying!"

So clearly it's not realistic – it's practically children's theater. *Z-Cars*, on the other hand, is a landmark piece in the

Elizabeth Sandifer

development of gritty realism. (Though as Miles and Wood point out, why is it that realism is the only aesthetic to come in a peanut-butter like crunchy variation? Which really is a fair point. I want gritty impressionism, dammit. Or smooth realism, a strange cousin to smooth jazz.) It features cops with personal problems who face morally ambiguous situations. Of course it's more realistic. And in one sense it is.

Except that Z-Cars is estimated to have an average shot length of twelve seconds. This is turgidly long by modern standards, but is blazingly fast by the standards of 1962, when the show debuted. (For comparison, Dixon of Dock Green started in 1955. It ran to 1976, while Z-Cars went to 1978.) Which means that Z-Cars was presenting its stories heavily via editing and cutting.

The thing is, editing and cutting are non-realistic. Well. At least by another very sane definition of realism – namely that it means you try to minimize or eliminate the presence of the television so that watching a TV show is as like being a fly on the wall of real events as possible. In that case – and I think that's very close to what a lot of realism ostensibly strives towards – the editing-based storytelling of Z-Cars is profoundly non-realistic. And the staged theatrical storytelling of Dixon of Dock Green is relatively realistic, in that it simply provides a scene and observes it.

What about content? On the surface, Z-Cars seems to have the edge in realism again. The show is set in a clear analogue to Liverpool. Regional accents are on full display. You'll recall from past entries that Liverpool was a fading industrial city and also the center of the emerging youth culture. It's not an accident that Vicki has a Scouse accent. It's another part of the concentrated effort to have her be the iconic representation of the youthful future. And so centering Z-Cars on Liverpool consciously allies it with a real investment in the urban. This is why it comes in crunchy flavor. And that effort to capture the spirit of a real place is intensely realist.

Except let's think about this for a moment. *Z-Cars* is Liverpudlian, yes. But it's manifestly not trying to represent Liverpool to the audience. Rather, it's using the tropes of Liverpool – the fact that it's a rough, working-class city with angry, rebellious youth like those Beatles fellows – to tell its stories. Now, to be fair, *Z-Cars* pre-dated the explosion of the Beatles, but the Merseybeat scene they emerged from was at least a known quantity, and anyway, the show may have started pre-Beatles, but that has little to do with how it developed. It would quickly be the case that *Z-Cars* is not depicting youth culture, but rather using the existence of an anarchic youth culture as stage dressing to make the stories more exciting.

Compare to *Dixon of Dock Green*, where Ted Willis, writer of all 432 episodes, insisted the plots were based on actual police cases. Which means that, regardless of whether the representation was accurate, the show was actively positioning itself as showing what police life was like. Which is consistent with its moralizing tone – in order for it to make the continual claim that the police are what ensure a polite, civil society, it has to have the conceit that it is showing the police accurately. Whereas *Z-Cars* is not a moralizing show – it's an exciting show. It's not trying to show us what Liverpool is like, it's trying to show us cool police cases and is (as its editing shows) happy to toss reality out the window if it needs to.

So when I say that I despise realism, let's be clear – I am talking about *Dixon of Dock Green*, not about *Z-Cars*. What I oppose is the idea that art directly represents life in a straightforward way such that its lessons can be ported to reality. And that flashy storytelling techniques (as the editing of *Z-Cars* was for 1960s television) should be eschewed in favor of more "representational" techniques. No. Television – any narrative medium, really – should use every storytelling technique it has available.

And more to the point, a model of understanding television that doesn't take into account the medial reality of television is, to my mind, an actively useless model. Television is constructed and does, in point of fact, use techniques like editing and staging to communicate information. A model of television that tries to ignore these in favor of the suggestion that television in some way captures reality is fundamentally flawed. After all, what defines television is precisely the set of medial constraints and conventions that make it different from just observing the real world.

(To be clear, I have no objection to naturalism, which I take to mean that the show uses the assumption that the world being shown basically works the same way as the real world. Both *Z-Cars* and *Dixon of Dock Green* are naturalist. That is, the assumption is implicitly that, for instance, gunshot wounds are fatal. As opposed to Doctor Who, where the assumption that, for instance, police boxes are not bigger on the inside than they are on the outside does not apply.)

OK. So what do these two shows teach us about Doctor Who? Well, quite a bit. For one thing, its central image was straight out of *Dixon of Dock Green*. The sturdy police box is, in *Dixon of Dock Green*, a symbol for the sturdy, reliable police who use it. And so to travel around time and space in a police box evokes that image of safety – which is part of why Doctor Who is consciously British. Because the Doctor travels around bringing an image of British culture – an image that means safety and stability – all over the universe.

But Doctor Who is miles from the didactic realist ethics of *Dixon of Dock Green*. The Doctor may be bringing the police box to the whole universe, but the show is ultimately subversive in some crucial ways that we've already seen in the last few stories. If anything, Doctor Who is a complete rejection of the sort of authority-based stability that *Dixon of Dock Green* lionizes. The Doctor may be a reliable force that protects you, but he protects you by destroying your world.

And in many ways, Doctor Who is more easily allied with *Z-Cars*. Indeed, one of the original concepts for the show was a sci-fi *Z-Cars*. But that hardly lasted either. Perhaps it was in play back in, say, *Marco Polo* – though making any conclusions about editing in a serial from which not a frame of footage exists is rough business. Still, the tone of the serial, where sci-fi is rough, dangerous, and grueling, does evoke the original *Z-Cars* style.

But since then? Not really. The show has, by this point, largely abandoned grit in favor of the theatrical – as we'll see very clearly in the next few stories. So what we're left with is a sort of dialectical evolution from the two shows. The basic ethics of *Z-Cars* re-wedded to the theatrical tradition of *Dixon of Dock Green*, albeit with the visual flare that's characteristic of "modern" productions like *Z-Cars*.

Which is to say what should not be a huge surprise to us – that Doctor Who genuinely and meaningfully advanced what television was. It moved meaningfully and concretely beyond other popular shows of the time, and started merging techniques and styles from two very different traditions and views of television to produce, well . . . something new. Which is something to keep in mind as we move into the next stretch of stories. We noted at the end of *The Romans* that Doctor Who's basic identity has clearly, by this point, crystalized. Given that, the next run of stories, which constitutes the series' most extended engagement with the outright weird to date, is almost an inevitable development.

Elizabeth Sandifer

A Place Where Nothing Is Impossible (*The Web Planet*)

It's February 13, 1965. The Righteous Brothers are at number one complaining that you've misplaced your loving feeling. Over the next six weeks, we'll also see the Kinks with "Tired of Waiting For You," the Seekers' "I'll Never Find Another You," Tom Jones with "It's Not Unusual," and the Rolling Stones with "The Last Time." Other artists of note are: the Animals, the Moody Blues, Wayne Fontana and the Mindbenders, and Herman's Hermits. The album charts are mostly the Rolling Stones, with the Beatles taking the top spot for fun one week.

What you have to realize about these times is that, looking at what was popular, it is very clear that the world was changing. Things that had previously bubbled under the mainstream have, at this point, broken through in a big way. The Rolling Stones and the Beatles are the visible part of what (it is increasingly clear) is a ninety-percent obscured iceberg. In America, the civil rights movement is at its boiling point. White supremacists are beating demonstrators to death. Malcolm X is assassinated. Elsewhere, The Gambia obtains independence from the UK, the first spacewalk is conducted by Aleksei Leonov, and the Indo-Pakistani War of 1965 begins. This is not the present day by any stretch of the imagination. But it is also impossible to argue that 1965 is in any way more normal or understandable than the present day. The world of 1965 is staggeringly complex and weird.

I bring this up because for these six weeks, Doctor Who is showing *The Web Planet*. This is easily the weirdest Doctor Who to date, and a strong contender for weirdest ever. It is also among the most popular stories ever, in terms of viewers, and one of the least popular stories ever by most other metrics. It is also, however, largely misunderstood.

The word used in almost every review of *The Web Planet* is "ambitious." It's easy to see why. Every character save for the TARDIS crew in this story is non-human. You've got the Zarbi – bipedal ants who make a constant beeping sound. You've got the Menoptra – butterfly people, and the Optera – sort of grub creatures. And you've got the Animus – a giant tentacle monster. The episode is a special effects bonanza as a result.

And here's where people misunderstand it. Much is made of Doctor Who's wobbly sets and poor effects. And it's true – the effects on Doctor Who are often a bit cheap. (Although as Toby Hadoke will rush to point out, the sets only wobble a handful of times.) Pointing this out is fine. And because it has so many effects, *The Web Planet* has become exhibit A for those who want to talk about bad special effects.

The problem isn't with the accuracy of this claim. *The Web Planet* has some special effects howlers, including a Zarbi walking into the camera. The problem is with the implications of the claim, where the bad special effects are described as being "unrealistic," "unconvincing," or, my personal favorite, "unbelievable."

There's a moment on the DVD commentary for a Russell T Davies-penned Doctor Who episode where the show briefly appears to have killed off Rose. And Davies and Phil Collins, one of the other executive producers, are talking about whether children would believe that they really did kill off Rose. Collins says that he hopes children would not be so cynical as to say, "Oh, they wouldn't really do that." And Russell T Davies, in what is, to my mind, the most revealing thing he has ever said on a DVD commentary, says, "That's not cynical. That's wise."

That, right there, is the heart of the issue. The fact that Davies understands that this is why he was able to make Doctor Who as successful as it had ever been. And it's telling that one of the times in its original run where it was that successful was *The Web Planet.*

Apologists for the episode usually fall back on a defense along the lines of "watch it from a 1965 perspective and it's more convincing." This is, essentially, an argument about suspension of disbelief. The idea here is that viewers in 1965 could overlook the silliness and get themselves to believe what they were seeing, but that we can't anymore.

This is ridiculous. Even viewers in 1965 could tell that William Hartnell was flubbing his lines left, right, and center, and could notice when one of the Zarbi actors walked into a camera. William Hartnell trails off in mid-line after identifying the planet as Vortis and William Russell sort of wearily says "What galaxy is that in, Doctor" to prompt him; it does not take some savvy modern viewer to know what's going on. I'll go so far as to say that even some of the children watching in 1965 were savvy enough about how television worked to see a monster hit a camera or to recognize when an actor flubbed a line.

Modern viewers, for some reason, assume that the much beloved *TV Tropes* website represents some new understanding of narrative. And so they assume that, for instance, viewers in 1965 were somehow more convinced by what that site calls "People in Rubber Suits" than they are today. This is worth considering. So here's your assignment. Go find a picture of the Zarbi online.

Now, looking at that picture, what seems more likely? That viewers in 1965 could not tell that two of those legs were not like the others, or that viewers in 1965 were well aware that those were men running around in ant costumes? It seems to me that any argument that is dependent on the idea that anyone, ever, in the history of the planet has looked at a Zarbi and seen anything other than a man in an ant suit is extremely, extremely strained.

But why would that be a problem? Outside of television and film, we don't really get very worked up about this sort of thing. Nobody has ever read a book and gone "Ooh, these ink stains on this piece of dead tree pulp don't look much like what they describe." Painting didn't get to photorealism for centuries. And most of the great advances in art – impressionism in the form of Van Gogh and Monet being perhaps the most obvious example – are based on finding interesting ways to distort reality, as opposed to finding techniques that depict it more slavishly. The idea that art might be non-representational is not actually very complex or hard to accept to anyone but a TV/film obsessive.

And yet in all the discussions of *The Web Planet* – and the Lawrence Miles/Tat Wood *About Time* books spend a thousand words on the issue of influences on this story alone – nobody seems to mention one of the most obvious ones: George Méliès's early film *A Trip to the Moon*. *A Trip to the Moon* is a loose adaptation of both H.G. Wells's *The First Men in the Moon* and Jules Verne's *A Trip to the Moon*. Filmed in a lavish and ornate style with tons of elaborate costumes and pageantry, the film is probably best known for the sequence in which the rocket hits the man in the moon squarely in the eye. Its point is clearly not to ask seriously "what is it like on the moon," but rather to provide a compelling spectacle.

Comparing to this sort of approach clarifies *The Web Planet* tremendously. For instance, there's a scene in the first episode where the Doctor and Ian appear to stare up at a massive stone edifice. It's an obvious effects shot, and emphasized by the way it's edited into the episode. (The Doctor and Ian walk off screen, we cut to the massive edifice shot, and then we cut back to the previous set with the Doctor and Ian walking back from the edifice.) The only point of the shot is to show off that they can have that effect. In fact, much of the episode is structured around that effect shot. But crucially, if that effects shot is meant to be believable, that makes no sense. That kind of effort only makes sense if the effect is going to be noticed – i.e. if it's going to be visible as an effect. (This argument applies to almost any special effects that are hailed as centerpieces of their texts.)

In this interpretation, *The Web Planet* is interesting as a series of set pieces – as a six-week long exercise in spectacle that was not going for convincing illusion, but rather for striking visuals. This is well-supported by the story at large. Take, for instance, the bizarre lighting effects used for all shots of the surface of the planet Vortis, produced by smearing the camera lenses with Vaseline. Or, for that matter, the decision to have Roslyn de Winter, a choreographer, work with the Menoptra to make them seem suitably alien. All of these make *The Web Planet* extremely visually distinctive.

The result is, in fact, stunning. Realistic? No. But all the same, stunning, in the same way as *A Trip to the Moon* – a spectacle. And if *The Web Planet* is read in this way, which, as I said, is almost certainly the way it was read by its initial audience, it makes a lot more sense. It certainly explains why it was one of two stories from the second season to be novelized in the 1960s.

Ah. Right. The novels. I've actually devoted the entirety of the entry on *The Smugglers* to them, so for now, let's note simply that in 1964, David Whitaker's novelization of *The Daleks*, titled *Doctor Who in an Exciting Adventure with the Daleks*, was published, and in 1965 two follow-ups based on this story and the next were published. And these were the first instances of something that would eventually prove to be quite important for the series.

The thing that you have to realize is that in 1965, there was nothing resembling home video. When *Doctor Who and the Zarbi* came out, six months after airing, it was the closest thing to a personal copy of *The Web Planet* as existed. In fact, more to the point, it was the closest thing to a personal copy of the story that could possibly exist – the idea of a personal copy of a film or television episode was completely inconceivable. That wasn't how those media worked.

With this in mind, we can see that purpose of the book was to spur memories of the popular serial *The Web Planet* – essentially the sort of role that illustrated guides to the Doctor Who monsters and the like satisfy today. Notably, like the modern day equivalents, the book was illustrated. The illustrations are nothing special, but they are telling in that they emphasize the points of visual spectacle more than the crucial twists in the narrative. So, for instance, the special effects shot of Ian and the Doctor staring up at an impossibly large stone edifice is recreated in the book, even though its plot relevance is basically nil. This strongly suggests that the point of the exercise is not to be exciting on its own merits, but rather to jog memories of an exciting TV story. (A canny reader may also notice that the book refers to the Doctor as Doctor Who. We'll deal with that, but again, in another entry.)

The thing about spectacle is that it provides an opportunity for a very specific sort of horror. Much is made of Doctor Who's supposed scariness. Much of that scariness, as I've already suggested, comes from making the familiar strange. In this regard, the fact that *The Web Planet* was visibly produced is a major asset, because its bizarre visual landscape is not entirely alien. The frisson produced by the serial is precisely because what we are seeing is clearly a human design that does not look like human design is supposed to look.

And so there's some real horror here. Not merely scary bits, but horror – a sustained, conscious attempt to make things scary in general, as opposed to at specific moments. A major plot point in the first few episodes is a gold control harness that turns whomever it's put on into a mindless drone controlled by the Animus. After an extended sequence in which Barbara is taken over by the gold bracelet she happens to be wearing, we get a truly awful set of plot twists in which the harness is several times forced onto Vicki, and we watch the young companion figure – the supposed image of the future of Britain – suddenly go blank, her entire personality taken away. It's scary. It is genuinely psychologically horrifying. One moment she's fighting and screaming, and the next all that personality is just gone.

And that's not the only really horrifying bit. There's one cut in the serial where the camera suddenly jumps to a completely unclear image as the soundtrack takes a turn into a sort of proto-Diamanda Galas screaming. It's completely alienating – a refusal to conform to the normative visual grammar of television storytelling in 1965.

This is crucial. It is not so much that *The Web Planet* was ahead of its time and trying to do more than was capable in 1965. It wasn't. *The Web Planet* feels as though it existed in a wholly parallel time. The entire visual style of the story is focused on the task of making it seem nothing like television in 1965 seems like. And so when we get put off by it, that's not us failing to think like 1965. It's us failing to realize that we're actually having the exact right reaction. People, frustratingly, miss this. Miles and Wood accuse the episode of failing to try to make the world credible, saying:

Faced with an overwhelming mass of insect-flesh, what we really need here is for all those involved – both behind and in front of the camera – to play it casual. If everyone on Vortis acted as if this were their natural environment, and as if butterfly-people were a perfectly normal pan of the terrain, then after an episode or so we might forget the weirdness of it and treat it as a place where interesting things might happen.

Baloney. *The Web Planet* is supposed to be shockingly weird. So that, in Part Five, when there's a bit of a comic interlude about a tamed Zarbi that Vicki insists on nicknaming Zombo, the comedy does not so much fall flat as make the entire situation even weirder. It's a strikingly bizarre moment, but it's hard to laugh at it because the series has just taken us completely off the map so that even comic beats like this leave us uncomfortable.

For instance, in the same episode you have a sequence where Ian and some of the Optera are walking through some caves and find a spot where the way is blocked. The story has already spent a good deal of time establishing the alien characters as, well, alien – the Menoptra, for instance, have monologues including lines like "light was our god and we existed in light flying above thought," which is both oddly poetic and alienating. This sequence with the Optera begins by picking up on that tendency, describing the problem as "A silent wall. We must make mouths in it with our weapons. Then it will speak more light."

Then it goes nuts. They break through the wall, and it turns out to have been holding back deadly acid. At which point one of the Optera shoves her head into the wall to block the flow of acid. The remaining Optera calmly leave her body behind, saying that this is part of the dangers of living below ground, leaving Ian standing beside a giant insect corpse with its head shoved in a wall. If the sequence sounds bizarre, it is. It's easily one of the strangest things I've ever watched. But when this sort of absurdity abuts comedy about Zombo the Friendly Zarbi the resulting effect is a striking alienation.

This sort of thing is the *point* of Doctor Who. The entire concept of the series is that it's a means of taking ordinary people – Ian and Barbara – and thrusting them into bizarre situations where they don't belong. Then the series revels in the bizarre tensions this sets up. *The Web Planet* takes this approach to a new and higher level. The entire normal structure of narrative is juxtaposed with the world. Pathos, exposition, and comedy are all made strange. Not so strange that we don't recognize them when we see them, but strange enough that they jar. Ian and Barbara aren't the only things that don't belong on Vortis. The viewer, heck, the *camera* doesn't belong there.

All of this comes to a head with the story's villain, the Animus. This is the first time that Doctor Who has provided a villain of this sort – an almost godlike being. Later writers engaged in a kind of ham-handed retcon that proclaimed the Animus, along with some other classic villains, to be explicitly part of the Cthulhu mythos (Animus is apparently Lloigor, a 1932 creation of August Derleth – i.e. not even a proper Lovecraftian monster). Although this retcon was, all told, a pretty dumb idea that does some real injustice to Bill Strutton's creation of the Animus, the observation that there's something Lovecraftian about this monster is pretty on target.

The Animus appears in two distinct stages. At first it is simply something that the Doctor talks to by walking into a sort of weird speaking tube. Although the Doctor covers with glib humor (and a kind of brilliant lampshading), referring to the Animus as a giant hairdryer, the fact of the matter is, it's clear that this being is something the Doctor fears. The Animus is both vastly powerful – it controls all of the Zarbi – and intelligent. Although its second form is mocked along with the other effects, it too is deeply creepy – a mass of bizarre lights and fleshy tentacles that is profoundly weird even with the rest of *The Web Planet* to lead up to it.

The result is a strong sense that Vortis is a place that the Doctor and his companions should not be, and that this is a scarier adventure than usual. This sense of fear is heightened by the fact that this story involves some real assaults on the TARDIS. The story is the first time that the trope of the TARDIS being pulled down to a planet appears. The Doctor has not inadvertently landed on Vortis, he's been trapped there. For the first time, lengthy TARDIS scenes exist in which the TARDIS is a prison, not an opportunity. It's not malfunctioning here – it's been taken over. And since the TARDIS is central to the idea of what Doctor Who is, when it's in danger that means something very different. We know by this point that the companions are replaceable. The TARDIS isn't.

This story is also the first time that a monster enters the TARDIS. The overwhelming message is that the Doctor and his companions are just completely out of their league. And when the story finally resolves, with Barbara managing to kill the Animus, the victory feels like luck – the Doctor and Vicki have already failed, and Barbara can barely get the weapon she uses to work.

It would be one thing if these constant creepy and unnerving set pieces got in the way of the characters, but they don't. The Doctor is anarchically manic, continuing the odd sense of characterization as a young man we saw last episode. Ian and Barbara have a deepening relationship – Barbara's resolve to destroy the Animus is given a crucial boost by Ian appearing at the last second, a sort of Power of Love ending that will become standard under Russell T Davies. Vicki and Barbara's banter provides the first episode, which is otherwise a kind of lengthy trudge around an empty planet, with considerably more energy and fun (although it's very difficult not to get the sense that Vicki is trying to seduce Barbara).

The story, in other words, is unmistakably a case of familiar, well-loved characters thrown into an impossibly strange situation full of bizarre spectacle. The audience does not need to "believe" the spectacle to get into this, because the main dramatic tension is in fact how weird and strange everything is. Immersion and belief are anathema to what's going on here – bizarre and unsettling theatrical staging does a much better job of making the audience feel uncomfortable and lost (much like the characters) than any sort of realism possibly could. If we were to understand and believe Vortis, all of its horror would drain away.

And yet the default assumption on this story – and apparently why Spooner accepted the script – is that it's a parable about Communism, with the Zarbi being the deluded working class. Miles and Wood suggest that the story is about the working class, making much of the fact that the Zarbi are portrayed as cattle. The only problem is that, by all appearances, that's exactly what they are. At no point is there any serious suggestion that the Zarbi are anything other than oversized ants who are being controlled by the malevolent Animus. There's no politics to be had with the Zarbi for the simple reason that they have nothing resembling autonomy or will. They look like ants. They act like ants. If they were portrayed as having any will apart from what the Animus forces them to do, that would be one thing, and possibly a parable about Communism. As it stands, the story is not some expressly political parable. It's a creepy-ass story about the weirdness of its own special effects.

In other words, the biggest mistake that you can make about this story – and, maddeningly, the mistake that people most often make in discussing the story – is to treat it as a realist piece of science fiction that's a direct parable about the world of 1965. The truth is far more complex, and far more interesting – *The Web Planet* is a story about freaking out the audience and making them uncomfortable. Because the big problem with people's assumptions regarding this story is simple – they assume that because it was made in 1965, it's less modern than Doctor Who is now.

It's not. If anything, *The Web Planet* goes further than almost anything on television today. See for yourself. Add the story on Netflix and watch it for the spectacle. Or, better yet, find a scratchy VHS copy. This is not a story to enjoy in VidFIREd high-resolution glory. This is television to watch in a darkened room on a flickering TV set with a hazy image – much as it would have been in 1965.

Substitute for a Sound Character (*The Crusade*)

It's March 27, 1965. The Rolling Stones still hold number one, although that weird tendency for totally rubbish pop trash to take over whenever the show goes into historical mode promptly rears its head with Unit 4+2 and Cliff Richard ready to pounce over the following three weeks. Elsewhere in the charts we can find Tom Jones, the Searchers *and* the Seekers, the Yardbirds, Donovan, Bob Dylan, the Supremes, and the Who.

If *The Web Planet* felt like it was going out into a world of bracing and sudden change, *The Crusade* feels like it's going out into a world that's a bit dull. Even the major acts in the charts are either off their game (the Who chart with "I Can't Explain") or cliché (Dylan is in with "The Times They Are A-Changin"). Indeed, the most interesting thing to happen during the four weeks it's airing is *Mary Poppins* winning a bunch of Oscars. *Mary Poppins* is interesting for presenting a ridiculously nostalgic look at British culture that, effectively, was a love letter to Victorian children's literature so effusively written that people actually believed Victorian children's literature was like that.

I mention this because *The Crusade* is Doctor Who's pseudo-Shakespearean story – quite distinctly, with bits of the script written in iambic pentameter. There's something odd on the face of it here – the possibility of saying "the X story" for Doctor Who suggests an oddly definitive power for the show. Miles and Wood (who, if it's not obvious, I have the sort of tremendous respect for that it is only possible to have for people with whom you disagree almost completely) point this out explicitly – the odd thing about the historical stories, in specific contrast to the monster stories, is their unrepeatability. If the Doctor faces the Daleks or the Zarbi, it's an attempt at creating a popular and marketable monster. Those stories are designed to recur. But the Doctor is not supposed to return to a historical location – especially not those like the French Revolution or the court of Kublai Khan where he meets historical figures. We expected to see something like *The Dalek Invasion of Earth*. We do not ever expect to see a sequel to *Marco Polo*.

And so for Doctor Who to do the pseudo-Shakespearean story is definitive. This is meant to be the one story of this type. Which poses something of a problem when, as is the case with this story, half of it is missing. Indeed, the bulk of it was missing for years until a series of unlikely events caused the first episode to surface in New Zealand. (Short form of the story – the TV station that had been airing Doctor Who in New Zealand was destroying film it no longer had the rights to. A collector bribed a huge lot of it out of the dumpster blind, and then this print bounced around collectors in New Zealand for years without anybody realizing it was the last surviving copy of the episode.)

This means that its release came in 1999 – which, you may remember, were some dark days for the program. The sort of floundering that was going on is actually visible on the quickly released VHS copy of the two surviving episodes, for which William Russell provided in-character linking narration that makes an oblique reference to *The Witch Hunters* in a sort of bizarre attempt at cross-promotion. I say bizarre because it's not as though anyone cared about the show anymore. The only people who wanted to see the recovered episode of *The Crusade* were the hardcore Doctor Who fans with bad enough taste that they were probably actually reading the BBC Books.

In fact, it may well make more sense to read this reference as a nod to a knowing segment of fandom who read the books, as opposed to advertising. (The book isn't mentioned by name or anything, after all.) Which is to say, the people putting out the video clearly believed Doctor Who had consolidated on its core audience of diehards who would buy anything.

The weird thing is that it's hard to imagine an audience less suited to *The Crusade* than, well, Doctor Who fans. This is the thing about the historical adventures – because their central concepts are singular and they (by necessity) represent a different sort of storytelling from what Doctor Who eventually settled on as its default, they feel like exactly what they are. They're not even a dead end of Doctor Who so much as a different show that inadvertently got made under the name of Doctor Who. So that watching them, the major work becomes trying to explain how the heck this story fits in between giant ants and whatever comes next week.

And to be fair, the first few times we did this, that's a pretty valid question. *Marco Polo* was a bizarre thing to shove between *The Edge of Destruction* and *The Keys of Marinus*, and its major contribution to the series frankly has to be taken as showing that any attempts to predict what the hell the series is about are doomed to failure. *The Aztecs* is a similarly dissonant note, though one with more unambiguously successful contributions to the evolution of the show. But both *The Romans* and, in particular, *The Reign of Terror* felt like bizarre intrusions on the show.

Perhaps the strangest thing about *The Crusade*, then, is that it actually fits quite well between *The Web Planet* and *The Space Museum*. Which, without getting too far into *The Space Museum*, is actually a completely bewildering task. Much of this is down to a positively inventive opening. The trope, basically invented by Whitaker in *The Rescue*, of starting in the world of the story and having the TARDIS enter it is used again. Thus the pseudo-Shakespearean tone of the story is strengthened –

because the story is about Shakespeare world being visited by the Doctor, not about the Doctor visiting Shakespeare world.

Much of this is down to the writer. David Whitaker, now free of the burden of editing every script, here begins the second phase of his involvement in Doctor Who. Where before he was responsible for making everything work, here he becomes the first writer to really push the format and ask what sorts of things it can do that aren't obvious. He is, in effect, the first writer to attempt experimental Doctor Who.

To wit, and for the first time, when the TARDIS crew shows up, they drop immediately into action – there's basically no establishing dialogue before Barbara gets kidnapped. The result is that the first episode picks up as though it's recovering from a cliffhanger.

Which is actually perhaps the best starting point to get into this story, and something we should probably talk about anyway. See, classic Doctor Who is, as a general rule, not consumed as intended these days. Doctor Who was a weekly show where adventures lasted a month or so, coming, usually, in four-episode chunks. Each chunk (save the first part of a story) would end with a cliffhanger that led into next week's episode.

In fact, in these early days, this was true between stories. Episodes were not sent out as *The Crusade* Part One, but with individual titles, and usually each story picked up with a cliffhanger direct from the previous. This is much of why so many stories up to this point have featured plots based around something happening to the TARDIS – because it's one of the few cliffhangers that can readily be built around "And now we're going to a place!"

The thing is, other than these trans-story cliffhangers, the cliffhangers were generally not exciting as such. I mean, picking up on Davies's "That's not cynical, that's wise" observation, odds are pretty low that any audience member – including the children the show is (idiosyncratically) for – actually thinks a member of the TARDIS crew is going to die.

The TARDIS crew is self-evidently safe. So the ostensibly obvious purpose of the cliffhangers is pretty rapidly defused.

This is not to say that the cliffhangers are bad. There's a reason that the new series has chosen to put a few two-parters into the mix, and it's the classic appeal of cliffhangers. This is one of those cases where understanding the classic series is probably easier in light of the new series. So take, for instance, the cliffhanger at the end of *The Time of Angels*. The Doctor is in a trap. The Doctor basically says "Ooh, blimey, I'm in a trap." Then he points out that putting him in a trap is a really dumb idea, and fires a gun into the air. And, cliffhanger.

There's no actual tension here. The Doctor says he's going to get out of the trap he's in. Then the Doctor does something. It does not take a particularly advanced understanding of narrative technique to figure out that whatever he did was probably a way of getting out of the trap. So the cliffhanger is not "Is the Doctor OK?" He is. We know that. The cliffhanger is "Why was firing a gun the right thing to do?"

In other words, the point of a cliffhanger is not to leave the audience in any sort of doubt as to what's going to happen to the leads. John Byrne, in a moment of epic stupidity, describes the contrary position to this approach.

When I was a lad, I worried every time Superman fell into a kryptonite death trap. Usually I only had to wait four or five pages to find out that he was going to be okay, but it never occurred to me to shrug and flip to the next story to see if he survived. Only when reading *Superboy* was I ever aware that there was no "tension", since we knew Superboy would become Superman. (I refer to this as "Superboy Syndrome", and caution writers to be very careful about it when doing flashbacks or, more significantly, flash forwards.)

If you reach a point at which you "know" no real harm can ever befall the main characters, and you are unable to simply accept that (without commenting that there is "no real tension") then you have crossed an important line, and there is no point in you continuing to follow this kind of fiction. Accept it for what it is, or move on – but don't find fault with the ocean because it is too wet.

Here's the thing. John Byrne is an idiot here, and it's a wonder he ever managed to write a decent comic if he actually approached them the way he did. (Infuriatingly, however, he actually is quite a good comic writer.) I mean, the problems here are enormous. First of all, why Byrne would even need to flip to the next story to see if Superman survived is beyond me. Is there a next story? In a comic called *Superman*? Then I'll wager that the odds are pretty damn good Superman is in it.

Byrne tries to handwave this away by saying that it's essential that you pretend you don't know what's going to happen. But how the hell that's any harder with *Superboy* than it is with *Superman* is a mystery to me. Not even the most credulous of childhood readers of *Superman* thinks Superman is going to die in a kryptonite death trap. They know he has to survive because otherwise there's no next issue, and they have to have a next issue. They recognize *Superman* as something that appears with regular frequency at a store. Just like any viewer of Doctor Who recognizes it not just as a bunch of characters, but as something that reliably happens on Saturday night.

The tension of the cliffhanger is not – and never has been – whether the characters are going to be OK. Rather, the tension of the cliffhanger is how. That's what the page gap in Superman comics, or the week-long gap between Doctor Who episodes is. It is a space in which the reader or viewer has to fill in their guesses as to what's going to happen.

It's why serialized media begets fans. The entire reason there are still hardcore *Star Wars* fans frankly comes down to the fact that *The Empire Strikes Back* ends with Han Solo frozen in carbonite. Because serialized media encourages its viewers to compete against the writers – to try to see if they can come up with a better next move – and thus to act like fans. Which is why the week-long gap in Doctor Who matters. Because it is actually a beat of the story – one that gets erased when you can just hit "next episode" on the DVD and resolve the cliffhanger.

This is very clear in the first cliffhanger of *The Crusade*. Barbara has been kidnapped by Saladin. The Doctor and Ian are trying to persuade Richard the Lionheart to make a deal with Saladin for her release. He refuses, saying he'll never deal with Saladin, and storms off. Ian goes to follow him, the Doctor holds him back, and the credits roll. Clearly this is not a situation of particular danger. So why is it a cliffhanger? Because the challenge facing the Doctor is clear – he has to figure out a way to rescue Barbara, and asking the king isn't going to cut it. So the Doctor is left pondering his next move . . . for a week. Which means the audience is pondering the next move as well. That's the major point of a cliffhanger – the writerly moment whereby reading the text and constructing it become conflated.

The thing that you miss if you watch the show on DVD – the thing that is not intuitively reconstructed if you stop and think about this – is that in a given 168-hour week, Doctor Who is on for 25 minutes, and in the midst of a cliffhanger for 167 hours and 35 minutes. The bulk of the show is in fact the writerly moment – trying to figure out where the narrative is going.

And this is why John Byrne is so transparently and idiotically wrong in his Superboy Syndrome idea. Because the whole point of Superman comics is those moments of trying to fill in the gap – the moment of participating in the story. The would-be credulous reader he imagines who ignores the fact that Superman is going to survive is, in fact, a stupid reader. A smart reader plays along, and engages with the story as a story. (Of course, the fact that John Byrne thinks comics are for stupid readers is fairly clear to anyone who has actually read a John Byrne comic, but that's neither here nor there.)

So when *The Crusade* picks up acting as though it had a cliffhanger leading into it (when in fact it didn't), this is actually a supremely interesting moment. First of all, it extends the writerly pleasure distinctly into the episode itself – the viewer is simultaneously anticipating developments and trying to reconstruct past events. I mention this mostly because the next story takes this even further, so let's set it aside for the moment.

Instead, let's focus on the way in which this cliffhanger business ties in with what I said last time about *The Web Planet*. There, you'll recall, I talked about the idea that Doctor Who is dealing with non-representational techniques. I made passing reference to a synonym for this, which I'll expand on here. Doctor Who is theatrical. Which is closely related to why it's at home in a serialized tradition with cliffhangers – because the cliffhangers are, as I said, a case of presenting the show to the audience instead of immersing the audience in the show.

Which is why Doctor Who can follow giant insects with pseudo-Shakespeare and have it feel like anything other than the weirdest thing on television. But, ironically, this depends on dropping the inter-story cliffhanger. In order to work properly, *The Crusade* has to be a Shakespearean world that the Doctor and company drop into. Which is why Whitaker uses the fast start from within the pseudo-Shakespearean world instead of the normal TARDIS arrival sequence. This is the first major step towards abandoning individual episode titles – which will finally happen in a little over a year.

But the thing is, this theatricality was not in the least bit experimental. I mean, don't get me wrong – Doctor Who is, on the whole, massively experimental, and Whitaker here is being more experimental than usual. But theatricality is in no way part of its experiments. The show, after all, is on the BBC. Which is something that it's easy to lose sight of.

Let's pause for a moment and help out those who are in less fortunate countries with poor education systems that don't teach them important things about the world – like America. The BBC is a publicly owned non-profit corporation. When you buy a television in the UK and start using it for anything other than watching DVDs or playing video games, you have to pay a license fee of 150 pounds a year for a color TV. When Doctor Who started, that fee was four pounds a year. And that fee is a tax. It is not like a cable bill – it's a government tax that it is illegal not to pay.

So, for Americans. You know how conservatives want to slash the modicum of funding for NPR and PBS? In the Britain of 1965, that viewpoint would mean that you want to eliminate fifty percent of television outright. Television and radio were, in Britain, offered as a public service. And as you might imagine of 1960s Britain, that meant that proper art had to be shown on them.

Not exclusively, of course – the looming competition of ITV was sufficient to establish at least partially that making some commercial programs was a good idea. But Doctor Who was not, strictly speaking, a commercial mass hit either. Rather, it was a bizarre sort of hybrid program. It's a show anchored by an elderly character actor that's meant to entertain kids and secretly educate them, but that airs in a family slot and so has to entertain everybody. This sort of mad concept could only happen in the name of the public good.

But it also meant that Doctor Who had to occasionally go and do things like *The Crusade*. Not out of some sort of BBC mandate, but just because that was part of being the public service program that it was. Because Doctor Who was never particularly subversive to what the BBC was. And so of course it did a high culture, theatrical Shakespeare story. Because the BBC was about the arts, and when it came to drama, the arts were theatrical. Which is why the concept of nipping off to do a bit of theater in between stints on the most popular program on the BBC is still not that weird an idea in England. (For a comparison, imagine if NCIS went on an eighteen-month hiatus with only a few ninety-minute episodes to air sporadically through the time so Mark Harmon could do *King Lear*. See?)

So *The Crusade* has Julian Glover, who's actually a Shakespearean actor of non-trivial repute, tromping about alongside the regulars. Because this is a particular sort of theater, and the BBC is well-equipped to put on that show. Which, again, is profoundly non-immersive. You're not supposed to go "Ooh, Richard the Lionheart!" You're supposed to go "Ooh, Julian Glover as Richard the Lionheart." You're supposed to recognize that the rules, this week, are Shakespearian rules. Which is, again, why we start the serial in the world – because the rules apply to the Doctor here too. (Hence his extended comic set piece about clothing theft in the first episode.)

But here's the thing about Doctor Who. On the one hand, it's happy to play along and do its Shakespearean duties. On the other hand, (and this is where Doctor Who in March of 1965 differs from Doctor Who, say, a year earlier) doing a historical serial meant playing it all very straight and doing an epic. Now, however, there's enough of an idea of Doctor Who and its sort of mad cap ethos starts to run up against its own setting.

And so here we get the absurd meta-conceit of Vicki cross-dressing as Victor for no discernible reason whatsoever. Why? It's funny, yes, and as this episode leaves Vicki with no room to give a monster an amusing diminutive nickname, her comedy beat has to come from somewhere. But, notably, it's specifically a joke about the Shakespearean theatrical tradition – namely its convention of having the female characters be cross-dressed males. (A situation which, I hasten to add, was played for laughs at the time because nobody has ever actually seriously suggested that immersive narrative is a good idea prior to about Wordsworth. Nobody took it that seriously until the mid-to-late twentieth century, and if I had my way nobody would ever take it seriously again because it's absolutely idiotic.)

I want to focus on this for a couple of reasons. First, it's campy and theatrical in a big way, and evolving an ability to revel in theatrical camp is kind of a survival instinct when it comes to watching Doctor Who after about 1963. Second, it's a staggeringly meta joke that puts the lie to the idea that

Doctor Who is for children in any sort of exclusive way – no ten year old is going to get the humor of dropping in on a Shakespeare play and cross-dressing your female character as a male so that they're allowed to be there. Third, anyone wondering when drugs entered the Doctor Who production office can probably make a pretty safe bet that it's somewhere in the vicinity of the tentacle-rave bouncy castle at the end of *The Web Planet* and the introduction of cross-dressing comedy to Doctor Who.

But fourth, and perhaps most interesting, we see again here a way in which Whitaker is experimenting with the structure of Doctor Who. Ironically, given that this story in a concrete sense advances Doctor Who from a continual serial to a series of discrete stories, this is structured in an unusually serialized way. Each episode moves from its seeming premise to a decent cliffhanger. But there's very little sensible progression over the course of all four episodes. Whitaker abandons the idea of a meta-story that connects the four episodes in favor of a continually shifting adventure that simply tries to get through the high points of its premise. But because the story *was* four serialized adventures with large gaps, this works. Watched over a month, it's easy for the overall details of the plot to get a bit hazy while the look and feel of it is remembered. Whitaker writes the story with visible awareness of how that works, and abandons traditional narrative structure to embrace what works in this format.

Some other quickies to notice about this story. This is the first time people who actually have dark skin appeared on the set. Albeit not in any scenes with the Doctor. I wonder why. (I know full well why, but that's another entry.) And there's another bit tailor made for those who quote obsessively, as Joanna, sister to Richard the Lionheart (and, in the original script, kinky incestuous lover until William Hartnell objected) describes the Doctor by saying "There's something new in you, and yet something older than the sky itself." Once again, the mythic nature of the Doctor is established – in this case necessarily so, as otherwise he has no chance of standing up against Shakespearean King Richard in the plot.

As it stands . . . he still doesn't really manage to do anything over all four episodes, but as I said, that's not the point. This story hasn't aged that well, but taken as part of its time, it's easy to see why its reputation is so high.

Decadent, Degenerate, and Rotten to the Core (*The Space Museum*)

It's April 24, 1965. The Beatles have number one again, with "Ticket to Ride." Those of you who are obsessive Doctor Who fans will glean the particular significance of that. The more normal folks will find out in two essays. (The really obsessive fans now know exactly what book is up in the next essay. If you are one of those fans, congratulations.) In the fourth week of *The Space Museum* it will be unseated by Roger Miller's "King of the Road" in what is very possibly the single most jarring transition on the charts until "Do The Bartman" unseats The KLF in 1991. I will not say much about Roger Miller, because, well, he's Roger Miller. I will, however, point out his future number-one hit in his native US, "England Swings." The Animals, Donovan, the Rolling Stones, the Supremes, and Bob Dylan, now with the far more interesting "Subterranean Homesick Blues," all chart as well.

It is easy, at this point, to think that the world is coming unstuck. Protests in Yerevan, Armenia begin to bring the horror of the Armenian Genocide to light. Protests in Berkeley, California involve torching draft cards. All of this suggests that things are starting to come to a head. The ball that started rolling with the Kennedy assassination – the sense that the world is somehow coming apart – has gathered something like critical mass. While the most powerful man in the world was a dashing young technocrat, there was something resembling stability – a sense that things were moving forward. When the most powerful man in the world is a drawling Texan career politician, even though he's probably a more effective champion of liberal causes than Kennedy, things come unstuck. The youth get uppity. They evolve. They rebel.

At the center of all of this, however, quite bizarrely, is London. Never mind that the UK has missed a rather epic series of beats and gone from world-spanning empire to fallen power in a generation. None of that matters. The UK has the Beatles. The UK has Carnaby Street. The UK has the miniskirt. The UK, in short, is mod. And the world is starting to recognize that. As the youth rebels and starts to change the world, the coolest place in the world is London.

If we view the 1960s as in part a struggle between youth culture and establishment culture, this story marks the point where Doctor Who unambiguously picks a side. It should be no surprise, given the last four stories, what side it's going to pick. Its newest character is a futuristic star-child with a Scouse accent. Its old man lead has turned into a giggling anarchist. The show has adopted a wild theatrical style that lets it look and feel like nothing else on TV. Is it going to side with the mod youth or the entrenched establishment? Take a guess.

No, what's surprising about *The Space Museum* is not its successful execution of a host of mod clichés. It's that it's doing it in what are still the early days of the mod fad. And, more to the point, it's that its doing it well and more complexly than it has any right to, going beyond mod culture and getting towards its successor, psychedelia, before mod culture even has a chance to arrive on the scene.

The usual brief on *The Space Museum* is this: the first episode is almost universally recognized as being completely brilliant. The other three episodes are considered to rank somewhere between "disaster" and "hidden gem" with most descriptions using the word "disappointing" in some fashion or another.

Frankly, this is due more to the high quality of the first episode than the low quality of the back three. The first episode is indeed stunning and complex, and almost deserves an entry on its own. Instead it'll get a few paragraphs, like so:

Back with *The Crusade* we talked about cliffhangers, and how the story took advantage of a ludicrously fast start. *The Space Museum* takes this in a different direction. The story opens with the lights going out in the TARDIS, then coming back on. From there on out, strange things begin to happen – Vicki drops a glass of water, and it jumps back up into her hand. The TARDIS crew does not leave footsteps, and seems invisible to everybody else on the planet. The mood alternates between the first episode of *The Daleks* and *The Edge of Destruction*, veering from lonely and scared exploration to a looming sense that something weird and terrifying is going on. It's not until about three-fourths of the way through the story that we finally include the cliffhanger that leads in from *The Crusade*, with the TARDIS crew in their clothes from that episode "jumping a time track" and landing on Xeros. Which is just wonderful playing with the show's structure, again – putting the actual resumption from last episode's cliffhanger in the wrong part of the episode.

But underneath and alongside it is a completely different story. There are reports that the writer of this one, Glyn Jones, was displeased with Dennis Spooner's rewrites to his script. Ironically, Spooner removed most of the jokes, then substituted ostensibly less funny ones. This may be so, but the episode is still hilarious. Notably, it's a flagrant parody of Doctor Who. Jokes are made about how the crew shouldn't split up. The TARDIS crew rounds a corner and a suspenseful music cue mounts as we discover a Dalek in the Space Museum. And then it turns out to be an empty museum exhibit of a Dalek, and the musical cue deflates into comedy, with Vicki lampshading the Daleks by saying they don't particularly look scary. (Ian reassures her that they're unlikely to encounter one. This will be funny in a few paragraphs.)

And then there's the . . . I don't want to say unintentional humor, but at least idiosyncratic humor. I'm getting a bit ahead of myself in terms of the development of the series, but there's a strain of thought about the show that posits a significant gay subtext to it. Just, you know, something to keep in mind. Completely unrelatedly, here's the opening dialogue of *The Space Museum*.

IAN: Doctor, we've got our clothes on!
DOCTOR: Well I should hope so my dear boy, I should hope so.
BARBARA: No, Doctor, our regular clothes.

So that's funny too.

But in amidst that humor is some real creepiness. The Doctor and companions wandering invisibly around a museum trying to figure out what has gone wrong and where they are is scary. The characters remark on how they don't seem to belong here, and on the unnerving silence. Given that the episode uses minimal incidental music (due mostly to being done on the cheap and recycling music from other episodes), this comment about the unnerving silence works well. Especially because even the recycled music features the harsh electronic sound characteristic of Doctor Who, so when it flares up at the end as the wibbly-wobbly, timey-wimey stuff happens it's still scary and alien in a way that nothing else on television compares to yet. Perhaps the best moment of the episode – a fair contender for one of the best moments of the series to date, really – is when the TARDIS finally catches up with its crew. Suddenly the world of the people onboard the TARDIS is, for the first time, rocked by the TARDIS arriving into it. For the first time since *An Unearthly Child* the TARDIS is made to seem completely unnerving and alien.

The flip side is that the episode is dense with technobabble. Which William Hartnell is as good as ever at delivering, which is to say, terrible. This is actually one of the major virtues of bringing Vicki on board as a companion – her futuristic ways mean that the show can safely dump technobabble off on her, where she'll handle it with a surprisingly satisfying to-camera address.

And then, in most people's view, the whole thing goes off the rails. And look, I understand why. I do. The first five minutes or so of the second episode are absolutely brutal to watch – one of the worst exposition dumps this series or any other has ever belched onto a television screen. Thrill to such gripping scenes as "I've got two more minims before I can go home. Yes, I say it often enough, but it's still two-thousand Xeron days." (A bit of dialogue that manages the impressive double of being awkward and unintelligible at the same time.) And the equally natural-sounding, "I'm the governor of this planet, you're supposed to show some respect." The dialogue clatters along at roughly this level of quality, including one of the classic bad lines of the series, "Have any arms fallen into Xeron hands?"

So, fine. The exposition is a train wreck. Of course, much of this is down to the artificiality of the structure. Because the first episode goes with the isolated TARDIS crew for cost reasons, when the second one picks up we're twenty-five minutes behind where we want to be on exposition. So we get the exposition dump. Even a few minutes of folding this into the previous episode – having characters who walk by the TARDIS crew talk, or something – would have helped tremendously.

But let's look at what else is going on in the episode. You've got Barbara in "criminally underused" mode, yes, but the show has never managed to use all four regulars well through an entire story, and until it manages to pare the cast down to three and, finally, two, this is just what happens. Ian, on the other hand, is unusually compelling. William Russell's myriad of skills do not, with this part, include a particularly large range of emotions. Yet his tendency towards stunned fascination/terror serves this story well. Ian is played as having just completely snapped, as though fighting to change the future so he does not become a museum exhibit is, finally, too much for him. (Rewatching the last episode of *The Web Planet* makes one wonder why this is the straw that broke the camel's back, but oh well.) When he picks up a gun and mimes firing blindly around a room seemingly for his own amusement, it takes the character, for the first time, to a new place. Of course, it's also flagging his imminent departure, but hey.

The Doctor, on the other hand, is in low form – spending the third episode out of the picture and most of the fourth recovering from being out of the picture. But he has the scene of the episode in the second episode. And it's not even when he hides in a Dalek. No, it's when he's sat down in a chair that reads his mind and shows his thoughts on TV. Which he promptly foils by just thinking about whatever he wants to instead of what the interrogator wants him to think about. First he bluffs with a penny-farthing, in a strange anticipatory nod to *The Prisoner*'s more psychedelic tone. But then comes the high point. The Morok interrogator demands to know where he comes from. The Doctor says to look at the monitor . . .

Which is showing a huge number of walruses rolling around on an iceberg. Walruses. Not Gallifrey. Not the constellation of Kasterborous. No. Walruses.

And then there's Vicki. Right. Let's tie this entry together a bit more. See, the main plot of the episode is that the Moroks – who are fat, middle-aged men – are cruelly dominating the Xerons – the young beatniks. And Vicki gets the heavy lifting on this plot, running around talking about revolution with a giddy joy that makes her pyromaniacal adventures with the Doctor in *The Romans* look positively low key. Vicki clearly wants nothing more than to overthrow civilizations and give guns to hot young men. She gets the charismatic clever person plot – the one usually reserved for the Doctor these days – and shows the kids how to overthrow the government. It's very probably the high point for the character.

OK. So here's where this episode settles into odd brilliance. Historically speaking, as we go along, here's what's going to happen; right now we've got the rise of the mods. But the mods, with their bright, colorful styles, are easily co-opted. The mods look good, and so they can be sold. Eventually less family-friendly counterculture like psychedelia, punk, and new wave will come along and have their huge influences on Doctor Who. But right now, it's the mods' day. Right?

Except look at what's in this episode as a whole. Yeah, you've got your mod rebellion. But it's over the backdrop of a massive existential dilemma with all the characters walking around trying to figure out how you make a choice in the face of an apparently proscribed future, and having all sorts of debates about free will. The mod rebellion is only an incidental step in resolving the larger existential crisis. In other words, this story, which ostensibly glorifies the mods, is also stepping beyond the mods and hinting that there's something more than just a smiling Scouse lass calling for revolution . . . something considerably deeper and weirder.

Specifically, it seems to be foreshadowing psychedelia. We're not going to talk a huge amount about psychedelia in this book, although it starts to play up in the last few essays. The main psychedelic era of Doctor Who is Patrick Troughton's tenure. But in reality, mod culture and psychedelia led into one another more sensibly than people assume, and here we see that transition beginning.

And then, at the end, as if to remind us that the episode has actually been kind of brilliant all along, it ends with a long pull back. For a good twenty seconds or so, the viewer is left trying to figure out where they've jumped to and what's going on. Then the answer comes into shot. The fake-out of the Daleks earlier in the episode is, in fact, a fake fake-out. That Dalek may not be real . . . but the real Daleks have learned how to travel in time, and have decided to hunt and kill their greatest enemy.

Which, ooh. The Doctor is now formally the Daleks' greatest enemy. Ever since he last faced them, frankly, it's been building to this. They were the fascistic force that left London in ruins. So the Doctor went and got the embodiment of youth culture and has taken her around the universe. The show has embraced a wild, theatrical style. The Doctor, secretly a young man (there's a throwaway line about how the Doctor has always assumed there must be a museum in space, but he's never seen one. Fans of the Matt Smith era will grin), is first and foremost a force for the impishly mad. So now it's time for another round with the Daleks – the ultimate force of control and power for its own sake.

Oh boy.

Time Can Be Rewritten: *The Plotters*

So here's the thing about Doctor Who that we may not have talked about quite enough yet. It has fans. Exactly when it acquired this potential affliction is hard to pin down, but the answer probably has something to do with 1980. And it's been a solidly mixed blessing. If it weren't for fandom we wouldn't have, well, Doctor Who from 2005 on. But, on the other hand, if it weren't for fandom, we wouldn't have had Doctor Who from 1985 to early 1987. Which, in the eyes of a fair number of people, would have been nice.

But Doctor Who has fans. It has fandom. And it's had it for a really long time – indeed, at this point for a majority of its existence. In fact, given that Russell T Davies and Steven Moffat are two of the biggest anoraks on the planet, as is David Tennant, it's pretty safe to say they've taken over the asylum. Seriously, track down the old Podcast commentary for *Forest of the Dead* with Davies, Moffat, and Tennant just geeking out over Doctor Who in general and basically ignoring the actual episode. Aside from the fact that it is in no way a commentary track, it's the best commentary track ever.

So the fact of the matter is that we're now at twenty-one years in which fans have been running the asylum, versus at most twenty-six where they weren't. We're nearing the point where fans have run Doctor Who more than normal people have. (In fact, due to events we'll cover when we get to Season Twenty, arguably we've already crossed that point.)

And one consequence of an extreme and chronic case of fandom is that tastes have changed.

Which is why things like the Missing Adventures are so interesting. Because this is a book written in 1996 that is about the pleasures of a TV show from thirty-one years earlier. And it's by a writer who was twenty-eight at the time he wrote it. So the one thing we can safely conclude about Gareth Roberts' take on late second season Doctor Who is that it is not in any way based on the experience of actually watching late second season Doctor Who in 1965. Further making this interesting is that Gareth Roberts is one of the writers of the new series, having contributed five episodes to date. So this novel is actually, ignoring some stray comics and short stories, the earliest set piece of Doctor Who by a writer to have written for the new series. Giving Gareth Roberts the interesting distinction of having the widest span of Doctor Who writing – 195 televised stories take place between this novel and his Season Five episode, *The Lodger*.

This poses an interesting question, because it means that we are forced to make sense of a single view of what Doctor Who is that encompasses a jaw-dropping span of the series. Which is fine. Because there are countless eras of fandom's viewpoints all overlapping on any given era of Doctor Who, and countless re-conceptualizations of eras to be had. Ask people what the second season of Doctor Who is like and you'll get as many answers as people you asked. Thus far we've been treating the William Hartnell era as an era of boundless wonder and creation, in which this amazing show is forged. And it was.

But here's another truth about it. William Hartnell was a cranky old man who was suffering from the early stages of arteriosclerosis that would eventually leave him unable to work and kill him. He couldn't remember his lines at all, which is why he fluffs them nearly every episode. And it's really tough to watch it in 2011 sometimes knowing that. In particular it's hard to watch something like *The Crusade*, where you know that one reason given for why the Doctor and the black people don't get any scenes together is that Hartnell was an unrepentant racist who probably would have gotten along swimmingly with Mel Gibson. And so they kept him away from the black people.

Here's another truth about Doctor Who. You remember how the last few entries have stressed repeatedly that Doctor Who is theatrical? And how that was used to explain how to understand the men in butterfly costumes talking in a sing-songy voice? OK. Let's phrase that in another way – one we alluded to last entry. Doctor Who is massively beloved by gay men. And Gareth Roberts is a part of gay Doctor Who fandom – a segment of fandom that, as anyone vaguely aware of Russell T Davies's life and aesthetic knows, turns out to be rather important to the history of the show.

There are a lot of complex reasons for this. Homosexuality was illegal in Great Britain until 1967. But within art and theater circles, it was accepted as a sort of open secret. (This is why the generation of actors like Derek Jacobi, Simon Callow, and Ian McKellen exist. And hey, look at how two-thirds of that list have appeared in the new series.) Even William Hartnell, hardly a paragon of progressiveness, was apparently fairly accepting of gay people he actually knew – tolerating, for instance, Waris Hussein as the director of the first episode. So any TV drama had some significant advantages within the gay community.

Then add to that the fact that the show is, as we've seen, extremely theatrical. I'd say bordering on camp, but no. It blazes past that line in to open camp. Not just in its wobbly sets and rubber monsters, but in its celebration of them. The brilliant central twist of *The Rescue* or the full insanity that is *The Web Planet* work because the show is well aware that it is absurd. And this is before the periods in the show where the gay subtext is one of the major things going on in it. Suffice it to say that the '70s and '80s, for a variety of reasons, caused Doctor Who to have a massive contingent of gay fans.

But let's be fair here. As flagrantly suggestive as the start of *The Space Museum* is, and as much fun as we know children's entertainment makers have slipping things in, most of the double entendres in early Doctor Who are probably wholly accidental. (Later Doctor Who is a different matter. *Love and Monsters* is as pervy as you think it is.) So the gay Doctor Who fandom has always been a bit revisionist, finding hidden meanings in old stories.

Which is, of course, exactly what Gareth Roberts is doing in writing a story set in a era he knows only from VHS tapes, most of which, in 1996, would have been personal recordings or things traded at conventions – *The Space Museum*, for instance, didn't see an official VHS release until three years after Roberts wrote this book, which ostensibly takes place immediately after it.

This would never have been – and could never have been – televised in 1965. The reason for this is simple – the book openly portrays King James I as homosexual. Which there's plenty of historical evidence for, but it obviously was never going to be on television. Compare this book to the also-probably-gay Richard I, who appeared two stories ago in glorious straightness, and you can immediately see that the sense of how we're going to treat British monarchs is completely different. And the theatrical cross-dressing of Vicki from *The Crusade*? It makes an appearance again here, but this time to instigate an extended subplot about King James wanting to sleep with "Victor." The book even has the Doctor grumping about King James calling him a "winter apple" in comparison to Victor/Vicki, saying that "In my day, I was considered quite a looker." Now try to imagine our grumpy racist of a leading man delivering that line.

And yet despite that, it's clear that this novel is written out of real love for the era it's set in. The novel, more than any of the books we've looked at thus far (indeed, more than most in general), holds to an episodic structure. It's broken into four parts, titled individually like Hartnell-era episodes, with clear cliffhangers between parts. And the basic format – as the frontispiece of the book notes – is a straight-up homage to a sort of story that only existed in this era of the show – the willfully inaccurate historical in the vein of, say, *The Reign of Terror* or *The Romans*. The purely historical story, of which this is an example, in fact does not survive much longer than where this book is set. So in this regard, the book is clearly a William Hartnell story.

There's also real effort made to capture the characters that were on TV – Vicki's strange obsession with naming pets (Sandy from *The Rescue* and, of course, good old Zombo the Zarbi) comes up again when she names the horse she and the Doctor acquire Charger. Then there is the aspect of it that has proven (somewhat puzzlingly) to be substantially controversial. The novel is unusual for a Hartnell novel in that it includes the so-called Billy Fluffs that are, in practice, a mainstay of the Hartnell era. That is to say, the Doctor several times in the novel becomes tongue-tied and offers malapropisms of various sorts – as anyone familiar with the show itself will know Hartnell, historically speaking, did. (For instance, "Do you imagine I purchased Char-this mangy creature for no good reason?") In practice, these flubs came from the pressure cooker filming environment (where unless a take was completely ruined beyond all usability, it was used because doing a second take was a real pain) combined with the fact that, as mentioned, Hartnell's health was steadily failing. (Or at least, that's the assumption. There are persistent claims that a fair number of Hartnell's flubs were actually scripted.)

Roberts uses these flubs for storytelling and meta-commentary – most notably when the Doctor says "I thought this episode – I mean to say this episode of my life – was going in a different direction" when it briefly appears that there might be something supernatural going on. Some reviewers in the Doctor Who Ratings Guide accuse *The Plotters* of being insulting to its era for including the Billy Fluffs, accusing the novel of mocking Hartnell by including the scenes. Which is baffling mostly because it seems as though doing things like having him regret that King James doesn't find him attractive is considerably more insulting to

Hartnell than making his dialogue sound like it would have once he delivered it. The book certainly does appear to be asking what the Hartnell era might have been had 1965 been a more enlightened time, but fundamentally, the dialogue is the place where the novel *isn't* changing the basic tone of the televised era.

In the end, though, that's the essential tension of this book. On the one hand, it is an extremely faithful recreation of the tone of its era. On the other, it's an unabashed revision of it – fitting given that it has adopted the inaccurate historical subgenre of Doctor Who story, i.e. a genre that is already about revision of history. And Roberts uses that to craft a story that could never have been made for television, but is consistent with what we see on television instead of what we know was going on behind the scenes. Roberts writes a book in a world where William Hartnell was nothing more (or less) than a kind old man who loved children and loved the possibilities that Doctor Who offered. (Which, it's key to note, he also was alongside being an ailing racist. Hartnell, like any person, is complex.) Roberts writes a world where he, and people like him, aren't criminals.

And there's something oddly wonderful about this. Because it is hard to watch 1960s Doctor Who sometimes. It's hard to get past the visible racism of, say, *The Aztecs* and get to the fact that the story, while behind our time, was still ahead of its time. It's hard to see the character I love in William Hartnell. The experience is, actually, well-summed up with one of the (quite meta-textual) monologues Steven Moffat gives to River Song:

You know when you see a photograph of someone you know, but it's from years before you knew them. It's like they're not quite finished – they're not done yet. Well . . . yes, The Doctor's here. He came when I called just like he always does. But not "my" Doctor. Now my Doctor, I've seen whole armies turn and run away. And he'd just swagger off, back to his TARDIS. And open the doors with a snap of his fingers. The Doctor. In the TARDIS. Next stop: Everywhere.

And that's the real magic of what Roberts does here – the thing that makes you see why the writer of this novel still gets to write for River Song's Doctor. Because he is, perhaps, the only writer to have been able to see her Doctor in William Hartnell. (Even Steven Moffat has trouble with this, snubbing the Hartnell era in several interviews.)

Far from being disrespectful to Hartnell and the era of Doctor Who he represents, this revision is, I think, the ultimate kindness. Here is a man who has every reason to hate the conservatism of William Hartnell's Doctor – a gay man who is old enough to vividly remember the horrific fight over Section 28. And yet he doesn't mock. Even in a novel that takes seriously the ugliness of the past (the novel has a substantial and kind of upsetting description of a bear baiting), the ugliness of the past of Doctor Who is, in the end, forgiven.

And in an odd way, this is perhaps the most compelling refutation of Hartnell's many flaws that can be offered. That the man we grew up to recognize as The Doctor, the most wonderful man in the universe, was still, in the end, a part developed by a senile old racist. That a man who embodied many of the worst qualities of his times could still help build the character of a man who embodies the best qualities of all of time.

Elizabeth Sandifer

Was William Hartnell a Bigot?

A disturbing feature of the folk history of the Hartnell era is the often-stated truism that William Hartnell was a bigot. Usually, this is focused on his supposed dislike of minorities, Jews, and homosexuals. In recent years there's been a pushback against this, with many people rushing to defend Hartnell from any critique along those lines. In truth the evidence on all sides of the debate is thin, and the debate is more about the larger question of how, if at all, the possibility of racism in the classic series matters.

First, the facts – somewhere between 1966 and the present day, William Hartnell went out of vogue in a big way. Actually, in some ways it's tough to say he was ever in vogue. Those who claim him as their favorite Doctor often fall into two categories – cranky fans who have keyed on to the fact that they can win any "how stodgily misanthropic a fan can I be" contest by asserting that the show isn't as good as it was when William Hartnell was in it (here Alan Moore holds the crown with his assertion that all of Hartnell's successors act like pedophiles) or younger fans who want to have "distinctive" views within fandom (a phenomenon that also accounts for an uncomfortable number of Paul McGann fans).

But there's a difference between dislike of the era and dislike of the man. The Colin Baker era is widely regarded as a failure, but Baker himself is widely loved. Tom Baker, on the other hand, remains widely criticized for his behavior while on Doctor Who, but the Hinchcliffe era remains the gold standard of the classic series. So the fact that the Hartnell era is widely viewed as slow and a bit dull, and that it's not exactly the most popular classic era, is hardly an indictment of Hartnell himself.

So, why is so much energy spent on the personal condemnation of Hartnell? Part of it stems from a hatchet job in 1966 itself. Wanting rid of their lead actor, who was, to be fair, temperamental and at times very difficult to work with, the production team portrayed Hartnell as a senile asshole. As these accounts became increasingly known in fan circles, those who had worked with him and liked him – Carole Ann Ford in particular – began defending him actively, as you'd expect. Then Anneke Wills hit the convention circuit and threw that rule out the window, dishing freely about Hartnell despite having worked with him for a total of twelve weeks, specifically the ones where he was at his frailest. The result is that Hartnell, as a person, is a contentious figure.

That Hartnell could be difficult to work with and was in failing health is indisputable, although suggestions of senility or incompetence are difficult to square away with any of his actual episodes. Trickier is the claim that Hartnell was a bigot. There are some scattered pieces of evidence for this. The big three are a comment he made to Nicholas Courtney specifically pointing out a crew member as a Jew, a racist tirade against a black janitor, and his alleged refusal to work with Max Adrian in *The Myth Makers* because he was a gay Jew.

The counter-evidence is compelling as well – his willingness to work with Warris Hussein on the first story, despite Hussein being a gay Indian, his willingness to work with Carole Ann Ford, a heterosexual Jew, and the observation that he had worked with Max Adrian just fine before *The Myth Makers*, suggesting that any fight they may have had was not based on racism but, more likely, about the fact that Hartnell hated that particular script.

But most of the attempts to divine absolute certainty out of shreds of historical data are difficult. In the end, Hartnell was a product of racist times. The probability that he held racist beliefs is reasonably high. But the thing that we forget about racists is that "racist" is not actually a complete character description. There are actually numerous settings between "contemporary liberal intellectual" and "KKK member," and most people are better described by one of these shades of grey. William Hartnell's bigotry was nowhere near that of the virulent racists of his time, but that does not mean it didn't exist.

On the other hand, when Enoch Powell set off a powder keg of racial tensions with his "Rivers of Blood" speech in 1968, many of those who praised him for saying "what needed to be said" were people who went through their day-to-day lives without committing any overt acts of bigotry or hatred. Racism's nastiest teeth come from the skinheads and extremists, but they exist because a vast willingness on the part of ordinary people offers them various levels of support, both tacit and explicit. That's what racist times are: times where ordinary people believe terrible things.

To put the metaphor in American terms, when a black man is lynched for having consensual sex with a white woman, it requires more than a small gang of racist men to do the job. It requires a police force that will look the other way, a woman and family who will not stand up for the truth, and a community that is willing to accept lynching as a substitute for legitimate justice.

William Hartnell was in no way a frothing bigot who screamed at minorities whenever he saw them. But I am strongly inclined to believe that he was the sort of bigot who stood by, perhaps made some deeply inappropriate comments, and who offered the tacit support that bigotry required to remain a viable force in the larger culture. His bigotry likely came in isolated instances, and was of the common flavor whereby individual exceptions would be granted to people he liked. His was, in all likelihood, the sort of bigotry whereby, when frustrated with a script, he would allow homophobic and anti-semitic language in as a part of his larger outburst at another actor. Which is to say that while it's unlikely that he hated Adrian for being gay or Jewish, it's very much believable that he would use homophobic and anti-Semitic slurs were he to start shouting at Max Adrian for another reason.

But it's vital to note that this is one facet of a man's life. It does not explain all or even most things about him. "Racist" is not an identity, but an endemic social problem that plagued the society William Hartnell was a part of. Accepting that Hartnell probably had some racist beliefs – and more to the point that he was almost certainly not the only person on Doctor Who in the 1960s who did – is part and parcel of accepting the material reality that Doctor Who was made in the 1960s, and that Britain in the 1960s had profound problems with racism. That is not the only thing that is true about the 1960s. But it is true about them, and it is probably true about William Hartnell. It doesn't erase the many good things that are true about Doctor Who, William Hartnell, and the 1960s. Nor, however, do those good things erase the reality of racism.

Elizabeth Sandifer

Anybody Remotely Interesting Is Mad (*The Chase*)

It's May 22, 1965. Number one is going to pass among four artists for the next six weeks: Jackie Trent, Sandie Shaw, the Hollies, and Elvis. So, basically, a mélange of pop acts. This is once again fitting for Doctor Who, which airs *The Chase*, a story that is, basically, a mélange of set pieces punctuated by occasional Dalek attacks. Other artists in the charts include the Beatles, Burt Bacharach, the Everly Brothers, Donovan, and the Kinks. In real news, opposition to the Vietnam War begins to heat up with demonstrations and teach-ins. But all told, it's a quiet six weeks.

Let's start by being honest here. There are, to my mind, two ways to read this story. Either it's a flawed but mostly edgy, brilliant piece of early post-modernism, or it's a complete crap-fest.

I won't lie and pretend the latter case is not, on paper, stronger. Terry Nation is, as we've discussed, a tough writer to love. He parlayed his brief description of some robotic monsters into copyright on one of Doctor Who's two most iconic images, managing to run roughshod over Ray Cusick, who was the one who changed Nation's description into an iconic design. Nation is credited whenever the Daleks appear on screen while Cusick . . . isn't. On top of that, of Nation's many Doctor Who scripts, it's a braver man than I who can argue that several do not feel phoned in. Not the least of them is this story's most obvious antecedent, *The Keys of Marinus*. On top of that, there's a general feel with this story that everyone sat back and trusted the inclusion of the Daleks to make everything else work. When all boundaries of good taste kicked up their feet for six weeks with *The Web Planet*, the sheer mad ambition of the thing carried it through. Here you don't even have that.

On the other hand, Nation was able to put together *Genesis of the Daleks*, which is rightly considered one of the best Doctor Who stories ever. And it's basically impossible to argue that he is anything less than one of the most influential creative figures in Doctor Who history. Looking even at his three stories prior to this, we can see that it was Nation who introduced the capture/escape sci-fi model, the Doctor's love of pioneers, genre juxtaposition, and, of course, monsters. And that's the root problem with Terry Nation. He's a genius who is perfectly willing to be a hack instead.

So with this story, it's genuinely tough. Because I do think there's a reading to be had that mostly makes this story work and work quite well. I'm also very much uncertain that this reading has anything to do with anything that Nation or anyone else involved with this story had in mind at the time. It is not just a redemptive reading of the sort I usually do, but the creation of an almost entirely new version of *The Chase*.

Still, this book is not entirely (or even primarily, really) about reviewing stories in the context of their time (there's been enough quality writing on Doctor Who that does that, most notably Miles and Wood's sublime *About Time*). It's about understanding a story of Doctor Who that continues to this day. And the version of *The Chase* that I can bring myself to quite enjoy is a version that seems to me to have been tremendously influential on, say, *The Stolen Earth/Journey's End*. And even if, on paper, it seems more probable that this is a warmed over piece of hackery from Nation that got maimed by Richard Martin when it was directed . . . maybe they were just ahead of their time. Let's pretend.

Here's the key to *The Chase*'s redemption: narrative collapse. By which I mean that the Daleks, in *The Chase*, are not merely threatening to exterminate the Doctor and his companions. The Daleks are threatening to completely destabilize the entire narrative foundations of Doctor Who such that further Doctor Who stories cannot be told, and the Doctor has to figure out a way to stop them.

This is established quickly in the opening episode. The first ten minutes are occupied by the TARDIS crew operating the Time-Space Visualizer picked up at the end of *The Space Museum*. As explained here, the visualizer is a time television, allowing them to watch any historical event on television. So we get ten minutes of the TARDIS crew watching TV instead of having adventures, culminating in a bizarre sequence of Ian dancing to the Beatles' "Ticket to Ride." (The Beatles make their sole Doctor Who appearance here via a tape made from *Top of the Pops* – although it appears that the Beatles were all in favor of it, and in fact a photo of John Lennon chilling with a Dalek exists and is easily Googled. Note, however, that Vicki expresses surprise that the Beatles played classical music – in other words, as mod and hip as the Beatles may be in 1965, Vicki is way, way hipper.)

This, needless to say, destabilizes the narrative considerably. It is, in fact, basically the end of Doctor Who as a concept. If the TARDIS crew can simply watch the universe on television, why voyage into danger? Indeed, the Time-Space Visualizer effectively reduces the TARDIS crew to the same position occupied by the viewer – watching events on television. Thus the first ten minutes are not, as they might appear, a kind of boring stretch of nobody doing anything, but rather a significant challenge to the entire structure of the show.

Especially when one realizes that the TARDIS crew is contrasted with the Daleks, who have developed time travel themselves. I'm going to talk about the Dalekmania craze in two essays' time, but suffice it to say for now that the Daleks were massively popular, readily rivaling the show itself at this point. And now, in the opening episode, the Daleks have literally usurped the show. The TARDIS crew is sitting around watching television, and the Daleks are adventuring in time and space. They've even gotten to where they break into a mass chorus affirming the last line of their orders, leading to the first really classic moment of Daleks sitting around screaming "EXTERMINATE!"

This continues as the TARDIS crew heads out onto Aridius and . . . sits around sunbathing. Really, Ian and Vicki go and wander, while the Doctor sunbathes with Barbara in a nice throwback to the old Doctor/Barbara scenes, which we haven't really seen much of this season. But they don't do anything. It's not until they see the Daleks on the Time-Space Visualizer – by which point, as the Doctor points out, the Daleks must already be on Aridius, since the Visualizer just sees the past – that they actually start acting like there might be a plot.

In other words, the show opens by having us be more inclined to sympathize with the Daleks, who are actually giving us a plot, than with the TARDIS crew, who are painfully boring. But in the very end, this inverts again and we are reminded that the Daleks, awesome as they may be, are still a force of narrative collapse, and one more overtly dangerous than a time telly.

Way back in *The Dalek Invasion of Earth*, I talked about how the cliffhanger at the end of the first episode is a matter of delayed gratification. We know the Daleks are coming, and so the episode of withholding them finally pays off with the iconic shot of one emerging from the Thames. The first cliffhanger of *The Chase* is superficially similar, with a Dalek emerging from the sand. Except that there is no delayed gratification. The Daleks are all over this episode prior to the one that rises from the sand. So instead, the cliffhanger is nothing more than a twenty-five second shot of a Dalek, which we've already seen tons of in this episode. There's no pleasure to be had; it's just a rote recitation of standard narrative beats. The episode even mocks this by having the

Dalek cough and grunt as it works its way out of the sand. Even the Dalek knows it's stuck in a rubbish cliffhanger. And this is the central threat of *The Chase* – the possibility of the entire narrative structure of Doctor Who collapsing.

You'll also recall, in comparison to the last Dalek story, that the Daleks' plan there made no sense at all, and appeared to involve driving a hollowed-out Earth around the galaxy as a sort of space Volvo. I didn't make much of the bizarreness then, largely because the point of the story wasn't why the Daleks were invading the Earth, it was that they were. Having a completely bizarre explanation for it only highlighted the fact that the story was really just about the set piece of Daleks in London. I mention it here because that logic is pushed to its endpoint in *The Chase*.

The entire story, as we find out in the second episode, is based on a chase through time. Now, if you're sitting there thinking "But wait, El, a chase implies a time gap between pursuer and pursued. If the chase is through time, why doesn't the pursuer just nip forward a few minutes and catch them?" then congratulations – you have identified the gapingly obvious flaw in this story that everybody else who has seen it has also mentioned. The story makes no sense at all and has a completely incoherent view of time travel. Which, to be fair, so does Doctor Who, where you can't rewrite history, not one line, at least, not on Earth and before the seemingly arbitrarily chosen date of 1963. But even Barbara, who is usually quite good at this sort of thing, has a rough time keeping a straight face as this bit of exposition is spat out at her.

No. *The Chase* is, ultimately, a story about dropping the Daleks into existing stories and watching them screw everything up to remind us that they can do that to Doctor Who as well. The second episode, thus, is on the one hand a story about the problems of the desert planet Aridius, where the native Aridians are helpless against the Mire Beasts. The Aridians are classic *Web Planet*-esque presentationalist monsters – in fact, they seem in some ways directly modeled on the Menoptra. Except for the fact that instead of that story, we get Daleks running around exterminating stuff. (This includes the best double entendre the show has had yet. Ian: Barbara, give me your sweater. Barbara: What, again? Ian: It's not for me, it's for the Dalek!) And so that story never happens.

Instead, we quickly jump to another story, in which the TARDIS crew ends up on top of the Empire State Building confronting a country bumpkin from Alabama (played by Peter Purves, who will be appearing again in a few episodes). This sequence is the easiest to criticize in the story. It's slow, not that funny, and seems pointless. There are a couple of interesting bits – most notably when Vicki suggests that New York has been completely destroyed by her time. But mostly, it's tough to love.

Even here, though, I think we can make something out of it. Most significantly, there's the fact that our Alabama yokel assumes that the TARDIS and the Daleks are from the movies. Because apparently America is all about the movies. But again, we can parse something pretty good out of this, in that the Daleks are explicitly threatening basic storytelling. The joke, after all, is that Morton Dill doesn't realize that he's already in a fictional story.

Nowadays, of course, this sequence would end with the Daleks arriving after the Doctor leaves and exterminating Morton Dill. And, let's be honest, it would have been a better ending. Its absence, when a modern audience can see clearly that it's "supposed" to be there, is probably the thing that makes this sequence the hardest. But you can still see what they're trying to do here, and the idea is sound.

A quick side comment, incidentally, about the completely nutso Dalek ship that is being used – named by fans as the DARDIS. The inside of it feels so excessively 1960s as to seem more like the pastiches of it from *Austin Powers* than the real thing, with tons of big spirally things swirling about in mod/psychedelic patterns. It's another thing that makes clear the underlying tension. The show has, over the last few episodes, explicitly allied itself with youthful culture. But the Daleks are part of that culture too. Cusick's iconic design is completely at home in this blur of psychedelia. And this is what makes them more than just monsters – they're fundamental threats to the narrative structure.

Next up we get one of the oddest sequences in the story. Basically, the TARDIS crew lands on a boat, then leaves, then the Daleks land and everyone on the boat is scared into jumping off in a mass suicide. And here the story seems to just have no idea of what it's doing. The mass suicide is played for comedy – the Daleks trip off the boat, and there are slapstick shots of a woman jumping overboard holding her baby. On other hand, it's a sequence of mass suicide in which a woman jumps overboard holding her baby – a shockingly intense moment. And after the Daleks go, we get a lengthy series of pans around the empty boat before we finally learn that it's the *Mary Celeste* – that these people really are dead, and dead because the Daleks fell into their world.

It's a horrible, awkward, and upsetting moment that the story completely swallows as a narrative beat while refusing to give the audience the room to be upset over the reality that they want to see this. The collapse, in other words, is accelerating as the Daleks close in. The story is coming apart at the seams here. We've gone from having no adventure because the TARDIS crew has decided to watch television, to having no adventure because we no longer have a world that even makes sense.

Which brings us to the fourth episode, which seems to me the most misunderstood episode of the lot. Most commentary on the episode inexplicably assumes that the end reveal – that it takes place in a haunted house in an amusement park – is known throughout. But watching the actual episode makes it clear that this final revelation is meant to be exactly that – a final revelation.

In fact, through most of the episode one assumes the audience is going to be trying to figure out what sort of story they're in. After all, the last episode was a comedy that ended with a mass suicide, and the one before that was fairly standard Doctor Who sci-fi. This story is genre-hopping like mad, so when they land in a seemingly haunted house, we the audience don't know what to do. (Ian, however, quickly notes that there are stairs, which should be useful with the Daleks. I bet you didn't think that joke would show up this early in the series.)

In fact, most of this episode plays on exactly that aspect – the fact that the audience is going to be guessing what sort of show they're watching. So when the Doctor suggests that they are inside the collective unconscious and that's why Dracula and Frankenstein are attacking them, it seems plausible. After all, we've been everywhere else.

Then from there we get the insane spectacle of the Daleks inadequately fighting off Frankenstein and Dracula while the TARDIS crew escapes and we get the pan back to learn it was just a haunted house. But by the time we get that explanation, it already doesn't make sense – how on Earth is a carnival haunted house going to fight off Daleks as successfully as it does? So in this story, the narrative undercutting has sped up to the point where sense is no longer even possible.

Here another dramatic moment comes up that one immediately senses would be done differently today. Vicki is apparently left behind in the haunted house. However, the audience gets to see her sneaking onto the Dalek ship before they see the TARDIS crew react. In other words, the TARDIS crew being horrified and upset that Vicki is missing comes after the audience knows she's all right. Especially in a story like this that seems to be throwing out the rules, it would have been a powerful scene to withhold Vicki's survival. But alas, the show avoids that.

Instead, we get a robot duplicate of the Doctor, played by Edmund Warwick as a reward for his stepping in and doing some scenes in a wig as a fake Hartnell when he was injured in *The Dalek Invasion of Earth* and had to miss an episode. The problem is that Warwick looks nothing like the Doctor, and that the evil duplicate is still voiced by Hartnell and played by Hartnell in close-ups. Warwick only plays him in medium and long shots.

This is the cliffhanger leading into the fifth episode, "The Death of Doctor Who." Now it's certainly possible to take this as one of several pieces of evidence that the Doctor's name is actually Doctor Who (more on this later). But it also seems like a meta-commentary on the story thus far. The fifth episode is where the narrative structure of Doctor Who is finally directly threatened as opposed to theoretically threatened.

This episode takes place in the jungles of Mechanus – a weird, alien place that evokes Vortis in its hostility. And we get a fairly typical runaround with the TARDIS crew and the robot duplicate. Finally, Ian gets the chance to fight the robot duplicate, and, crucially, gets it wrong, fighting the Doctor instead. The robot duplicate implores Ian to bash the Doctor over the head with a rock, and Ian goes to do it when Barbara (who has already had a fantastic scene arriving on Mechanus and giving a sense of genuine wonder and fear – through all she's seen, she has lost none of her sense of awe) realizes that Ian has the wrong guy.

Now the question is, is this a deliberate callback to *100,000 BC* where the Doctor nearly brains a caveman? If so – and I am inclined to say that it is – it's the dramatic turning point of the show, because it is where Barbara asserts boldly that the show has changed and evolved. She can now identify the real Doctor most easily through how he has changed. The Doctor can now be identified precisely because he wouldn't engage in the same behavior that, a year and a half ago, he did. The TARDIS crew escapes this one not just by walking into the TARDIS before the Daleks get in their way (as they did in the last three situations) but by changing the rules. This is, dramatically speaking, crucial, because it sets up the last act.

The cliffhanger between the fifth and sixth episodes is a straightforward one. A new alien race appears – the

Mechanoids. A Mechanoid, as it happens, basically looks like a d20 with a flamethrower. But we can see that the show proposes them as a major monster for the simple reason that their unveiling is a cliffhanger. (Once again, the narrative coding of *The Dalek Invasion of Earth* is crucial to understanding this story.)

The thing is, in the sixth episode, it's quickly clear that the Mechanoids are rubbish and everyone knows it. (Well, except Nation.) The episode opens with a hilarious shot of a Mechanoid and the TARDIS crew in an elevator, with the TARDIS crew crowded to the edges and clearly uncomfortable at the space-hogging Mechanoid. This is followed by them walking out into the Mechanoid city and gasping "It's huge!"

The next shot after that is an obvious model shot. And it's impossible not to laugh at the contrast. Shortly thereafter we get a thirty-five second scene of two Mechanoids talking. Which amounts to them bleeping unintelligibly. The Mechanoids, in fact, are among the most incoherently speaking monsters we've ever seen. And the show is clearly mocking them – in fact, Barbara and Vicki even get in on the Mechanoid-mocking action.

After a quick meet-up with Steven (also played by Peter Purves), a marooned pilot with a stuffed panda he keeps at all times, we go into another burst of plot. The Doctor sets the Daleks up the bomb, leading to what is easily the best Dalek moment we have ever seen (beating out even the crowdsurfing of *The Dalek Invasion of Earth*) as a Dalek spins around the room for an extended period of time shouting "AM EXTERMINATED! AM EXTERMINATED!" Meanwhile, Ian, Barbara, and the Doctor have to blindfold and tie up a screaming and protesting Vicki to lower her down a rope out of the Mechanoid city, providing what I am sure is some very disgusting fanboy's dream.

Meanwhile, in the Mechanoid city, the director, Richard Martin, serves up a truly amazing fight scene. The direction is often flagged as the weak point of this story, and it's a fair cop; Martin picks some truly terrible camera angles throughout, and does feel a bit over his head. But the final fight between the Mechanoids and the Daleks is fantastic. Starting with a montage, the sequence cuts faster and faster, and then begins overlaying multiple scenes until it is no longer able to be parsed by the viewer and is just a blur of fire and ray gun effects. And this is telling. In the end, narrative resolution comes when the TARDIS crew decides "the hell with this" and runs off, leaving the Daleks to fight the ill-conceived Mechanoids. The TARDIS crew has nothing to do with defeating the Daleks. They just waited around until another monster arrived and slipped out the back while the narrative re-stabilized itself. And in the end, it's nothing to do with Doctor Who that saves the narrative, but rather with the Daleks who, despite being terrifying conquerors of the universe, ultimately are just another silly robot.

But here's the thing – which is crucial about narrative collapse storylines like this. Yes, the narrative can be restored. That's the whole point of Doctor Who in these narrative collapse stories – that ultimately there is no such thing as threatening the fundamental narrative logic of Doctor Who because, eventually, it just shrugs its shoulders and does something random to get out of it.

But there's a flip side. The narrative restoration always comes at a price. The Doctor can get out of anything, but the flip side is that he is always going to be alone. The Doctor's fundamental move – the first trick we ever saw him do – was to fall out of the world, i.e., to escape. He can do that even from narrative collapse. But when you escape, you are, in the end, alone.

And so, in a sickening collapse, we go from the TARDIS crew joking around (including Ian pretending to be a Dalek) to Ian and Barbara realizing they can use the DARDIS to get home. And it's clear, under a careful reading, that this is, ultimately, because of the Daleks' destabilization of the narrative. Because on the Empire State Building, they were there in their own time – closer to home than they'd ever been – and they made no effort to get out of the TARDIS and go home. But now, as soon as they see the DARDIS, they realize that they want to go home.

As I've said, I'm not confident in my reading up to this point. The story really might just be a silly mess. But from here on out, I'm rock-solid confident because Ian and Barbara's departure is brilliant. The only question is whether it's a brilliant scene at the end of a rubbish story, or the brilliant culmination of a brilliant story.

As soon as Ian and Barbara mention wanting to go home, the Doctor loses it. He reverts to the sort of childish anger we haven't seen from him in ages – the raw crankiness of the Doctor who might bash someone's head in, and who sabotages his ship to force his companions to explore. This is the very Doctor Barbara rejected just an episode before. He screams at them. He rails at them.

And here we see what a great TARDIS crew we've had for the past six stories. Jacqueline Hill, unsurprisingly, sells it. Flattering the Doctor and begging him at once, as she was always the best at doing, she tells him openly and honestly how much traveling with him has meant to her. But also that, unlike him, they have a home to go to, and they want to go there. And it's a heartbreakingly beautiful scene.

And then there is Ian. I've been down on Ian as a character in the past, to the point where Simon Guerrier, who wrote *The Time Travellers*, has called me absurdly wrong on the point. I still think there are some major problems with Ian – most notably that he's the exact sort of manly action hero that the show usually sends up a bit. Which is why you have him with ridiculous scenes dancing to the Beatles and pretending to be a Dalek – because he is faintly absurd, and the show knows it.

He's also hampered by the fact that his character isn't one we recognize in Doctor Who anymore (although Rory is very close). He's the companion who least gets to react to the strangeness of the world around him, which leads to the sort of one-note acting I've previously complained about. He's stoic in a way that Doctor Who avoids later. But there is one later companion that Ian is a clear inspiration for, in a weird way, and that character is the one that, I think, can give a clear lens on how to read Ian as a great character. And that's Wilf.

It's clear from a couple of points throughout his time on the TARDIS that Ian served in the military. If he's the same age as William Russell, that would put him in World War II, and about the same age as Bernard Cribbins and thus Wilfred Mott. They are, in other words, characters with very similar origins. But where Wilf has stayed on Earth and been passed by, becoming a quiet, respectful patriot who looks at the stars, Ian got to go there. They are, essentially, the same character, and had Ian never traveled on the TARDIS, he'd have grown old to be Wilf. And if you can project that backwards and look at Ian that way, you can see the noble bearing and quiet dignity that was bottled up torturously in Wilf allowed out. When, years down the line, Wilf chokes back tears while begging the Doctor to take Donna with him, because "she was better with you" (in an episode whose structure owes more than it would like to admit to the reading of *The Chase* above), the subtext is that Wilf, too, would have been better with the Doctor. And in Ian, we can see exactly what he means. Ian is a better person for traveling on the TARDIS. He was always a good man, but the Doctor gave him the opportunity to be a great one, and one senses he will never go back.

And then there is Vicki, who is a few stories away from an unceremonious writing out largely because she allied with Hartnell against the new producer. It's Vicki who in this scene does what Susan never could. She stands up to him. She tells him to let them go. And she does so lovingly – loving the Doctor as a man. Not in a creepy sexual way, but also not in the paternal way that Susan loved him. There are shades of Lewis Carol and Alice Liddell. Which is still an unnerving relationship. The Problem of Susan has not gone away. But that's another story.

In the end, we are denied the actual goodbye between Ian and Barbara. Which is a beautiful decision. Instead we get something better. Ian and Barbara ride off into the sunset, returning to beautiful, contemporary, swinging London. There's a great bit where Ian is momentarily terrified by . . . a police box. They've returned to our world full of joy and wonder. This is the completion of a story arc, and is done better than we will see it done for almost a decade.

And as the episode ends, we pull back and see the Doctor, now watching his friends on the Time-Space Visualizer. The natural order of things is restored. Now the Doctor watches us on television, just as we watch him. And as the episode ends, the Doctor at last, for the first time, admits that he will miss them.

This, I should note, is why one of the few continuity points I am adamant about is that there are basically no pre-*Unearthly Child* stories. I mean, you can give the Doctor one or two adventures, but there's no real way to say that he adventured substantially before that. Because if you compare this Doctor, choking up with sorrow at losing his friends, to the one who, when caught in the Cave of Skulls in *100,000 BC*, just gives up, it is clear that Ian and Barbara have changed the Doctor. Being with them has made him into a hero. And if you give him adventures before he meets them, you cheat them of that story role. I'm fine with retcons and contradictions in continuity, but I'm loathe to accept one that actively invalidates the emotional core of another story. And giving Ian and Barbara any position at all beyond the two people who taught the Doctor to be a hero cheapens them. Watching these first sixteen stories, it is clear that they are not just the first companions for the viewer, they are the first companions for the Doctor.

And he misses them.

He'll miss others. This sense of loss is essential to the show. But to everyone who complains that they miss Rose, or Donna, or any other later companion, remember this:

It is June 26, 1965. The Hollies are at number one with "I'm Alive." And we miss Ian and Barbara – more even than Susan, whose absence was, ultimately, for her own good and the Doctor's own good. This is the first departure to truly hurt. Fourty-six years later, it still hurts. And if, in 2052, *Doomsday* turns out to have had the staying power of this last scene, maybe then we can talk about how much you miss Rose. Assuming that, eighty-seven years later, we've stopped missing Ian and Barbara.

The Doctor certainly won't have.

That Jackanapes (*The Time Meddler*)

It's July 3, 1965. The number one single is going to trade back and forth between Elvis and the Hollies before the Byrds storm in and take number one with their cover of Bob Dylan's "Mr. Tambourine Man." Although the Byrds are American, this still seems like the completion of a deal that started back in *The Reign of Terror*, when Bob Dylan introduced the Beatles to drugs. In turn, the Beatles, indirectly through the Byrds, introduce Bob Dylan's sort of music to rock, creating folk rock. The day after the last episode of *The Time Meddler*, Bob Dylan plays his infamous electric concert at the Newport Folk Festival. The Kinks, the Who, Donovan, the Yardbirds, Lulu, and Dusty Springfield also chart.

In other news, Edward Heath, future prime minister, becomes leader of the Conservative party, and cigarette advertising is banned on UK television.

The comparisons to *The Reign of Terror* are apt, as this is the second time Dennis Spooner has been tapped to write a season finale. While Spooner has not distinguished himself as one of the best writers in Doctor Who's sable, he's been the script editor since *The Rescue*, which is the first sustained run of high quality in the series. (Meanwhile, behind the scenes we have here the first script edited by Donald Tosh, who has no solo scripts on Doctor Who and is thus hard to judge in comparison with Whitaker and Spooner.)

With very few exceptions, it's hard to draw clear lines of "eras" in Doctor Who. The usual method, and the one I defaulted to in splitting these books up, is changes of the lead actor. These changes certainly provide some sense of the major changes in the show, but they're not the whole story. Of the eight actors who took the part over while the show was running, as opposed to doing so in new launches, only two – Pertwee and Smith – have ever had their debut story also serve as a companion debut. Furthermore, only twice has regeneration also marked a wholesale change in the major production staff (producer or script editor for the classic series, executive producer for the new) – Tom Baker and, again, Matt Smith – although the Pertwee and McCoy had a reshuffle. And so there is often more continuity across an actor change than is imagined, and the equally important producer changes are largely ignored. *About Time*, in one of its bolder and more satisfying decisions, uses season changes as its markers, which is compelling, capturing the production team changes at least somewhat better (although there's often an oddity at the start or end of a book). But whatever measure you use there are problems, and the changing of the guard often happens invisibly within any given history.

I say all of this because, muddy as it is, there's a clear transition between eras going on here that is worth remarking on. The first season of Doctor Who was largely defined by its inconsistency. Significant chunks of it were not very good – *The Keys of Marinus* being the most uncontroversial example. Nobody involved had a clear sense of what Doctor Who was good at yet, which led both to stories that were brilliant but not the direction the show would go (*The Aztecs*) and stories that were just out in left field (*Marco Polo*, frankly, and *The Edge of Destruction*). Even the story most obviously like future Doctor Who, *The Daleks*, is more distinct in its differences from what we expect Doctor Who to be than its similarities. Amusingly, the story from Season One most like future

Doctor Who, *The Sensorites*, is reliably the one that comes in last in fan polls about the season.

Somewhere in the transition to Season Two – I'd put it at *The Dalek Invasion of Earth*, personally, but there's a case to be made for putting it one story earlier or later – the show found its footing, and we got a chain of six or seven stories of which, frankly, the worst that ought be said is that *The Romans* is a bit fluffy. (Fan consensus would have you believe otherwise. We'll talk about the changing nature of fan consensus and what it means for evaluating the program with *The Gunfighters* later on.)

Crucial to this change was that the show embraced a youthful and mildly anarchic view of the world, and took a real joy in it. I say this era is better than Season One largely because it is at least possible to find a set of criteria that the show appears to be judging itself by. In Season One, it was a real challenge to figure out why *The Sensorites* and *The Reign of Terror* were part of the same show. In Season Two, it was possible to make sense out of why *The Web Planet* led into *The Crusade* and *The Crusade* led into *The Space Museum*, as different as they were. You can, in this season, use a fairly consistent yardstick of what the show is to evaluate all of them. Even if that yardstick seems at times to strain credulity, you can, for the first time, look at an extended chunk of Doctor Who and say, "this is what they were doing here."

Starting with the last episode of *The Chase*, however, we enter a fourteen-episode stretch of Doctor Who in which we get three companion departures, two companion arrivals, a change of script editors, and a change of producers. More broadly, the run from *The Chase* in the summer of 1965 to the beginning of *The Ark* in the spring of 1966 forms the closest thing to a distinct multi-story arc that Doctor Who will do for some time.

Now that we have a rough roadmap to take us through the next few stories, then, let's look at this one starting with the new TARDIS crew. The Doctor and Vicki's relationship is re-stressed here, and is worth remarking on, as Vicki assures the Doctor, quite touchingly, that she wants to travel with him. In practice, she departs after only two more appearances, both of which are completely missing from the archives, so this is actually the last existent story in which we see Vicki. So let's take a moment and talk about her, as she's terribly underappreciated.

The first thing to say is that Maureen O'Brien is fabulous, and makes a lot out of a character who is all too often given writing that can charitably be described as flat and phoned in. Anyone who thinks she is not a successful companion should fire up *The Space Museum* and watch her happily tell the computer she's planning revolution. Then consider the fact that the character who loves all that the Doctor represents and loves traveling through space and time with him was invented by Vicki. Susan loved her grandfather, and Ian and Barbara were reluctant passengers. Vicki is the first companion from the mould that will bring us Sarah Jane, Ace, Rose, Donna, and Amy – the eager adventurers.

We also properly get Steven here, since he previously seemed like a one-shot character. This ends up hammering home how much the Doctor has changed since *An Unearthly Child*. He accepts Steven quickly, and even seems spurred to be unusually charismatic and charming, explaining the workings of the TARDIS to him with what is possibly his best line to date, "That is the dematerializing control. And that, over yonder, is the horizontal hold. Up there is the scanner, those are the doors, that is a chair with a panda on it. Sheer poetry, dear boy!"

Steven is, at this point, unsurprisingly undeveloped. Just as Vicki was very much Susan rejigged to be a mod fantasy of future youth, Steven is, at this point, a youthful Ian. Perhaps the most interesting thing is that we finally get a detailed explanation of why the TARDIS looks like a police box, which, when it occurs, seems like an incidental detail, not like a significant piece of setup for the plot.

Ah, yes – the plot. For a while now, with few exceptions, Doctor Who has been alternating between historicals and science fiction. So following *The Chase*, the audience was primed for a historical. That, along with the fact that the stories still have individual episode titles here (meaning that the first episode title "The Watcher" doesn't give the premise away in the same way that *The Time Meddler* does), is absolutely crucial to understanding how this story works.

Thus far, when we see a historical with Dennis Spooner's name on it, we have a pretty good idea of what to expect. Any careful and attentive viewer will remember *The Romans* and *The Reign of Terror*, and, when they see the eleventh-century Britain setting, assume they know exactly what they're going to get, namely an episode of Doctor Who that will probably, when they get around to having titles for these sorts of things, be called *The Saxons*. One of the major story beats of the first episode is the Doctor working out the history of AD 1066 and what's going to happen, which, again, sets us up for a story we know – in which we find out the ways in which the Doctor was secretly responsible for some aspect of history.

Which is the key thing people overlook in this story. It's not just that we don't expect to see another time traveller in AD 1066. It's that we don't expect to have a plot involving history other than the Doctor either scrambling to rescue the TARDIS crew or secretly being responsible for some major event in history. Spooner, however, continually subverts those expectations, making the story far more interesting than all of that.

That said, I'm not sure he's quite as clever as the story's reputation would suggest. The first episode is where most of the praise centers, largely for an admittedly brilliant sequence in which the Doctor is wandering around a monastery with sounds of chanting in the background. He turns a corner and finds a record player, which he lifts the arm of, revealing that the chants were being played on a record in AD 1066. And yes, this is a fantastic sequence that plays with our expectations of what the music in a story is. (The sequence immediately following is also great, in which a trap door slams shut in front of the Doctor and the Monk emerges to give us our first proper, insane, and villainous laugh of Doctor Who.)

On the other hand, it might have been a bit more clever if, in the scene immediately before, Steven hadn't found a modern wristwatch and thus if the discovery of modern technology in AD 1066 was still as much a surprise as the discovery that the music was fake. Or if, a few minutes earlier, we hadn't heard the record skip. This sort of repeated use of the same revelation has been a problem before. The *Mary Celeste* sequence of *The Chase* is wrecked in part by the fact that the story spends a while panning around the empty ship before revealing that it's the *Mary Celeste* – a perfectly reasonable way to do the reveal – and then immediately jumps to the TARDIS in which Ian tells Barbara the exact same thing. Thus we get the "reveal" that it's the *Mary Celeste* twice. Which is, no matter how you cut it, one too many times. Likewise, the first episode's cliffhanger would be far more shocking if the discovery of the record player were actually a complete surprise as opposed to one we've already seen, basically, twice before in the episode.

And so watching *The Time Meddler* clearly requires a healthy level of "yes, well, let's give them a break because no one had ever done it before." Which is a skill that, to some extent, the whole Hartnell era requires, but this story requires it more than others. And, I mean, it is fair. Much of what is obviously done wrong about *The Time Meddler* is only obvious because we've seen fourty-six years of Doctor Who in which the basic ideas of *The Time Meddler* were repeatedly dusted off and done better. *The Time Meddler* has to get some sort of a break for doing it first.

And if Spooner failed to quite realize that the cleverest idea he had in this script was the frisson between the historical and the science fiction, he did at least partially realize it. Notably, look at the use of comedy in it. Spooner's historicals have, as I said, been established as "the funny ones." (And keep in mind, we've only seen six historicals before this – two Spooner, two Lucarotti, a Coburn, and a Whitaker. That the codes of the genre are well established enough that we can distinguish Spooner-style historicals from Lucarotti-style ones is an astonishing testament to how memorable and distinctive even the relatively rubbish ones are.) And this one is no exception. But the primary comedic figure is the villain – the Monk himself.

This, as much as the subversion of history and science fiction, is where the frisson really comes into this story. We've seen the comedic bumbling figure through history, and the pleasure of it has always been that the Doctor gets the joke when he doesn't. Consider, for instance, Nero in *The Romans*, where the whole joke is that the Doctor knows where the history is going and so can outwit the comedic fool. Here, the comedy risks outwitting the Doctor, which is oddly terrifying. But it's terrifying in a way that tends to get overlooked in favor of the story's more familiar legacy.

Because the story's legacy, of course, is its third-episode cliffhanger where Steven and Vicki enter the Monk's secret hideout and discover that it's a TARDIS. This is the story where we meet another Time Lord except, no, it's not. Other than a repeat appearance by the Monk later this season, the Time Lords, and those words never actually appear in this story, are still invisible until the end of the sixth season. And once the Time Lords proper appear, the Monk never does again. The Monk was, in other words, designed independently of the Time Lords, and the Time Lords were never designed to accommodate the Monk. To read the Monk, as fans tend to, as a sort of proto-Master is to spectacularly miss the point of this story. The Master comes from taking a Time Lord like the Doctor and making him into a villain. The Monk comes from taking a comedic historical villain from the Spooner tradition – a tradition that no longer even existed when *Terror of the Autons* aired – and making him like the Doctor.

In fact, one thing that's interesting about the Monk is how poorly he fits with later conceptions of Time Lords. The Doctor suggests, for instance, that the Monk is "about fifty years later" than he is. This jars with the later presentation of the Time Lords, who seem to have a clear "present" at all times. Curiously, their "present" seems to coincide with the present of Earth. (The latter sense of the present, however, does apply to this story. The Monk and the Doctor clearly consider 1965 to be the present.)

Which is why the usual fan complaint that the story is dull whenever the Vikings are around misses the point. This may be the first pseudo-historical, but comparing it to something like *The Time Warrior* or *The Unquiet Dead* misses the point. This story is "The Meddling Monk invades *The Saxons*," not "The Doctor versus the Monk."

Really, this is another example of narrative collapse. It's a more targeted one than *The Chase*, because for some reason the Daleks are the ones that really lend themselves to that style of plot, but it's a narrative collapse story all the same. The story hinges on the fact that a character like the Monk is aberrant to Doctor Who – he doesn't belong.

But crucially, he's not a villain. Honestly, if he were a villain, he'd probably fit better into the tradition that includes the Daleks, Yartek (leader of the alien Voord), Lobos, the Animus, etc. But no, the Monk is a variation on the Doctor. Where the Doctor delights in turning out to be the reason history happened, the Monk likes chaotically rewriting history. And, notably, he's put on the same level as the Doctor. We're told explicitly that Stonehenge only happened because the Monk, for instance, provided the delightful possibility that our own human history is fundamentally wrong. You can, it seems, rewrite history.

So we are forced to choose between the chaotic, funny Monk's approach to creating our history or the Doctor's. And for the first time, we get something resembling a real challenge to the Doctor's role as an anti-establishment figure. This is a theme we are going to see play out over the next few stories – a sense that there might be something darker to the youth rebellion that Season Two spent so much time advocating.

Even still, though, one gets the sense that the Doctor is a sort of rebel. The Doctor quickly identifies the Monk as a particular and known type of time traveler. The Monk, on the other hand, seems far more cautious about the Doctor, and seems not to know what to make of him. The Doctor is still, in other words, clearly a rebel. It's just much less clear, now, exactly what sort of rebel he is. Put another way, it's interesting to see that the first attempt at an evil version of the Doctor is not a black-hatted Moriarty figure but a malevolent trickster, suggesting by implication that the Doctor is still not so much the hero as the good trickster.

Which makes this story a nice endpoint of the arc that began with *The Dalek Invasion of Earth*. Having done its narrative collapse, the show is working towards a new status quo that is not entirely clear yet. But it is one that seems distinctly purposeful. In a fundamental sense, it is only because the Daleks made a concentrated effort to dismantle Doctor Who that it can be rebuilt in this strange new sense, where we can no longer expect with confidence that we know what kind of adventure we are having.

And so the second season of Doctor Who comes to a close, seeming to have, for the first time, told a real set of stories where the show knew what it was. The third season is coming, with, at least for its first half, an equally sure sense of what it is. But between now and then, there's something very big that is going to happen to Doctor Who – something with as big an impact as anything we've seen before.

Elizabeth Sandifer

You Were Expecting Someone Else: *Dr. Who and the Daleks*

It is August 23, 1965, a month after Doctor Who left television for its summer break, and a little under three weeks until it returns. As it should be, the Beatles have the number one spot with "Help!" And, in order to fill the sad gap in our lives between July 24 and September 11, AARU Productions helpfully released *Dr. Who and the Daleks*.

More than anything, to understand this we need to back up and look at British culture in the summer of 1965. We've done this to some extent already – we know about Swinging London and the rise of mod and post-mod youth cultures. We know that we're in the midst of a Labour government, and that there's a strong sense of overthrowing the old and putting in the new. We know that the Beatles are big, and that they brought with them a wealth of other bands that, at least temporarily, put the fallen industrial power of Liverpool at the center of the cultural map, second only to London.

We know perhaps less well that the Daleks are massively popular. The term "Dalekmania" that describes this era is perhaps overstated, if only because it obviously attempts to equate the Daleks with the Beatles. But on the other hand, there is a mass of Dalek merchandise including: little rolling action figures, Dalek play costumes (which are ludicrously valuable today), Dalek board games, and far weirder things like Dalek White Boards to draw on, or Dalek View-Masters.

The Daleks, then, up to this point sat exactly on the line between Doctor Who's public service duties as a good and proper BBC series and its status as a commercial hit. On one level, Doctor Who was like air. For almost two years straight, it aired faithfully on Saturday evenings as part of a family programming block. You watched it whether you liked it or not. (In fact, the steadily climbing AI figures for the program over its classic run are probably less a product of the show getting better and more a product of the fact that the changing nature of television meant people who didn't like it stopped watching it. Notably, AI figures in general – for all shows – improve over time.) It was clear that a secondary market of people who really liked it existed, because the toys sold, but the show was not "for" that market in any overt way. (Although the producers were not so foolish as to pass up the opportunity to use Dalek stories to boost ratings and get attention.)

And so the first thing to realize about *Dr. Who and the Daleks* is that it is the first time Doctor Who was made entirely for fans. Because this was Doctor Who for people who cared about it enough to pay for it. This, more than any other fact about the movie, including that it was in color, is the most important thing about it.

Thought of this way, one of the most striking things about the movie is how much it changes given the modern-day obsessions of fandom whereby failure to completely and slavishly adhere to everything that has ever gone before is cause for extensive denunciation. Most obviously, of course, the Doctor has become Dr. Who. This is explicit – he is repeatedly referred to as such. (Presumably, then, his daughters – Susan has moved up a generation, and Barbara has joined the family – are Susan Who and Barbara Who. Which probably explains Barbara's eagerness to find a mate – so she can get a proper last name.) Equally significant, however, is the fact that Dr. Who is a human inventor. We'll talk about the former in a later entry, but for now I want to focus on this other change to the Doctor's origin.

Of course, calling it a change is slightly off-target. In the original version of *An Unearthly Child* – the unaired pilot – the Doctor was a futuristic human inventor, not an alien. And even after that got changed, Doctor Who stories well into the second season presume that the Doctor built the TARDIS himself and that it is one of a kind. It's not until the Monk shows up at the end of the second season that this notion gets overthrown. And so this change is not so much a violation of what's on television as a return to the mean.

Which is unsurprising. It is not as though this movie was made with no attention being paid to the TV series. Some of its Daleks were lent to the TV series for *The Chase*, and when Terry Nation was unavailable to adapt his script to film they turned to David Whitaker for an uncredited rewrite. So the writers, at least, were familiar with what Doctor Who was. And remember, the Doctor's alien origin is, at this point in the series, an ambiguous signifier. The Daleks were still treating him as human in *The Chase*, and although the Doctor has a home, that home is thus far defined as little more than the place he cannot go. The Doctor and the Monk we saw a month ago were merely not of this Earth, not Time Lords as such, and any attempt to read them otherwise is a retcon. (Not invalid – just a retcon.)

So the change to make him a human inventor is not as drastic a change as it seems, given that his original design is much closer to human inventor than to immortal Time Lord. But where this fact really comes into its interpretive own is when it's combined with thinking about the movie as being in color. (Well, colour if we're localizing properly.)

In any case, a quick glance at the movie poster gives you a very clear sense of what the movie's selling points are. In ranked order, these are: Daleks, colour, and Dr. Who. We've talked a bit about Doctor Who as pop spectacle, and this is the embodiment of it. The use of color is not about realism, but about spectacle. Which is why Skaro is, in this film, a technicolor monument to retrofuturism, complete with lava lamps. And the fact of the matter is, once you see Daleks with lava lamps, there's no going back. I guarantee it. Even if you go watch *Genesis of the Daleks*, with the most explicit Nazi Germany version of Skaro ever seen, you'll find yourself going "Hmm, maybe if there were a lava lamp or two . . ."

This film is also where the dominant visual look of the Daleks comes from. If you're wondering why the New Paradigm Daleks introduced in *Victory of the Daleks* look the way they do, go look at the poster for this movie. This is where that idea came from. And since, ironically, this "for fans" version of Doctor Who has had more re-airings on television than any actual episode of Doctor Who, these technicolor Daleks are actually the most iconic image of the Daleks around. Which is part of why fans (who have, by now, mostly rejected the Cushing films as non-canonical fluff) are considerably grumpier about the Dalek redesign than normal people.

Actually, one thing to note about this movie is the degree to which it is clearly influential on Moffat's version of Doctor Who. The gleaming blue TARDIS exterior, for instance, is explicitly modeled on the movie. The TV ones were always much duller and older-looking. The TARDIS interior made up of cobbled together objects similarly finds its start here. And look at Peter Cushing's delivery of "We could be anywhere in time and space, which is rather exciting" and ask yourself if Matt Smith would change a single thing about that delivery if he were playing the role.

But there's one more very significant thing to note about the intensely visual style of the film, and it's what connects the Dr. Who as doddering inventor to the rest of the film. Consider, for a moment, the opening shot of the film – a pan across Dr. Who's living room. Susan and Barbara Who are reading serious works of science. Then we get to Dr. Who, who is reading a *Dan Dare* comic.

But for our purposes, the thing to look at is actually the war movies. In the immediate aftermath of the Second World

War, one thing to note was that the British victory was connected to a longer tradition of British greatness. This tradition, if you extend it back, eventually gets you to the Victorian adventurer. Consider the Jules Verne or H.G. Wells style hero, or, perhaps most obviously, the protagonist of *The Time Machine*. So this is actually part of his characterization as an eccentric inventor in the Victorian tradition. It's clear from the moment we see him and realize he's Dr. Who that he is a skilled scientist. So his choice of reading material is not a comment on his lack of commitment to science, but rather a comment that he is so well versed in science that he can move on to the next stage of a man's life: adventure. (It also marks the first real hat-tip on the part of Doctor Who to *Dan Dare*, which was a significant influence.)

Why does all of this matter? It matters because the TARDIS console is a cobbled together bunch of machines much like, as I said, the TARDIS in the current series. We can see here that this view of the TARDIS has its roots in 1960s memories of the tradition of the Victorian inventor. Now, when you do things like that and then create a TARDIS full of gleaming metal, levers, and cobbled together wires in 2010, everybody knows what to call it. In 1965, there wasn't a word for it, or a visual aesthetic. But make no mistake – this film is where the basic roots of Doctor Who as steampunk come from. Even if the film lacked the visual vocabulary to go full-out steampunk, and even if it opts for a bit of a blend between 1960s and Victorian aesthetics, this is clearly where the image of the Doctor as an old-fashioned Victorian inventor hits its zenith.

The other thing to happen in this film, visually, is Peter Cushing's performance. Cushing plays, basically, a prettied-up version of the Hartnell Doctor – all of the wandering eccentricity, none of the snappish irritability. But what's most interesting about Cushing's portrayal is that he turns the part into a broad character performance. Cushing always walks with stooped legs, giving him an artificial gait and visual style. And, whereas Hartnell had to characterize his Doctor via smaller hand gestures, Cushing can characterize Dr. Who via broad motion that takes up the whole screen with a full body performance because he's acting on a much larger movie screen.

Over time, however, television has become much more cinematic in this regard. This is much of why, in 1980, the change was made to give the Doctor something much closer to a costume than the mere clothing style he'd had before that point. Because suddenly, on television, you could do what you could always do on film, which is use design to have your main character be recognizable from any angle and visually distinct on the screen at any time. (Moffat, on the DVD commentary for the first episode of *Sherlock*, talks about outfitting Sherlock with his "hero coat" and about this exact visual issue.) Though Cushing is doing it here via physical acting and not costume, the basic point remains; this performance exemplifies a certain approach to playing the Doctor in which he is not just the hero because of any character traits he has, but because the entire visual logic and structure of the show is designed to highlight him as the hero. Dr. Who is not the mythic hero because of years of past stories in which we know the character, nor is he the mythic hero just because someone says so. He's the mythic hero because he has his own set of visual iconography and signifiers that the film specifically uses to highlight his presence on screen. When it comes to how the film is put together, the world really does revolve around him.

Unfortunately, the companions suffer badly from the elevation of Dr. Who and the Daleks into mythic forces in the visual logic of the film. Ian is reduced to a pure comic relief character. Barbara makes no sense and has no meaningful role. Her most iconic contribution to the original TV story – being the person menaced by the unseen, advancing Dalek – is removed. She screams at some unseen threat, but we see nothing of the Daleks. Their appearance is instead held off until Dr. Who can meet them. (This shot is impressive, taking place in a room shot to feel constrained.

Eventually the camera is positioned in close to Dr. Who, Ian, and Susan Who. As they turn to see the Daleks, the camera pulls back quickly, and the Daleks have filled the space we had been led to marginalize in our conception of the shot. Again, this heightens the degree to which the Daleks and Dr. Who are both mythic forces in the film – every shot is centered around them.)

Susan, ironically, is the one character to fare pretty well in all of this. The casting of a twelve-year-old girl who plays her even younger goes a long way here because it removes the Problem of Susan entirely. By making her the small, precocious child in every shot where she speaks, the show gives her a sense of the mythic that, while far less than that of the Daleks or Dr. Who, is still bigger than that of any other humanoid character.

The Thals suffer less, not because the film is terribly interested in them – it's not – but because they're dressed as sparkling proto-Ziggy Stardusts seven years too early. This does clear up the creepy racism of their first appearance, but it's no less distancing.

On the whole, though, the film feels sharper than the television serial. It's not just the bright colors and simplified characters. It's that the film moves along at a much nicer pace. It's about half as long as *The Daleks* itself was, and this reveals just how much padding there was in the original story. Now to be fair, this is only a partial criticism. The original story is meant to be watched over seven weeks in twenty-five minute chunks. It's not a huge surprise that the story doesn't hold up quite as well when you shotgun it in one nearly three-hour sitting. The movie is meant to be watched in one sitting, and is paced like it.

But on the other hand, even within a given section of the story, the movie works at a much faster and more exciting pace. I recognize this as a deeply unpopular view within fandom, but the fact of the matter is that if you sat ten people in front of this and ten people in front of *The Daleks* and told them they could leave if they got bored, you'd lose audience on *The Daleks* way, way faster. *Dr. Who and the Daleks* shows how much better the pacing on Doctor Who could be, and provides an extremely compelling case for why the serialized format is less than ideal for Doctor Who.

And yet despite all this, it's almost impossible to say that the film is better than the TV series on the whole. Part of this is that the increased production values mean that the show loses some of its manic charm. Compare the final fight between Daleks and Thals in the movie – an immaculately choreographed affair – to the fight between Daleks and Mechanoids in *The Chase*, where the whole thing becomes a blur of superimposed images. Yeah, the movie fight scene looks better. But *The Chase*'s is much more interesting, telling the story of the climactic fight in an unusual way.

But more than that . . . in the end, the genius of Doctor Who is not the fact that it has Daleks, or anything else. This is one of the things we easily forget when we look at *The Daleks* today. What made it a classic serial was not just its well-designed monsters. It is a classic serial because it follows three episodes about cavemen with radioactive jungles and robot monsters. What is brilliant about Doctor Who, in other words, is that any two stories are likely to have no connection and, often, not even a common look or feel to them. The point of Doctor Who is not any one story, but the fact that there are so many very different stories.

(The film makes a token effort to accomplish this by landing the TARDIS in an ancient Roman battle at the end, but here the special effects are so bad as to be laughable. The open TARDIS doors are used to project what is obviously stock footage of Romans running, giving the impression that the TARDIS is buried in the ground, as the Romans are clearly running over it. Rather than suggesting new adventures to follow, it mostly suggests that the budget ran out.)

This is why I've never managed to get excited about the constant rumors of a Doctor Who movie. Because even a well done Doctor Who movie – and the fact of the matter is that this is a pretty well done film for what it's trying to be, which is a big action story (and let's face it, that's what *The Daleks* is trying to be too) – is still not going to work. Doctor Who can work as audio plays, as television, as DVDs, or as comics quite well. But film, in the end, is just not a medium it's well suited to. Because what makes Doctor Who brilliant is there's no such thing as the iconic Doctor Who story that captures the feel of the show. The feel of the show is the vertigo when you're pulled from one story to another. Film, focusing as it does on individual stories, can never capture that.

Time Can Be Rewritten: *The Empire of Glass*

It's November of 1995. Somewhat surprisingly, this is the first time we've dealt with a novel from this period – the prime years of the Virgin line. Which makes this the first real glimpse we've had into that era. Andy Lane is a good author for this as well. He's not one of the absolute lions of the Virgin range, but he is strongly associated with it and a writer the Virgin line turned to for at least one major book in the line. So this is a good place to look at the line.

Well, sort of. There may be thirty-three novels in Virgin's Missing Adventures line, but the fact of the matter is that the books Virgin is known for, and that their importance to Doctor Who really depends on, are the sixty books in the New Adventures line. TARDIS Eruditorum is going to cover many of those books when we get to them. But one of the big controversies surrounding those books was that they were for adults in a way that the series wasn't. Except that's not really the complaint. More accurately, that's the defense. The complaint is that the New Adventures embraced sex and violence in a manner usually reserved for twelve-year-old boys at their first sleepover with nudie magazines.

The truth, of course, is subtler than either position, and as I said, we'll talk more about it when we hit 1991 and begin our surprisingly long exploration of the interregnum. What's interesting here is the somewhat bizarre spectacle of seeing the Virgin era's approach applied to the tail end of the Verity Lambert era.

As is often the case with Time Can Be Rewritten entries, the first thing that jumps out when one of these novels is read more or less in sequence is how jarringly different from the televised era they are. In this case it's not just the appearance of Irving Braxiatel, another renegade Time Lord who, in later life, is a major player in several Virgin books and spinoffs thereof. It's also things like explicitly setting this novel after the events of *The Three Doctors*, future continuity always being a bit of an odd card to play.

But equally strange is the characterization of the main characters. Steven is characterized as constantly impatient, mistrusted by the Doctor, and, perhaps most interestingly, bisexual. Which is not a problem as such. I mean, it's not inconsistent as such with anything we see on screen, given that he's depicted, basically, as a sexless character. But equally significantly, it's not consistent as such with anything on screen – it doesn't add meaningfully or significantly to his character. I mean, there are characters in the history of Doctor Who where the revelation of bisexuality would make sense. A bisexual Turlough or Mike Yates would be a completely different story. But Steven just isn't a character that codes with a particularly intense level of sexual ambiguity, making the revelation seem hollow and for its own sake.

Still, Steven fares better than Vicki, whom Lane seems at times to actively despise as a character. The book includes numerous snide comments about her (the Doctor and Steven agree, it seems, on only one thing, and that's that Vicki shouldn't have a TARDIS key), and her main plotline involves having her be heartbroken when her alien lover turns out to be evil. One is almost tempted to ask why Lane didn't just set the book between *The Daleks' Master Plan* and *The Massacre* and get just Steven as a companion, except that the answer seems unlikely to be satisfying. (Vicki does, admittedly, have a lovely scene in which she suggests that the

Doctor only cares about people in the way that one cares about pets. But as great as this observation about Hartnell's Doctor is, it doesn't quite seem right coming from Vicki.)

And then there's the Doctor. It's not that the Doctor in this book is wrong for Hartnell as such. He's not. But he's also not quite right. A few "my dears" and "hmms" are thrown in as is traditional when writing Hartnell, but again, this is not the character we recognize from the screen.

Of course, this is also not the sort of story we recognize from the screen – one involving dozens of elaborate alien species, jumps in location from Venice to England, chases, explosions, and appearances from Galileo, Shakespeare, and Christopher Marlowe in a pseudo-historical. It's nothing that could even be conceived of as happening on television in August of 1965, the gap in which this story supposedly falls.

None of that, of course (except maybe the bits about Vicki) is a criticism as such. Nothing about the book gives a strong sense that it was ever supposed to be taken as an imitation of Hartnell era stories. Nor, however, is it akin to something like *The Man in the Velvet Mask*, which we'll talk about later as a conscious attempt to show a new spin on the Hartnell era.

Rather, what this book represents is an attempt to reimagine the Hartnell era as an antecedent to the Virgin era. The result isn't quite the Hartnell era that was on television, but it remains connected enough to be firmly rooted there. But on the other hand, the novel introduces a ton of future continuity – references to *The Three Doctors*, *Carnival of Monsters*, *The Time Warrior*, and, of course, in the form of Braxiatel, the New Adventures line abound. But unlike many continuity-dense books, *The Empire of Glass* doesn't throw all of these things up primarily to fit them together as a sort of intellectual puzzle.

The best hint to what the book is really doing comes when Braxiatel is explaining to Vicki his general plan and describes the Doctor as having "a growing reputation" based on his handling of the miniscope affair. This is, in many ways, the heart of Lane's concept in this novel. The Doctor is in the sort of adventure he'll eventually be known for, but isn't quite there yet. He's still getting established and becoming the hero. And what Lane is doing here is consciously showing us an adventure at a sort of halfway point. This is not quite a New Adventure and not quite a Hartnell adventure. By putting feet in both worlds it shows that the worlds are not as far apart as they might initially seem.

Which is to say that the book, odd as it might be, works. It's an interesting story with some neat ideas and fun twists. A few moments jar – the Doctor's lengthy monologue about his agnosticism that tends towards atheism is both preachy and unnecessary, explaining more of the Doctor's worldview than is strictly necessary. (Compare it to the relative deftness with which the same issue is handled about a decade later in *The Impossible Planet/The Satan Pit*.) The inclusion of an undead Christopher Marlowe comes off as a bit too much.

But all of these are incidental. Nobody comes to a Doctor Who novel expecting perfection. At the end of the day, this is an exciting and interesting story with feet firmly in two very different aspects of Doctor Who. The result is a story that provides a reminder of something that is all too easily forgotten in the endless factionalizing of fandom: there actually are things in common beyond the superficial across all eras of Doctor Who.

You Were Expecting Someone Else: *1966 Annual, The Dalek Book,* and *Dalek World*

Let's talk about canon. These days everybody knows the refrain: there's no such thing as canon. But a broader question is what that means. I mean, it's all well and good to do some hand waving and proclaim that Doctor Who has no canon and all works of fiction are equally valid in the Doctor Who mythos, but it comes awfully close to the literary criticism equivalent of technobabble. I mean, yes, it's trivial to show that Doctor Who does not have a canon in the traditional *Star Wars* tiered sense of things. (Though it's worth doing so, as *Teatime Brutality* demonstrates. If only so you can quote that hilarious line from the *Transformers Wiki*, "Indeed so little attention is paid to it that the franchise is riddled with countless, irreconcilable continuity clashes despite being presented as a single continuous story, even in the TV movie and continuing television series that were made many years after the original series was cancelled." It's the hilarious implication that we poor Doctor Who fans are somehow living with a terrible affliction in this regard. Hey, Transformers fans. We just have a lack of canon. You have three Michael Bay movies. We win.)

So let's look at it with some historical perspective via these three books, which are among the earliest instances of something that may or may not be Doctor Who canon. First off, what are they? Well, they're about a hundred pages each, though I don't imagine that was exactly what you were asking. The Dalek books are a mixture of four color comics and prose stories with single color illustrations (red, as it happens), published by Panther Books. The Annual is all prose stories with four among the first published Doctor Who fiction. (The other two big examples are some comic strips in a title called *TV Action* and the three early Doctor Who novels – adaptations of *The Daleks*, *The Web Planet*, and *The Crusade*.)

Lawrence Miles and Tat Wood, in *About Time*, make great snide references to the entire body of non-televised Doctor Who as "professional fan fiction," which is perhaps true, and in any case surely needs to be taken in context given that Lawrence Miles has written reams of the stuff. But calling this fan fiction would be wrong. The Dalek books are written by Terry Nation and David Whitaker. The Annual has no listed author, but it's well known that Whitaker ghost wrote most of this stuff. So these are people with tremendous real involvement on the show. Nation, for all his flaws, is one of the most influential writers in the show's history, and Whitaker is both among the most influential and the best.

But it's equally clear that this is not straightforwardly part of the series. I mean, the Dalek books seem to have Skaro as part of our solar system, and to assume that the bulk of planets in our solar system are habitable. And the Annual features the return of that character so popular from the movies, Dr. Who. Neither of these reflect future directions in the series well at all.

On the other hand, watch *The Dalek Invasion of Earth* immediately followed by *Bad Wolf/Parting of the Ways*, or, better, by *Doomsday*. You'll immediately notice something about the Daleks in the two stories. The Daleks of the Russell T Davies era fly around, have massive spaceships, and there are oodles of them. For obvious reasons, in *The Dalek Invasion of Earth* there are five of them, they wobble around, and they are very, very terrestrially inclined. And that gets lampshaded in *The Chase*. (Which also has a great shot where a Dalek clips the side of a door and the suit visibly bounces open. But to be fair, the set doesn't wobble.) There's a bit of a disparity here between the Daleks we see on TV and the Daleks we imagine.

That disparity came from the spin-off fiction. Because things like these Dalek books were the first time we saw massive armies of Daleks swooping around and conquering things. They were the first time we saw an Emperor Dalek. I mean, yes, he looks absolutely ridiculous, but that's hardly the point. It's the Emperor of the Daleks. You see that and the first thing you imagine is the Doctor facing that thing down.

But, of course, the nature of television is that you're never going to get the massive field of swooping Daleks. At least, not when these books were coming out. It's just not technologically possible. And so the books are providing a genuinely important service to the show in that they're providing context for the episodes. Once we see the Emperor Dalek in a comic, he's always there. Even if we don't see him on television, we can imagine the Daleks we see as a tiny subset of a much larger set. Doctor Who uses this kind of approach all the time. It's absolutely crucial to modern Doctor Who. Look at *The Stolen Earth/Journey's End* for a brilliant example. Throw in two or three CGI shots of a Dalek fleet and you can get away with having the entire rest of the episode be the Doctor and Davros chinwagging at each other and still have it feel epic. Or *The Web Planet*, which introduced the atmospheric density jackets (mentioned twice in the Annual) just in order to have the Doctor and Ian in white to make the special effects shot of the massive stone edifice work. Because once you see the massive stone edifice, you can get by with just showing some men in silly ant costumes for the rest of the story.

And so these books did a tremendous amount of work filling in the possibility of a larger context for the series. By giving us a glimpse of what existed beyond the episodes, the episodes became better. Likewise, every story in the Doctor

Who Annual takes place on other planets. Basically, in terms of sheer strangeness, they start where *The Web Planet* left off, all of them featuring hard-to-televise monsters and massive set pieces. Which, again, once you can regularly see the Doctor engaging in that sort of adventure, ironically, the restrictions of television become easier to accept.

But there's a flip side to this, as the argument is coming perilously close to suggesting that Doctor Who might be better as comics or prose pieces. And that's not really shown here. The fact of the matter is, these three books are slogs. It's really, really tough to get too excited about them. They feel appallingly rushed, and any quality they have is clearly due to the fact that Whitaker has a refreshingly high, minimum quality he achieves. Still, the lack of an editor is visible. The low point comes in "The Lost Ones," when on page forty-six it is clearly stated that the Doctor is "prevaricating, because, of course, he did not come from Earth," but then two pages later it's established that he doesn't want to let a spaceship go to Earth because "To send it back to modern Earth would condemn his world to destruction or slavery." I'd say the copy-editor should be exterminated for this, but the fact of the matter is, there probably wasn't one. The Dalek books, on the other hand, mostly feel like characters so two-dimensional even Isaac Asimov rejected them acting out "Dick and Jane Get Exterminated." (See Jane scream. Scream, Jane, Scream!)

On top of that, the books have dated in a way that the show hasn't. It's not just the depiction of Venus as lush and teeming with life, or "The Crab People," a truly horrifying piece of work in which the Doctor is implored by a dying civilization that has nearly destroyed itself with genetic engineering to take 100 test-tube babies from the civilization to safety. When the embryos die in transit, the Doctor writes it off with a shrug and a comment about how it served them right for tinkering with genetics and making things like test-tube babies in the first place – easy to write twelve years before Louise Brown. One can even, in the early, speculative days of the technology when it was merely a scary theory, understand why Whitaker would write it. But today, in a world where IVF is a common procedure, it reads horribly.

But it's more than all of this. It's the fact that the books are visibly not trying to be anything better than average quality pulp science fiction for the time, such that even when they do have the odd moment of ambition (the central image of "The Crab People," a civilization that has gone so far with genetic engineering that they cannot hold their own form and transform into unspeakable and unfathomable horrors in the grand Lovecraftian tradition, is great) it just highlights how lazy the whole thing is. (Another corker is the use of screencaps from *The Daleks* to tell a completely different story.) The fact of the matter is, these books do nothing so much as make one want to watch the much better TV series.

There is something – and we'll deal with this much more when we get to the '90s and Doctor Who is a book series – special about television. Doctor Who, for some reason, works better there. And these annuals aren't portraying a new vision of Doctor Who. They're portraying the fringes of the existing vision.

So are they canon? On one level, the answer is clearly no. Nobody would complain if the Doctor visited the Crab Nebula and it wasn't like it was described in "The Crab People." People do, on the other hand, complain when a new series episode like *School Reunion* directly contradicts a classic series episode like *The Five Doctors*. So clearly there's a differing status between the two. On the other hand, it's not like *School Reunion* was made by people ignorant of *The Five Doctors*. The real point may be that the series is perfectly willing to contradict itself.

On another level, the answer is clearly yes. The Dalek Emperor makes his way to the TV show, as does the basic vision of Daleks on offer here. In the Annual, you can see several wild ideas that, years later, the show would finally tackle. (Giant spider, anyone?) These stories are part of the cultural memory of Doctor Who, and influence the show. If canon is the established body of literature the show can draw on, these are canon.

I prefer that definition, by and large, because it seems to perform the useful function of actually having canon work more or less the way the writers treat it as working. Canon is the menu of things you can reference. And so the Dalek annuals, with their gleaming space marauders of Daleks, are canon because it's screamingly obvious that's where Russell T Davies got his images of Daleks. Because the alternative, as we'll talk about way down the line, is to argue the fact that the Virgin New Adventures aren't canon. These, of course, are the books that were so important to Doctor Who's development that Davies went and commissioned Paul Cornell to rewrite his book *Human Nature* as a TV story. Which is, of course, used as evidence that the book version can't count. This is canonicity at its most perverse – books that are so important to Doctor Who that they can't be canon.

Accepting everything may lead to deep-seated weirdness. But surely it's no weirder than the alternatives.

Eat Crisps and Talk About Girls (*Galaxy Four*)

It's September 11, 1965. The Rolling Stones are at
number one with a more Rolling Stonesy recording than
they've charted with previously, "(I Can't Get No)
Satisfaction." They'll give way to some less interesting stuff,
namely, the Walker Brothers for one week and Ken Dodd for
a staggering five weeks with a song I have never heard of. A
quick listen suggests I was not missing anything. In fact,
hearing it, I think I might be missing the blissful unawareness
I had before. (But we'll give Ken Dodd a slight break for
appearing in *Delta and the Bannermen* in 1987.) Also in the
charts are Sonny and Cher, the Beatles with "Help!," Bob
Dylan, and Barry McGuire's staggering piece of apocalyptic
folk "Eve of Destruction," notable for one of the worst
rhymes in all of pop music, in which "coagulating" and
"contemplating" are rhymed.

Since we last saw Doctor Who, the Beatles invented the
stadium concert, playing Shea Stadium in New York City, and
the India/Pakistan conflict increased its simmer towards an
open boil. Meanwhile, while this story is on the air, a
smattering of coups and revolutions, both successful and
unsuccessful, goes on. *Thunderbirds* debuts on ITV to the
delight of puppet fans everywhere, or, at least, puppet fans in
the UK.

Meanwhile, Doctor Who is starting up its third season with *Galaxy Four*. For years this was one of the outright missing stories, and the start of a long run of missing stories. That's changed recently, but it's worth discussing the general concept of the missing episodes.

This is a complex topic, and it's not going to be until the end of the Troughton era that we finally finish with most of their implications (although the phenomenon affects stories into Season Eleven). First of all, they are among the least seen episodes of Doctor Who. That's not to say they're completely unseen. The soundtrack of every episode of Doctor Who exists, and a group called Loose Cannon has done superlative reconstructions based on the soundtracks and photographic evidence of the stories. For most of the missing stories, this is made easier by the existence of Telesnaps – a service provided by a man named John Cura where he would point a camera at the television screen and take photos throughout an episode in case the production team wanted a handy visual record.

Unfortunately, *Galaxy Four* is not among the stories Cura did this for, meaning the visual evidence was for a long time particularly thin. Thus Loose Cannon had to make up the slack via photoshopping existing photos together to make decent guesses at what the scenes looked like, and, in the case of *Galaxy Four*, building their own version of the monsters to recreate scenes of the monsters from scratch. But these, for copyright reasons, had no official distribution, instead filtering out online and in fan circles.

So the stories were available, and in versions that give an extremely good sense of the missing episodes, given the obvious limitations. It's just that they're obscure in a way that the stuff the BBC formally releases on DVD isn't, making these stories less seen than others. And, of course, not everyone likes watching a slide show and listening to the soundtrack. But even among those who have seen them, there's something odd about reconstructed episodes. The reconstructions have an overt artificiality to them, with Loose

Cannon having an understandable but idiosyncratic tendency to favor getting motion into a shot whenever possible, often meaning that unusual attention is called to relatively banal scenes that they can recreate well as opposed to the more catchy scenes which often involve actors and are harder to copy. The result is a lot of obviously spliced together footage of robots gliding along photo backdrops with no shadows and things like that, while the nuances of acting performances get understandably swallowed. And so for ages we had very little that we knew about *Galaxy Four* – so little, in fact, that for years we didn't even know what the Rills, the primary "monsters" of the story, looked like.

This helped contribute to something of a misunderstanding of *Galaxy Four*. Because on paper – which is essentially the only way we had it – *Galaxy Four* is by far the most phoned-in story we've seen yet in Doctor Who. It is, in many ways, less a Doctor Who story than a stitched together remake of half-remembered bits of Doctor Who stories. It doesn't look or sound bad, but it is still the first time that Doctor Who has really felt like it's just doing the Doctor Who thing by default instead of trying to push itself. Eventually this will become more normal, if only because eventually Doctor Who will have pushed itself in so many directions that there are more types of retread to be done. But this, to be honest, is the first time Doctor Who has just decided to do a story that plays it totally safe and feels like Doctor Who is "expected" to feel.

And for the most part, it's a thinly veiled redress of *The Daleks* and *The Sensorites*, with a few overt references to *The Space Museum* and *The Web Planet* (featuring the unexpected return of the Astral Map). But perhaps the most obvious "Doctor Who by Numbers" moment is the latest attempt at creating the next Daleks, the Rills' robotic servants, named by Vicki in her last act of cute naming as "Chumblies," (a name that, inexplicably, everyone including the Rills immediately adopts).

And then there are the behind the scenes details. Verity Lambert, about whom we'll say more in the next essay, had by this point decided to leave the role of producer, and was in any case spending more of her attention on the next story than this one and leaving the work on this story functionally to the incoming production team. The result is a story that feels a bit cobbled together. Steven is stuck spending the entire episode delivering lines originally written for Barbara, and although Vicki at least has a plot, Maureen O'Brien apparently picked enough holes in the dialogue during rehearsals to drive incoming producer John Wiles to sack her after this story, resulting in her hastily being written out in her next appearance.

Usually after a full change of production staff we get one or two episodes that are odd holdovers from the tone of the last regime. Here we have it in the other direction – an episode that feels like a greatest hits collection released too early in a band's career – a handful of clever bits in a sea of "meh." Mostly this feels like all the bits of the youth rebellion theme we've seen for episodes mashed up senselessly. Steven youthfully rebels against thinly veiled communism. Vicki youthfully rebels against whatever is put in front of her. Everything is very sparkly, mod, and pretty much exactly what you'd expect. And there are Chumblies.

Or so we all assumed. But perhaps we should have known better. Derek Martinus, the director of *Galaxy Four*, has been well established as one of the good directors despite, for a long time, only twelve of his twenty-six episodes existing and two of his stories – this one and *Mission to the Unknown* – being totally unrepresented in the archive. The possibility that there was something we were missing here was always felt.

And then, in December of 2012, we found "Air Lock," the third episode of *Galaxy Four*, alongside the second episode of the Troughton story, *The Underwater Menace*. The latter was straightforward – it was the exact right time to find a Troughton episode, and the relative weakness of the existing episode of *The Underwater Menace* meant that people were primed to re-evaluate that story favorably. A preview clip of Troughton doing a typically good job acting sealed the deal.

But *Galaxy Four* was trickier, in that we had to formulate first impressions. In many ways, what was striking about "Air Lock" was how competently it was shot. Martinus favored high and low camera angles, so that we either stared upwards at the characters or peered down at them. The Rill spaceship turned out to be surprisingly well designed, and Maaga's monologue early in the episode was shot as a terribly interesting direct address to the camera. It was not just well directed, but lushly so.

The result is something that initial impressions of the story simply couldn't give us. Because while the world of *Galaxy Four* is not the most innovative world Doctor Who produced under Verity Lambert, it turns out to be one of the best-realized. In this context the comparison between the Chumblies and the Daleks (who were, if we're being honest, generic monsters elevated by brilliant design) makes more sense. The Chumblies are generic robotic servants, but the idea is that they're placed within a vibrant context of design such that they become iconic. They miss, but only just, and not because they're "too cute" or have silly names. The Chumblies are an attempt to do with sound what the Daleks did with visual design. It doesn't quite work, but the fact that it was being tried speaks volumes.

Behind the scenes we know that Verity Lambert all but skipped this one to make sure that *Mission to the Unknown* went well. But instead of leaving this the hollow exercise in the generic that it appeared, what we have is everybody trying their damndest to make it work without Lambert's supervision while exercising a polish on a script that didn't deserve this sort of quality. If we praise *The Space Museum* for the fact that, under its generic runaround with youth revolutionaries, there's a really interesting concept about time and predestination, then we can just as easily praise *Galaxy*

Four for being a well-meaning space adventure that's done with impeccable presentation.

Throughout this volume we've held that one of the basic purposes of Doctor Who in its earliest conception was to be strange. Typically we assume this strangeness should come conceptually – that it should be strange by subverting a story that looks like it should be *The Saxons* to be about a malevolent trickster version of the Doctor, or by doing Méliès on television. But it's equally valid and important to accomplish strangeness through design. *Galaxy Four* is an example of the BBC pushing the limits of what they can do every week to their aesthetic max just to see what it looks like. We might wish they did this more often on scripts that could have used the help and less often on cut-rate pulp storytelling, but the fact of the matter is that virtually every story since *Planet of Giants* has managed to succeed admirably in at least one regard.

Nevertheless, in hindsight it's also important to realize that this is something of a last hurrah for a given approach. Martinus makes a desperately generic script sing by focusing on the visual and sonic production to crank up the strangeness, but it turns out that he's gone in the wrong direction for where the program is going to go next. The program's plan turns out to be to abandon estrangement as its primary aesthetic in favor of being a more generic adventure serial. *Galaxy Four* is shot like the pinnacle of the Lambert approach, but it's written like what's going to come up a lot over the next four years. Watching "Air Lock's" majestic sense of world is oddly elegiac, because it's the last time anyone is going to put quite so much effort into world building on Doctor Who for a long time.

Which brings us to the final moments of the last episode, in which Vicki, in rapid succession, sprains her ankle and wonders what's happening on a random planet beneath them. The former sets up an odd parallel with the end of *The Myth Makers*, more about which in two essays, while the latter is the direct lead-in for *Mission to the Unknown*, about which more next essay. But what we have here, in the dawn of a new regime, is something we've not actually seen on Doctor Who before. Starting with *The Time Meddler*, the show has been building inexorably towards something. It's going to, with the next two stories, begin moving faster and faster towards the endpoint of that.

As inauspicious as this start to a new regime is, things are getting very, very interesting.

Elizabeth Sandifer

My Mother Verity (*Mission to the Unknown*)

It's October 9, 1965. Ken Dodd's "Tears" is still at the top of the charts, with no real changes to the underchart since last week. Post Office Tower, the tallest building built in London in the 1960s, opened yesterday and is the biggest visible monument to the cultural capitol that is London. And Doctor Who is doing something unusual – the only single-episode and Doctor-free story of the classic run, *Mission to the Unknown*.

I've talked about the way in which the stories are, right now, building towards something. It's probably worth talking about what that something is right now, because more than any story under the script editorship of Donald Tosh or John Wiles (who was producer in all but official name during the whole of this season), this episode exists first and foremost to build towards a later payoff.

One of the things that was settled on quickly after *The Chase* was that instead of doing two Dalek six-parters on either end of the season, they'd do a massive twelve-part Dalek epic in the third season. However, due to a quirk of accounting stretching back to having to re-film the first episodes of both *An Unearthly Child* and *The Daleks*, as well as condensing the last two episodes of *Planet of Giants* into one, it became necessary to produce an extra episode at the end of the recording block that started with *The Rescue*, and, ideally, to give the entire cast a break at the same time. So a single-episode, TARDIS-free prelude to the Dalek epic got put on the schedule, and this is it.

That's the lens through which this story is normally approached. And it is, factually speaking, true – that is why this episode exists. But it has the unfortunate side effect of turning a very interesting episode of television into a lesson on the intricacies of BBC budgeting in the 1960s. And, I mean, I say this as a ridiculous pedant who actually finds BBC budgeting in the 1960s interesting, but that does a real disservice to the episode.

For one thing, it's one of those annoying approaches that prefers the archivist lens of fandom to an approach that's actually invested in the history of what Doctor Who was and how it was experienced. Nobody watching this story in 1965 was thinking about it in terms of BBC budgets and "the only single episode story of the classic series." And nobody making the story was primarily making a historical document to illustrate BBC funding. This is purely an invention of hyper-knowledgeable Doctor Who fans trying to develop a history of the show. While this is usually a wonderful thing, and the fact that Doctor Who's production is so well documented is part of why the show is important, here it's a bit of an irritation. Part of it is no doubt that, being yet another missing episode, for most fans the received wisdom and history of the story is all we've got. This is especially telling when we consider that *Mission to the Unknown* and *The Daleks' Master Plan* were among the last stories to get a novelization, with John Peel's two-volume adaptation not coming out until 1989. So prior to 1989, detailed information on this story just wasn't there.

But these days we can do better. Not only do we have reconstructions, we've had them for long enough that an alternative take on this story has started to spring up thanks to the efforts of things like *About Time*, *Running Through Corridors*, and *The Discontinuity Guide*, all of which I freely admit to being perched giddily atop the shoulders of.

The first thing to realize about this story, then, is that it must have been completely mind-blowing to the viewer, who would have settled in and watched in increasing bewilderment as the TARDIS fails to show up. Even in the present day, that's unusual. At least now we usually get told in advance what the Doctor-light episode of a given season is going to be, as opposed to here, where it was a complete surprise. There's nothing that indicates this as a Doctor-free episode. Instead we settle in and assume that we have an establishing shot of the world before the Doctor arrives in it – something that has become a fairly standard category of opener by this point.

Except the establishing shot never ends. The tension mounts and mounts, and the audience keeps waiting for when the Doctor is going to arrive and the situation will start looking better, and it never comes. What we normally think of as the intro to the story keeps going until the tension finally reaches a breaking point and everybody dies. And all the while, the TARDIS never comes. The episode is just a massacre of all of its sympathetic supporting characters at the hands of the Daleks, and there's no Doctor at all.

This does a couple of things. First, it pokes a massive hole in the Doctor's mythic heroism. Starting with *The Dalek Invasion of Earth*, we've been told over and over again that the Doctor is fundamentally a hero who makes everything OK. Now, with a story occupying the exact same slot that *The Dalek Invasion of Earth*'s second episode did – the one that had the Daleks nervously reassuring themselves that "We are the masters of Earth" in response to their meeting with the Doctor – we get the exact opposite story. We get a story where the Doctor doesn't show up, nothing is OK, and the Daleks exterminate everybody. While it is still true that the Doctor can save the day, this episode is a sobering reminder that sometimes he doesn't.

To a highly engaged viewer inclined to take a conceptual look at the series, this is significant. The Doctor has a time machine. He's defined by now as a character who can show up anywhere and any time. But this episode is a brutal reminder that he doesn't. To some extent we know that – he refuses, in a significant way, to save the day in both *The Aztecs* and *The Reign of Terror*, instead allowing death on a massive scale because he won't interfere with history. But the implication has always been that the future is fair game – that he will save the day there. But now we know that he doesn't show up. Much as *The Web Planet* was in part significant because Doctor Who never had to show such an extremely alien planet again, this is significant because it reminds us that every time the TARDIS touches down and the Doctor steps out, that's a choice. He has a limited life and doesn't show up at every point of danger in existence. When he saves the day, it means something. (This is actually the best argument against making the Doctor truly immortal – an immortal time traveling hero will eventually save every day. For the Doctor's actions to mean something, he has to be genuinely unable to save everybody in the entire universe every time.)

The other thing it does is finally put the Daleks from the *Dalek Book* onto the screen. These are not the swooping armies of space Daleks, but they are the Daleks we know as proper, galaxy-conquering terrors. Nation has, it should be noted, put four different sets of Daleks on the screen now – horrible monsters lurking in a ruined city so desperate to survive that they've lost all that made them "human," daft '50s alien invaders, the comedic legion of *The Chase*, and now the ones from the comics. And one thing that is very clear here is that Nation is much more interested in these Daleks than in the others. And in fact, he's much more interested in them than in the Doctor. For the first time since *The Daleks*, one gets the sense of Nation just writing something he wants to write as opposed to writing for the paycheck. And it's the best writing we've seen from him to date, frankly. The episode is tense and exciting in a way that past stories of his haven't been.

But when all twenty-five minutes are over, what, exactly, is the audience supposed to make of it? It is significant that the story ends not with the slaughter of Marc Cory and his crew, but with the establishment that his warning survived. In other words, although the Doctor didn't show up to resolve the immediate crisis of this episode, there is still another crisis, and the show is still Doctor Who. Eventually the Doctor is going to walk into this story, presumably next week . . . but more on that later.

OK. So let's draw a line under that, and take a quick turn to the other thing about this episode – the thing that, actually, makes treating it as nothing more than a prelude to *The Daleks' Master Plan* really egregious. *The Daleks' Master Plan* is a John Wiles produced story. Yes, it was commissioned before he took over, but he was still in charge of it. This is a Verity Lambert produced story. In fact, it's the last Lambert story. The reason she was off ignoring *Galaxy Four* was so she could make sure she went out on a truly spectacular note. Mission accomplished. But more to the point, any list of the ten creative figures with the biggest influence on Doctor Who has to include Verity Lambert. She's as transformative as David Whitaker, Patrick Troughton, and Russell T Davies. And of them, it's Verity Lambert who has by far the most interesting story.

Doctor Who was, on paper, created by Sydney Newman, the incoming head of drama at the BBC. He'd been poached by the BBC to make them more competitive with commercial broadcasting. It would be easy to assume that he was thus a ruthlessly populist figure who went for the lowest common denominator, but he wasn't. He was clearly working with the mandate of figuring out how to do BBC-type stuff and having it be commercially successful – not with changing what the BBC was.

And so he developed Doctor Who as an educational program. Which didn't last long, but as we saw in the early episodes, was there. But he also developed Doctor Who to be big, popular entertainment. Which is why one of his first decisions about it was so striking. Not a lot of people in 1963 would put an inexperienced, twenty-eight-year-old Jewish girl in charge of a flagship series.

Of course, not a lot of twenty-eight-year-old Jewish girls were Verity Lambert. By that point in her career, she'd already managed such accomplishments as keeping a live TV show running on camera after the lead actor dropped dead between scenes, and keeping order while the proper director scrambled to rewrite the script. She was known by anyone who met her as a force to be reckoned with, and rightly so.

And so there was Verity Lambert, in her first TV production job, holding it together as Doctor Who figured out what it was. It was Lambert who told Newman he was wrong not to like Delia Derbyshire's theme music. It was Lambert who managed to talk Newman into being OK with the Daleks, to obvious results. It was, over and over again, Lambert who managed to get temperamental William Hartnell to work well with the crew, and Lambert who made virtually every decision that kept Doctor Who from the unfortunate fate of flaming out early on.

By all accounts, Lambert was a wonder – capable of standing up and fighting with anybody who she thought was getting in the way. Most accounts are demure, but the strong impression is that Verity Lambert was someone who could rely on winning an argument if it came down to a screaming match, and so was perfectly willing to let it if need be. On top of that, she had an unfailing eye for what would be popular. She, more than Newman, was responsible for the decisions that made Doctor Who a mass success, drawing it away from the frankly dull didacticism Newman had in mind and towards the weird and wonderful show that produces things like *The Dalek Invasion of Earth*, *The Rescue*, *The Web Planet*, and *The Space Museum*.

And she did it at the age of twenty-eight, as a girl, in 1963. She did it so well that after proving Newman wrong on both the theme music and the Daleks (and having the guts to tell her boss to sod off, she knew what she was doing), Newman stepped back and let her run the show, basically ending his direct involvement until he stepped in and helped rescue the transition to Patrick Troughton. Needless to say, especially given that Lambert was, to be blunt, absolutely gorgeous, the rumors were that she slept her way to the top.

She didn't. She worked, fought, and occasionally knifed her way to the top, going head to head with everyone who disagreed with her and usually getting her way, which was unerringly right. Frankly, you can look at the list of contributors on the first two seasons of Doctor Who, and with the exception of David Whitaker, there's nobody who it's completely impossible to imagine the show working without. Even the Daleks, being an equal product of Terry Nation and Raymond Cusick, don't have a single name that you can point to and say "That's why the Daleks made it on screen and worked."

Except Verity Lambert. Who at the same age I am now, did eighteen months of work that were, let's be honest here, more important to the world than anything I am ever going to accomplish, and probably anything you are ever going to accomplish. Doctor Who exists because a brilliant, beautiful, and strong-willed lady named Verity Lambert spent eighteen months fighting tooth and nail to make it happen.

Doctor Who will, over the other forty-six years of its existence, become a number of things, some of them miles from anything we saw on screen in Lambert's time as producer. But at the end of the day, there is nothing about Doctor Who that is not completely dependent on her. And her influence never left the show. Flip forward a decade or so, and think about where the people working on Doctor Who might have gotten the idea for a brash, strong-willed, capable female who worked alongside the tempestuous Doctor. Ask yourself where a model for a character like Sarah Jane Smith, or Romana, or Tegan, or Ace, or Martha, or Amy might have come from. The answer is obvious. The Doctor always had a companion like that – from day one. It's just that she never stepped out in front of the camera before Lis Sladen stepped out in The Time Warrior.

So screw the foreshadowing, screw the epic plot *Mission to the Unknown* sets in motion, screw the mythic significance of the Doctor as an ontological heroic force in his own unceasing narrative. Screw it all. You want to know what *Mission to the Unknown* is about? It's about saying goodbye to one of the greatest women who ever lived.

Verity Lambert died in 2007 at the age of seventy-one. She lived long enough to see the show she started her career on impossibly come back from the dead. There's a gorgeous interview with her and Russell T Davies from 2006, where her love for the show in its current form is as clear as Russell T Davies's massive admiration for her. And reading it, knowing her history, knowing what she managed to do, it's impossible to read it and not tear up at it.

Years later, in the *Time Crash* mini-episode, there's a beautiful moment where David Tennant, only half in-character, tells Peter Davison how influential his playing of the Doctor was on Tennant. And he ends with the wonderful line that "you were my Doctor."

In the interview, Russell T Davies doesn't say it in as many words. But he means it. Verity Lambert was his producer. So let's give him the last word.

Like I said, a lot of it was also about taking it back to the '60s . . . no Time Lords, proper people as companions who had histories and real lives, seeing the wonder of the TARDIS, travelling into the future and the past . . . And that's what you did. There have been so many different versions of Doctor Who since then, but I sat down and said we need to get back to that '60s version, where Daleks were mysterious and powerful and had empires and things like that . . .

Goodbye, Ms. Lambert.

You bloody well rocked.

Elizabeth Sandifer

There Should Have Been Another Way (*The Myth Makers*)

It's October 16, 1965. Ken Dodd's "Tears" continue to rule the chart. It will continue for the next three weeks, beating back Andy Williams, Barry McGuire, Sandy Shaw, and Manfred Mann. We'll deal with the history in a bit.

For once, let's start with the opening shot of Doctor Who. After all, last week left us in such a strange place. And we open with . . . Achilles and Hector fighting in the fields of Troy, with Achilles killing Hector when the materialization of the TARDIS distracts him. So immediately, we know that we are not in Dalek country.

We also know, by sight, that we're in a comic historical. We've seen them enough before. Perhaps somewhere in the back of our minds we remember that the last comedy historical, *The Saxons*, was unexpectedly interrupted, but one genre-breaking story does not erase the existence of the genre. So whatever shock we might have in the unexpected failure of the Daleks to show up again, we can at least settle down quickly.

And indeed, the first episode of this story is pretty straightforward. By the end of it, we know we're in a typical historical. This is something that really can't be stressed enough. I've said that Doctor Who is building to something in these stories over and over again now, and we're almost there, but that's an easier claim to make today when I know what the next sixteen episodes of Doctor Who are and have seen them. In 1965, this tonal shift was jarring and confusing, and it was in no way clear where all of this was going. And so the fact that the episode appears to offer some foothold – that it looks like something resembling normal service – is probably nice. After something as weird as *Mission to the Unknown*, the historical version of the *Galaxy Four* phoning-in is pretty welcoming, even to someone who really wants to see the Daleks.

But as the episodes play on, a couple of things are clear. For one thing, this is funnier, at least to modern tastes, than any past historical. There's a scene in the second episode in which Paris slips out to the battlefield to make a token effort at challenging Achilles to single combat, and happens upon Steven, who wants to fight him. Paris visibly dislikes of the idea of combat, and wants nothing more than to get out without dying. Similarly, in the first episode, there's a wonderful scene of Menelaus complaining that, honestly, after ten years of Trojan War, he doesn't even care that Paris stole Helen, and he'd rather just go home.

Much of this is down to the source material, which is actually far funnier than people give it credit for. But more is down to a new writer, Donald Cotton, who has the sense to use the comedy of the source material and to trust that it's still going to be funny. On the early evidence, he appears to be quite a sharp, clever writer who one hopes will make a return to the series down the road – because this is a really sharp, funny story. The acting is also good – Max Adrian as Priam is fantastic (even as his homosexuality allegedly caused serious tensions with an increasingly temperamental William Hartnell), as is Frances White as Cassandra, retooled as a villainess who demands Vicki and Steven's execution as Greek spies. Her counterpart on the Greek side is Odysseus, who gets some fantastic scenes with the Doctor as the Doctor tries to bluff his way out of having to solve the

Trojan War before finally giving in and just proposing the Trojan Horse.

So it's a return to form. Like *Galaxy Four*, it's an attempt to go back to what Doctor Who is known to be good at, but unlike *Galaxy Four*, it's a profoundly non-lazy attempt that makes a real effort to be interesting, funny, and better than what's come before. Right?

Not so much.

It's November 6, 1965. At long last, Ken Dodd goes away and is replaced by the Rolling Stones ordering people off of their cloud. It is worth, for once, looking at the immediate history surrounding this moment. In Britain, two things of extreme note are going on. First, the transmission of this story coincided with the breaking of the Moors murders, a series of five brutal child murders committed around Manchester. The murders are named thusly because two of the graves were discovered in Saddleworth Moor. We should take a quick moment to define "moor" here – rural, uncultivated hilly areas of Britain. They'll be worth knowing around 1970 or so.

The other thing to know about the last month or so of British culture is that there has been an escalating crisis in the colony of Rhodesia, which we now know as Zimbabwe. You may recall from a few previous entries occasional remarks about the UK losing another African colony now and again. Mostly these went pretty well. The fact of the matter is that the UK was really good at losing colonial power, that is, up until Rhodesia. Rhodesia was a disaster.

The main problem was that the UK's policy under Harold Wilson was that it would not grant a colony independence unless the ruling powers in the country were the ethnic majority. That is to say, the UK actively declined to have a situation where it would liberate a colony in such a way that white colonists and their descendants formed the government. Ian Smith, prime minister of Southern Rhodesia (as it was known to the British), disagreed, and over the four weeks that *The Myth Makers* aired, the situation hurtled towards its resolution, which came five days after the end of the serial when Ian Smith and his supporters signed the Unilateral Declaration of Independence, separating from the UK and establishing a white minority government. The situation was a complete disaster – the UK was under enormous international pressure to stop Smith from declaring independence by whatever means necessary, while within the UK opinions were divided on whether a minority white government was actually all that bad. Remember, after all, that the whole kerfuffle with Gandhi in India was only resolved about twenty years ago. The British Empire was clearly dying, but that didn't mean that there wasn't a vocal chunk of people who would fight for it until the bitter end.

I say all of this to stress that the first three episodes of *The Myth Makers*, with its broad comedy of the impersonal irritations of war, would have had a particular tone airing in this climate. With the real possibility of a British military action looming and the general darkness of horrifying child murders in the news, the dark and pessimistic humor of *The Myth Makers* must have struck a very particular and frankly powerful chord. Which is crucial for the fourth episode of the story, which may be the best-timed episode to date.

Because come the final episode, the comedy drops out horrifyingly. The story veers abruptly from a comedic historical to something that feels like it's just shredding the basic structure of Doctor Who. Some of the tropes of narrative collapse from *The Chase* come in – a character called Katarina is hastily introduced amidst a wave of everyone acting like they've known her for three episodes now. But unlike *The Chase*, this is not a funny episode. This is, instead, an episode where half the characters brutally murder the other half, and the Doctor runs around trying desperately to collect the TARDIS crew and escape.

It's something we haven't seen before. The Doctor doesn't save the day here. He barely escapes with his life. Not since *The Aztecs*, really, have we seen the Doctor simply get out of a situation at all costs instead of saving the day. And there, the only real loss was the perfect victim, and it was a moral parable about changing history. Here it's a bloody massacre. The massacre may have been unavoidable, but the reversal wasn't – after all, *The Reign of Terror* and *The Romans* both involved inevitable calamities, but remained comedic as they reached them. The decision to pull the comedy out from under this story wasn't necessary.

And it does become anti-comedy. The most striking sign of this is the end fates of the two villains of the piece. Odysseus goes from a vaguely comedic figure to an extremely dark, threatening figure. Cassandra, on the other part, goes from a snarling antagonist to a tragic figure who is ultimately cut down by Odysseus.

Meanwhile, in the chaos of things, the Doctor loses Vicki. I mean loses. Not that she dies – she doesn't. Instead, she runs off to be with Troilus, taking on the name Cressida. But, notably, we are denied a proper farewell sequence for her. By all appearances, she makes it into the TARDIS, until we see her later on the battlefield with Troilus promising to help him rebuild – specifically to go help Aeneas found Rome, which is oddly circular given that her first adventure after joining the TARDIS is *The Romans*. But, more significantly, her entire departure is consumed, along with her name and identity. She loses her status as a companion of the Doctor's and becomes a Trojan woman. This, I think, is some of why Vicki is marginalized as a companion – she really was fantastic, and did a ton to establish what the role of the young female companion was. I've praised her before, and will not belabor the point here, but Maureen O'Brien is undoubtedly one of the overlooked gems of the Hartnell era.

Katarina, meanwhile, gets all but kidnapped onto the TARDIS – taken onboard in the chaos of their departure. She, being an ancient Trojan, does not understand what is going on. She believes herself to have died and gone to the afterlife, and believes the Doctor to be a god – much to his consternation. She's only there because Vicki sent her and told her all would be well. We will see, next story, how well that goes for her, but it is worth tracking her character arc – thrust into the TARDIS because the Doctor destroyed her world with his Trojan Horse idea, promised that all would be well, and was very, very wrong.

As for Steven, in the closing minutes of the story he suffers a gruesome wound in battle, paralleling Vicki's sprained ankle at the end of *Galaxy Four*, but taking now a much more sinister tone. The Doctor admits that he needs to seek medical assistance for Steven. What has changed so that the essentially similar endings – a member of the TARDIS crew carrying an injury – take such different tones? The answer, it seems, is *Mission to the Unknown* – the reminder of the fact that the Doctor can't save everybody. After the Doctor's failure last story (a failure he doesn't even know about) his status as an absolute hero who saves the day is endangered. Now it is shattered. Sometimes the Doctor can't win.

In this regard, *The Myth Makers* is by far the best historical we've seen. The last episode is a brutal sucker punch that advances the themes we've seen. This is the weakest we've seen the Doctor. When we saw his cowardice in the Cave of Skulls, it was because he was still learning to be the Doctor. By now he knows, and his failures are a sign of something far more troubling. Perhaps being the Doctor isn't enough. Which is an interesting and even appealing point, but there's something more unsettling underneath it: it doesn't seem to be a point the series is making. It seems to be the new concept of it. It seems to be what the series has to say about itself right now. The note that the Doctor doesn't always win is only interesting when juxtaposed against the frequency with which he does. As a point unto itself, "the Doctor is kind of rubbish" is horrifying.

Two stories in a row we've been told that the Doctor is insufficient and not fit for purpose. Next week, we are told, "The Nightmare Begins." The horror is the idea that it hadn't already started.

Elizabeth Sandifer

Doesn't It Just Burn When You Face Me (*The Daleks' Master Plan*)

It's November 13, 1965. The Rolling Stones are still on top. They'll be replaced by the Seekers. The Beatles will take the Christmas number one, hold it for five weeks, then turn it over to the Spencer Davis Group, followed by, finally, on January 27, the Overlanders. I'd list other artists in the charts, but it's just going to be exhausting.

The Rhodesia thing worsens. The UK passes the Race Relations Act, its first attempt to combat racial discrimination legislatively. *Rubber Soul*, *Doctor Zhivago*, and *A Charlie Brown Christmas* all debut. The first Acid Test occurs in San Francisco, there are coups in both Nigeria and the Central African Republic, and India and Pakistan successfully negotiate peace. Finally, Indira Gandhi is sworn in as prime minister of India.

Those of you who like arithmetic may have noticed how we've covered twelve weeks there. That's not a mistake. The story for this essay, *The Daleks' Master Plan*, is a mammoth twelve-parter, not counting its prequel, *Mission to the Unknown*. It is by far the longest Doctor Who story ever, running nearly five and a half hours. And not for the first time, but thus far the most important time, we're going to have to pause here and look at what this story means to Doctor Who as a whole. It's the pinnacle of John Wiles' tenure as Doctor Who producer, which admittedly only began last story and ends two stories hence. It is, in other words, absolutely epic, and everybody knew it. It said so in our handy 1980s books on the series that listed all the episodes. Really, I quote Peter Haining's *Doctor Who: A Celebration*, which says that this story is "quite simply the longest-ever Doctor Who story and also one of the best."

Seventy-five percent of it is also missing. So for a long time, that description was what we got. *The Daleks' Master Plan* was the big Hartnell epic that was really good and missing. And seventy-five percent gone is an improvement. The second episode was only found in 2004. Prior to its discovery, major characters from the story simply didn't exist anymore. It wasn't novelized for years, because it was just too long. (Finally in 1989 John Peel did it as a two-volume set.) In other words, it was one of the great, lost epics of Doctor Who. There are a couple of these scattered through Doctor Who history – stories that were allegedly among the greats of their era but were missing and couldn't ever be seen.

To put it another way, in the '80s Doctor Who got into the habit of remaking some of its old classics for new viewers. Mostly these were disasters, and we'll talk about them when we get there. The point is that this practice didn't start in the '80s. It started in 1973, when two six-parters were quietly welded together to form a twelve-part epic that, after some misdirection in the first story, turned out to be a Dalek epic. That's how good this story's reputation was. It was so good that there was a desire to redo it eight years later.

Life's been hard on the story since the 1983 guide, though. In 1992, the two surviving episodes at the time, the fifth and tenth, finally made it out for home viewing on a documentary called *Daleks: The Early Years*, sparking a bit of a rethink. The problem is that what we knew about the story before seeing those episodes was that it was a massive epic of Daleks in which tons of people died. The novelization had come out super-late in 1989, so hardly anyone had read it. A few hardcore fans would have seen screenings of the missing episodes at conventions, but the fact of the matter is, this was the first time most people saw anything of this allegedly brilliant epic.

The problem is that the two episodes that were surviving were completely not what people thought this story was or, at the time, wanted it to be. (They're still not really what people want *The Daleks' Master Plan* to be, necessarily, though this is more of a problem with people than with the story.) The fifth episode involves some bizarre comedy involving Daleks, mice, and the possibility of mice inventing teleporters (Yes. Douglas Adams did watch this at the age of thirteen. Why do you ask?), and the tenth episode is a strange farce about Daleks, intergalactic emperors, the Monk, and a bunch of Egyptians. They're miles from the dark epic we were promised – so violent it never got sold abroad, Peter Haining told us! Where was our violence? Why were there mice?

And so the great re-evaluation began, and the story was ruled a brilliant idea that was way too long and brought down by the silliness (which was, predictably, laid at the feet of Dennis Spooner, who had done cleanup on Nation's apparently functionally non-existent scripts. While it's probably true that the funny bits were Spooner, this badly misunderstands the nature of his contribution). And so it was for a while, until in 2004 the second episode was discovered and finally people actually saw one of the bits of the story that looked like what we'd been promised in our 1980s episode guides. 2004 was also when Loose Cannon got their reconstruction out, making the story even remotely available for people. And the new consensus is . . . well, there isn't really one yet. There's only been two top-down attempts to review Doctor Who done post 2004. Miles and Wood make a good case for the idea that the story works but is so far afield of what we think of as the Doctor Who format these days as to be impossible to judge. Rob Shearman and Toby Hadoke seem to like it, but get a bit burnt out on it.

OK. So we've got all that down? Good. Now throw it all out. Absolutely nobody understands this story. Miles and

Wood come closest when they say that it doesn't work like modern Doctor Who, and are right to suggest that viewing it as a weekly serial makes it make more sense, but they don't actually explain how it works. And it's worth explaining how it works, because this is, in many ways, the most '60s Doctor Who story. It's not in terms of its cultural references (although those are deeply 1960s as well), but in terms of its structure, pacing, and approach to storytelling. Understand how this works and almost all of the rest of '60s Doctor Who clears up.

I've talked in passing about how Doctor Who aired in the 1960s and how modern conceptions of Doctor Who are unsuited to it. Never has that been more important than here. So let's review. Doctor Who was on around fourty or so weeks of the year. It aired on one of the two channels that existed at the time it debuted, and by the time of *The Daleks' Master Plan*, one of three. Television transmission in the 1960s was on the old 405-line system – that is, there were 405 lines of information used to constitute a television picture, as opposed to the later 625-line system, which is in turn distinct from modern digital television. In technical terms, what this means is that the image was made up of less information – it was . . . I'll go ahead and just quote from Miles and Wood here, because they do a bang-up job of explaining it:

Its mode of address was both to convey the viewer to somewhere extraordinary, and to visit people in the intimacy of their living rooms. Intimacy is a key word here, because 405-line broadcasting was a dialogue with the viewers.

Specifically, they clarify that the issue was that the 405-line broadcast screen, in a literal sense, worked differently and thus interacted with viewers differently. The screens did poorly in light, and so had to be watched in dimmed rooms. The pictures were fuzzy, requiring the viewer to engage in an act of explicit interaction with the screen and to actively interpret the images as representing things. This is another aspect of the lack of realism in Doctor Who. The images of Doctor Who never seemed like reality in the first place.

The overall format of the experience – commercial-free and linked together with continuity announcers so that a given show was something that was part of an unceasing experience of The Day's Transmission – encouraged this sort of interactive approach. The television would tell you what you were going to see, and then you did the work of seeing it. Doctor Who was scary because it was part of a defined space in the televisual day and week marked out for being scary. This also explains the oddly presentational style we've seen – both at its high points (and I will defend *The Web Planet* as a high point of the series tooth and nail against the mobs of people who just don't have a clue what it is they're actually watching) and its low points (namely the *Mary Celeste* sequence of *The Chase*, where the show veers way too far in the "tell people what they're seeing" direction).

On top of that, episodes had individual titles, and cliffhangers often extended from one into the next. We really see this here, with this story picking up immediately from the panic at the end of *The Myth Makers*. This is in marked contrast to the modern approach, where these stories are reskinned as discrete entities and packaged as individual movies. So instead of being able to watch Season One of Doctor Who on Netflix, you can get DVDs of "The Beginning" (the first thirteen episodes), *The Keys of Marinus*, or *The Aztecs*, each treated as discrete stories that are marketed more like films than television.

This is not how the show was actually written or experienced. Yes, individual stories had separate writers and directors, and you could see where one left off and the next began, but what you didn't get was the idea that the episode entitled "Volcano" was "*The Daleks' Master Plan, Part 8 of 12*." Nobody even knew the phrase *The Daleks' Master Plan* in 1966. It was just another episode of Doctor Who, aired on Saturday evening that the family sat down for and made an experience out of. Yes, it was clearly part of a larger Dalek story that had been going on for a while now, and didn't seem terribly near to finishing up, but first and foremost it was the thing that happened around six o'clock on Saturdays, and had been basically every week for two years now. It was part of a serial, which went on over real time with cliffhangers, which we've already established were moments for the audience to engage with the show for the week between episodes. Thought of like this, *The Daleks' Master Plan* isn't five and a half hours long. It's four months long, counting *Mission to the Unknown*. And as I've been saying, really it's longer than that; it's been paying off plot threads that started way back in *The Time Meddler.*

This is a mode of interpretation we just don't have anymore. There's no vocabulary for it. It's impossible to reconstruct in the mode we watch television in today. For instance, I watched it via some DVD rips and a digitization of a VHS tape from Loose Cannon being streamed over a wireless network to an Apple TV hooked up to a 30" HD LCD television via an HDMI cable. Even though the word "television" appears in the description of both this and *The Daleks' Master Plan* as it aired in 1965/'66, we're not really talking about the same medium here. Watching it today you get one of two choices – actively try to reconstruct the experience of the original medium, or deludedly pretend this is television as you understand it. If you pick option B, you get a conclusion along the lines of "this is neat, but a bit of a mess." If you pick option A, you suddenly realize why everyone in 1983 remembered this story so fondly from when they were growing up.

So let's try to translate this into modern terms. First of all, let's rubbish the idea that this is a twelve-part story. It's not. It's really about four separate stories, two of which are nested inside others, one of which is a direct sequel to another, and all of which are contributing to the larger serial that is Doctor Who.

The first story is five episodes long. The first of these was *Mission to the Unknown*, and the second of them is "The Nightmare Begins," more commonly thought of as the first episode of *The Daleks' Master Plan*. In the middle of that was the second story, *The Myth Makers*. So what we had was a story that opened with a reminder that the Doctor doesn't always show up, then took a brief digression to show that even if he does it might not be so great. Then it returns to the situation where he previously didn't show and has him show up. All of this is part of the storytelling of *The Daleks' Master Plan* – if the five episodes previous hadn't been an extended exploration of the possibility that the Doctor could fail, this story would not have the tone and resonance it does in the first episode.

In other words, there's a huge amount of this story that has already been established the moment we see the TARDIS actually show up. The TARDIS shows up in a state of panic. As viewers, we immediately recognize that we're landing back in the Dalek story from a month ago. We arrive in chaos. Katarina is in the TARDIS clearly out of place and confused. Steven is critically injured. Daleks are conspiring to take over the universe. And at this point, after the last five weeks, there is no real reason why we should expect the Doctor to be able to save the day. Even he seems out of his depth, unaware of the direness of the situation. He quite likes Katarina, and once he makes it out of the TARDIS seems almost to forget about Steven in favor of a nice romp around the deadly jungles.

Then comes the real genius of these first four episodes. This is something that, again, people miss. Another one of the reasons this is a big epic of a story is that it's Nicholas Courtney's first appearance in Doctor Who as Bret Vyon. This is touted as one of the big parts of the story. Reading about it, you'd think he was in practically the whole thing. He's touted more than Mavic Chen, the Guardian of the Solar System who spends all twelve episodes plotting with the Daleks and generally being a ridiculous and awesome villain. He's actually only in four episodes. But man, what an impact he has.

Early on, he encounters the Doctor, and tries to demand the key to the TARDIS. The Doctor engages in his usual chinwagging and charisma to try to talk his way out of it. And in response, Bret Vyon does something we have never seen anyone do to the Doctor before. He simply says "Give me the key, or I'll kill you." And this quickly re-establishes the theme of the last five episodes. The Doctor is not the toughest thing in the universe. (Bret Vyon goes on to an even better scene in the second episode, in which he takes over a spaceship by walking onto the bridge, pulling a gun, and saying, and I quote, "I'm taking over this spaceship." The point is clear. He is every bit the ontological force the Doctor is, epic and heroic because he says he is.)

These four episodes are a tense runaround with enormous stakes. The Daleks have a bunch of delegates from across the universe, all with strange alien mannerisms. They have Mavic Chen, Guardian of the Solar System, selling out the whole solar system and suavely helping the Daleks. Their goal appears to be the conquest of everything – ever. They have a super-weapon called the Time Destructor. And the only thing standing in their way is the Doctor, his injured friend, his worshipful handmaiden, and Bret Vyon, the British Nick Fury.

We should take a moment to expand on this claim. There is zero reason to think Steranko was directly influenced by Doctor Who, as he almost certainly didn't see it when he started making Nick Fury a straight mirror of Bret Vyon in 1968. This is amazing, as anyone who looks at the two would immediately conclude that one must be a straight rip-off of the other. As we have already seen, this is not the first time that Doctor Who has managed the puzzling feat of obviously inspiring something without actually having any direct link to it. Honestly, it rapidly becomes easier to just assume that Doctor Who is some sort of mystical phenomenon that leeches into the zeitgeist than it is to try to make sense of this. See also the first shot back in *An Unearthly Child*. What's particularly strange is how these moments of ridiculous prescience on Doctor Who's part – doing one of the most acclaimed runs in comics history three years earlier – get put right alongside hilarious anachronisms like the importance of magnetic tape in the far future.

As you might imagine, this builds stressfully. The Doctor manages to escape Kembel with the Tarranium core of the Dalek superweapon (which, despite its name, bears more than a passing analogy to a nuclear bomb), but an escaped convict makes it on board with them.

And here we get the climax of this story. So let's talk for just a moment about Katarina. She's a character who has very little to do in this story. Three episodes into it, on her fourth appearance overall, she reiterates her near worshipful attitude towards the Doctor, and prays for divine intervention. The Doctor treats her with loving patronization. She is, by all appearances, our new female companion, replacing Vicki. And towards the end of the third episode, she reiterates how she knows that she's safe with the Doctor.

Mere seconds later, she's grabbed by the convict and lets out the most blood-curdling, horrifying, anguished scream we have ever heard a companion give in Doctor Who. And that's our third-episode cliffhanger.

And then, less than five minutes into her fifth appearance on Doctor Who . . . she's dead. She sacrifices herself by blowing herself and her attacker out the airlock. That's the cliffhanger resolution. Remember that cliffhangers are primarily about audience interaction – part and parcel with the interactive dialogue of the 405-line era. The question isn't "What happens to the Doctor?" It's "How are they going to get out of this one?" And in the first minutes of the next episode, we get the answer.

They don't. Katarina, the innocent, naive girl who was all but shoved onto the TARDIS by Vicki, dies. And this is hammered home. It's like nothing we have ever seen before. She dies in a lengthy, anguished, painful sequence that just spits in the face of the audience. And look at what it comes after – four episodes of dark, brooding tension and real suggestion that maybe the Doctor isn't good enough. This has been built to over the course of the story thus far. And here, again, he isn't good enough. He loses a companion. And the show rubs it in – shrieking music plays over an effects shot of her dead body floating away in space.

As brutal as this is, to really understand what's going on here we need to go a little further and learn some production details. See, Katarina wasn't supposed to die here. Katarina wasn't actually supposed to exist here. She's by far the most minor companion ever – she never does anything, and appears in five episodes total, one of them only for the first five minutes. And she's a fill-in.

It was supposed to be Vicki.

Vicki – the Scouse future girl who represented the mods and the youth rebellion that was at the heart of cultural Britain – was supposed to be flushed out an airlock in a shock cliffhanger resolution. Think of how that would have played out – especially after the second episode of *The Myth Makers*, where Cassandra declares that Vicki is a spy and must be killed, and then we get "Next episode: Death of a Spy." Clearly this is meant to make us think Vicki might die, and to make us spend a week trying to find some other way to account for the title. And of course Vicki makes it out just fine. The cliffhanger always turns out OK. And on the surface, this looks like a similar cliffhanger – how is the companion going to get out of this? Had they carried through with it and killed Vicki here, it would have been the single cruelest, most cynical moment in Doctor Who history. The plucky joy of British youth, slaughtered. And all of that would have aired right as Vietnam War protests really kicked up in the US, and as the UK careened towards a possible war with Rhodesia. This isn't just reactionary. It's savage – a declaration of the fundamental failure of '60s counterculture made in late 1965, right as it was really starting to kick up to its heyday.

And then to cap it off, at the end of the episode, after some hype about Kingdom, the crack special agent coming in to clean this up, we learn that Kingdom is Sara Kingdom, decked out in a catsuit with a laser gun. She strides into the ship and guns down Bret Vyon – the seemingly unstoppable character who the Doctor has just been treating like a companion mere moments before. It's odd that Katarina and Bret – who have basically the same amount of screen time – are treated so differently by later fandom, with Katarina being the first companion to die (even though it wasn't until 2004 that we actually had an episode she appeared in to watch) and Bret being "that part Nicholas Courtney played before the Brigadier." Within the episode, they're clearly meant to be of equal importance, and this episode is meant to be an even more shocking punch in the gut than the end of *The Myth Makers*.

That's the first and second stories of *The Daleks' Master Plan* done with two to go. And these two are going to be nested again. So, to recap, it's December 11, 1965. The Seekers are at number one. And after the most brutally cruel episode of Doctor Who to date, we get ... comedy about mice.

We get Jean Marsh striding around imperiously in her catsuit of awesome and William Hartnell doing some truly impressive writhing around in pain (by truly impressive I mean absolutely ridiculous). Clearly we're watching "Counter-Plot," known as, for a long time, the one of two *Daleks' Master Plan* episodes we actually had. And it's one that is just completely misread, because we took it in isolation and assumed it was all like this. Had the fourth episode survived instead, one imagines the reception of this story would have been radically different for years – especially because, since we do have the clips of Katarina's death, we know how brutal that episode really is.

And here's where that serial thing really comes in. It's December 11. Every Doctor Who story since October 9 – two months ago now – has come to the same conclusion. The Doctor doesn't always win. He's 0–3 in the last three outings. And here we're starting up another strand of the plot, and it goes comedic and light, with silly bits and mice, and Daleks exterminating the mice because they might be powerful alien overlords. Nobody watching this who has been following the serial thinks this is a daft comedy episode. The comedy is bleakly unfunny. This is where Spooner's genius really shows through, in fact. By now, we've been better trained to expect the other shoe to drop than we have been to enjoy the Doctor Who stock tropes. And so the comedic bits – so striking when the episode is watched in isolation – take on a very different, uncomfortable tone. Look past them at the actual plot of the episode. The panic and tension mounts faster and faster – the Doctor gets teleported back to Kembel, the Daleks hunt him down, and he escapes only because Steven – in an oddly unfamiliar role as the slow one, being from earlier in human history than Sara and obviously less knowledgeable than the Doctor – risks life and limb to make a fake Tarranium core that the Doctor can fake the Daleks out with.

The mice are not a stupid digression or a time-waster. They're a reset button – a clear marker that we've finished one story and started another, and are back to a status quo. But that's terrifying. We know this is going to go wrong. As soon as the action speeds up again, after three sucker punches, we're just waiting for the inevitable.

But then, to make everything even more confusing, that story gets interrupted after two episodes by another. So let's use that nice vertical line trick I worked up for *The Myth Makers*, and deal with the fourth story that is *The Daleks' Master Plan* . . .

It's December 25, 1965. It's the Beatles at number one now, for those playing at home.

So, as I said, the seventh through tenth episodes kind of come out of left field, interrupting the story in progress. Basically, this is a four-episode redo of *The Chase* that opens with a Christmas episode in which the Daleks don't even appear. For some bizarre reason, this is what fans fixate on. In particular, they fixate on the fact that the Christmas episode ends with the Doctor breaking the fourth wall to wish the viewers a merry Christmas, but more broadly the fact that the episode is half set in a Liverpool police station and half on a Hollywood silent film set.

I will say that I have no clue whatsoever why anyone objects to this. I mean, jump ahead to the eleventh episode of the story, and pretend that had followed straight from the sixth instead of taking a detour. Plotwise, this is quite easy – it would have been nothing to cut the story down to eight episodes. But imagine sitting down on Christmas to watch the eleventh episode. Or, better yet, imagine the twelfth episode on New Year's. It would be the most jarring, tonally inappropriate thing imaginable.

The show was airing in December on a year that Christmas fell on a Saturday. There was surely no question of putting apocalyptically dark Dalek fights on the holidays. So the show had to find an excuse to go do something fun instead. So we got two pure comedy episodes of the Doctor running around various set pieces. A Liverpool police station (which is not an arbitrary choice after *Z-Cars*), a silent film set, and, in the New Year's episode, landing on a cricket green, at which point the commentators just try to figure out if this has ever happened before. (Yes, I already told you, Douglas Adams watched this when he was thirteen. Why do you keep asking?) This is followed by the return of the Monk from *The Time Meddler* (thus establishing why I claimed this storyline was as long as I did).

So why the next two, which feature Mavic Chen, suavely evil Guardian of the Solar System, the Monk, the Daleks, the Doctor, Steven, Sara Kingdom, and a bunch of Egyptians? Mostly because the Doctor is now off Kembel and has the Tarranium core. The Doctor can't steer his TARDIS, as we know, so we have to find some way of getting him back to Kembel and getting the Tarranium to the Daleks. And that's all the ninth and tenth episodes are – two episodes of getting out of the detour forced by Christmas. The Monk is brought in to give the Doctor a way back to Kembel, and we do a quick Egyptian runaround to follow on the two comedic episodes so we can get back to the main plot. That's all these four episodes are – an extension to the story caused by the intrusion of the holidays.

Which means that if you want to bludgeon *The Daleks' Master Plan* into a normal structure, the thing to do is to just cut the seventh through tenth episodes entirely. Drop them. Don't even watch them. Jump straight from the sixth episode to the eleventh, and pretend the Doctor had to give up the real Tarranium core instead of a fake one. You can just pick it up and go from there, and get a proper eight-part Dalek story in two clear four-part chunks. The only thing that's majorly going on in these four is some Christmas fun, some plot hole filling, and the establishment of Sara Kingdom as the new companion.

I mean, there are a few neat things. We can do some nice commentary on the genre-bending abilities of Doctor Who and Hollywood, and how it picks up on the Morton Dill segments of *The Chase*. There's a line about the Doctor's human form just being a disguise that's chilling and mysterious and something someone should have picked up on since 1966. There's the best technobabble explanation in the history of the show, namely the Doctor just openly refusing to explain something to Steven and literally handwaving it away with not so much as an "I'll explain later." And there's a bunch of stuff that heavily reiterates the fact that the Doctor is not, in 1966, a Time Lord and that it is next to impossible to read the whole Time War business into these episodes and have them make a damned bit of sense. (This storyline would feel so much more normal to today's audience if the Master instead of the Monk were in it, as it did to a 1973 audience.) And, tellingly, these four episodes, once again, end with the Doctor losing and having to relinquish the Tarranium core, putting him at 0–4. We can note all of those and have.

But really, this is here because the scheduling in 1965/'66 demanded it. It's not part of a twelve-episode epic to be watched in one shot, or even in two or three shots. It's part of an ongoing, always-on serial that happened to be airing on

Christmas. It made perfect sense in 1965/'66 when it was aired, and it was only designed to air then, once. Any questions about how it "holds up today" or of the pacing of it when taken as a twelve-part epic just miss the point, which is that those are arbitrary standards to judge the story by in the first place.

In any case, let's head back to the story in progress with the eleventh episode. And again, to reiterate we really could have jumped straight here. The sixth episode could just as easily have ended with the Doctor having to cough up the real Tarranium core, and then cliffhangered straight into the eleventh episode. It would have made total sense from a plotting perspective.

Given that, the eleventh episode, "The Abandoned Planet," plays brilliantly. It's one of the periodic Doctor-free episodes, a nice parallel to where we started in *Mission to the Unknown*. Steven and Sara have the bulk of the work, trying to figure out where the Doctor is and what he's up to. Meanwhile, Mavic Chen gets the endpoint of his plot, going from valued ally to the Daleks to utterly superfluous. As the episode plays on, it becomes clearer and clearer that the Daleks will, in fact, eventually kill him too. But not a lot happens. It's easy to mistake this episode as a seventh consecutive episode that doesn't up to the genius of the fourth episode. But that misses the way that audience expectations are being played with.

No. This is bold and clever. The Doctor has, as I said, suffered four consecutive defeats now. And so he's removed from the picture, and the audience is invited to remember the fact that, flawed as we now see him to be, he's still far better than the alternatives. We miss him and want him to be found. And when the episode ends without him showing, with Steven and Sara being led alone into the Dalek base, it's scary. Sara ends up being our audience identification character, by and large, stressing over and over again that it's important to find the Doctor (while Steven seems, all told, fairly competent on his own). All of this builds the tension extraordinarily.

And so we come to the finale. Mavic Chen, our charismatic villain, has fallen completely, seeming almost delusional in his demand that the Daleks respect him and clearly doomed. It's not even clear whether he wants power, at this point, or whether he's just desperate for the Daleks to approve of him. And eight minutes into the finale, the Doctor finally returns.

This should be good. This should be where he wins, and it's all OK. The Doctor seems determined. He has a plan. But Hartnell is good. He really is an extraordinarily good actor when he is well enough to do it. And in this episode he is. He has a plan, but he seems frantic, perhaps even scared. He tells Sara and Steven to get back to the TARDIS, and he runs off with the activated Time Destructor.

But Sara believes the Doctor needs her. She goes back for him.

After four consecutive defeats – *Mission to the Unknown, The Myth Makers*, and twice now in this story, perhaps we expect victory. That is, after all, what the Doctor's disappearance from the eleventh episode seems to set up – that the Doctor will return to the story and save the day. That's why you remove him from the story – to show that he's still needed. Surely we've seen the worst in the fourth episode, if nothing else. Surely.

No.

The Time Destructor is horrifying like nothing we have seen before. We expected a straightforward superweapon – a bomb. But no. Instead we get a glowing, shrieking ball. Seemingly, it's harmless, even silly at first. But then it turns awful and horrible. It is shredding the Doctor and Sara, savagely. Sara ages before our eyes, well aware of what is happening to her. She knows she's dying. And when this starts to happen . . .

This isn't suspense. This is tragedy. After four defeats, the Doctor – never quite a hero anyway – seems miles from

Elizabeth Sandifer

iconic and mythic. He's so . . . vulnerable. And as he staggers
back to the TARDIS with a dying Sara Kingdom at his side,
we know how this is going to play out. All Sara's youthful,
sexy power – her catsuit and laser pistol – is gone now. What
remains is a shell to hold a fragile old woman, disintegrating
before our eyes. It's brutally long, taking place over minutes.
The horrific, shrieking shot of Katarina drifting off into space
at least came after the death. Here the sense of anticipation –
the thing that was the entire justification of things like *The
Dalek Invasion of Earth*'s first episode, where we wait endlessly
for the Daleks to arrive – is turned against us. We know how
this will play out. We're forced to watch anyway.

It works. And it works because of the structure – because
of the weird serialized nature of it. It works because we have
had the structure of Doctor Who taken apart in front of us
over and over again for nearly three months straight. It works
because the show has been setting us up for this for months
now, showing us worse and worse defeats, showing us how
powerless the Doctor can be. This payoff can only happen in
the serialized structure of a show that is constantly on. This
payoff is absolutely a product of everything Doctor Who is in
1965 and 1966.

The Doctor collapses. Steven charges out of the
TARDIS, trying to save him, and manages to flip the Time
Destructor into reverse, making it run time backwards
instead. It's too late for Sara, but just enough for the Doctor
to be dragged to safety. And we see the Daleks return . . . the
Daleks, who by now are the Daleks as we know them, the
ultimate foe of the Doctor, perfectly matched, each side well
aware of the other and full of nothing but hatred. It's time for
the final showdown, after all of this.

But we're denied that. Instead, we get the Daleks
screaming as they are regressed. This is the first meaty death
of the Daleks – the first time they have seemed like flesh, not
robots. The Dalek casings collapse, revealing the shriveled
mutants within. It's physical. It's grotesque.

And in the end, Steven is left to mourn the stupidity of it all. Katarina, Bret, and Sara, all dead. Kembel destroyed.

The Doctor has failed. Again. This was the consequence of everything that went before. That all the youth and hope he represented would be dashed on the rocks.

A flip through the news gives context: Rhodesia, the brutal coup in Nigeria, another former British colony, the Vietnam War. There is horror and death in the world.

Previously, we had thought those things were opposed by the Doctor, and balanced. We thought that he could save us. Now, on Kembel, where the lush jungle has been reduced to a barren desert full of bodies, we know the truth: the Doctor loses sometimes.

There's an episode next week, of course, as impossible as it seems. Something actually follows from this. The story continues. Surely, after all of this, after five defeats, after this horrible, gruesome death of Sara Kingdom, things must turn around.

Surely tomorrow must be better?

Time Can Be Rewritten: *Guardian of the Solar System*

It's July of 2010. The series is in great shape. Steven Moffat's first series just wrapped to massive acclaim if not to fantastic ratings towards the end, although those proved to be a small blip rather than a lasting problem. This is the first time we've gotten to deal with something released in an era where everything was hunky dory for the series in a Time Can Be Rewritten entry. Sure, we did *The Time Travellers*, which was between the Eccleston season and the first Tennant season, but that was the death spasm of a being-cancelled book line, and it's hard to really enjoy it. And everyone was more than a little nervous about how the regeneration would be taken by the public. This? This is a release in the still healthy and fun Big Finish Audios line well into the point where the new series had become a fundamental British establishment again. This is Doctor Who in an era where we can kick up our feet and enjoy ourselves.

Amusingly, as with the last time we dealt with something from a healthy period in Doctor Who history, this is written by Simon Guerrier, whose praises I already sang earlier in the volume. At this point, I think we can safely say that Guerrier has established himself as the person to go to for compelling stories set in the Hartnell era – a task that, as a perusal of the Time Can Be Rewritten entries in this book shows, no shortage of writers have failed to be up to. But in many ways, this takes the cake.

There are, as this book points out in several places, some aspects of classic Doctor Who that are fetishized as Stuff Doctor Who Fans Know. For instance, there is an official list of companions. (There are several, actually, to deal with disputes about the original.) But one consequence of the existence of an official list of companions is that we know for certain that Katarina and Sara Kingdom are companions, even though Katarina appears in five episodes of Doctor Who and Sara Kingdom appears in eight, all of which are part of one story. (Although as we just saw, calling *The Daleks' Master Plan* one story is misleading.)

So here's Simon Guerrier doing the further adventures of Sara Kingdom. Which, on the one hand, feels like a moment of ultimate fanwankery – let's bring back the most obscure character imaginable. And on the other hand, seems like what continuity and a deep history of Doctor Who is for. If you can't dig deep and brush off the most obscure and bizarre ideas in the series and try to make them work, what's the point in having the classic series?

And so Guerrier, taking off from an idea John Peel came up with when novelizing *The Daleks' Master Plan* in which a few months of adventures are inserted between the seventh and eighth episodes (thus giving Sara room to be a proper companion) expands on her story. Except he goes further than that. *Guardian of the Solar System* is actually the third in a trilogy of Sara Kingdom audios that deal with the idea that in one of these adventures, Sara's consciousness became embedded in a house and has been running the house long after Sara herself died at the end of *The Daleks' Master Plan*. This second Sara, across the trilogy, relates her story to Robert, who comes upon the house and ends up staying there.

Thus these stories each offer both a main story and a frame story. This allows Guerrier to develop Sara Kingdom significantly beyond what we see on screen. And Guerrier uses this opportunity to show something unique about Sara Kingdom that other Hartnell companions lack. Hartnell companions, good or bad, tend to be general roles rather than developed characters. Even the best of them – Ian and Barbara – are ordinary people who are forced into standard sci-fi roles. There's nothing comparable to, for instance, Martha's unrequited love plot running over all her stories, or the tangled soap opera dynamics of Amy, River, and the Doctor.

But for Sara Kingdom, there is. Her plot over the course of *The Daleks' Master Plan* involves her killing her brother and then turning on the faction that made her do it, renouncing everything she previously believed in along the way. That's a huge character arc that doesn't get room to be explored in her one televised story, and it's this that Guerrier builds up on, expanding Sara from those episodes and giving her a proper character arc.

This story, then, is the climax of that effort, and it serves to resolve Sara's story in two ways simultaneously. First, and in some ways least interestingly, this story wraps up some plot holes in *The Daleks' Master Plan* by having Sara run into her boss Mavic Chen and her brother Brett Vyon about a year prior to the events of that story. Besides clearing up Mavic Chen a bit as a character and making sense out of why he was working with the Daleks, it also takes the not-entirely-surprising but clever twist of having Sara inadvertently cause many of the events of *The Daleks' Master Plan* and being integral to why Chen allies with the Daleks.

Oddly, all of this is wrapped around a plotline involving old men who continually mill about inside of a gigantic clock, initially seeming to operate it, and then later turning out to be continually trying to break it and failing as the clock feeds off of their minds. This gives the entire story an odd poetry – an almost lyrical feel. This is appropriate since so many of the actors from this period of the show had passed on by the time this was recorded, necessitating that a large number of characters be kept to the sidelines.

And so this isn't quite a William Hartnell story. It's a story in his era – not just, as in some returns-to-eras, a story set in his era, but a story that is fundamentally about his era. But it's not of that era. It's a fugue upon that era, a little story unto itself hidden amongst its lesser facets. And this is just a wonderful little thing grafted into the era.

And so its real story is the one outside that. The one seemingly so removed from Doctor Who – a copy of Sara Kingdom saved into the memory of a house. In her time as a house, Sara spent a great deal of time – perhaps centuries – with a man named Robert in the house, providing for him, serving him, conducting a strange new version of her vows as a soldier. This version is changed by the intersection of her life with the Doctor's. It's a version that's now living a sort of fairy tale, to put it in terms of the Steven Moffat season it appeared after.

And in this fairy tale, we've come to the end. Robert cannot stand to see Sara hurt and torture herself with guilt for killing her brother – a guilt she's trying desperately to assuage by living her entire life as a meaningless copy of the vow he represented in her life – and asks of her that she let him take control of the house and set her free. And though she does not want to, she has vowed to serve him, and so must.

And so Sara Kingdom is forced to live her life – to live again after her travels with the Doctor. She's forced to try to pick up the pieces somewhere with a whole new life. She is forced, in other words, to complete her story without the death Terry Nation and Denis Spooner set out for her end. And she can't do it. She comes crawling back to the house and forces herself to finish her story to Robert, which he had made her abandon to let him take over the house. And in doing so, she's forced to admit her complete culpability in killing her brother – that she not only betrayed him in killing him, she betrayed him in causing the situation that led to his fatal confrontation with him. And in doing so, she finally forgives herself.

This isn't an arc that could possibly have taken place in the televisual medium that existed in 1964 and 1965. It couldn't have been a William Hartnell story. It feels, in most regards, like a Matt Smith story. It's of that caliber, certainly. And yet it is woven into the loose strands of the Hartnell era. It is unmistakably a product of the Hartnell era, a love letter to the Hartnell era, and an homage to the Hartnell era.

This is the sort of celebration Doctor Who, in 2010, can still do of itself. This is the sort of history it has. Such that, in its earliest days, stories of the caliber of its most cutting-edge glories can be found.

This is a damn beautiful show.

Not Always. I'm Sorry. (*The Massacre*)

It's February 5, 1966. The number one single is the Overlanders' "Michelle," which will be unseated by Nancy Sinatra with "These Boots Are Made for Walking," which, actually, I'll be able to make something out of later on in this essay, so that's nice. The Spencer Davis Group, Cilla Black, the Beatles, the Beach Boys, and the Rolling Stones all also chart.

News-wise, the most interesting things going on are that the Russians landed a thingy on the Moon, a bunch of governments go up in flames, and military coups. Oh, and the Naval Minister of the UK resigns. Which I suppose is worth mentioning, if only because Christopher Mayhew holds the wonderful distinction of being (I think) the only major politician overseeing a military force to be filmed tripping balls on mescaline. Which, and this is the really good bit, has nothing whatsoever to do with why he resigned. He was just cranky about a change in military policy towards land-based aircraft launches instead of aircraft carriers.

Doctor Who is not going to get around to becoming a full-out drug trip for another eight weeks, though, and it's not even going to be a very good trip. Instead, well, let's recap: twelve-week Dalek epic, massive death toll, and Doctor at the lowest point we've ever seen him and completely frail and mortal. So things must be looking up this week, eh?

Well, OK, perhaps not if you read the title of the story. But as has been pointed out by others, this, more than any other story, is one that visibly loses something when you turn it into a movie with its own title. The official title – *The Massacre of St. Bartholomew's Eve* – is rubbish. For one thing, the massacre in question is on St. Bartholomew's Day. The usual defense of this teensy problem – that the story ends the day before the massacre, and that the story is thus about the eve of the massacre – opens the far larger problem that the title of the story now turns the slaughter of thousands of people into a holiday. For comparison, this would be like setting a story in Nazi Germany on November 8, 1938, and calling it "Kristallnacht Eve."

The alternative title – *The Massacre* – does considerably better, but is still a deeply flawed title in that it gives away the end. It would be like renaming *The Rescue* "The Guy Who's Disguised As a Monster."

Because the thing is, this story hinges on the fact that it's a historical that isn't about a well-known historical event. As has been frequently pointed out, the audience, watching this, would not have a clear idea of how this is all going to play out. It's a story that works precisely because its component parts are not called *The Massacre*, but are instead called, in order, "War of God," "The Sea Beggar," "Priest of Death," and "Bell of Doom."

Let's back up for a moment. We've talked about missing stories, and how good the reconstructions are. Every once in a while, though, you hit one where the reconstructions just aren't up to the task. It's not their fault. Other eras of Doctor Who have the advantage that the producer employed John Cura to point a camera at his TV screen and take pictures throughout the program, giving us pretty high quality images at the rate of about three a minute. Except the producer for these stories – John Wiles – didn't employ him. So instead the reconstructions have to work off of a meager set of publicity photos.

But even if there were telesnaps, I think this would be a strong choice for the story I'd most like to see recovered, for one simple reason. Watching it, there's a gaping ambiguity where I don't think there's supposed to be.

Let's start with what we know for sure about this story from the existing reconstruction. In it, the Doctor and Steven arrive in sixteenth-century France. The Doctor quickly wanders off to go explore, leaving Steven in a tavern where he gets dragged into some political intrigue between the Protestant Huguenots and the Catholic majority in France. Steven blunders about as the situation deteriorates rapidly, meeting a young girl, Anne Chaplet. At the end of the story, the Doctor reappears and tells Steven that they have to go. After they depart, the Doctor reveals that Steven has been witnessing the buildup to a brutal massacre of thousands of Protestants across France. Steven, enraged that the Doctor left Anne to die, storms out of the TARDIS, and then some other stuff happens that we'll come back to later.

One thing that's immediately clear is that, far from *The Daleks' Master Plan* being the culmination of all of the plot threads we've seen since *The Time Meddler*, this story is where they actually come to a head. After a string of brutal failures, this is where the Doctor fails so dramatically and so drastically that even Steven abandons him. (Indeed, one way of looking at this extended plot arc is as Steven's big test of faith in terms of the Doctor.) This is where the Doctor's string of failures finally resolves as a plotline, leaving him at the lowest we have ever seen him as a character, with a bit that is some of the best acting Hartnell ever gives in the series where he stands, alone in the TARDIS for the first time in his life, and he almost decides to give up and go home before realizing that even that choice is lost to him.

But this scene is also the thing we can't figure out from the reconstructions. Is Steven right to leave him? Is the Doctor's monologue – in which he continues to insist he did the right thing and that Steven just doesn't understand – one where we are meant to be sympathetic to him and cross that

Steven left? Or are we meant to be frustrated that our hero doesn't understand why he's doing the wrong thing?

Most of that hinges on a specific ambiguity within the story. See, the Doctor only appears in the first and fourth episodes of the story. But William Hartnell appears in all four. In the second and third episode, he plays the Abbot of Amboise, a savagely anti-Huguenot priest heavily involved in the conspiracy to assassinate a key Huguenot leader. The entire interpretation of the story rests on when the audience and Steven realize that the Abbot is not, in fact, the Doctor.

Certainly given the Doctor's fondness for taking on other people's identities and getting involved, Steven's hypothesis that he might be impersonating the Abbot is a valid one. But is it the most likely circumstance? Within the reconstruction, it's tough to tell. The first episode appears to have a scene in which someone obviously recognizes who the Doctor is as he leaves the pub, and follows him. In theory, that scene should establish firmly that the Doctor is misrecognized as the Abbot early on, and thus that it can't be that he takes on his identity later (as clearly he shares the same face at the start).

But the evidence for that is basically a caption on a reconstruction. Without seeing how that scene of the Doctor being recognized by a Catholic actually played out, it's impossible to tell whether or not it should have been a major clue that when the Abbot appears at the end of the episode and looks just like the Doctor, he's not actually the Doctor. And, of course, the fact that this is a cliffhanger suggests strongly that we are meant to doubt that the Abbot is the Doctor. After all, the revelation that the Doctor is doing his normal impersonation thing is hardly a cliffhanger. If the point of a cliffhanger is, as we have repeatedly understood it, to lead into a week of active engagement with the show where you try to figure out what's going to happen next, then the entire point of that cliffhanger must be trying to figure out whether or not this is in fact the Doctor. Which only makes sense as a cliffhanger if we have some active reason to think that the man who looks just like the Doctor isn't.

Which is where the earlier scene comes in. Looked at from this perspective, it must have given us a reason to think it was not – namely that someone clearly recognized the Doctor.

The other big clue that would be nice to have is Hartnell's acting. By the sound of the recording, it does seem that he's acting the Abbot differently than the Doctor. This is actually one of the biggest debates about the episode, though. Let's give Mad Norwegian Press some more free publicity. On the one hand, we have Tat Wood and Lawrence Miles, who declare in *About Time* that Hartnell's performance is "so radically different from his portrayal of the Doctor as to warrant separate consideration. After this, it's impossible to think of Hartnell's Doctor as anything but a concerted acting performance. The Abbot is cold, ambitious, and word-perfect, with none of the apparently spontaneous 'hmms' and giggles we're used to hearing from the Doctor." Rob Shearman and Toby Hadoke, in *Running Through Corridors*, the other amazing comprehensive review of Doctor Who out from Mad Norwegian, say that "it feels pretty Doctor-ish to me; Hartnell sounds a bit posher, perhaps." (I should note that's Shearman, specifically, and not Hadoke, as the book does distinguish between its two authors, whereas *About Time* does not, making it occasionally tricky to figure out whether it's Wood or Miles I want to denounce at a given moment.)

In the end, it's a case where one really wants to see it. Judging television acting from audio recordings is extremely hard. So much of Hartnell's Doctor is in his poise, how he looks around, and in particular how he uses his hands. Lacking all of that, it's tough to tell whether the Abbot is meant to be read as Hartnell playing a cold, calculating villain or whether he's meant to be Hartnell playing the Doctor playing a cold, calculating villain. The remaining evidence is a split decision. Steven believes the Abbot to be the Doctor, which is telling, but the credit sequences just credit Hartnell as playing the Abbot, dropping his Dr. Who credit. (Of course, whether he ever played "Dr. Who" is an issue too, but we'll deal with that later.)

The reason this is so significant is that judgment of Steven's actions depends on whether the audience agrees with him about whether the Abbot and the Doctor are the same person. And here there are two completely different interpretations of the story that, on the evidence we have, it's impossible to figure out which is correct.

In option number one, Steven's major failing in the story is his choice to delay and wait for the Doctor, who he thinks is impersonating the Abbot, to work it out. He spends an episode and a half trying to figure out what the Doctor is doing. If the audience was supposed to know that Hartnell was playing two different roles, Steven's deference to the villainous Abbot is his major error, and his decision to leave with the Doctor instead of insisting on taking Anne with them is primarily his failure. In this interpretation, the Doctor could have been persuaded to take Anne with them, but Steven continued his deference to the Doctor at the expense of taking action for himself and, just as he was unable to help the Huguenots avoid the massacre, he also failed to help Anne.

In option number two, however, the Abbot is an unfortunate coincidence that screws over Steven. But the primary failure then belongs to the Doctor for simply dropping out of the story with no explanation for three days, and in that time failing even to realize when in French history they are exactly, what's going to happen, and, furthermore, for failing to even save one person. (Contrast this with *The Fires of Pompeii*, where saving one person is precisely what the Doctor does in order to resolve the dilemma of how to handle tragedies of history.) In this interpretation, Steven's anger at the Doctor is the natural culmination of a story arc that's been functionally running for months now.

Notably, in either interpretation, leaving Anne to die was wrong. The question is whether the primary responsibility for that failure lies with Steven or the Doctor. Clearly the idea of the TARDIS crew simply failing to save the day continues in this story, but it's not clear whose failure it is from the reconstruction. (In this case the novelization is no use – Lucarotti's script was heavily rewritten by Donald Tosh, and his novelization restored his original script, meaning that it does not give us a clear idea of how the actors involved were playing their parts. Though, has anyone asked Peter Purves about it?) And it's an amazingly frustrating failure, as it's the difference between this story being the lowest point the Doctor has been brought to, and this story being a story about how Steven is just as imperfect as we know the Doctor to be and is naive for trusting in the Doctor so much after seeing what happened on Kembel.

It's also relevant because of the end of the fourth episode, in which a new companion, Dorothea Chaplet, better known as Dodo, is introduced. While we had Vicki on board I mostly set the Problem of Susan aside, in no small part because Vicki was, by and large, a model for how the problem could be more or less handled. There was obvious affection between Vicki and the Doctor, but it was affection based on genuine friendship that seemed undoubtedly chaste on both sides, and, more to the point, for a reason. One could understand why Vicki liked the Doctor, and why the Doctor liked Vicki. And Vicki had a meaningful role as our starchild mod future.

Dodo forces us to return to the problem. So let's recap it. In a nutshell, the problem is this – given that the Doctor has been cast as male in all eleven incarnations to date, thus resulting in a tendency towards female companions, how does the show deal with the intrusion of sexuality and sexual awakening into its landscape? It is named the Problem of Susan for two reasons. First, it's because I like giving homage to Neil Gaiman. Second, it's because the problem originated with the Doctor's first companion, Susan Foreman, who was ostensibly the Doctor's granddaughter, thus setting up a dynamic by which the Doctor is simultaneously forced to be a protective father figure and a provocative adventurer, two roles which naturally fall on opposite sides of the relationship with developing and emerging sexuality.

In other words, either the Doctor wants to go on madcap adventures with young women (and as the Doctor has a granddaughter and has displayed romantic affection for women on screen, it is hardly difficult to understand why he might like doing that) or he wants to protect his companions from harm. But the two positions are contradictory, in no small part because the role the companion can take in each position is sexualized. If she's on madcap adventures with a magical man, then she's growing up and sexually awakening – she's an empowered woman in control of her desires. Her boots, if you will, are made for walking. If she's being protected, she's a female in peril, and we've sexualized that because we have a bit of a problem with that sort of thing. The companion here is frankly a sex object. Her boots are made for running down corridors screaming. They are never going to walk all over you. (I told you I'd get something out of that song. Not that it would be good.)

Virtually every female companion other than Barbara has had to grapple with that problem. Some do it successfully – sexualizing Vicki is just not that big a problem, because she is explicitly allied with a sexually awakened youth culture. She was unambiguously a character who was having madcap adventures with the Doctor, and if the Doctor she was traveling with were played by Matt Smith instead of William Hartnell, well, watch the last few minutes of *Flesh and Stone* and you'll see how that one plays out. (Heck, Doctor/Vicki is one of two pairings you can plausibly make with the First Doctor. Ironically, the other one is Barbara.)

Dodo, on the other hand, does not so much fall into the Problem of Susan as throw herself into it full-force. She's depicted as a working-class English girl. OK – that's pretty straightforward. Her parents are dead, and her aunt wouldn't care if she ran away from home – that's less straightforward, but OK. We're clearly wedding the youth culture of Vicki to a contemporary London idiom, right?

Except for two big problems. First, the Doctor takes her on board in part because she reminds him of Susan. Which flings her right on the pyre, really. Second, Steven ends up forgiving the Doctor because Dodo's surname – Chaplet – means she might be a descendent of Anne Chaplet. In other words, she's proposed explicitly as a replacement for the girl the Doctor failed to save. But here's the thing, as Miles and Wood slyly point out in *About Time*. Surnames don't pass matrilineally. Which would mean that if Dodo shares Anne's surname because she's a descendent, Anne must have had her out of wedlock. Which is an unusual enough thing that Steven shouldn't assume it. Unless, of course, he has specific reason to think that Anne might have gotten knocked up . . .

So with Dodo, we have a sudden, jarring introduction of a new companion who is, from day one, frankly fraught with problems. Not the least of which is that she is somehow used as the pretext for Steven to return to the TARDIS. (Contrary to some accounts, he does not decide to stay with the Doctor because of Dodo's surname – he has already entered the TARDIS and they've taken off by the time he learns her surname.) In other words, this character, for no clear story reason, serves as the interruption and return to order after the chaos that started with *Mission to the Unknown*. There's no justification for it – she plows into the TARDIS and interrupts the Doctor's self-pitying monologue, and that's it for that sentiment.

Which is the biggest problem with this story, really. On the one hand, the run from *Mission to the Unknown* to this has been extraordinary. If we take the stories on their own, *The Myth Makers* is really staggeringly good, *The Daleks' Master Plan* is quite good once you learn to watch it, and *The Massacre*, up until Dodo charges in, is a fair contender for Hartnell's best story. Even with Dodo it's still pretty clearly the best historical we've seen, with the possible exception of *The Myth Makers*. The Season Three historicals have, by and large, been amazing, and come the closest we've seen to a clear justification for why these stories should be a part of the Doctor Who formula. It's hard to imagine why they'd give them up after a run like this, really. But here we realize something – for all the incredible drama that's been wrung out of the Doctor's repeated failures over the last twenty-one episodes . . . there wasn't a way out for the writers. The fact of the matter is, Hartnell's monologue, stunning as it is, has nothing that can follow it. This is the story where the Doctor is finally broken completely. And they had nowhere to go from there. All they could do was bring on another companion, have Steven take back his storming out for no discernible character reason, and call it a day.

Steven is really the one who suffers the most from this. Prior to this, he'd been a fantastic companion – a leading action man in the Ian tradition, but one with the mad energy of Vicki. This story, however, just breaks the character. It's not Peter Purves's fault – he gives the part his all, and holds the screen when called to. There's a reason he made a great presenter on *Blue Peter*, and it's because he has a real charisma that begs you to watch him – something Hartnell, honestly, doesn't have, which is why he needed the male companion role so much. But as a character, with this Steven goes from the Doctor's second in command and a worthy backup to a character who just doesn't make sense and lurches chaotically from plot point to plot point.

Now, you can make a case that this is another narrative collapse à la *The Chase*, with Dodo being the intrusion of the ridiculous that restores the order of things after the collapse. But *The Chase* was one story. This has been four stories and twenty-one episodes. *Mission to the Unknown* was over four months ago. This darkness and failure on the part of the Doctor is not the content of a story, but a major theme that's been running through the show for a long time now. And in the end, all the writers can do is say, "Well that ran its course" and abandon it.

Which is true – they did push it to beyond the point where the show could recover without an insane side jump like Dodo. But in the end, that begs the question of why they took the show down that road in the first place if they didn't have anything to say or do afterwards other than shrug their shoulders and walk away from it. Which is to say that, although this story sings when taken on its own, after making such a fuss about why we shouldn't do that for *The Daleks' Master Plan*, it's tough to turn around and praise this one when it poses so many problems in its original context. *The Daleks' Master Plan* was an excellent culmination to a storyline about the failures of the Doctor. This, good as it is, just feels like kicking him when he's down.

But worse, there's an underlying cynicism to the approach that's starting to peek through. We commented back in *The Time Meddler* that it was interesting that an evil version of the Doctor was a malevolent trickster, not a mustache-twirling villain à la, say, Mavic Chen. But by this point we're starting to get an alternate take on the character. Here the Doctor is treated as inadequate to a certain type of plot – as if the mercurial trickster figure he represented is just not suitable to big, crashing adventure plots with Dalek armies or massacres, and what the show really needs is a square-jawed action hero like Steven. Put this way, it's difficult to get excited even if the last few stories have been well made: after all, so was the entire season before them. And it was good without being cynical.

Elizabeth Sandifer

Ready To Outsit Eternity (*The Ark*)

It's March 5, 1966. Boots continue to be made for walking. The Walker Brothers will, come March 17, discuss how the sun ain't gonna shine no more. This seems flatly contradicted by the episode of Doctor Who that airs five days earlier, in which the sun expands and burns the Earth to cinders.

Thankfully, that takes place in the far future. In 1966 itself, these weeks are fairly tame, presenting a nice tableau of what we might call stories about the British character. The Jules Rimet trophy for the World Cup is stolen, and dug up a week later by a dog named Pickles. The Archbishop of Canterbury courts controversy for having the gall to sit down and talk to the Pope. And Ronnie Kray, one of the two Kray Twins who basically run organized crime in London, commits the murder he'll finally be sent away for when he walks into the Blind Beggar pub and shoots George Cornell in the head, causing a record of "The Sun Ain't Gonna Shine No More" to skip endlessly on the word "anymore." Kray would manage to get away with this for three years by virtue of the fact that nobody was actually stupid enough to testify against a man who walked into pubs and shot people dead. There's a certain tautology to the logic behind something like this, actually. If you have the insane hubris needed to shoot someone in the head in front of numerous witnesses because you believe yourself to be untouchable, you also have the insane confidence needed to actually be untouchable – at least for a while.

It's not that these are dark days. They're not. It's that they're deeply schizoid days, in which the sort of rampant corruption needed to have the Kray twins exists side by side with the charming nationalistic glee of Pickles the trophy-finding dog.

"Deeply schizoid" is an apt phrase, really, for talking about the end of John Wiles's brief tenure producing Doctor Who, which happens with this episode. He was only on board for four stories, though of course, one of them was rather long, and yet it seems difficult to overstate his importance to the show. Even if, under him, the ludicrous failure to resolve *The Massacre* well (a problem that really is constrained entirely to the last ten minutes of the story, as the rest of it is phenomenal) meant that the series never quite resolved the ongoing plot arc of the Doctor's inadequacy, the fact of the matter is that, on quality, *The Myth Makers*, *The Daleks' Master Plan*, and *The Massacre* have been among the best Doctor Who stories we've seen. And now we have his finale, and the lone story of his tenure to be complete in the archives.

Oddly, though, *The Ark* is the first and only time under John Wiles that we'll get something that feels more or less like a normal Doctor Who story. It's actually been six months since we last had a story in which the Doctor and company arrive on an alien world and have to learn the rules and situation of that world, as opposed to a historical or a big story about Daleks, who are great villains, but require no learning or exploration from the Doctor. The introduction of Daleks pretty much brings to a conclusion any speculation as to what the story might be or what's going on.

Watching the opening of *The Ark*, then, one thing that is very clear is how much faster and more confident the program is in its third year. For all the complaints about the pacing on *The Ark*, it's very difficult not to notice that its first two episodes are basically *The Sensorites* done in a third of the time. Under Wiles, the show has learned to get to the point and tell a story. It will get better (the pacing of Doctor Who basically accelerates constantly over the years, and frankly, this is almost always a good thing), but Wiles has done a lot to tighten the storytelling.

The biggest loss to make up for this is, frankly, not that big a loss to anyone over the age of about ten – the show is much less didactically educational than it used to be. As tedious as the opening of *The Ark* in which Dodo walks around the jungle identifying animals is, just imagine if this had been a Season One story, in which case biological features of the animals would have been crucial to the resolution. Instead we get a remarkably savvy and clever sequence that fools us into thinking that we're looking at a stock footage elephant (complete with a shot-reverse-shot cut to Dodo's face that seems designed to hide the lack of a real elephant) only to have the TARDIS crew stride up and touch the elephant. And honestly, that's better than an educational digression about elephants.

Similarly, even though it takes over half an episode to get the Doctor to the plot, the plot starts moving before that. We don't spend the entire first episode on a mystery about where the TARDIS has landed this time. Nor, in the second episode, is the race to find a cure for the outbreak of disease on the Ark delayed by a runaround through the sewers. Instead, things happen with considerable frequency. So much so that, two episodes in, it looks as though we may have watched a two-parter and be on our way out of the story.

Then something interesting happens. The Doctor, Dodo, and Steven are driven off to the TARDIS (this is one of my favorite details of this story, by the way – the little golf carts that are used to transport people around the Ark, giving it a sense of scale). The golf cart drives off, we watch the TARDIS dematerialize, and then . . . it reappears.

And it's here that *The Ark* simultaneously reaches its maximum genius and runs smack into what is, in the end, the biggest problem I have with John Wiles's tenure on the show.

See, in the first and second episodes of *The Ark*, in the background, there was a plot going on about the Monoids. Basically, the Monoids are tall aliens played by men with ping pong balls in their mouths painted like eyes, and weird Beatle wigs on top of their costumes. We're not told a lot about them – they were refugees who came to Earth when their own world was dying, and are valued as a servant class. They seem friendly enough throughout the first two episodes. There are a couple of things that are unsettling – they're clearly second-class citizens. For instance, when the TARDIS crew is on trial for their role in spreading the plague across *The Ark*, the trial only gets really serious when a human dies of the plague, when previously it had just been Monoids. And there's a really uncomfortable scene where the Monoids have a funeral procession for one of the plague victims, and Dodo says they look like savages.

All of which is remarkably subtle set-up for the second episode's cliffhanger, in which the statue that the humans were building, which we were told would take 700 years to build, is now complete. Oh, and it's a statue of a Monoid.

And unfortunately, after twenty-two episodes of incredibly high quality, which left me expecting to watch *The Ark* and write up a nice retrospective on John Wiles that talked about him as an overlooked creative genius in the history of Doctor Who, we got the two episodes that made me completely re-evaluate his entire tenure.

I mean, not that he's talentless. The last two episodes of *The Ark* are great to watch, making him one of two Doctor Who producers to oversee zero turkeys (the other, Derrick Sherwin, only produced two stories). That's not the problem. The problem is . . . well, OK. The usual criticism of *The Ark*'s latter half is that the Monoids, once they're in charge and oppressing the humans, are utterly stupid villains who do things like inadvertently explain their whole plan, out loud, to the humans. And they have a Security Kitchen (though to be fair, eventually when the show comes up with ideas like a kitchen/prison, we decide it's brilliant. To my mind, if you hate the Security Kitchen, you'd better give up immediately on the Yeti, the Axons, Erato, the Eternals, Varos, the Kandyman, Cassandra, the Adipose, and the Star Whale too).

Except here's the thing . . . I don't think it's poor plotting that makes the Monoids stupid. I think, actually, they're supposed to be stupid. I think that's completely deliberate, because this story is a piece of colonialist, imperialist, and downright mean-spirited crap.

Let's look carefully at the Monoids again: refugees who arrived in a world otherwise full of white British people and were dutiful servants. They are "savages" (or so says Dodo). They can't even talk in the first two episodes. Does this sound remotely familiar to you? Perhaps if we threw in some poetry:

> Take up the White Man's burden--
> Send forth the best ye breed--
> Go bind your sons to exile
> To serve your captives' need;
> To wait in heavy harness,
> On fluttered folk and wild--
> Your new-caught, sullen peoples,
> Half-devil and half-child.

I mean, by any modern standards, the Monoids should be sympathetic. Though they are treated like servants and second-class citizens, they only rise up, we are told, because of a genetic defect that makes the humans docile and unfit to lead. And even then, they are only capable of rising up because the humans are foolish enough to arm them and give them the ability to talk. In a modern Doctor Who story, we'd want to see the Doctor on their side – fighting for their independence. Surely treating an entire race as a class of servant-like savages is wrong.

Except it's not, in this story. The Monoids rise up and are moustache-twirling villains. And their tendency to give away their plans to anyone around them? Well, I don't want to glorify it with an entire essay, but we can jump to another show on the BBC to get a sense of what was going on there, namely *The Black and White Minstrel Show*. Make no mistake, the Monoids are flagrant minstrel characters. Their blabbing of their plans and incompetence is meant to be funny. I mean, they act like minstrels, are treated like they're from the same ethnic background as minstrels, and look dark skinned. It's kind of hard to get around. They're incompetent because the whole point is that savages like them can never actually run a country, and we'd be fools to turn one over to them.

In fact, even being nice to them – giving them more power like speech and weapons – is wrong. The Monoids deserve to be a race of servants, because that's all that savages like them are good for. And when, at the end of the story, the humans are ordered to make peace with the Monoids, one does not sense that it will be a peace of equals, but rather the return of the Monoids to being a well-treated servant class. And it's just sickening. It's a sickening, vile piece of racism and neo-colonialism that, while not wholly out of step with its times, was reactionary and nasty in 1966, and is only worse in the present day.

But the real problem is that once you see it, you see what was going on in the rest of John Wiles's tenure. It starts with a seemingly innocuous detail – that the Monoids have Beatles haircuts. The Beatles, of course, are the icon of youth culture. It's very, very difficult to come up with a reading of the decision to make the irredeemable savages have Beatles haircuts as anything other than a savage condemnation of youth culture. Especially when combined with the decision to write Vicki out of the show unceremoniously, and the near-decision to actually kill her. Or, for that matter, the decision to replace Vicki, our Scouse revolutionary, with the bumbling and naive idiocy of Dodo – a jaw-droppingly harsh reconsideration of how to portray youth culture. Much is made of the fact that Dodo is a (poor) attempt to add a contemporary London girl to the cast, but not nearly as much is made of the fact that she's played as stupid comic relief.

She's not an icon of youth culture like Vicki. She's a vicious condemnation of contemporary youth. She's an explicit comment that they're stupid, ignorant, and worthless.

And suddenly the running plot of how the Doctor sometimes just has everyone die seems a lot more sinister. The Doctor, who a little over a year ago was a pyromaniacal figure of revolution, is now a force of destruction. Time after time he shows up and people die. Even here, he shows up and just gets people sick and calls for the overthrow of the nice British people. And all put together, it's very difficult – for me, at least, impossible, to get away from the message. Revolution is bad. Youth are stupid. Dark-skinned people are savages who cannot be redeemed. And if you, like the Doctor, side with those people and help them, you will cause untold death and destruction.

For all his skill in making a good program, the fact of the matter is, the twenty-four episodes produced by John Wiles are mean-spirited, reactionary, and, frankly, in the final analysis, racist. They're well made. But then again, "The White Man's Burden" is a well-written poem about being a racist imperialist. It doesn't make it good. And just because Wiles broke new ground in the idea of pushing the Doctor to the limit, it doesn't mean his tenure was any less of a racist, reactionary mess.

The Ark is fun to watch. But it's sickening, and by the end, quite frankly, one is glad to see the backside of this regime. The script editor changed over after *The Massacre*. Now the producer has as well.

Frankly, thank God. Surely things will look up now?

The Most Totally Closed Mind (*The Celestial Toymaker*)

It's April 2, 1966. The sun continues not to shine. In two weeks, the Spencer Davis Group will require someone to save them. So the singles chart isn't that interesting at the top. Lower in the charts are the Hollies, the Yardbirds, the Kinks, the Beach Boys, the Who, and Cher.

Flipping to current events, then, we have . . . not a heck of a lot. An artificial heart is installed in Texas. That's a bit funny, actually, given that the story we're talking about today was almost Hartnell's regeneration story, whereas his actual regeneration story features a villain based on paranoia about things like artificial hearts. So yes, we're stretching a bit. Except for one thing, which we'll get to.

So this story and the next one are a bit interesting. I mean, Doctor Who is always interesting. Even when it gives a complete turkey of a story, it's still usually interesting. But these stories are interesting because they are a consecutive pair of stories that have both had dramatic and significant re-evaluations within fandom. We'll talk about the actual process of re-evaluation with *The Gunfighters*, but for now, let's note that this was, for a long time, considered one of the great lost classics of Doctor Who.

It's understandable on paper. You've got an unusual setting, a first rate actor in Michael Gough, and a bizarre and terrifying villain. Everything looks like we're set for a story that works well. So in the absence of anyone actually taking a look at the thing, of course everyone thought it was good. The fourth episode wasn't found until 1984, which is after the cut-off for initial impressions, and didn't get a mass release until 1991. Loose Cannon didn't get to it until 1999. There was plenty of time for everyone to make assumptions about the story before anyone saw it.

Sometimes this process masks a hidden gem. Nobody quite knew how good The Massacre was for a very long time, because on paper it didn't look like much. Here, however, that process led us to assume that this story was brilliant. After all, we started with a nightmarish realm of toys ruled over by an insane demigod that forces the Doctor and his companions to play a bunch of nefarious games with odd titles like the Trilogic Game. That sounds great. Clearly a departure for Doctor Who into something new and exciting, and an ambitious idea that introduced new kinds of threats for the Doctor.

Then people actually saw the thing, or, at least, its fourth episode and the audio of the first three. And that's the problem. In practice, this story is a complete trainwreck. The pacing is excruciating. Even if you make the standard accommodations of remembering that it's not supposed to be watched in one shot, it's tough to get over the fact that there is no emotional content to this story. It's just the Doctor playing the Trilogic Game for four episodes while Steven and Dodo meander through a series of arbitrary, deadly challenges. The reason it's four episodes long is . . . that's how long it is. It could have been one. It could have been three hundred. It doesn't matter, because the plot does not build at all, at any point, anywhere in the entire story. They just eventually run out of games and go free.

I mean, watching the reconstructions you can find a little leeway. Yes, it's almost certain that the fourty second dance sequence in the third episode would have played better if you didn't have to stare at a single photograph for fourty seconds while music played. But then you get to the fourth episode and realize that, no, the whole thing actually is as dull as you were afraid.

And on top of that, the whole thing is just . . . not even trying. It makes literally zero effort to be good. There's an interesting bit that comes up occasionally in which Dodo tries to treat the opponents the Toymaker creates for them seriously because they're real people who got trapped by the Toymaker. But her and the Toymaker saying so is the only actual evidence we have for this. She makes a vague claim that their remaining humanity is why they let them win, but it's a tell-don't-show moment. Nothing, watching the episodes, makes them look like anything other than generic villains. That's par for the course here. "Ooh, that's an interesting idea, let's ignore it in favor of fifteen minutes of hopscotch."

The central example of this – the one that I spent most of the four episodes laughing at – is the Trilogic Game. Which sounds delightfully esoteric when you just read the name, or hear the Toymaker's description: "The Trilogic Game. A game for the mind, Doctor, the developed mind . . . difficult for the practiced mind. Dangerous for the mind that has become old, lazy, or weak." I mean, wow! What a great idea! A devilish, difficult game that is so savagely difficult as to be actively dangerous for a lesser mind! How does it work?

Well, as it happens . . . it's Towers of Hanoi. If you're not familiar with the name, you're surely familiar with the concept. There's a tower of discs of varying sizes, stacked with the largest on the bottom and the smallest on top. You must move the tower from one location to one of two others, one disc at a time, and never putting a larger disc on top of a smaller one. For my part, I first encountered this game in a computer game – I believe *Sesame Street* themed – in which the discs were layers of a cake. I was very good at it. I was also three.

In other words, the diabolical logic puzzle is, in fact, an idiotically simple puzzle that children can and do solve and that is trivial to write an algorithm for. Which would be one thing if the sodding Toymaker didn't routinely shout for the game to advance itself. Which kind of establishes the game as the linear execution of an algorithm that it is. I mean, it's a bit puzzling why the Toymaker constantly goads the Doctor about whether he has the sequence right when the Toymaker has been making half the moves himself. (Really, about the most fun you can have with this episode is trying to come up with elaborate explanations for why the Toymaker is as stupid as he is. Unfortunately, as we'll see in a moment, the most sensible explanation is a deeply unpleasant one.)

This may also be the story that functionally kills Dodo as a character. After an introduction in which she's maddeningly stupid, here she has nothing to do. I mean, nobody has anything to do in this story, but for Steven or the Doctor that's not so bad, because we at least know them well as characters. But Dodo has gone from stupid to nothing to do, meaning we've had eight episodes of her not working as a character. Even if she's extraordinary in her remaining ten, she's kind of up a creek now, and it's no wonder she got dropped.

To some extent, there are excuses to be made. The original idea for this story was apparently to have it be an implicit sequel to a play called *George and Margaret* by Gerald Savory. *George and Margaret* was a minor piece of absurdism that got to the central idea of *Waiting for Godot* a decade and change earlier than Beckett did. The play is about a dinner party for George and Margaret in which the titular characters never show up. This episode was going to actually have George and Margaret, until Gerald Savory decided he didn't like the script and demanded they be taken out, which necessitated a hurried rewrite of the script to remove its central concept. Probably the whole story would have been spiked there and then, except the show needed a cheap story and this story fell right on the transition from John Wiles to Innes Lloyd as producer, so Lloyd didn't really have time to kill it, even though by that point even Wiles, who'd commissioned it, wanted it killed. In practice, though, much of the blame for what got on screen has to go to Gerry Davis, the script editor, who apparently basically wrote the episode as it actually turned out.

But this background is only so helpful. You could try watching the story as a piece of absurdist theater, except it's lousy absurdism too, because absurdism is ultimately about something. This story isn't. It's not exposing the capricious and arbitrary rules that tyrannically govern the world. It's just faffing about with musical chairs of doom. It may use the tropes of absurdism, but it doesn't get at the point of those tropes, making them an empty exercise, and making the absurdist explanation little more than an interesting production detail.

But here's the really brutal part. It's not enough that this story is complete rubbish. I mean, it is, and it boggles the mind that this was once thought of as a classic. (They were going to bring the Toymaker back in Season Twenty-Three, before the 1985 hiatus killed that plan. Doctor Who fans should thank Michael Grade for sparing us from that trainwreck of an idea.) But that's not actually the biggest problem with this story.

So let's get to the real problem – the thing that takes this story beyond "Interesting idea with completely botched execution" into "Oh for God's sake, just kill me." That is, the fact that this story is unrepentantly racist.

And, I mean, seriously. I'm certainly deliberately including race as a running theme in this book, but would the show mind cutting me a little slack so I don't have to point it out every single episode? I mean, I suppose at least the racism has changed slightly. *The Ark* is racist deliberately and ideologically. Everything about it is racist. Which is oddly more tolerable than this, where the racism is wholly incidental. *The Ark* was racist because some people with racist beliefs decided to write a story about what they believe. *The Celestial Toymaker* is racist because some people with racist beliefs just couldn't be bothered not to put them in.

There's two big aspects of racism in this story. One is more commented on than the other. The less commented aspect is this – the Toymaker himself is a vicious caricature of the Chinese. You may have missed this reading about the story. First of all, let's note that the Toymaker is explicitly dressed and described as a Mandarin. This would be one thing, except the title of the story – *The Celestial Toymaker* – reiterates this. Celestial does not mean "cosmic" here. It's old slang for Chinese. (Fire up an episode of *Deadwood* and you'll see it thrown around.) Specifically, at least according to some sources, it implies drug use, which sets up an interesting interpretation of this story as a condemnation of the entire idea of psychedelic culture, but is probably neither here nor there. So we have a racial slur in the title, and a villain dressed in the appropriate ethnic clothing.

But wait, you say, Michael Gough was white. Yeah, but so was most of the cast of *Marco Polo*. He's playing the role in obvious yellowface. For proof, look at him when he shouts at the Trilogic Game (also of Asian origin, at least by legend, although exactly where in Asia varies, and the legend is likely an apocryphal backstory to explain a nineteenth century invention) to advance some number of moves. Hear that clipped, shouting speech with an accent that isn't quite English? Sound familiar? That's because it's the same exact parody of East Asians speaking English still in use whenever you want an ethnically stereotypical Asian. The entire story is based around having a Fu Manchu style villain who is evil precisely because he's Chinese. To an audience watching and even remotely aware of these stereotypes, the fact that he is Chinese is how we know the moment we see him that he's evil. And just think about the xenophobia here – his toys and games are all classic Victorian stuff. So this is a nefarious, evil Chinese man who twists good Victorian children's culture into sadistic and evil games.

If for some reason you still don't buy the argument, try Gerry Davis's novelization of the story, which contains the following sentence: "The Toymaker was lounging in a black

Chinese chair behind a lacquered Chinese desk inlaid with mother-of-pearl and scenes of Chinese life, after the style of the Willow pattern." And later, "The Toymaker stood up, a tall imposing figure, dressed as a Chinese Mandarin with a circular black hat embossed with a heavy gold thread, a large silver red, and blue collar and a heavy, stiffly embroidered black robe encrusted with rubies, emeralds, diamonds and pearls set against a background of coiled Chinese dragons." In case you didn't get the subtext, by the way, the Toymaker is Chinese.

Honestly, I am stunned and kind of upset that the Toymaker is still considered a classic Doctor Who villain. Big Finish has been using him in audio stories as recently as June of 2010 despite the fact that he's a flagrantly racist caricature. And you can't even rewrite him to avoid that, because the racism is in his name. It's not like you can just shave off the pointy bits and have a character that isn't racist. You're pretty much stuck with it. The fact that anybody trots this character out as a classic part of Doctor Who history is a black mark on Doctor Who fandom.

And that's not even all! The other, better known bit of racism, is that the nineteenth century American version of Eenie Meenie Miney Moe is recited in the second episode. That would be the version in which "tiger" is replaced with "nigger."

For those who defend the slur as being acceptable in 1966 . . . no. The slur was not acceptable in 1966. Agatha Christie's *And Then There Were None* had its title changed to not include the slur in the 1940s. It was racist then. It's racist now. It's just plain racist. There's not a defense of this one to mount. You can't hide it behind "Oh, times have changed." Yeah, they have. But that's not one of the things that's changed.

I mean, for God's sake, the American Civil Rights Movement is international news by now. The word is an American slur. *The Oxford Dictionary of Nursery Rhymes* establishes conclusively that any UK usage of that version is picking up on the American version. To use that version is explicitly a reference to American culture, and in 1966, shortly after the heyday of Martin Luther King and the Civil Rights Movement in America, there's no sympathetic reading here. There's no way to pick that version of the rhyme without making a conscious decision that you're perfectly fine with calling Martin Luther King the same thing.

Nor can it be chalked up to it being the UK, where the race issues weren't as bad. It was, after all, during this story that Enoch Powell made his famed "Rivers of Blood" speech, a viciously racist anti-immigrant speech that was widely condemned while also, inevitably, attracting a sizable "Powell was right" contingent. If you're going to pick a week where racism was clearly an issue in the UK, it's the one between part three and four of *The Celestial Toymaker*. And, perhaps more to the point, Martin Luther King won the Nobel Peace Prize two years earlier. The idea that Europe's eyes weren't firmly on the Civil Rights Movement is absurd.

And yet there are still people who insist on defending it. So let's try one more observation. The bulk of racism was not performed by moustache-twirling villains. The bulk of racism in the 1960s was performed by ordinary people who were on the wrong side of history. Enoch Powell was not particularly unusual in his viewpoints. He was unusual in being stupid enough to blurt them out in a major speech. But millions of people quietly agreed with him. Millions more didn't think about it too much, but weren't above using a racist slur in their conversation. This is the real face of racism in the 1960s, and if we reduce the racism of the 1960s to overt white supremacists we lose sight of what was so horrible about race in that time period. The ordinary, banal racism of deciding to use the word "nigger" instead of "tiger" is what racism in the 1960s was, most of the time. Giving it a pass as not being that bad or being typical of the era is, in effect, saying that racism in the 1960s was limited to a handful of bad eggs. In truth, it was a massive, endemic problem.

So it's not "a product of its times" or anything like that. Nor was *The Ark*. Or, rather, they are a product of their times, but they're a product of the worst and most reprehensible instincts of the times. I mean, I'm OK with sympathetic readings of racist texts of the past that acknowledge the failings even as they celebrate what's good about them. Hell – I freely admit that *The Ark*, and the entire John Wiles era, is gripping television, even if it is largely ethically bankrupt. And it certainly doesn't help that *The Celestial Toymaker* is crap to start. But there's also no excuse for this or *The Ark*.

Yes, there were more unrepentant racists in 1966, and so in that sense racism was "part of the culture." But so was the idea of racial equality, and the sense that maybe colonizing people and oppressing them wasn't a very nice thing to do. I mean, the entire Rhodesian conflict we've been talking about puts the lie to the idea that racism and colonialism was unambiguously accepted. Frankly, the ideas that are needed to label this story and *The Ark* as reactionary bullshit were just as present in 1966 as the racism they embody. Possibly even more so, in that this was an explicit debate going on at the time, and these stories unashamedly associate themselves with the wrong side of that debate.

And I just can't do it. I can't. The show I love doesn't pull stunts like this. It doesn't do stories that exist to revel in stereotypes and crass racism. It certainly doesn't do them a week after a ringing endorsement of the idea that brown people just aren't fit to govern themselves. This isn't Doctor Who. I take back what I said about every story being a Doctor Who story. That's not true. Stories that are fundamentally about racist ideologies and oppressing people because their culture isn't as good as yours? Those aren't Doctor Who stories. No matter what theme music you put at the top and what actors you cast, they aren't Doctor Who stories. I'll accept the Paul McGann movie, the Peter Cushing movies, hell, "A Fix with Sontarans" and *Death Comes to Time*. Those can all be canon if they want to be – fine and dandy.

The Ark and *The Celestial Toymaker*, though? Not canon. Plain and simple. I flatly refuse to let these two into the clubhouse. Doctor Who is not a show in which reactionary imperialist ideology wins the day. It's not a show where the Doctor fights racist caricatures, unless he's fighting someone for producing them. It's not a show about xenophobia and racism. It's just not. And stories that try to make it into one are far, far bigger violations of what the show is about than most of what constitutes a canon debate. The fact that there are far more fans outraged about the fact that the Doctor maybe was in love with Rose than there are about the fact that in 2010 we're still using a racist caricature as a recurring villain is, frankly, disgusting. This is a real and major failing of Doctor Who fandom, and one of the few points over which I feel kind of dirty being associated with it.

Stetsons Are Cool (*The Gunfighters*)

It's April 30, 1966. Dusty Springfield is politely disclaiming the necessity of us telling her we love her, and next week Manfred Mann is going to sing about a "Pretty Flamingo," which certainly sounds exciting. Lower on the charts are your usual mix of mid-'60s artists – forgettable pop groups and American imports aplenty, with occasional outbreaks of Cher, the Who, or the Beach Boys. The most interesting thing you get is the chart run of "Wild Thing," which never hits number one, but at least does help illustrate the way in which a dirtier, rougher sound was entering mainstream pop music.

In other news, the first episode of today's Doctor Who story aired on the same day that Anton LaVey formed the Church of Satan, which, as we'll talk about, must be hilarious for a certain segment of fandom that considers this story to basically be the Devil itself. Other news over the next few weeks will include the launch of some pirate radio stations off the coast of Britain, the resolution of the Moors Murders we talked about way back when Donald Cotton was last writing for Doctor Who, more Rhodesia problems, and more Vietnam War protests. Oh, and *Pet Sounds* and *Blonde on Blonde* both come out on the same day, which is actually kind of awesome.

So there's not exactly any thrills going on in the culture of Britain here. Things are boiling along. The stylized optimism of mod culture and Vicki are not gone, as such – if anything, they're entering their most important era. But they're counterbalanced by the fact that the world is as scary a place as it's been since Hitler was busy taking it over. This is one of those periods that history seems ill-suited to. We know the ending, both the Summer of Love in America and the Underground in the UK, and the final collapse of it all in '68. At the time, though, everything is up in the air, smoldering tensely.

But that's OK, because *The Gunfighters* is one of the few Doctor Who stories it is nearly impossible to take primarily as a product of its times. Because *The Gunfighters* is, more than any other Doctor Who story, and I include the fanwankiest depths of the John Nathan-Turner era in that, the story that symbolizes Doctor Who fandom.

Let's have a bit of history, shall we? Up until the 1980s, Doctor Who fandom in the sense we know it today wasn't really possible. With no Internet and no home video, Doctor Who fans were left mostly with the novelizations and some hazy memories for the bulk of the show's run. In the 1970s Terrance Dicks and Malcolm Hulke put out *The Making of Doctor Who*, and that was actually the first time a complete list of Doctor Who stories was ever published. It wasn't until the 1980s that publishing the list became routine, due to a swirl of factors we'll learn more about when we get there, but that, to be very brief, had to do with trying to repackage the show to be more like American cult sci-fi and the buzz over the twentieth anniversary. So it was that, in the 1980s, Doctor Who fandom was invented.

One of the first and most important consequences of Doctor Who fandom was Peter Haining's 1983 coffee table book *Doctor Who: A Celebration*. We've mentioned this book before, and with good reason – it was massively important in its time. This book featured the earliest attempt to systematically review all Doctor Who stories up to that point, in a section written by Jeremy Bentham (Yes, Foucault fans, he is related). Bentham was the head of the Doctor Who

Appreciation Society's reference department, the fandom before fandom, which, through their diligence, is why we have things like "any Doctor Who stories from the 1960s" and "detailed knowledge of production." And so this section represented Holy Writ for a long time – the assumed default consensus of fandom.

It's impossible to overstate how important this book and section is. Even still, it's the starting point for assessments of the show. Any time you start discussing and debating a story, frankly, you start with Bentham. *The Celestial Toymaker* is known as a classic in a large part because it was written up as one by Bentham. If you, as I do, say it's actually rubbish, you know full well that you're arguing against Bentham here and that you will never, ever actually remove its status as a classic. The story will become a classic that's fallen from grace, but never a bad story. So what is the default consensus on *The Gunfighters*? Let's just quote the review outright, shall we?

If ever reviewers feel tempted to pour scorn on the attempts by America to emulate British costume drama, a good lesson in humility could be learned from studying this serial as a demonstration of how the British can not do westerns. It was billed as a show about the gunfight at the OK Corral, but it was more the massacre of the OK Corral.

So badly was this show received by the public that its audience viewing figures dipped below the horizontal axis line on the ratings graph in the Doctor Who producer's office for the only time in the programme's history!

What made this serial so poor is the cumulative effect of so many bad points which on their own would be forgiven in most other stories. The script was pure Talbot Rothwell, the acting was not even bad vaudeville and the direction was more West Ham than West Coast.

It was not good. It was bad and it was ugly. It was certainly the story that decided in the mind of new producer Innes Lloyd that the time had come to rethink the policy of using historical stories in Doctor Who's framework.

Ouch. And it's the only story in the book to get a drubbing like that. Some other stories are widely disliked, but only *The Gunfighters* has the status of clearly and unambiguously being the worst Doctor Who story ever made. And for over a decade, that was all there was to say about it. *Doctor Who Magazine* took the Bentham position as gospel. The CMS fanzines had a pseudonymous review taking the story to task for historical inaccuracy (but note that Bentham is one of the writers of that issue, so his hand is pretty clearly there). And the Howe-Stammers-Walker Doctor Who handbook (Howe being Bentham's successor as head of the DWAS reference department) from 1994 declares, "After the high drama of the previous story, *The Gunfighters* is a disappointment. This is a rare example of Doctor Who attempting something previously untried and failing... Ultimately the attempt to stage a full scale Western adventure in a small UK TV studio proves too much of a challenge and is what lets the story down."

So it is written, so shall it be. But even now, we should be able to see that there just might be some problems here. For one thing, complaining that the BBC can't do a realistic Western seems to ignore the fact that the BBC has some obvious problems with a realistic planet of insects, a realistic generation starship, or, as Moffat pointed out regarding *Z-Cars*, realistic cars. It seems bewildering to suddenly get on the realism bandwagon here of all places. Yes, the moment you hear the Clanton brothers talk you know full well you're in a British Western, but... well... you are in a British Western. Just like a month ago you were on a British starship in the far future, and before that you've been in British sixteenth-century France, British Rome, and British Mexico. I mean, they can't even keep a consistent accent for Dodo at this point in the series, and she's actually supposed to be British. How are the American accents the problem?

And historical inaccuracies? What? I mean, yes, the story is full of them, but this is a show that less than a year ago was dropping gramophones and wristwatches at the Battle of

Hastings, that had just recently done the Trojan War with Cassandra as proper prophetess, and has had the Doctor at the center of Nero burning down Rome and the fall of Robespierre. Oh, and in the first historical ever, *Marco Polo*, so botched the actual history of Marco Polo that Wood and Miles spend a page and a half in *About Time* advancing the argument that the character played by Mark Eden is not actually Marco Polo at all. Again, why is this suddenly the breaking point for historical inaccuracy?

Perhaps the greatest moment in "wait a moment, what show do you folks actually think you're watching here," however, comes from the Howe-Stammers-Walker guide, in which they suggest that it is in some way surprising that Peter Purves is a good comic actor. Would this be the same Peter Purves whose first appearance on the series was as a drawling Alabama hick in a comic role? And who would go on to be a highly successful host of children's television? It's surprising that a host of *Blue Peter* would be funny? How do you even get to the point where you say things like that?

I mean, if these weren't some of the most devoted Doctor Who fans in the world, I'd be forced to wonder if they actually watched the episode, or simply made things up. Instead, however, we're left with an even more unsettling prospect. The clue is back in the Bentham review, when the script is described as "pure Talbot Rothwell." Talbot Rothwell being one of the great comic writers of the twentieth century, voted in 2007 as having written the best cinematic one-liner in British film history. And yet Bentham clearly intends it as a swipe at the story. Which suggests, perhaps, that the problem is a belief that Doctor Who isn't supposed to be funny.

But the result is that this story is still widely hated. Case in point, the hilarious anecdote from Shearman and Hadoke's *Running Through Corridors* where Shearman talks about a woman who stood up at a panel at a convention in LA and proclaimed "as if she were delivering Holy Writ, that there were two monsters she didn't want to see make a return appearance in Doctor Who. The Zarbi were one, and the Gunfighters were the other." Which captures, I think, the basic issue here. Because "monsters" in the modern Doctor Who sense have very little to do with the Hartnell era. Certainly treating the Clanton brothers in *The Gunfighters* as having some semiotic similarity to Daleks requires a catastrophic failure to have a clue what is going on in this story.

But let's be generous here. This is 1980s fandom, in which memory of past stories was as important as actual textual evidence, and in many cases more so. Although I'm pretty sure Bentham had seen *The Gunfighters*, and sure Howe, Stammers, and Walker did as well, the fact of the matter is, Bentham was the only source on *The Gunfighters* most people had for a decade. The novelization didn't come out until 1985 (after the novelizations were switching to collectors items, not, you know, books, although Cotton's three novelizations are hilarious, including a take on *The Romans* that is far funnier than the original), and the VHS wasn't out until 2002. This isn't some flaw in the readings of past stories or fan consensus. 1983 was the first year any Doctor Who came out on VHS. Prior to that, treating the history of Doctor Who as something you could visit instead of reading about was not so much wrong as not even conceivable. So inasmuch as *The Gunfighters* was remembered poorly, poorly rated, and a sort of story that wasn't like most Doctor Who, it became a scapegoat for utterly understandable reasons.

Then came what we might call the second wave of criticism, in which the '90s came, and Doctor Who fans from all over the world started nattering on at each other on the Internet. And without an actual show to watch, and with a healthy release schedule on VHS coupled with the relative ease with which tape trading to acquire other stories occurred, Doctor Who fandom began the Great Re-evaluation.

The key text here is Paul Cornell, Martin Day, and Keith Topping's 1995 *The Discontinuity Guide*. Its reviews were short, but, crucially, the book was an irreverent romp that was perfectly willing to throw received wisdom out the window. It was idiosyncratic in the extreme, but such a massive breath of fresh air that its idiosyncrasies seemed (and still seem) beside the point. But their summary of *The Gunfighters* – "With Hartnell, Purves and Anthony Jacobs in amazing form, and such a great script, this is a comic masterpiece, winning you over with its sheer charm" – was remarkable because it was more or less the first time anyone had publicly said anything nice about the story. Its significance was not that it was terribly well argued – how the acting went from terrible to amazing and the script became great and a masterpiece in a decade is never quite explained – but that it rang in an era where a motley crew of keyboard slinging Doctor Who fans were going to re-evaluate everything.

The thing about the Great Re-evaluation is that it was not a rigorous examination of the history of Doctor Who. It was starting from the received wisdom of '80s fandom, and then arguing with it. Every Doctor Who fan had their pet eras that they could defend the genius of, and their pet eras they wanted to dump on. The result was that every single Doctor Who story save a narrow handful of barely disputed classics acquired a good reading and a bad reading. You can see this clearly if you look at the *Doctor Who Ratings Guide* on *The Gunfighters*; basically what you get is fans arguing between the two poles. So for *The Gunfighters*, that means "it's ridiculous and cheap" on one side, and "it's funny" on the other, and to talk about the story you stake out a position somewhere on that line and stick to it.

The archetypal example of this is probably the 2002 review of the VHS release in *Doctor Who Magazine*, which ends up taking the neutral position of pointing out the flaws in most of the arguments against it, before finally suggesting that the root problem is just that Doctor Who fans don't much like Westerns. Which is vintage Great Re-evaluation – an argument that is less about the TV episode than it is about reconciling a mass of past consensus on the story. Ultimately, the Great Re-evaluation is less about the stories themselves than it is about negotiating the nature of fan consensus in a fandom that is becoming more egalitarian. Which makes sense. We're still dealing with an era where the less-classic stories are hard to find. This is still, much like 1983, a period where it's easier to find what everyone else has said about *The Gunfighters* than it is to watch it for yourself.

Which brings us to the third era of fan consensus, the one that by and large began in 2002 when the VHS era came to an end with a hurried release of all surviving material. It had clearly begun by 2006 when Loose Cannon got the last of their reconstructions out (and when there was a new series to care about, and so everyone could take a nice big chill pill about the classic series without sacrificing all their fan credibility. Why hate a Hartnell story when you can hate the entire Russell T Davies era?). Basically, this was the era when it was finally the case that an average fan could fairly easily get their hands on any story they wanted. This has only grown more and more true – these days if you want to watch a Doctor Who story, you need know nothing other than the url of a BitTorrent site. They're all up. And especially with the avalanche of new fans who came in post-2005 and don't give a crap what Jeremy Bentham said in 1983, we have the era of Reconstructionist Criticism.

The magnum opus here is, as you might guess, the six-volume Miles and Wood set *About Time*, which is notable for attempting to provide a thorough overview of Doctor Who stories based primarily on watching the stories and looking at the influences at the time. It's difficult in some ways to wrap one's head around this, given that the show has been around for so long, but in many ways *About Time* is the first serious and thorough attempt to look at stories primarily in the context they happened in as opposed to primarily through the lens of post-1983 fandom. The books are amazing, and anyone who likes this book should really own them.

That's since in the process of being joined by Rob Shearman and Toby Hadoke's *Running Through Corridors*, a more personal approach that is based more heavily on the experience of watching and responding, but is done by actual TV professionals who are thus good at and qualified to talk about nuances of acting, camera work, etc. And again, shockingly given the age of the show, Shearman and Hadoke provide the first significant times anyone has actually bothered doing close-readings of individual scenes from some episodes.

And that's a tradition I'll happily slot myself into as well. My goal, and I freely admit that it's made massively easier by the fact that I'm the third one to go over the Hartnell and Troughton era, is to tell the story of how Doctor Who got to where it is today, and to tell this story primarily from the perspective of the episodes themselves, rather than from a production-based perspective. (Since the making of Doctor Who from 1963 to present is extremely well covered by existing sources.)

Because one thing that's very clear about the Reconstructionist era of Doctor Who criticism is that it is a contemporary phenomenon. For one thing, it depends heavily on the fact that the new series, particularly under Steven Moffat, has made media critics of us all. These days a sixty-second trailer for the new series is taken apart frame by frame to see what's revealed. The new series hinges on active, savvy viewership. I mean, the entire dénouement of *The Big Bang* is based in part on a fake blooper from an earlier episode – an incredibly precise, hyper-engaged sort of twist. The Reconstructionist approach is, in the end, based on watching old Doctor Who with a mind towards history and the tools embraced by new Doctor Who.

Reconstructionists, by and large, seem to love *The Gunfighters*, and I'm certainly among them – this is one of Hartnell's best stories. Shearman and Hadoke unrepentantly enjoy the story, and Woods and Miles are more than happy to defend it. So let's, for once and for all, figure out what this story actually is instead of what decades of ossified fan-lore say it is.

First off, let's note that the writer of the story, Donald Cotton, is not a hack. If we remove this story from consideration, we're left with *The Myth Makers*, which is, as I've already argued, sublimely good (in part because it gets in early on the "the Doctor loses" bandwagon so that its ending is novel and exciting, not expected), and with his novelization of *The Romans*, which is by miles funnier than the original script. To be perfectly frank, on the evidence of *The Myth Makers* alone, it's pretty easy to argue that Cotton is the funniest writer to write for Doctor Who until Douglas Adams wanders by. So whatever is going on in this story, the odds are pretty good that it's well written. Certainly a writer who has written two great bits of Doctor Who should probably be given the benefit of the doubt on his third.

The main thing that Cotton brings here, aside from a fantastic sense of humor, is that he understands something very important to writing good stories in a serial format. The concept of the story is not the story. The concept for this story – the Doctor in the wild West – is easy. Anybody can, very rapidly, come up with two-dozen good concepts and settings for a Doctor Who story. A mediocre Doctor Who story – in any era – stands out because that's all it is. It's my essential problem with a story like *The Reign of Terror*. At the end of the day, the story isn't about anything besides "the Doctor and company get stuck in revolutionary France." And even that is only accomplished because the Doctor is written out of character in the first episode. Compare to something like *The Massacre*, which is not about a bunch of Huguenots getting killed, but rather about Steven's failure to display sufficient independence, and you quickly see why one story is great and the other isn't.

Cotton gets this. This story is about something.

You can get that, really, from the first shot – a low shot, peering from beneath a wagon, as horses ride down the street and the "Ballad of the Last Chance Saloon" plays. The ballad is one of the most talked about aspects of the episode. Some people claim it's disruptive and distracting. Others get it stuck in their head. For my part, I love it, because it is a line in the sand that declares that the world of the Western is different from everything else. More than any establishing shot thus far on the series, more even than the bizarre landscape of Vortis or the jump-start of *The Crusade*, this makes it clear that the TARDIS is visiting somewhere with its own defined set of rules. Which is quickly re-enforced by the ballad giving way to the sound effect of the TARDIS, a massive tonal contrast. This tonal contrast is used for every cliffhanger as well, as another verse of the ballad gives way to Delia Derbyshire's shrieking rendition of the theme with bewildering frisson.

This idea that the TARDIS has taken them somewhere they don't quite fit is quickly reinforced by the scene after the TARDIS crew realizes where they are, in which Dodo and Steven giddily run back to the TARDIS, Steven declaring that he's always wanted to be a cowboy, and Dodo wanting to be a cowgirl as well. They re-emerge in ridiculously overdone Western clothes (including Dodo with an idiotic wig), drop a cowboy hat on the Doctor's head, and start playing at being in a Western. They are, of course, terrible at it – Steven trips over his spurs and drops his guns.

The dead giveaway, however, is how the Doctor introduces the crew to Wyatt Earp. The Doctor decides to pawn off the entire TARDIS crew as a theatrical troupe. This is where the story firmly takes its shape. It is, in the end, about the genre of the Western, a world where the TARDIS crew doesn't really belong, and about their attempt to play as if they do belong there. Which, to a meaningful extent, parallels the production – a BBC television studio being used for a genre it doesn't really belong in, and a bunch of actors attempting to play as if they're doing a real Western. It is less about the Western genre than it is about the theatricality of it. Bizarrely, it watches particularly well if you watch an episode of *Deadwood* first, since the theatrical and stylized dialogue of that and the British trying to do a Western are actually strangely similar.

Most specifically, however, this story is about the degree to which the Doctor just doesn't belong in this story. The first episode's cliffhanger is the key moment here, as the Doctor, after having his tooth removed by Doc Holliday, staggers down the street towards an ambush by the Clanton brothers. On the one hand, it's a classic Western shot – the main character walking alone down the street towards a battle. On the other hand, the main character is oblivious, has a toothache, and is staring in bewilderment at his gun.

For the first two episodes, at least, this is played for fairly straight laughs. Hartnell, Purves, and even the usually spectacularly narrow-ranged Lane are having an absolute blast with these scenes, which helps. Lane gets what is probably the best scene of her time on the show, where she pulls a gun on Holliday and demands to be taken back to Tombstone. The scene is hilarious, particularly when she nearly passes out after he agrees, and then again when he lets her know he could have overtaken her, and has an odd charm, as Holliday agrees despite not being in any real danger. It may well be the first time Dodo works as a character, which means we'll have to write her out immediately.

Purves, on the other hand, demonstrates an odd skill. Looking at this next to his performances in *The Celestial Toymaker*, *The Massacre*, and *The Time Meddler*, it's striking how different they are. Part of this is down to an inconsistently and hazily-defined character in Steven (think of how little his origins and nature have come up compared to any of the companions before him), but part of it is down to Purves being a chameleon of an actor, capable of filling in whatever spot is needed in a scene or story. This is particularly useful given that he's acting alongside the erratic William Hartnell. Though Hartnell, in this story, is more on the ball and on target than we've seen him in ages. It's well known that by this point he was being eased out of the lead role by the production team, and that the entire set was tense from his tendency towards outbursts and tantrums, so seeing him appear to have fun at this late a stage in his run is genuinely nice. (Also nice is watching an apparent Billy Fluff – calling Wyatt Earp "Werp" – played off of by Peter Purves to make a small joke while reminding us that not every fluff is actually an error.)

But there's also the sense of something looming over these episodes. It's perhaps clearest towards the end of the second episode, in which the Doctor is warned that "the boys don't want words, they want action." The Doctor, after all, is at home with words. This is reinforced throughout the script with bits of clever wordplay and the like. But lurking is the fact that the Doctor, Steven, and Dodo are not well suited to this world. This world takes action.

And then in the third episode, things start to get darker. Johnny Ringo shows up, and as his first major act guns down Charlie, the barman, because Charlie knows who he is. It's a horrifying scene – Ringo takes obvious delight in the murder, and the sequence revels in its contrasts. Charlie falls over dead with comedic flopping, and the ballad strikes up again to add a bit of levity, but the camera stays for a perversely long time on Charlie, stressing the fact that this is the first death of the story, and Ringo's icy pleasure in the kill adds another dissonant note. The end effect resembles the brutal turn of *The Myth Makers*, but does something that story did not – sits for a while right on the cusp of comedy and darkness, and lets the viewer twist uncomfortably.

And then in the fourth episode, Cotton redoes his *Myth Makers* trick, and it's just as good as the first time he collapses a comedy into a tragedy. The inevitable gunfight is a long, gorgeously filmed sequence with shots paralleling the establishing shots from the first episode, leading into a lengthy stretch of savage violence. Never before in Doctor Who has the soundtrack been reduced to the drumbeat of gunfire as shot after shot is fired. And suddenly the Doctor's continual reluctance to carry a gun in the story – a reluctance that is reiterated so much that this story, more than any other, has to be taken as the basis for Terrance Dicks's famous "never carries a gun" mandate – takes on further depth.

Ironically, and contrary to most readings, in the end, this is a story about why Doctor Who isn't a Western. Here Doctor Who stakes out the essential difference between itself and *Star Trek* before *Star Trek* airs its first episode. At the end of the day, *Star Trek* is about a man of action on the frontier. And Doctor Who is about a man of words wandering freely through the world. This is a story about that difference. The Doctor is ill-suited for a world of action, and a world with a TARDIS has no frontiers. But more to the point, by collapsing into the brutal violence of the final gunfight, this is a story to persuade us that we'd rather be in Doctor Who than the wild West. That as much fun as Steven and Dodo may have playing cowboy and cowgirl, in the end, this world of brutality and guns simply is not as good a place as the world of the Doctor.

In a way then, perhaps it's not until Doctor Who fandom reached its era of Reconstructionist Criticism that this story could have been appreciated. As clever as it is, it seems also impossibly ahead of its time, depending on a mode of viewing that is much more modern than it is 1966. And perhaps the best evidence of this comes not from the tomes of Reconstructionism, nor from the Great Re-evaluation, nor even from the 1983 roots of modern fandom. The best evidence comes from the one era we rarely consider with regards to the Hartnell era – the Hartnell era itself.

As this episode aired, Sydney Newman, head of drama at the BBC and co-creator of the series, criticized it with a lengthy memo taking the story to task for being too silly and too much of a send-up. In it, he suggested that none but the most sophisticated viewers would appreciate the story. And the episode's viewing figures – both in numbers and audience appreciation – bear his guess out. The story was not well liked at the time (perhaps part of why it became Bentham's sacrificial lamb in the Haining book).

The Gunfighters is unmistakably an oddball in 1966 – a largely comedic story in amongst the serious and apocalyptic, a historical as the genre was already in decline, and a Hartnell-heavy story amidst stories that have consciously been written to marginalize his character. And, of course, a story set in a foreign country in a subgenre that the BBC had never done before. But in the end, this is much more faithful to what Doctor Who is than *The Celestial Toymaker* or *The Ark*. We're all sophisticated viewers now. Maybe we should finally admit it. Stetsons are cool.

Elizabeth Sandifer

The Right to Experiment (*The Savages*)

It's May 28, 1966. The Rolling Stones have the number one single with "Paint It Black." Also in the top ten are "Wild Thing" and "Rainy Day Women Nos. 12 and 35," alongside conventional fare. Although Frank Sinatra takes over number one after one week, holding it for the remaining three weeks of *The Savages* with "Strangers in the Night," the remainder of the charts retains the increasingly hardening edge of music with the Animals and the Yardbirds both notching top ten hits.

In other news, two days ago the South American colony of Guyana was granted independence from the UK. The rest of the news is fairly typical '60s stuff. The Space Race continues with the US doing its second spacewalk, American cop shows evolve suddenly when the Supreme Court rules in Miranda v. Arizona, and the Vatican finally gets rid of the Index Librorum Prohibitorum.

On television, we get one of the least heralded episodes of William Hartnell's tenure on the show. Certainly it was one of the least watched, with this entire period of the show being the lowest sustained drop in ratings the series would experience until 1980, and the second least watched story of Hartnell's era. And on top of that, it's another missing story, this one with no episodes in existence and a post-1983 novelization (see *The Gunfighters* if you don't know why 1983 matters here).

One of the harder things in writing these is marking the ends of things. Since in the classic series a new creative team for the show always inherits some spare scripts from the previous team, the end of an era tends not to be an emphatic "out with a bang" in the style of *The End of Time*. Rather, it's some faint whimper down the line that you don't even realize was the end until you look at the next seven stories and notice that nothing is being done the way it used to be.

So it's easy to miss that this is basically the last William Hartnell story. I mean, he sticks around for three more, but in terms of the tone and type of adventures that make up a normal Hartnell story, the historical checked out back with *The Massacre* (but more about that when the historical itself checks out) and science fiction checks out here.

Once upon a time, you see, Doctor Who didn't always have monsters in it. Eventually that came to an end, and somewhere in Season Four or Five we reach a point where the norm is for stories to have monsters. But up to now, the only proper monsters we've had are the Daleks. The other attempts to create "the new Daleks" have been interesting visual designs, but not the sort of lurking Otherness of a proper monster. Look at something like the Chumblies or the Mechanoids and you get an alien, but the point is their strangeness. They're objects of wonder. The Zarbi are the closest thing to proper monsters we've really seen, and they're really just benign cattle under mind control. Doctor Who monsters in the proper and traditional sense really just haven't been a part of Doctor Who thus far, leaving the Daleks to be the one thing you can turn to when you need ultimate and inconceivable evil.

In fact, the Jeremy Bentham section of the Haining book calls this story out as one that would be better with monsters in it, a claim that Wood and Miles take considerable issue with in *About Time*. But more to the point, the introduction of monsters meant that a particular mode of science fiction story – one that is about the contours of a given future society – was largely ruled out. For science fiction throughout the

Hartnell era, the questions have been what kind of world the TARDIS has arrived on – see in particular the opening episodes of *The Ark* or *The Web Planet*. The Doctor rarely arrives at moments of crisis and intervenes. Instead, he arrives at relatively normal moments and makes chaos.

The Savages is a work in that style, and, as is usually the case for these post-regime change holdovers, not a hugely remarkable one. In particular, it displays one of the cases where I solidly do agree with complaints about pacing in the classic series. Usually I'm inclined to argue that it's less that the classic series is paced badly than it is that the classic series is paced to be watched weekly, but is widely consumed as a single unit to be watched in one go. Unsurprisingly, when you completely change the medium from "television serial" to "films" without changing the actual content, things go wrong. So I'm perfectly willing to forgive a story whose problem with pacing is that the middle episodes could be taken out. What I'm less forgiving of is a story that takes ten minutes to do what could be done just as well in two minutes. And that's where this story errs. The revelation that the Elders are evil moustache-twirlers is painfully obvious to the audience ages before it's actually clear on screen, which makes for television that is flat-out tedious.

But even if it is a slightly wobbly episode, *The Savages* is useful because it lets us actually look at this era. One of the things that we're going to see as we navigate the transition into Patrick Troughton is that the series is going to develop a very new take on counterculture and the future. That change coincides with the collapse of alien races into humanoids and evil, but it's not actually the same change. And we can see that really clearly if we compare this story to *The Ark*, since they are in fact basically the same story.

Both stories are intensely and clearly about colonialism. But they take exactly opposite views. *The Ark* was, in the end, about how the Monoids were clearly unsuitable for self-rule. *The Savages*, on the other hand, is about how the eponymous savages are unjustly oppressed and are perfectly capable of dignified civilization.

The clearest clue here is that the original title of the story was *The White Savages*, a title that would have on the one hand somewhat undermined the point, and on the other hand made the point even clearer. Instead it leaves this story with the slightly uncomfortable holdover that Frederick Jaeger plays Jano blacked up. I should stress, however, that he does not play the role in the American blackface style. It's not a minstrel part, and is barely noticeable in the telesnaps. Much of this comes down to the fact that makeup worked differently in black and white television, and blacking up actors was not jarring in the way that it is today. The biggest sin of blacking up in the sense employed here is mostly that it ended up keeping jobs from actual minority actors.

But you can see right away that the transition to "human good, funny-looking thing bad" has already happened, because the central difference between the two stories is not just that one is pro-colonialism and the other is anti-colonialism. It's also that one has a funny-looking alien and the other doesn't.

In this regard, actually, Bentham is right and Wood and Miles are wrong, although to be fair, I don't think this is what Bentham had in mind when he complained about the lack of monsters. Think of how much more interesting *The Ark* would have been if the Monoids looked exactly like the Guardians, and it was only cultural differences that existed and distinguished the two. Or, for that matter, how much more interesting *The Savages* would be if the oppressed "savages" were visibly different from the Elders so that the Elders are not quite so self-evidently moustache-twirlers. And here we can really see the sort of thing that has fallen off since Verity Lambert left the show. Compare both of these stories to something like *The Web Planet*, where the entire point of the story is the fact that nobody looks like humans and we actually have to judge them on their actions instead of their anatomy, and you see immediately the collapse that's leading to "funny-looking aliens are monsters." Or, for that matter, compare it to the beginning of this season, where *Galaxy Four*, for all its flaws, explicitly inverted this trope with the pretty people being evil and the ugly monsters being good. The xenophobic turn had already happened, really, back in *The Ark*. And like most endings in the series, we missed it.

One ending we don't miss in this story, however, is the departure of Steven. Again, though, this is a case where you can see the amount of work and development the series still has ahead of it. In the first episode there's a great scene in which Dodo taunts Steven for being unable to make his own decisions and for just doing what the Doctor says. In a modern episode, this would be what the story is about: Steven's successes and failures of being independent from the Doctor as a set up for the Doctor volunteering Steven to help rebuild the society.

Instead, we get glimpses of this – in particular after the Doctor's life energy is drained and Steven is forced to take charge and make decisions. It's enough that, if you put your mind to it, you can almost pretend that this story was designed as a counterpart to *The Massacre* so that, where that story was about the failure of Steven to take charge, this story is about him finally being able to. Almost. But we never quite get the sort of definitive "this story is about Steven" moment that we take for granted in the new series where a companion departure gets an entire episode that is basically devoted to that theme. Frankly, and we'll really see this in comparison to *The War Machines*, it's a wonder Ian Stuart Black managed to get in as much thematic content about Steven as he did.

But as we have a longstanding tradition of pleasant memorial episodes whenever a major departure happens, let's do our Steven memorial. But first, a quick rundown of other things worth remarking on; this is the first story to abandon individual episode titles in favor of the story getting one overarching title. The result is a slight step away from the serial nature of the show. It's not a move to the movie-like approach that the DVD/VHS releases take, but it is at least a move towards codifying the idea that every few weeks Doctor Who changes everything. This story also has one character – Jano, the leader of the Elders, who partially takes on the character traits of the Doctor and is another dress-rehearsal for the interchangeability of the character, something we know in hindsight was only a few stories away from being very important. This story also has a fascinating conceit that, to my knowledge, no other story ever used – the Elders have tracked the Doctor's trajectory through space and time and have known he was coming for years. This is a great idea, and one that I think has some real potential for future stories – the idea of people having years to prepare for the Doctor's arrival because the TARDIS, as a time machine, is visible over time. And this is the first time a rock quarry is an alien planet – a conceit that on the one hand is stereotypical Doctor Who, and on the other hand frankly works pretty darn well.

OK. So, Steven then. As I've said previously, the thing about Steven is that the actor exceeds the character by a great margin. A strong case can be made that the show could never have survived without its year of Peter Purves. Where William Russell had a narrowly defined character who was, in the end, extremely useful, Peter Purves was never given much with Steven. A futuristic pilot who mostly just had to look credulous, Purves's job on the series very clearly increasingly became to pinch-hit for an increasingly erratic William Hartnell. With Hartnell being written out of every other episode, and really never being ideally suited to the leading man role, Purves was forced to be a chameleon, filling in whatever a given story needed him to fill in. It's difficult to meaningfully memorialize Steven. But Peter Purves kept the series together for a year, and thank God for it. And if his departure is sudden, it is by miles the least sudden and least bewildering departure we've had thus far on the show besides Ian and Barbara. (And even they puzzlingly miss the fact that they were back in their own time four episodes before they suddenly risk life and limb to return there.)

But by and large, this episode is . . . transitional. Although it's not formally the case that Hartnell is on his way out, the fact of the matter is that Innes Lloyd has been angling to remove Hartnell since *The Celestial Toymaker*. Rumor says the only reason the Doctor wasn't played by a different actor when he rematerialized in that story was that the BBC accidentally renewed his contract. And so in many ways, since then the series has been quietly evolving – trying new things. This story may have been the last return to the style and themes that dominated the first two seasons of Doctor Who. But with as much in the air as it was, even those styles and those themes seem strangely . . . off. (Another thing I could have spent a lot of time talking about is the strange and alienating effect of string-based music in this story.) By now, the series can't go back to the Verity Lambert days. But until Patrick Troughton shows up, it can't go forward to what it will be either.

Time Can Be Rewritten: *The Man in the Velvet Mask*

So this one ought to be fun. Daniel O'Mahony's *The Man in the Velvet Mask* is pure Marmite. Ostensibly one of the most hated Doctor Who books, it apparently came in dead last in *Doctor Who Magazine*'s poll about the novels. But that claim carries a metric ton of assumptions with it. I don't want to do a whole post like *The Gunfighters* about the various factions of fandom during the interregnum, mostly because I intend to actually cover the interregnum when we get there. So suffice it to say that this book also has passionate defenders. (I suppose I should, as part of my continued commitment to helping Americans work through their stages of grief at discovering that there are actually entire facets of foreign cultures that have nothing to do with them, mention that Marmite is a savory, salty, yeast-based spread used in the UK on sandwiches, toast, crackers, and other such things. Its use is somewhere between that of peanut butter and mayonnaise, neither of which it tastes remotely like. Among those for whom it is part of their culture there are exactly two opinions available – passionate love or utter hatred. Thus "Marmite" is, in the vernacular, an adjective describing something that produces extremely polarized views with minimal middle ground.)

Most of the dispute centers on whether or not the book simply goes too far to be a Doctor Who story, and, secondarily, whether it goes too far to be a Hartnell story.

Which is to say, the objection is over the fact that Dodo spends an awful lot of this book naked, then also has sex and gets infected with an alien virus that slowly corrupts you. There is some dispute over this, with some people claiming Dodo gets a fatal venereal disease or syphilis. She doesn't. The description of the virus is that "Once infected, you cannot be sure whether your actions are of your own free will or directed by him." By the end of the book the him in question is dead, But given that in the next story televised Dodo succumbs to mind control, the implication is that it leaves one susceptible to mental domination in general, and the virus is later described as "eating through her nervous system and her brain."

Back with *The Celestial Toymaker*, I called into question the idea that every story was a Doctor Who story. And as the delightfully brilliant Anna of *stringofbits.net* pointed out after that entry, there are more obvious problems with the claim – as she put it, "What about that story where the Doctor is a serial rapist?" Which captures at least one crux of the issue – that the notion of "Doctor Who story" is bounded on one side by the fact that the Doctor needs to act Doctor-like. But is there more than that? The problem with *The Ark* is not even that the Doctor does the wrong thing; the Monoids are, after all, portrayed as moustache-twirlers. The Doctor isn't wrong to overthrow the Monoids, the show is wrong to show us the Monoids the way it does. Likewise, it's not like the Doctor does anything wrong when confronted with a raging stereotype of yellow peril. He just never should have been confronted in the first place. The problems with those two stories are their premises.

Continuing on this thread, Paul Cornell once observed (in an interview I can't find) that the reason Sylvester McCoy was his favorite Doctor was that McCoy was the first Doctor Cornell could imagine encountering a concentration camp and still having the story work, whereas earlier Doctors would just not work, morally, in that setting. Whether or not one agrees that McCoy could work in that context, at the root of the observation is a fair point – imagining William Hartnell "hmmming" his way through systematic extermination while insisting on upholding history would be sickening. Which makes the fact that Brian Hayles was actively working on a story called *The Nazis* at this point in the show's history a bit of a jarring fact.

But frankly, saying the production team had any real confidence of what Doctor Who was at this point is a bit of a stretch. Once the show experienced the thirteen episodes from *The Time Meddler* through *The Myth Makers* – a series of episodes as long as the show's initially commissioned run over which every single major creative figure save for William Hartnell changed over – it began casting about and trying to find a clear sense of what it is. In many ways there's more dramatic shifts in tone at this point than there ever were under Verity Lambert. That's going to settle down over the next few televised stories, but if you asked someone in the week before the last episode of *The Savages* and the first episode of *The War Machines* what sort of show Doctor Who was, you'd surely get some pretty interesting answers, including ones that don't necessarily sound a lot like the show we know today.

None of which is to say that *The Man in the Velvet Mask* could ever have been made in 1966. Of course it couldn't. It's comical to imagine Hartnell agreeing to be in this story. There is no way whatsoever to read this as a "missing adventure" in the sense that it's some lost story that you can imagine being made. But we've already seen that the far more traditional *The Plotters* wouldn't really have fit into its gap even as it goes out of its way to feel like its era. Hartnell accepting a story about King James I's homosexual lust for his companions is just as improbable as him agreeing to do a pseudo-historical guest starring the Marquis de Sade.

But the thing is, *The Plotters* does go out of its way to feel like its era, whereas this seems to go out of its way to clash with expectations of what the Hartnell era is like. This book fits into a particular fan theory of the Hartnell era that is unmistakably a product of 1996. I mean, this is the entire point of the title of this entry – that what we're looking at here is the Hartnell era reflected through later eras. Or, to put it another way, we've got retcons aplenty going on here. Yes, there's no way that this is what the Hartnell era was doing at the time. I mean, a central premise of the book is that the Doctor knows he's about to regenerate and is constantly struggling against his own failing body. Whereas if you watch the stories from the period, the idea floated by O'Mahoney – that the Doctor has known his regeneration is coming since *The Celestial Toymaker* – is clearly revisionist. The story after *The Celestial Toymaker*, after all, is the one in which we saw the Doctor more animated than he had been in years.

Though this does give some idea of the weird way in which that story's reputation is distorted compared to what it actually did. Why pick *The Celestial Toymaker* as the point at which the Doctor's life begins to run out instead of the trauma he experiences at the hands of the Time Destructor in *The Daleks' Master Plan* or the draining of his life force by the Elders in *The Savages*, both of which would have an actual reason for a looming regeneration? Because *The Celestial Toymaker* is the "classic," and because it's got a weird and superficially avant-garde premise that appeals to writers who like deconstructing past eras of Doctor Who. And perhaps equally significant, because the fanlore that Hartnell was almost replaced after that story is well known, so it symbolically provides the beginning of the end of Hartnell's tenure. But again, this is totally unsupported by the actual episodes. Especially because, as we'll see over time, even if the decision had been made to replace Hartnell by this point – and while it was clearly Innes Lloyd's desire, Hartnell hadn't agreed to it yet, so it clearly wasn't made – the idea of regeneration as we think of it today wasn't invented until the mid-'70s at the earliest.

Given all of that, then, what do we make of a passage like this:

The first Change was coming. He'd felt the storm brewing months ago. He'd fought against it, but his efforts only seemed to strengthen it and darken its edges. The tide would pass across him, scouring his landscape, leaving scattered devastation in its wake. The clouds swirled, darting round him ready to swallow and consume his self. He felt the tears bulging on his eyelids, dribbling down a distant, detached face. The Change was more frightening than death. The Change would destroy part of his self forever. He'd know that for the rest of his lives, and the knowledge would torment him.

One heart, he thought blissfully. One heart, soon to meet its twin.

Well, OK, yes, it's gothically overwritten. But what else do we make of it?

Several things are introduced here that aren't really a part of Doctor Who at this stage – the idea that regeneration is the death of part of his self, that he has lives, that regeneration exists, and, of course most significantly, the whole two hearts business. The heart bit is probably the most quoted line of the novel, actually, and is probably worth talking about. What's going on here is an attempt to reconcile some continuity. You may remember way back in *The Sensorites* that the Doctor explicitly refers to his heart, singular. You may also know that way forward in *Spearhead from Space*, the Doctor clearly has two hearts. This led to the fan theory that the Doctor acquired his second heart in his first regeneration.

The trouble is, as Miles and Wood point out, there's some strong evidence that the Troughton Doctor only has one heart as well. They come up with a bold new fanwank explanation, but this all dances around the larger problem. As a matter of actual reading of episodes, there's just no way to argue that when we start up *The War Machines* we'll be watching William Hartnell play a character who knows he's dying and thinks he's about to get a second heart.

There are, of course, defenses to mount here, most obviously that authorial intent doesn't matter and that later developments force our hand into reinterpreting the Hartnell stories in light of later information. In this theory, *Spearhead from Space* forced us to retcon the Hartnell era, and that's just that. Or, in another interpretation, the bits of *The Sensorites* and *The Wheel in Space* that suggest a single-hearted Doctor are just "goofs" that should be ignored. Except, well, yuck. Surely the goof is in *Spearhead from Space* when the writers forget the bits that established the Doctor as having one heart, and a proper Doctor Who fan with loyalty to the continuity should insist on a one-hearted Doctor. But of course, we don't do this – for whatever reason, fandom is more prone to modify the past based on the future than to reject new stories for contradicting the past (although it certainly does do that).

The real problem we're running into is that there's no unified Doctor Who. Yes, the Hartnell era contradicts the Pertwee era. Given the multiple turnovers in production teams between them, this should hardly be a surprise. And as we've already discussed, the notion of continuity is ludicrous in an era where there was no chance of past stories ever being repeated. The past, at this point in Doctor Who, is simply assumed to be gone. Maybe a fleeting mention of it here and there – the throwaway reference to Ian and Barbara at the end of *The Massacre*, for instance – but let's face it, the notion of coherent continuity exploded within a few stories. Arguably the first major continuity error comes in *The Edge of Destruction*, where the Doctor strongly suggests having had an adventure on the planet Quinnis, despite acting in *100,00 BC* as if he'd never been in serious trouble before.

So the problem we have is that the Hartnell era wasn't assumed to be revisitable except in a hat-tip sort of way until much later in the show. But, ironically, doesn't that ultimately help O'Mahoney's case? If the Hartnell era was made with the idea that it wouldn't be visitable except via memory and reconstruction, what's so bad about a story that obviously doesn't fit in at the time? The Hartnell era's assumption, if it even vaguely imagined that anyone would care at all about it in 1996, would be that it would be a dimly remembered aspect of the show. So a novel that takes strands of dim memory and folds them into something strange and new is . . . not actually entirely unfair.

In which case perhaps the biggest problem this novel has is that it exposes just how much strain we put the Hartnell era under. I mean, at the end of the day, this is three seasons of hastily made television with a cranky leading man who was going senile and multiple production teams. And we rely on it to provide the design document for forty-five subsequent years of Doctor Who. Every subsequent era is assumed to have to justify itself in terms of the Hartnell era, and has be able to read the Hartnell era as a logical antecedent to itself. Which is rather a stretch, to say the least.

And in the end, one is left between a rock and a hard place. Ultimately, you can either depict the Hartnell era faithfully, or you can fix continuity. And ultimately, this book is an example of the latter. It goes back and tries to add context from the future into the past. And it's an interesting choice and an interesting experiment. Is it a Hartnell-era book? No. Of course not. But it's a fascinating commentary on the relationship between the Hartnell era and the aesthetic of Doctor Who in 1996, and a comment on the implicit gaps of the Hartnell era, which, particularly in this part of the era, there were a lot of.

The biggest gap this book tackles, however, is not the question of the Doctor's impending regeneration. It's Dodo, who is going to leave two episodes into the next story with basically no meaningful sendoff in what is easily the second worst companion departure ever. (The worst, of course, being Liz Shaw.) This book aims to fix that and explain her departure.

Dodo, as we've seen, was not a huge success as a companion. The part was not written well, in no small part because there seemed to be no overall direction as to what the character was supposed to be. More than any other companion we've seen, Dodo has spent virtually all of her time being stupid and getting into trouble, or being stupid and failing to get out of trouble. It's as if they took Susan from *The Reign of Terror* freaking out about rats and deciding the guillotine is preferable, and built an entire character out of it. I don't even want to criticize Jackie Lane's acting, because I see no meaningful evidence that she had a role to play in the first place.

Yes, it's a bit shocking given the era of the show in question for her to be having sex, although it's not like the book has any explicit sex scenes. But then again, if we stop to think about it, the idea that a teenage runaway from London is going to travel through space and time without a moment or two of experimentation is a stretch too. And Dodo is portrayed as being conflicted about sex. She's talked about as an innocent, and her sexual awakening is described as corrupting her (by the man she sleeps with, no less). In this context, the setting of the book seems particularly apropos, and we should perhaps look primarily to the major historical personage featured in the book, the Marquis de Sade.

Sade is an easily misunderstood figure whose writing blended reveling in explicit, fetishistic sex and philosophical discussions of liberty and art. The book is, in many ways, a Sadean story about Dodo, the innocent cipher of a companion. And so we return, once again, to the Problem of Susan, this time in its most explicit formulation. The central problem of the book – the entire issue that divides people on it, frankly – is whether or not the audience will accept the sexualization of an otherwise unsexualized character who, in any realistic portrayal, would have been sexually awakened. The book confronts the show's decision to take what was ostensibly supposed to be a working-class London girl from the swinging sixties and make her a sexless cipher with no clear character traits. And it makes the argument, a not entirely uncompelling argument, that the desexualizing of her was what made her not work as a character.

Certainly, sexualized or not, it's difficult to argue that the Dodo Chaplet created by O'Mahoney is not a far more interesting character than the one we ever see on screen. Yes, O'Mahoney's take is one that we never could have seen on BBC1 in 1966. But that's not the point. The point is to show us a version of the Hartnell era that is a strange, dark mirror of the version that was on television. Sure, it features a character that would never have flown on '60s television. But let's face it, Dodo was herself a bit of a flightless bird. Sure, the world and tone of this book isn't as good as that of Hartnell-era Doctor Who. But Hartnell-era Doctor Who is enriched by having this to contrast with, and by having this to bring to light some of the loose threads and ignored aspects of the world of that series.

Or, to pick up on an earlier analogy, yeah, it'd be shocking and garish to see the First Doctor walking through a concentration camp. But sometimes seeing the shocking extremes of what a Doctor Who story can be is necessary. You don't really know the shape of something until you probe its edges.

(For the handful of people for whom this information would be relevant, I want to point out that the plot of this is extremely similar to the early issues of Grant Morrison's comic book series *The Invisibles*, which had as its second storyline a time-travel plot about the Marquis de Sade and about extra-dimensional alien incursions into Revolutionary France. Given *The Invisibles'* notion of narrative, it becomes fairly easy to read this novel in the context of *The Invisibles* and as a Morrison-esque attempt to create a conscious revision of 1960s Doctor Who to be more compatible with the avant garde traditions of the time. We'll talk more about the avant garde and revolutionary traditions of the 1960s in a few essays, and even more in the Patrick Troughton volume, and we'll look at *The Invisibles* itself in the McGann/Eccleston volume, but I'd hate to have a reader tut-tutting that I missed this aspect of the novel. All of which said, according to O'Mahony, the similarity is purely coincidental.)

Pop Between Realities, Home in Time for Tea:
Quatermass

If you kidnapped somebody from November 24, 1963, and asked them about televised British science fiction, it would be self-evident that the most important thing to talk about is Nigel Kneale's set of three serials in the 1950s: *The Quatermass Experiment*, *Quatermass II*, and *Quatermass and the Pit*. Still influential well into the 1960s due to the adaptations by Hammer Films into *The Quatermass Xperiment* (1955, the X refers to the film rating they were going for), *Quatermass 2* (1957), and, in 1967, their version of *Quatermass and the Pit*, everybody knows that the Quatermass serials were major influences on Doctor Who, which is why Kneale refused to write for the program, viewing it as just a rip-off of his ideas.

And really, with even a cursory glance at the first three seasons of Doctor Who, you can see just how much the show relied on Quatermass. Just look at all the stories featuring intense paranoia about space, a government that is evil and untrustworthy out of misguided virtue, and broad global terrors of alien invasions that threaten to consume the Earth. It's a wonder Kneale didn't sue over the rip-offs, really.

Hopefully you see what I did there. If not, suffice it to say that up to this point, it's far easier to discuss the ways in which Doctor Who is a decisive break with the Quatermass tradition than it is to discuss the similarities. That won't always be true, of course. The first season of Jon Pertwee's tenure opens with a sequence of three stories each of which is directly and lovingly ripped off from one of the three Quatermass serials. Even then, Lance Parkin, in an essay reprinted in the first volume of Mad Norwegian Press' fantastic *Time Unincorporated* series, makes a fairly compelling argument that the influence of Quatermass on Doctor Who is egregiously overstated.

But perhaps easier than approaching this in terms of its influence, we should just look at the Quatermass series on its own terms first and then get back to Doctor Who. The three '50s Quatermass serials belonged to the old live transmission school of television. With only a few exceptions of inserted scenes in the later two, all of Quatermass was shot live. The original, *The Quatermass Experiment*, in fact has four missing episodes not because the BBC wiped the tapes à la Doctor Who, but because there were no tapes in the first place. There was no effort at all to preserve it for posterity. We only have the first two, in fact, because of an aborted plan to sell the show to Canada. Watching them now is . . . an interesting experience. As with most serials, they transplant somewhat poorly to the modern era, or at least, to the modern practice of watching them as a movie that occasionally runs the credits in the middle of the feature. As with Doctor Who, restoring the original tone of serialization helps a lot.

But one thing that does come across is an amazing sense of tone. The Quatermass serials throb with a growing sense of paranoia and panic. There's a constant sense that there are terrible things in the world and that humanity is on a slow and relentless march towards its own destruction with only the enlightened men of science able to stem the tide. The three classic serials have instantly memorable premises – the British Rocket Group's first manned launch goes horribly wrong and only one astronaut returns, and he's possessed by an enormous vegetable creature that wants to consume the Earth. Some meteors crash to the Earth and break open, exposing people to a pathogen that leaves them mind-controlled drones preparing for an alien invasion. And, perhaps most memorably, there's *Quatermass and the Pit*, in which a buried spaceship reveals that humans are actually evolved from aliens and that all of the classic British folklore about goblins and demons is really about aliens.

But in execution, there's something weirdly timeless about them. Not timeless in the sense of "eternally applicable," although they are that, but rather in the stranger sense of seeming slightly out of place in whatever time period they're considered during. The frenetic energy of the serials makes them feel ahead of their time in the 1950s, but by the time of the 1967 Hammer version of *Quatermass and the Pit*, there's already something stilted about the entire affair. Perhaps the weirdest and most educational version to watch is the 2005 BBC production of *The Quatermass Experiment*, in which a lightly abridged version of Kneale's scripts was used for a live-on-TV performance in the style of the 1950s, only featuring David Tennant, Mark Gatiss, and Indira Varma (as well as several very good actors and actresses who haven't appeared in Doctor Who or *Torchwood*). Watching modern actors try to find any nuance or depth in Kneale's dialogue is an at times actively painful experience. (Tennant, more than once, seems openly annoyed at the lack of rhythm or lilt to his expository monologues, and you can just about hear him praying that his upcoming scenes of technobabble in Doctor Who don't go like this. On the other hand, Mark Gatiss is better than I've ever seen him.) But on the other hand, for all the bizarre anachronism of it, what is perhaps most remarkable is just how watchable it is. It has no business working, but it does.

So I suppose that's one similarity with Doctor Who, which also has no business surviving from 1963 to 2013 and counting. And there are some other similarities, taken as a whole – Quatermass had three different actors on television, two in the movie series, and two more who have played the role since those. Lacking in a sense of clear continuity, Quatermass is a mode of science fiction that is unusual today – less a distinct world and setting than a style of story and a type of main character. The only other obvious example of this, of course, is Doctor Who. And, of course, as I've reiterated time and time again, the serialized format is crucial to both shows (and seriously, we did unbelievable harm to Doctor Who when we reduced it to an anthology series of movies instead of a proper serial). And I suppose both do have male scientists as protagonists.

But past a vague structural similarity and an uncanny endurance, it's easier to spot the differences. For one thing, Quatermass is much more grounded in England than Doctor Who has been thus far. I mean, yes, Doctor Who has from day one shown a bias towards contemporary Earth and particularly London. Since the show debuted, the TARDIS has touched down in near-contemporary England four times (*An Unearthly Child*, *Planet of Giants*, *The Daleks' Master Plan*, and *The Massacre*), and in contemporary New York once. Admittedly, that's way out of proportion to the number of times that, for instance, the Fifty-Seventh Segment of Time, Marinus, or fifteenth-century Mexico have been visited. But the stop-offs have mostly been brief. The only time the show used contemporary England as the primary setting for an adventure, *Planet of Giants*, the hook was that the crew was miniaturized – i.e. they were still on an alien world, even if it was one that we recognized as a strange variation on our own. And when we visited London proper, it was a ruined post-apocalyptic London. More often Doctor Who has either presented an alternative time period in Earth's history that we can compare our world to (whether it be historical or futuristic) or presented an alien world with similarities to ours in some fashion. The interest, in other words, is in presenting variations on our world. This is markedly different from Quatermass, which shows terrible things that could happen to our world.

The difference is perhaps subtle, but it is significant. Doctor Who featured a character from contemporary England in all but five stories in the Hartnell era. Of those five, three featured Vicki, a thinly-veiled Scouse girl, one featured a stop-off in contemporary England, one featured 1960s technology invading the Middle Ages, and the only one not covered by at least one of the above is just a one-episode teaser for one of them. But that was, mostly, its main contribution. The major thrust of Doctor Who was taking someone like Barbara – a regular old and solidly maternal schoolteacher – and dropping her in an alien jungle. It's thus far taken the mundane and dropped it off in the fantastic. Quatermass does the exact opposite: it takes the fantastic and drops it into our world. Which is closely related to the observation I already made that Quatermass is about a scary universe that might eat us, and Doctor Who is about an amazing universe we can explore.

This gets at what is perhaps the biggest difference between the Doctor and Professor Quatermass. For all that the Doctor is a scientist, he is by and large a troublemaker first and foremost. Quatermass is part of the establishment. Even if he is a firebrand who butts heads with the military, government, and his fellow scientists, he is still fundamentally a part of the British social order. The Doctor, on the other hand, has an intense disdain for the social order. As we've seen, given his druthers, he thinks burning it down is funny. It's the difference between an anarchist who's willing to play by the rules sometimes and a bureaucrat who's willing to get into trouble sometimes.

It's not that Quatermass is statist. *Quatermass II* is, at its heart, a piece about anxieties over the Welfare State. The serial's major set piece is a synthetic food plant that's actually a cover for a rapidly growing alien creature. To start, the idea of synthetic food – i.e. a technologically engineered solution to a social problem – ties easily to the basic idea of the Welfare State. Combine that with the motif, repeated throughout the serial, of Quatermass getting vital information from tramps or elderly rural folk, all of whom talk vaguely and ominously about the sense that something had been taken away from them. It's over that backdrop that Kneale does his *Invasion of the Body Snatchers* plot. (*Quatermass II* comes a year after the first publication of *The Body Snatchers* in the US, but a year before the movie. The book was mildly obscure, so I don't know if Kneale was aware of it, though there are other less famous antecedents such as *The Thing from Another World* and John Campbell's "Who Goes There," which was the basis of *The Thing*.)

Taken in context, then, the usual *Body Snatchers* interpretation of it as being a metaphor for McCarthyism or Communism stumbles fairly badly. Rather, Kneale is sketching a world here where the state is necessary (as it brings us people like Quatermass) but fragile, much like the rest of the world, and that if the state overreaches it is brought down much more easily. But it's crucial to note, the state is still indispensable. Even in *Quatermass and the Pit*, which makes much of Quatermass's frustrations with attempts to militarize space and his butting heads with the government, the story ends up with Quatermass as the wise technocrat cautioning the masses against the perils of mob rule.

In this regard, there's a fundamental incompatibility with Doctor Who. Now I should note that neither Quatermass nor Doctor Who are, most of the time, overtly political. Not that there are not Doctor Who stories that engage contemporary issues, nor that Quatermass isn't hugely invested in a political argument. But both stop well short of actual interventions in electoral politics. The Doctor never hangs a "Vote Labour" sign on the TARDIS.

On the other hand, there is no such thing as apolitical science fiction. Whenever aliens show up, one thing those aliens signify, necessarily, is the issue of immigration and otherness. Any time a scientist insists that we are all in grave danger and is laughed off by the political establishment, it makes reference to the climate change debate, or, in older times, the debate over atomic energy and nuclear weapons. Any time technology becomes too advanced and a danger to us we have a commentary on genetic engineering, the Internet, or some older object of paranoia. Science fiction, by virtue of its conceit, is about the world and how it changes, and that's necessarily political. And beyond that, mass culture is necessary political, in that it necessarily makes assumptions about the shared values of a population.

More broadly, it is not as though political philosophy operates in a vacuum. I'll use contemporary US politics here because they're the ones I'm more familiar with, but the fact of the matter is that a story about a highly educated man who loves other cultures, hates ignorance, overthrows governments, and gets full of moral outrage when he sees people suffering and demands that it be fixed is necessarily more allied with liberal politics than conservative politics. There's no way around this, because political ideology is linked to personal ethics and personal ideology. If you make a character who is defined by his beliefs about how the world ought to be, you're making a character who comments on politics. And when those beliefs are cosmopolitan, intellectual, anarchistic, and invested in social welfare, you necessarily end up on one side of the political spectrum.

We'll talk more about this in a few essays when we'll fill in some gaps about 1960s counterculture in Britain. (And in general, these Pop Between Realities entries are going to become more common. I apologize a bit for this, because I have the distinct sense that these little digression entries are wildly less popular than the ones where I actually watch Doctor Who, but we're dealing with a major transition in the tone of the series, and if we want to understand Patrick Troughton stepping out of the TARDIS as something other than a piece of received fan lore, we're going to have to make sure we understand television in 1966. So even though there's only three William Hartnell stories remaining after *The Savages*, there are rather more essays in the book after that.) But for now, let's note that the politics of Quatermass are distinctly conservative, and this is mostly a big difference with Doctor Who, which, while not always liberal, is at least always most comfortable with stories that are, broadly speaking, of a more liberal worldview.

So to recap the score, yes, both Quatermass and Doctor Who share a certain anthology flavor and a male scientist protagonist, although Quatermass (thus far) comes much closer to having a set formula than Doctor Who. But Quatermass is fundamentally conservative while Doctor Who is fundamentally liberal. And Quatermass is about the fragility of Earth and humanity, while Doctor Who is about the boundless potential of the universe. Thus far, Parkin is right – there are a lot of things that are much more obvious influences on Doctor Who in 1966 than the adventures of Professor Quatermass.

Basically, as long as Doctor Who is mostly a show about futuristic planets where thinly veiled allegories for colonial oppression take place, it's just not going to be much like Quatermass. Now if it were set in contemporary London and based around a horrifying non-human threat that could overthrow humanity as masters of the Earth, perhaps running out of some major recent landmark like Post Office Tower, maybe we'd want to talk more about the similarities between Doctor Who and Quatermass.

But frankly, what are the odds of that happening?

Very Sophisticated Idiots (*The War Machines*)

It's June 25, 1966. The Beatles are at number one with "Paperback Writer," and will trade it to the Kinks in two week's time. The remainder of the charts displays a fairly standard blend of irritating traditionalism and pleasant edginess as it proceeds towards a more contemporary style. In the news, not a lot happens – some shuffles of foreign leaders, France leaving NATO, and the Vietnam war gets worse and worse. Oh, and the 1966 World Cup started five days before the finale of this story. But it's not like that had any influence on British culture of the time.

Meanwhile, on television, the Doctor fights a renegade computer that's controlling people's minds out of Post Office Tower. So I guess the odds were fairly high after all, and we're going to have to talk more about Quatermass.

Much of the point of taking the Quatermass excursion was to make sure it was clear just how bizarre this story is in the context of prior Doctor Who. Doctor Who has felt a bit all over the map since Verity Lambert left, but never with the supreme confidence with which Lambert's Doctor Who simply assumed it could get away with whatever it tried. Since she left it's been desperately trying to find what it's good at, and, absent a hand as assured as Ms. Lambert's, hasn't quite found out yet. The amount it has changed in a year is staggering. More or less exactly a year ago today, the show was wrapping up *The Chase* and saying goodbye to Ian and

Barbara. To get from there to *The Daleks' Master Plan* is staggering enough. To get from there through that, through *The Massacre*, through *The Celestial Toymaker*, and out to this is . . . I mean, however bizarre the jump from *The Sensorites* to *The Chase* in one year is, it's nothing compared to the gap from *The Chase* to this.

But what, exactly, is different? Hartnell has changed, certainly, with his acting awkwardly deteriorating over the course of the season. The bigger change can be seen in the companions. A year ago, we had Ian and Barbara – the two ordinary humans – and Vicki, who, while not an ordinary human, fulfilled the promise of the first episode better than Susan ever did. She was very much *An Unearthly Child*, visibly from our world, but clearly an avatar of its future. The rapid shedding of this entire companion team in favor of Steven, the featureless chameleon and Dodo, the one where they forgot to have a concept for the character, marks a major change. With Ian and Barbara we could see mundane life in extraordinary people. With Vicki we could see a clear vision of the future. With Steven we have an effective character for plot resolution, and with Dodo we have . . . well . . . something very good at being kidnapped. We've gone from companions that set the tone of the show to companions that advance the plot well.

Which captures the heart of the change. Under Lambert the show was meant to be educational, or, at the very least, fascinating. Under Innes Lloyd, the show has increasingly morphed to where it aspires first towards being exciting, generally in an "action serial for young boys" sense as opposed to the broad family sense of the Lambert era, and only secondarily towards being interesting. And so where Lambert would never have tried a story like this, set in a contemporary London we are meant to recognize as our own, it's the obvious choice for Lloyd. If you want to have an action-packed thriller, why set it on Vortis or the Sense Sphere when you can set it in your backyard?

But even with all of that, there's something shocking about the change of tone here. It's not just that this is the first time a story has felt like unadulterated Innes Lloyd. *The Celestial Toymaker* was as much a John Wiles story as an Innes Lloyd one, *The Gunfighters* was all Lloyd in execution, but still a Donald Cotton script, and Cotton was a writer who started in the Wiles era. *The Savages* felt like an older sort of story. And here, suddenly, from the same writer as *The Savages*, we have a story that is like nothing we've seen on Doctor Who before. The only reason this looks even remotely familiar is that many of the things it's doing for the first time are things that the show will keep doing for the next eight years.

This isn't a new problem for us – since the show started, we've been caught between what we see on the screen and what we know we're going to see. To take just one example, the Problem of Susan is visible because we know about subsequent decades of vaguely problematic relationships between the Doctor and young girls, and we know that when the inevitable return of the Time Lords happens, the first thing we'll be looking for is a young girl that can wrap up some of the teased plot threads about the Doctor's family. But even if we see both ends of the Susan issue, we can at least easily tell which end is which.

But here we've got a real problem. Watched from one end, we know all the set pieces of this: the bizarre "Doctor Who is required" scene in which WOTAN decides on the importance of kidnapping the Doctor and sets off a thousand retcons as to why he flubs the name, the introduction of Ben and Polly, the ludicrously poorly done departure of Dodo, the central London stuff, etc. And we can fit them into our knowledge of Doctor Who and get it all to make sense, ignoring the fact that, taken as the culmination of three seasons of the show, this makes no sense whatsoever.

From the perspective of the show as it develops, this seems like it could be almost any show except for Doctor Who. The Quatermass connections are obvious – the entire world goes from business as usual to nearly doomed in a single day. Although the problem is purely man-made, WOTAN is not an evil computer in the familiar sense of *WarGames* (the movie with Matthew Broderick, not the Troughton serial). Where WOPR is misprogrammed, WOTAN is actually said to be able to think for itself. WOPR misunderstands the situation he is in and inadvertently endangers humanity, while WOTAN actually understands it perfectly. It's just that WOTAN honestly wants humanity to die. In this regard, WOTAN is, while man-made, strikingly alien. In fact, the nearest analogue to WOTAN that we've seen thus far is probably the Animus, a similarly impersonal entity. The result is a very Quatermass-like feel – a hostile and impersonal Other threatens the whole of humanity with extinction, and we see a government bureaucrat's eye view of saving the world.

But unlike Quatermass, there's no sense of mystery or discovery here. Come the end of the first episode, we know pretty much everything about the situation and the dangers, whereas the end of the first episode of a Quatermass serial tends to be the confirmation that there's danger in the first place. In this regard, the story matches more closely with *The Avengers*, a straight action/adventure series set in contemporary England, which we'll talk about soon enough. And those are just the two big ones – Wood and Miles in *About Time* identify a good half-dozen more in their write-up of the episode. And on top of that we have the show we're actually watching: Doctor Who.

The question is, how did audiences at the time take it? It's tough to tell, this being the '60s. The Appreciation Index started at forty-nine percent – decent but a bit low for the series in its third season – and careened down to a pretty dismal thirty-nine percent. By that measure, this story was distinctly less popular than either *The Savages* before it or *The Smugglers* after it. On the other hand, Innes Lloyd was not a stupid man with a solid sense of popular tastes. And he clearly decided that, AI or no AI, he was going to keep working in this vein. (Indeed, if you want to completely throw into chaos the received wisdom on *The Gunfighters*, try to explain based on AI figures why that was supposedly the reason why the historical should be abandoned in Doctor Who, whereas *The War Machines* model is the show's standard operating procedure for the next ten seasons.)

The fact of the matter is, it's tough to come up with a compelling reason why someone who had really enjoyed Doctor Who up to this point would watch this. In every regard, it feels like a complete departure. That's not unusual. We've had oddball stories before. *The Celestial Toymaker* springs to mind most readily. But before when we did a complete departure from everything we've ever seen, we got back to things that felt like Doctor Who shortly thereafter. That's not going to happen here. On the other hand, Doctor Who as we know it isn't quite dead yet. *The Savages* may have been the last traditional Hartnell story, but the transitory period is going to last a few stories, and this story is still unmistakably a Hartnell story.

So let's put the future aside, at least for another few stories, and try to clear the grime off our 20/20 hindsight to watch this thing. The first thing that's clear is that this is not merely set in contemporary London, it's full out embracing contemporary London. Its initial establishing shot screams London, and almost as soon as the Doctor lands, we get a shot of Post Office Tower, which had just opened when the episode aired. This is a complete inversion of Ian and Barbara, as I've said. Suddenly, instead of seeing the familiar taken into strange places, we see the Doctor, the avatar of strangeness, land in the middle of London and confidently declare that something evil is going on here.

We also get a new kind of threat – WOTAN, the evil computer. Again, I've already talked about his otherworldliness. More broadly, it should be noted that WOTAN is one of the elements of this story that it is hardest to watch now. The fact of the matter is, WOTAN does not work anything like a computer written in the twenty-first century would. But the thing is, as easy as it is to laugh at the

Doctor's lengthy explanation that the problem with these evil robotic tanks is that they've been incompletely programmed (and as comical as the dialogue about how WOTAN is going to be given control of all other computer systems in the world is), we're still talking about computer plotting that is as sophisticated as that of *Live Free or Die Hard* or *The Net*. (If you're the sort of bewildering masochist who likes badly written Internet thrillers and somehow haven't seen these "classics," you owe it to yourself.) Yes, "as sophisticated as *Live Free or Die Hard*" is not a statement that you generally want to aspire towards, but given that this was 1966, the goal is perhaps more ambitious than it sounds.

(I should add a parenthetical here for the reader I know will care. Yes, WOTAN is named after the Norse Odin, and the link is made even more explicit when the War Machines themselves are called Valkyries in the novelization. Unfortunately, there ends the fascinating Norse interpretation of this story, as it's pretty clear the only thing this is supposed to signify is the vaguely Nazi-like tone of the whole thing. Those looking for an epic confrontation between the Doctor and the Norse pantheon are just going to have to wait until 1989.)

Then there's Ben and Polly – numbers nine and ten in the official list of companions. As I already said, the companions are a mixed bag in this phase of the series. The fact of the matter is that Ian and Barbara were such strong characters that they have proven difficult to replace. And, actually, so has Vicki, going through three replacements. Although to be fair, two of these were always planned to be killed off. So I'm pretty pleased to say we have a pair of pretty good characters here. Steven was never a problem as a replacement for Ian, and Ben slots into that role pretty well but adds an edge to it we haven't seen before. He's the show's first, proper working-class character, and the class issues become visible in this story with upper class aristocrats dismissing him as "boy" and the like on an alarmingly regular basis. He's paired with Polly, who (even while spending half the story under

WOTAN's mind control) is magnetically charismatic in a way we have not seen in a companion yet.

The result is something that fulfilled its behind-the-scenes brief – a pair of companions that exemplify contemporary British youth culture. And it's no accident that the first place Polly takes the show is the Inferno nightclub, a tamed for TV but still recognizable version of a mod hangout. As soon as we see Ben, Polly, and Inferno, it becomes clearer than ever how inadequate of a companion Dodo is. Although she's ostensibly from this culture, she doesn't fit in at all, to the point where it's not her monotone delivery of the explanation (that she went and hung out with some friends) so much as it is the idea that she has friends and a life here that tips us off to the fact that she's under mind control. And so about halfway through the second episode, Dodo is left unconscious on a couch to sleep off the hypnosis – her last scenes being some bizarre close-ups of her being deprogrammed by the Doctor at his most strikingly alien. Goodbye, Ms. Chaplet. Sorry things didn't work out.

From that point on, the story is basically wall-to-wall action set pieces, including a truly fantastic sequence in which a comedy homeless guy is ultimately turned on and murdered by WOTAN's brainwashed servants. And there is an even better sequence in which the Doctor, who admittedly spends most of this story seeming out of sorts as Hartnell's acting reaches a new low, stares down an oncoming War Machine in a monster's eye shot that serves as the third episode's cliffhanger. This is a cliffhanger in the classic Doctor Who style. The tension is not "How is the Doctor going to survive facing down this awful machine," but "Oh man, what's he going to do to the machine?" The anticipation is not based on the Doctor being in danger, but on not getting to see him kick the machine's ass.

Unfortunately, that's about the only good bit Hartnell has this episode. It's tough to say why that is. Certainly the actor's health was in free fall at this point, and the fact that the production team very clearly wanted him to quit can't have made the on-set atmosphere very cheery. But perhaps more importantly, Hartnell's style of playing the Doctor just isn't well suited to the thriller genre. Technobabble has always been Hartnell's Achilles heel, so having him be the knowledgeable consultant to a bunch of men with guns is a rough proposition; he can't do very well getting physically involved with the action, and he can't do very well explaining the science.

In fact, if you look at Hartnell's best scenes from about *The Myth Makers* on, they are all when he is just going one-on-one with a quality actor. He's the only one who looks like he enjoys *The Celestial Toymaker*, in no small part because he gets to do scenes with Michael Gough and not worry about the rest. His comedy bits in *The Gunfighters* are gold, and his best bits in *The Savages* are when he's just chatting with Jano. A story in which there's nobody for him to chinwag with is not playing to his strengths. And this, more than anything, is where I think he falls flat in this story. His problem isn't that he's too ill to play the part – his energy level is pretty high throughout most of this story. It's that this just isn't the part he signed up for, and not a plot well suited to the character as he developed it.

Which is perhaps the largest reason why, paring the future context away from this story, it looks like a bit of a dud. All the moving parts are there, and the story seems fascinating and exciting. But it's not a story that seems like the Doctor fits in it. So unless the show plans on doing something completely crazy like recasting the main character and heavily altering his personality, the fact of the matter is, this story is as much of a failed experiment as *The Celestial Toymaker*.

Is His Name Doctor Who?

The correct answer, of course, is "of course not." This is, after all, one of the fundamental points of Doctor Who fandom. It's one of the basic questions that separates the anoraks from the wannabes (or, more often, the dontwannabes). Every fan knows that the way to identify a not-we is that they call the character Doctor Who when everyone knows he's just the Doctor. Sure, there are some slip-ups in the show, but they're all just errors.

Except that both Russell T Davies and Steven Moffat – as big a pair of geeks as the world has ever produced – call him Doctor Who in interviews from time to time. And not just morning-show stuff where you might claim they're pandering to non-hardcore fans. This happens on *Doctor Who Confidential.* So it's not that they're pandering to the ignorant, and they're clearly not ignorant. What's going on?

Actually, let's take a step back and look at what that whole "his name's not Doctor Who" thing is for anyway. It's basically a booby trap. You look at a series called Doctor Who and the natural assumption is that the character is named Doctor Who. The reason fans harp on it is to pull rank on the ignorant – to kick people who are insufficiently dedicated to Doctor Who out of the clubhouse. It's a way of saying "You don't know enough about Doctor Who to talk to people like me about it."

And beyond that, look at the list of errors. The character is credited as Doctor Who in a majority of the credit sequences for the show. He's called Doctor Who in the movies and in many of the comics. He's called Doctor Who on screen in *The War Machines*, signs papers as Doctor Who in early Troughton stories, uses Who as his license plate in the Pertwee years, and there's even a story that went out in the Pertwee years with Doctor Who in its title.

Miles and Wood, in *About Time*, go to heroic lengths to try to argue all of this along the lines that the Doctor's name must be Whovoratrelundar or something. Although certainly possible, there's something unsatisfying about this option – probably the fact that even if it explains everything, it is clearly not what was ever actually intended or thought by anyone making the program. Not to be a complete slave to authorial intent, but it seems like maybe somebody involved in the show should have thought of whatever idea we settle on for a question this basic.

But then, if we're being honest, why call the program Doctor Who? The standard answer – that the name refers to the mystery about who the Doctor is – makes sense, but barely. Certainly the general public hasn't caught on. Major newspapers still refer to the character as "Doctor Who." And it's hard to square that explanation away with *An Unearthly Child* and *100,000 BC*, on the evidence of which the program should have been called Ian Chesterton.

Actually, if one takes the overall evidence of the culture, on-screen clues, and the history of Doctor Who, it seems easier to ask the question of whether there's any good reason not to think his name is Who. Up until *The Girl in the Fireplace*, it's surprisingly hard to come up with a thorough case against it, and even there the phrasing of "it's more than a question" could be spun as compatible with a "his name is Who" theory. Dedicated fans have certainly come up with more bizarre spins to explain their preferred continuity points. It's not really until *The Wedding of River Song* that it becomes seriously difficult to argue that Doctor Who is actually his name. And it's equally difficult to avoid accepting that *The Wedding of River Song* finally and irrevocably confirms that the word "who" does in fact have some inherent connection with the Doctor's name.

The problem, of course, is that there are no dedicated fans advocating for his name being Doctor Who. For whatever reason, fandom is virtually exclusively on the side of calling him the Doctor and only the Doctor. Which is fine – the series gives ample support for that view, particularly in its latter years. But it gets at the real issue underlying this debate.

Which is what we glossed over at the start – that this entire issue exists mostly as a wedge for fans. It's no coincidence that the on-screen credits finally changed to "The Doctor" instead of "Doctor Who" at the start of John Nathan-Turner's fan-centric producership. At the end of the day, the debate became a shibboleth for fandom – the entry-level test. Except nowadays, it doesn't even function as that – the shibboleth is so well known that everyone knows the character's name is "really" the Doctor, and yet the biggest fans in the world – Moffat and Davies – still call him Doctor Who a fair amount of the time.

The result is an odd split whereby each name has its meanings. The character on the show is increasingly clearly the Doctor and not Doctor Who. The character in popular culture, on the other hand, remains Doctor Who. This is a simple fact of life, and arguing against it ends up being perilously close to arguing that obsessive fans have more of a right to the program than ordinary people.

But on the other hand, obsessive fans do have certain rights and privileges with regards to Doctor Who. What's different about today compared to the John Nathan-Turner era is that this isn't an exclusive proposition – the program doesn't have to choose between being for fans or for ordinary people. And so his name isn't Doctor Who. And his name is Doctor Who. It may not make a lot of sense, but at this point, we've had fourty-eight years to get used to it.

Elizabeth Sandifer

Pop Between Realities, Home in Time for Tea (*International Times*, Situationalist International, *Oz*, Kenneth Grant, the 1966 FIFA World Cup)

There is a '60s that we all know originated in San Francisco, and through the haze of marijuana we can still just about make out that there was some sort of revolution lurking underneath that tie-dye. Some aspects – sexual freedom, the de facto legalization of marijuana (which is, let's face it, not so much illegal to smoke as it is illegal to be caught smoking, with virtually no police forces in European or European-descended cultures actually bothering to seek out individual users), and certain hazy New Age concepts – have stuck around. But the hippie movement is, by and large, a desiccated corpse of a rebellion now defined primarily through its failure – i.e. as a symbol of a failed revolution whose proponents are too naive to realize that they have long since failed.

But in 1966, as mod culture is about to suffer a fatal capitalism hemorrhage and psychedelia is about to take the center stage, we have the opposite problem. Just as in *The War Machines* we were caught between the context that led us there and our knowledge of what was to come, 1966 is an impossible year to grasp. We cannot understand it without peeking at the future. The next two years, after all, are crucial – 1967 is the Summer of Love, and 1968 is the massive and catastrophic failure of the New Left in France and the US.

But 1966 itself is impossibly hard to see for what it was. Which is the point of this entry – a loose assortment of revolutionary and mainstream tendencies in 1960s British culture that will help us know what to keep track of as Doctor Who begins to change everything about itself.

The point here is not so much to identify styles as ideologies. If the hippies were a flamed-out failure of a revolution, they were also practically on the other side of the world from London. What did the fringes of British culture in the 1960s think, want, and do? As a result, this entry isn't going to talk about Doctor Who all that much. On the other hand, the next few years of Doctor Who are going to talk about this entry a lot.

The best place to start is probably the *International Times* and *Oz Magazine* – two of the leading counterculture zines of the 1960s. *IT* debuted in 1966, *Oz* in 1967, so we're looking here more at what is emerging out of the culture right now than what was strictly mainstream. *IT*'s debut in October of 1966 is distinct most immediately because of its sheer practicality. Its opening editorial, entitled YOU (except that the word is printed upside-down) gives a good sense of its attitude. Speaking of a boondoggle of a project to create a London poetry centre, the magazine writes:

No-one seems to have realized that a basement and a few notebooks, plus the necessary poets, could be a suitable starting base for a poetry centre. Everyone was too involved with the Arts Council and the money-power game such a body is bound to make you play. That is not to say that the people involved necessarily acted in bad faith, but more to point to where their approaches are confusing them.

What's striking about this compared with the stereotypical assumptions of '60s counter-culture is how well planned and pragmatic it is. No organic gatherings and be-ins are in sight here. Instead, *IT* is focused relentlessly on the business of doing. It wants action. The first page of its first issue is devoted primarily to a theater review that takes to task the Royal Shakespeare Company's production of *US*, a play about the Vietnam War, saying that "A century ago, the theatre's task, according to Chekov, was to ask questions. This has been superseded by a world-situation in which, if the theatre is to pull its weight, it must – at such times and on such themes – begin to supply answers." Practical results. Not mood, not art, not beauty, but action. And this existed across the page from an entire column devoted to tracking the use of cannabis and LSD across the world. The drugs, in other words, are tools, part of an arsenal of tactics being used to force change. But what sort of change?

Crucially, that seems to be somewhat more fuzzily defined. *IT* spends the first two pages of its second issue publishing twenty-year-old speeches by Ezra Pound during World War II, in which he was a raving fascist anti-Semite. Why? What significance did *IT* attach to this decision? "Because they exist . . . The fact is that despite Pound's treason trial, the speeches have never been published in their entirety." This is their style of revolution – printing anti-Semitic, fascist speeches they don't even agree with. This is a revolutionary act because of one key assumption: the world is so broken that simple depiction of it is a damning indictment.

By early 1967, this was clearly *IT's* official policy. Their lead feature on LSD begins with a lengthy explanation of why they've largely avoided the topic to date, noting that "London, 1967, is not ready for a completely flipped-out newspaper," and that "to keep in existence we are having to at least make a show of playing the right games with the law, the Establishment, the etc." One issue later, the magazine seems to be starting to let it hang out with pieces about UFOs and the like. And as time went on, it would get more aggressively weird.

But by and large, IT owes much to a movement that is, for one obvious reason, far less known in America and probably a fair deal less known in Britain than the hippies are – the Situationist International. Focused mostly in France, the SI, led mainly by Guy Debord, was a movement of avant garde Marxists.

Like most Marxists outside of the Soviet bloc, the bulk of SI work was theoretical. Actually, we should probably talk a little bit about what Marxism is. A lot of people tend to treat Marxism as a homogenous bloc of ideologies more or less akin to those of the USSR. This is roughly like declaring that Christianity is equivalent to the Catholic Church. Outside of the Soviet bloc, Marxism tended to be concerned less with trying to set up a functional Communist state and more with understanding how the hell the capitalist state kept surviving. Indeed, the dirty little secret of modern liberalism is that much of its understanding of the wealth gap and class issues is borrowed from Marxist theory.

The Situationalist International's approach was unusual in that it was based primarily on the concept of spectacle – that is, that it took media consumption as the essential metaphor for capitalism. It was not the only major school of Marxism to do so – the Frankfurt School's famed culture industry theory provided another and, in contemporary film and media theory, more widely influential approach. But SI's approach was unusual in that they went from a theory of media consumption that explained why the world was broken into being a primarily artistic movement.

First we should understand the spectacle. The spectacle isn't all of the media representations and sources in the world. Rather, it's the underlying social system those images support and maintain. Debord, in *The Society of the Spectacle*, writes about how actual, lived human experience has been replaced in society by images of human experience so that all actual/true understandings of society have been driven out.

To combat this, the SI created the idea of détournement. The idea of détournement is that it alters and parodies known and recognizable images into ones that disrupt the logic of the spectacle, providing gaps to debate and call into question ideological principles that are otherwise taken for granted. For our purposes, of course, the most interesting of their artistic approaches is psychogeography, an artistic movement from which my own approach to the history of Doctor Who owes a massive debt, but more on that later.

In the end, the SI movement sits on the edge of Marxism and anarchism, using a Marxist view of what's wrong, but offering no meaningful choice beyond "burn it down," even as it offered a compelling set of mechanisms for doing so. In effect, SI and its descendent revolutionary groups, such as those that created *IT*, reverse-engineered practical social justice movements and reduced them to their ideological core, creating a practical manual to burn down the world. Their sense of what to do next was . . . appreciably less well developed.

In practice, this will run aground merely two years later when the SI-supported wildcat strikes of May 1968 in France fail spectacularly. We deal with this more thoroughly in the Troughton era, but the capsule summary is roughly this – in France, the youth rebellion became a youth revolution, and it failed.

Returning to jolly old England, then, we'll look at the other big counterculture zine of the 1960s, *Oz Magazine*. If *IT* were anarchist revolutionaries masquerading as something resembling a proper newspaper, *Oz* was simply *Oz*: Exhibit A in British psychedelia. A glance at the cover of the third issue – swirling purple psychedelic blurs – shows the tone of the magazine, but this is perhaps the least interesting thing about it, which is an impressive thing to say of the post-modernist collage style that was being embraced. More interesting seems to be the content bemoaning "sad cells of anarchists, Marxists, pacifists and humanists who think they understand how power works." (That would be the SI they're insulting there.) So psychedelia with the same sense of social realism we saw in *IT*, and the same "DIY politics" approach.

But where *IT* foregrounded its practicality, *Oz* foregrounds its panache. Drugs are front and center, with ringing endorsements of cannabis: "At your first puff, muscles relax, tension dissolves and suddenly the world is benign. While your body takes a deep breath, your mind gains another dimension: perception sharpens and you discover a tremendous capacity for concentration and details. Your sense of hearing changes from mono to stereo, you look at mundane objects with child-like freshness, everything smells like frankincense."

Actually, that's a bit interesting I suppose. There are some key phrases in there. "Your mind gains another dimension," "child-like freshness," and perhaps "frankincense" are the bits that should be jumping out. And here we do need to talk briefly about Doctor Who, and perhaps a quick tour of other spots of counterculture. Things like *Gandalf's Garden*, a later zine that, as its title kind of suggests, explicitly mixes hippie culture and the classical children's literature sensibilities of nice old neo-Victorians like Tolkien. Let's quote their first issue, shall we?

GANDALF'S GARDEN is the magical garden of our inner worlds, overgrowing into the world of manifestation. GANDALF'S GARDEN is soulflow from the pens of creators – mystics, writers, artists, diggers, delvers and poets. A wellspring of love and anguish that those with searching thirsts may drink thereof. As in the Stone Gardens of the Orient, where Soul Wizards sit within the stimulus of their own silences, contemplating the smoothness of the million pebbles, so should we seek to stimulate our own inner gardens if we are to save our Earth and ourselves from engulfment.

And when we mention Tolkien, of course, we have to mention his good friend C.S. Lewis, who, intentionally or not, crafted what is perhaps the most literal metaphor for these inner worlds, magical gardens, and other dimensions of child-like wonder – the ordinary wardrobe, a plain wooden box, whose door leads to an impossibly larger realm within and invites us to fall out of the world.

Lewis died, by the way, on November 22, 1963, almost exactly twenty-four hours before Doctor Who debuted.

The concept of differing dimensions and worlds used by Tolkien, Lewis, *Oz*, and the rest has deep roots in British culture. The obvious ones are, of course, the Celtic legends of the fae – something like Thomas the Rhymer:

'O see not ye yon narrow road,
So thick beset wi thorns and briers?
That is the path of righteousness,
Tho after it but few enquires.
'And see not ye that braid braid road,
That lies across yon lillie leven?
That is the path of wickedness,
Tho some call it the road to heaven.
'And see not ye that bonny road,
Which winds about the fernie brae?
That is the road to fair Elfland,
Whe[re] you and I this night maun gae.

And of course there's the obvious door to another world, the TARDIS itself. But there's another important tradition of dimensions and worlds we need to look at – one that is, albeit very lightly, signified by the claim that cannabis makes everything smell like frankincense – the tradition of occultism in British culture.

By its nature, occultism is hard to summarize well. I've played with its concepts in some other writing you can find online – most notably in my blog *The Nintendo Project*, in particular with the two-part entry "Toward an Occultism of Video Games." So here I'll mostly stick to a top down summary of English occultism as an ideological system. Let me first note that almost every step of this is based on some dubious history – occultism tends to be based on exceedingly spurious claims of connections and influences in intellectual history. I'm presenting the history sympathetically to the occult tradition. Reality politely begs to differ at various points, and it is up to the reader how much that matters.

So, a long time ago, Rome was busy falling, and out of it came a couple of philosophical traditions. Among them were early Christianity, Gnosticism, and Neo-Platonism, all of

TARDIS Eruditorum Volume 1

which have well known and easily tracked impacts through the subsequent centuries. But the big weird one is Hermeticism – based on a set of writings dating to the second and third centuries, but organized in Renaissance Italy as the Corpus Hermeticum. These writings were attributed to Hermes Trismegistus, a fusion of the Greek Hermes and the Egyptian Thoth.

This process of fusing religions – known as syncretism – is central to Hermeticism, which mashed up various pagan and mystical beliefs into a not-entirely-consistent whole. In the fifteenth century, Hermeticism had a bit of a revival with the creation of the Rosicrucian orders, then petered out for a bit, then emerged full force in the late nineteenth/early twentieth centuries in England via the Hermetic Order of the Golden Dawn.

The Hermetic Order of the Golden Dawn is one of those surprisingly important things we like to overlook. Basically, anybody who was anybody for a while joined it. W.B. Yeats, Arthur Machen, Algernon Blackwood, and Bram Stoker were all members. Tarot cards as we know them today, particularly the most famous deck, the Rider-Waite-Smith deck, come from the Golden Dawn tradition.

Central to the Golden Dawn was a syncretism of a couple of traditions: tarot cards, an Italian card game/divination device, Jewish Kabbalah, and old-fashioned alchemy. These combine into a system that I'll spare you the extended details of (and give you a summary that would piss any self-respecting Kabbalist off), but that basically involves creating a world tree that has various planes of reality and human consciousness that one spiritually navigates. And this was huge in Britain in the early twentieth century. And one of the most important planes, known as Tiphereth, has as one of its symbols . . . frankincense. It is a plane particularly associated with spiritual enlightenment and contact with the divine; it's also the highest plane that man can aspire towards. (Not that I'm saying *Oz* was written by an overt occultist. Frankincense's association with solar imagery and spiritual enlightenment seeped into the broad culture to a great extent. The point is not to claim that *Oz* was selling cannabis as an occult practice. It's to claim that the spiritual dimension to cannabis *Oz* saw is adjacent to an existing spiritual doctrine.)

See where this is all coming together? You have a political ideology that is fundamentally based on tearing down the existing world, that is not invested in the details of what comes next, and that spends a lot of time on drugs looking for higher states of consciousness, i.e. doors into magic realms and other worlds. That's at least one of the central thrusts of British counterculture in the 1960s. Where France was invested primarily in material political change, and the US invested primarily in a narcissistic personal expression that psychedelic drugs aided, British counterculture split the difference, using psychedelic (the word, I should note, means mind-expanding) culture as a tool to try to make the world a stranger and more magical place.

But there's a complication. Let's circle back to that occult tradition. The Hermetic Order of the Golden Dawn basically imploded in an internal power struggle focusing on celebrity bad boy occultist Aleister Crowley. A thorough explication of what Crowley was all about is miles beyond the scope of this essay, but suffice it to say that he was not the moustache-twirling Satanist of legend. Reading Crowley one gets a compelling portrait of a social revolutionary with a flair for the mythic, and we'll see echoes of him throughout Doctor Who, but for our purposes, let's leave it at this – Crowley's vision of the world positioned it as a particular manifestation of much larger cosmic and mystical forces. In Crowley's view, history has a purpose, the future is inevitably moving towards something, and all of this is driven by the natural trends of spirituality. But as a result, the "real world" as understandable through tarot, Kabbalah, Holy Guardian Angels and, inevitably, lots of debauchery and drugs is big and alien. Not scary as such, but equally importantly, not a cuddly garden tended by a kindly old wizard from Tolkien.

It is safe to say, however, that Crowley's followers were by and large somewhat more drawn to the sex and drugs than other aspects. All the same, Crowley was, if not mainstream, at least plausibly well known – and in 1966, was only twenty years dead. To be fair, 1966 was not a huge year for English occultism by any stretch of the imagination. But it's useful to look at what was going on in it.

The main thing going on in it was Kenneth Grant. A protégé of both Crowley and the other great English magician of Crowley's generation, Austin Spare, Grant didn't start writing until 1972, but it was in the 1960s that he was busy having the formative mystical experiences of his life. So let's crack open Grant's 1972 debut text, *The Magical Revival*:

Writers in the horror genre, from Poe to Lovecraft, tended mostly to place a similar interpretation upon the intrusive presences sensed in dreams or abnormal states of consciousness, and many of them wove into their spells the barbarous names and monstrous speech of the ancient Grimoires. Goetic magic liberates the consciousness from the thralldom of individual existence. It permits it to billow into cosmic immensity. The result is a divine madness, an inebriation of the senses which is none the less perfectly and exquisitely controlled.

Intense stuff, to be sure. Don't worry about making sense of it. The thing I want to highlight is Grant's idea that the mystical experience of higher states of consciousness is what is gestured at by horror writers such as Lovecraft. Lovecraft, if you've never read "The Call of Cthulhu" or "Nyarlathotep," (and shame on you if you haven't) wrote horror stories about horrifying beings beyond all human comprehension that might one day happen to roll over in their sleep and annihilate all civilization by driving us mad. So Kenneth Grant was busy advancing the frankly terrifying idea that this was, in fact, the same process as psychedelic enlightenment. In other words, that expanding consciousness and exiting this world into a more magical world was not, in fact, a source of childlike wonder, but a source of utter terror.

It's not hard to see, in 1966, with international conflict, looming nuclear war, and aggressive culture wars within every developed country between the youth rebellions and entrenched power, why a vision of the world as on a precipice and about to plummet into madness would be appealing. That's just Quatermass, at the end of the day. What's bizarre is that this viewpoint and the revolutionary viewpoint are sitting so close to each other, and sharing tactics. The vast cosmic paranoia of Kenneth Grant doesn't mean Grant is anything short of eager to speak the barbarous names needed to attain divine madness, and the possibility that higher planes of consciousness will be terrifying experiences doesn't make revolutionaries any less willing to tear down the world to get to them.

So we are left with two competing ideas – on the one hand, it is necessary to fall out of the world into a better world. On the other, our world is a fragile thing surrounded by terrible monsters. That is the central tension right now in English counterculture.

And it's over that backdrop that the 1966 World Cup happened. Far from counterculture, it is possible that the 1966 World Cup is the single most mainstream event in British history. The country's most popular sport has its premiere competition in England. Five days before the finale of *The War Machines*, England plays its opening game against former champion Uruguay, coming to a 0-0 draw. 2-0 wins against Mexico and France send them to the next round of the competition. There they defeat Argentina, sowing the seeds of a rivalry that will be massive in years to come. That's followed by a semifinal victory against Portugal, setting up the final on July 30, in Wembley Stadium, against West Germany.

And so England plays Germany in what is inevitably billed and seen as World War III – the third decisive battle between the two countries. (Yes. Soccer, or as we call it in the civilized world, football, is that nationalist. In a later

England/Germany game, the chant from the crowds is "One World Cup and Two World Wars.")

Germany opens the scoring, with England pulling back the equalizer in the nineteenth minute, leaving the game 1–1 at halftime. In the second half, England takes the lead in the seventy-seventh minute with a shot from Martin Peters. Then, in the eighty-ninth minute, in a controversial goal possibly off of a handball, Germany equalized again, sending the match into extra time. Eleven minutes into extra time, England manages a controversial goal that ricochets off the crossbar and, arguably, into the goal – though the matter remains controversial to this day.

And then, mere seconds from the end, Geoff Hurst gets on the end of a long pass from the legendary Bobby Moore. As England fans begin charging the pitch in celebration, he lashed a vicious goal in, freely admitting that if he missed the net his second choice was to bury the ball deep in the Wembley stands to run out the clock. While on television, in the most watched broadcast in British history, Kenneth Wolstenholme provides one of the most famous moments of sports commentary: "And here comes Hurst. He's got... some people are on the pitch, they think it's all over. It is now! It's four!"

And with that, England won its first and to date only World Cup.

This is the height of the swinging '60s. Britain, already viewing itself as the cultural capital of the world, is now the home of the world champions of the world's sport. This is, quite literally, as good as it gets.

So to our already bizarre mix of higher states of consciousness and horrifying monsters, we add a tremendous sense of national pride. Nationalism, psychedelia, and cosmic paranoia. That's England, 1966.

And from our perspective, we should perhaps worry. That *War Machines* story we just saw was interesting, but let's face it, Doctor Who doesn't seem up to the task of doing a story like that. The cheery mod sensibilities of Vicki are long gone, and ever since confronting the possibility of a truly hostile universe, the show hasn't known what to do with itself. We should, perhaps, face the very real possibility that it is played out. The TARDIS has landed everywhere interesting it will ever land, and has nothing more to say to the world.

And yet despite falling ratings, the BBC renews Doctor Who to come back in a few months. Plus it's in the cinemas again with another Peter Cushing Dalek film. The question, then, is how and if it will reinvent itself into this strange new world.

You Were Expecting Someone Else (*Daleks – Invasion Earth: 2150 AD*)

It's August 5, 1966. The Troggs are at number one with "With a Girl Like You," a nice, proper, crunchy record. The rest of the top ten, however, is mostly pretty unambitious pop, with the Kinks chillaxing at number nine. Since we last saw Doctor Who, the news has been a standard mixture of war, mass murder, military coup, and the like. Beyond that, as mentioned last essay, England won the World Cup. Also, The House of Lords issued the Practice Statement, a somewhat important milestone in political liberalism in the UK in that it freed the House of Lords up to be more progressive, and August 3, 1966 happened, which is interesting only if you're a Simon and Garfunkel fan, as it happens to be the day the newscast for their most brilliant song, "Silent Night/7 O'Clock News," came from. Also, The Beatles' *Revolver* came out. And, as it's the summer break in Doctor Who, it's time for another Dalek film!

It's strange how different a position this film is in compared to the last one. I mean, first of all, this film flopped and killed plans for a third one (which would have been an adaptation of *The Chase*, a prospect that is mind-bogglingly weird). Second of all, the show is in a very different place. At the end of Season Two, the show was as strong as it had ever been, coming off an inventive season of hits. At the end of Season Three, the ratings were in the toilet, the star was being fired, and there was an increasing consensus that the TARDIS had landed everywhere worth landing. As a result, the last movie was in a position to remind us how wonderful Doctor Who could be and show us things bigger and grander than before. And it basically did that.

But what, exactly, is this film for? Most obviously, it seems to be an occasion for Doctor Who to make a case for its continued relevance – to say, "This is what the show can do." It's taking a Season Two episode – i.e. from the program's heyday – and doing it bigger and better. And ironically, given that it failed at the box office, the film is frankly a rousing success in that department.

I suppose we should deal with the film's flop status. Why did it flop? The argument that Doctor Who was also flopping at that time is certainly compelling, but it's worth noting that the film was not advertised as a Doctor Who film, it was advertised as a Dalek film. Admittedly the two were not entirely distinct in people's minds, and the Dalek craze was past its immediate prime, but Doctor Who's decline has been compellingly argued to mostly be down to the fact that ITV was aggressively counter-programming it with the Adam West Batman series, not due to actual problems with the snow.

No, to my mind the most compelling account for why the film flopped is that six days after a massive nationalist victory in the World Cup is possibly not the ideal market to release a film about a bombed out and decimated London. The film had a release date that went bad on it. Had West Germany beaten England, a film in which horrible Nazi-esque monsters who have decimated London are defeated by a dottering old Victorian man would very possibly have captured the national mood perfectly. Having won, though, and with England feeling at the top of the world, maybe bombing out London wasn't quite in step with what people wanted that week. Certainly we had reason to think there were more glamorous ways to fight against Germans than this. As delightful as Bernard Cribbins is, he's no Bobby Charlton.

The thing is, in most people's hindsight, of the two Cushing films this is decisively the superior one. And it's not hard to see why – if nothing else, Russell T Davies admonition that he cares about humans, not about aliens on the planet Zog, applies here. Fundamentally, it's easier to have a compelling drama about London than it is about Skaro. Just . . . not that week. There is, after all, a whole strand of thought on Doctor Who that says this – aliens invading London is what the show is for. It's not a strand of thought I particularly subscribe to, but on the other hand, it's tough to make a real argument that the occasional massive invasion of Earth isn't good fun. So even if the two films are almost equally well made, this film would have some natural advantages.

On the other hand, if we think back to the actual story this is based on, one of the things we'll see is that it's a story that's trying to be a much later version of Doctor Who than it is, and doing a mixed bag of a job at it. It's hard to oversell how absolutely essential Terry Nation's writing is to the style of Doctor Who, but the fact of the matter is that his ideas beat his execution a lot of the time, and that much of the fun of watching *The Dalek Invasion of Earth* is watching the series start to discover its potential, not watching it actually attain said potential. Exhibit A on this remains, of course, the spectacularly bewildering plot point of the Daleks planning on flying the Earth around as a space ship, a point that they manage to make even weirder in the movie.

On the other hand, Exhibit B in the "why *The Dalek Invasion of Earth* doesn't quite work" game is probably the Slyther, which, to its credit, the movie omits entirely as one of several fixes David Whitaker applies to Nation's script in order to shrink it to movie size/make the pacing not mind-wrenchingly excruciating. (As we saw in Season Three, and will see again in Seasons Four, Twelve, and arguably

Seventeen, taking Terry Nation's concepts and having someone else write them is generally a recipe for success.)

I'm dancing around it a bit, so I may as well come out and say it – almost everything that is well regarded about *The Dalek Invasion of Earth* is done better and more memorably by this film. In fact, I'll go so far as to say most people who have not watched either lately imagine the episodes to be much more like the film when they wax nostalgic about it. (Though there are reasons for this. The two Cushing films were mainstays of television in the '70s and '80s while the original Hartnell stories were impossible to see. As much as the novelizations, if not more so, these films served as the versions of old Doctor Who that could be accessed. Having served as fandom's memory of Doctor Who for decades, it is no surprise that the lines between the films and their originals has blurred.)

Watching *Doctor Who and the Daleks*, one got the sense of the TV show being done more competently but with less soul. That doesn't vanish here, but the fact of the matter is that when the series is flailing about trying to find what it's good at as much as late Season Three was, seeing a film that's at least confident about its strengths is oddly relieving. In some ways, watching the film clarifies just how odd the run from *The Ark* on has been – a series of experiments often (but not always) with dramatic high and low points, but never a show that felt like it knew what it was doing. That's going to settle out, though if you set the date where Doctor Who stopped knowing what it was doing at *The Ark*, we've got as many stories ahead before it settles down as we do behind. (Again, the original was, ironically, very much in the vein of Season Three – an experiment that tried to find new things the show could do. It wasn't entirely successful, but as with the first film, there is a sense of wonder it has that the film lacks. If nothing else, the cheap studio sets and hasty silent runs through London feel darker and scarier than the colorful pageantry of the film.)

But this film is useful, if nothing else, in that it shows us very clearly some things that work in Doctor Who that we're going to see integrated into the series proper over the next few entries. First of all, let's talk about Peter Cushing. Back in the first film, I observed the way in which he uses the visual space afforded to him in order to characterize the Doctor, using a stooped walk and physical presence to do what Hartnell does with small gestures, and how that lends a cinematic feel to the proceedings. Here he fine-tunes that even more. He drops the stoop slightly, and adds a proper, action hero edge to the character that, while short even of the Jon Pertwee era, little yet of a standard action hero, enlivens the action considerably. The eccentric Victorian inventor is still clearly the base, but the character has been reworked into a more viable leading man.

And for two of his three companions, there's some significant stuff going on as well. Susan Who, as in the first film, is played by child actress Roberta Tovey, and while she can be a bit overly precious, she still works better than Susan Foreman ever did. The dynamic of a child companion is intriguing, and one of the few aspects where movies may work better than television for Doctor Who. The logistics of a child actress on a shoot as grueling as Doctor Who, to say nothing of how many plot problems it would introduce, makes a child companion something of a non-starter in the series (although it is difficult, even as a dedicated Karen Gillan fan, not to wish that the Doctor had come back after five minutes and we'd gotten a seven-year-old Amelia Pond as a companion). But on the screen, it's a delight, with Susan playing it with a satisfying mix of precociousness and vulnerability.

And then there's Bernard Cribbins as Tom Campbell, our Ian Chesterton stand-in. It is, of course, impossible to mention Cribbins without pointing to his later turn as Wilfred Mott, one of the highlights of the David Tennant era. Especially because, as I said in the essay on *The Chase*, there are clear similarities between Wilf and Ian, so casting Cribbins as an Ian stand-in makes some real sense. Cribbins' stand-out scene is a lengthy comedic bit in which he, dressed in a Roboman costume, has to try to impersonate the mechanical Robomen and flails about trying to keep in lockstep with them. It's easy to see this scene as pointless faffing about akin to Roy Castle's comedic sequence trying to get a door in the Dalek base to stay open last movie. But where Castle's scene was just broad slapstick, Cribbins gets a scene with some real tension underneath it.

Yes, Cribbins is doing some physical comedy here (and he's great at it), but there's a genuine tension underlying the scene. It may be funny, but it's funny played out over a backdrop of immediate danger – every comedic fumble Cribbins makes is also a direct threat to his life. One thing that makes the Hartnell era of Doctor Who harder to watch for a fan of any later era is that there's markedly less comedy in it, and the comedy that is there is generally based more on broad concepts than on specific "gags." This scene is very much a template for the sort of humor that does come in later, and much as I love the Hartnell era, I confess, this scene was a welcome omen of the future.

There's also the Daleks, who are effective in a way they aren't necessarily on television. Part of this, to be frank, is that there are six of them and they can be used in action sequences, with explosions, at night. Yeah, the show isn't going to come close to that for decades. But the point is less that the Daleks are terrifyingly effective like this than that the movie highlights the importance of getting a set piece to work well. We'll see some startlingly good ones in both *The Tenth Planet* and *The Power of the Daleks* in which the show thinks about what it can manage and does that effectively – in a way that highlights the degree to which maybe having Daleks overrun London was a bit much for them. (The flip side of that night shoot is that the iconic shots running around London are replaced with some very generic cityscapes, and the action focuses heavily on the countryside. Of course, as soon as the UNIT era begins, we'll get lots of stories in which aliens invade everything in England they possibly can except for London itself.) Even if the story falls down here for its excessive reliance on action sequences, the movie is a sobering reminder that a good spectacle goes a long way. (See also the glam rock Daleks, five years too early and still just as fabulous as last time.)

The last thing we should note is something we didn't talk much about in *The Dalek Invasion of Earth*, and I should hat-tip once again to Wood and Miles's *About Time*. The normal brief on *The Dalek Invasion of Earth* and thus this film is that it's about the Blitz. But Miles and Wood compellingly argue that the story is best read as part of the "tear it down and rebuild" fervor of the youth culture in Britain. In other words, for all the darkness of the premise, this story, as with the television version, has a real sense of hope about the future. Yes, we might be slaughtered by Daleks, but we'll rise up, overcome them, and build something better (a sense that is heightened by the Doctor talking about the Gaia-hypothesis and "Mother Earth" while sounding positively eco-friendly).

Which is perhaps the big thing – Doctor Who works very well when it balances a scary universe with a genuine sense of optimism. The movie, for all its faults, captures that well, and that alone makes it a major influence on where the show is about to go.

Elizabeth Sandifer

These Books Are from Your Future (*The Smugglers*)

It's September 10, 1966. The Beatles are at number one again with the double-single of "Yellow Submarine" and "Eleanor Rigby." Also in the top ten are the Troggs, the Beach Boys, and Napoleon XIV. Over the course of the next four weeks we'll also see the Small Faces take number one with "All or Nothing," Jim Reeves will take it with "Distant Drums," and Roy Orbison, the Seekers, Sonny and Cher, the Supremes, the Who, and Manfred Mann will also pop around the Top Ten. Not on the Top Ten but still enormously important, the Doors released their debut album since we last saw Doctor Who. Also, the first episode of some American sci-fi show called *Star Trek* aired, which is surely just some cheap Doctor Who knockoff or something that we can safely ignore. And over in reality, while we were sleeping, the Cultural Revolution began in China.

Meanwhile, Doctor Who has returned for its fourth season with *The Smugglers*. Filmed at the end of the previous production block, as with *Galaxy Four* and *Planet of Giants* before it, it's in many ways the last story of Season Three more than it is the first story of Season Four – especially given the degree to which the next story represents, shall we say, a decisive break from what has come before.

As a result, it is possible that *The Smugglers* is actually the most undisputed story in Doctor Who history. Not undisputedly anything in particular – simply undisputed in a broad sense. Neither loved nor hated by much of anyone, this may simply be the Doctor Who story about which people care the least. (Which makes the decision to have *The Curse of the Black Spot* be an unstated prequel to it possibly the most beautiful moment of fanwank in the series' long and distinguished history.)

It's not terribly hard to see why – it's a completely missing story (Season Four, in fact, is the only season of the show with no complete stories at all), a historical (never a recipe for widespread acclaim), and was novelized all the way out in 1988. And on top of that, it's a story that just misses the milestones over and over again. It's the second to last Hartnell story, the second to last historical, the second story featuring Ben and Polly . . . just about the only thing it has going for it in terms of major milestones, actually, are that it is the first historical since *The Aztecs* to feature no major historical figures, which is kind of overqualified, and it is the first completely missing story to be novelized by Terrance Dicks.

Which, actually, is enough to make it absolutely crucial, at least in terms of how we're experiencing the story. Yes, it was a painfully late novelization, long after Terrance Dicks had passed his peak in terms of the books. (In fact, it's his third-from-last novelization.) But that's beside the point. Yes, there are other good novelizations of the Hartnell era, including Ian Marter's novelizations and the brilliant Donald Cotton trio. But somehow it seems unthinkable to introduce the Target novelizations properly with anyone but Terrance Dicks. (Except perhaps Malcolm Hulke, but that would mean waiting for Pertwee to do it right.)

A younger fan, or one more used to other science fiction shows, might reasonably ask why the novelizations are so important. Not a lot of other science fiction series have important book series at all, little yet ones that are just adaptations of the TV shows. But for Doctor Who, the novelizations are genuinely vital. Part of this is that for sixteen years of the program's history Doctor Who was primarily a series of novels, at least in terms of its newly produced content, and that it was the existing tradition of novelizations that, in part, allowed that to happen.

As a concept, Doctor Who novelizations have been around since 1964 when David Whitaker's adaptation of the first Dalek story, *Doctor Who in an Exciting Adventure with the Daleks*, was published by Frederick Muller Ltd. In 1973, Target Books republished that book, as well as adaptations of *The Crusade* and *The Web Planet*. Then in 1974 they started publishing their own material with Terrance Dicks's adaptation of *Spearhead from Space* and Malcolm Hulke's adaptation of *The Silurians*. The line ran until 1990, at which point it ended due to a lack of anything left to novelize. However, by that point the owner of the imprint and thus the Doctor Who license was Virgin Books, who went on to publish the New and Missing Adventures, about which we've already talked.

But more importantly, the novelizations were, in effect, the first things to make it possible to revisit classic adventures. Before VHS releases, and in a time when at best the BBC might run the occasional classic story as part of a special set of repeats (the famed *Five Faces of Doctor Who* series, for instance, and even that came six years after the novelizations started), if you wanted to revisit a favorite story the absolute only way you were going to manage that was if you could get the Target novelization. As the '80s went on and VHS became a viable medium for the preservation of Doctor Who, the novels started to take a backseat, becoming fannish collectables, even if, in many cases, the books were quite good. (The novelizations of the Seventh Doctor stories are particularly interesting and influential.) But, crucially, they weren't that to begin with. They were absolutely part of how fans experienced Doctor Who, in an era before "fandom," and it was Terrance Dicks who most defined the line.

As much stick as Dicks gets for his writing style (which is, admittedly, formulaic), there are some things we need to acknowledge. First of all, the odds are very good that

Terrance Dicks has done more to foster childhood literacy with the Doctor Who novelizations than you will ever contribute towards that cause in your lifetime, and for a lot of people, more than they will ever contribute to any public or charitable cause over their entire lifetimes. Literally thousands of people learned to read from Target novelizations stashed away at schools across Britain.

Second of all, if you can bang out a good novelization of a Doctor Who story at Target length limits in a weekend working only from the script, well, frankly, I suspect you're lying. Which is to say, Dicks routinely worked under crappy conditions and turned out pretty acceptable books regardless. As for the criticism that the books are short and threadbare, try reading one as you watch. Dicks expands as many scenes as he cuts down. The root problem is actually that four episodes of Doctor Who don't take more than about 130 pages to novelize.

Third, and perhaps most important, Terrance Dicks's biggest problem as a novelist is that nobody can write sixty-four Doctor Who books without repeating one's self a bit. On his own merits, frankly, Dicks is a capable wordsmith with some surprisingly deft touches. One thing that is quickly clear to anyone who reads even a handful of Dicks novels is that the man is a genius at beginnings. I mean, here's just a few highlights from Dicks's opening sentences (shorn of their titles, just to make that frisson of unfamiliarity Dicks is so good at stand out):

- It moved through the silent blackness of deep space like a giant jellyfish through the depths of the sea.
- Through the ruin of a city stalked the ruin of a man.
- Through the vortex, that mysterious region where time and space are one, sped a police box that was not a police box at all.

- Next to the crumbling Palace of the Emperor, on the edge of the sprawling ruins that were the capital of Skonnos, there rose the Power Complex.
- Night falls suddenly in the rainforests of the upper Amazon.
- In the gloomy, cavernous underground Hall of Learning, the assembled Gonds were waiting.

The thing that's most obvious from any of these (and you can take your pick as to your favorite, though for my money, the second is one of the best opening sentences I've read, period) is that they are remarkably deft at setting up compelling questions in one sentence. As for his larger prose style, it is remarkably well developed at what it is there for. It's easy to forget that the novelizations are children's literature, and specifically designed to be exciting adventures that are over quickly and that leave the reader looking for the next one. Dicks's prose style is perfectly adapted to that goal. It would, frankly, be a lesser writer who would add rhetorical flourishes and show off. Dicks has no such pretensions – he gets out of the way of the story, and tries to tell it as plainly and entertainingly as possible. Inasmuch as Dicks has a style, it is visible only because there are about 8,000 pages of his Doctor Who writing for it to show up over.

Unfortunately, *The Smugglers* ends up being the sort of Doctor Who story that Dicks's approach ends up being the most irritatingly formulaic at. Part of this is that the story is profoundly unambitious. We'll talk more about the decline of the historical when we get to the end of the road for the genre with *The Highlanders*, but suffice it to say that the genre was in terminal decline at this point. Having attempted its last ambitious historical with *The Massacre*, and its last one that looks like the historicals did in Season One with *The Crusade*, by this point the historical is a format for flat adventure in a standard issue genre (the pirate story, this time around). The result is a story that wasn't trying to be much at the time, leaving Dicks with little room to work. And since Dicks's gift really is as a novelizer, when he gets an unambitious, phoned-in story, the results don't exactly light up the page.

Where *The Smugglers* does work as a story is in introducing Ben and Polly as a new sort of companion – something that's clearest in the scene where they escape from prison not in what would have been the standard approach for any earlier companions (lure the guard in and whack him in the head), but through an inspired and lengthy bit of trickery and bluffing involving pretending to be evil magicians. The most striking thing about this is that it's the sort of clever bluff we usually associate with the Doctor (though it seems more callous from Ben and Polly than it would from him), indicating that we have companions now who can take a more active role in affairs. No doubt some of that is simply the show preparing for the possibility that Hartnell will not give up the role quietly, as he was asked to towards the end of filming of this story, and as he ultimately did. But it also marks a major shift in the nature of companions and what they do and don't do. It's just that the shift stays in place for most, albeit not all, of the twenty-two years separating the story from its novelization, meaning that by the time Dicks writes it up, it sounds far more generic than it did airing on television.

But by and large the sensation that the novel is a bit lacking sidesteps the fact that the novel is an extremely faithful adaptation of the television show in this case. Hardly anything is cut, and none of the cuts substantially alter the meaning of a scene. There are places where Dicks does change the meaning – having Hartnell's line at the start about how he thought he'd be alone until Ben and Polly blundered into the TARDIS suggest the Doctor resents their presence. In the actual episode, it is clear that he in fact was afraid to be alone. Also, a clarifying note on this, just to weigh into a fan debate: some sources say that Ben and Polly entered the TARDIS using Dodo's key. The same sources suggest that there is a goof in the fourth episode of *The War Machines* in which Michael Craze knocks a piece off of a War Machine with the Doctor's cloak. These sources are wrong on both counts. Careful viewing of the scene shows that the object Craze bends and picks up is the TARDIS key (contrary to fan rumor, he makes no attempt to re-attach it to the War Machine, and instead holds it up to the light to see what it is, which an actor would never do with a part of a prop during filming), and this is the key he returns later in the episode.

He also makes one significant structural change, opting to use Ben and Polly as POV characters for the start of the novel, complete with a lovely section in which Polly steadily realizes she has in fact traveled in time as she walks around Cornwall seeing nothing modern. In the episode itself, Ben and Polly's insistence that the Doctor is pulling their leg is played for laughs, in no small part because they are the less familiar characters and the Doctor is the more familiar character, so they cannot serve as POV characters. Because the novel affords Dicks an omniscient narrator, he makes the intelligent choice to have the story start focused on Ben and Polly's amazing trip and disbelief at what they're seeing in a way the show simply couldn't.

Other changes are milder – the Doctor drinks brandy in the book, while refusing it in the episodes. He does, however, drink wine in both. Dialogue is smoothed out, including several fluffs, the worst of which, for once, is not Hartnell's fault, as Terence de Marney flubs the rhyme revealing the location of the hidden treasure. Action sequences are cut from minutes in length to a few sentences, but this mostly is beneficial, as action sequences read poorly, and furthermore, the story was already stretched to fit four episodes. (There's a truly painful bit of plot extension as the Doctor decides he needs a fourth name to solve the riddle. Never mind that the riddle could work perfectly well with three names, and that there's only one thing in the riddle that could be a fourth name, we need to add a scene to this episode and that's that.)

But by and large, Dicks's novelization is a faithful recreation of what happens on the screen. For the missing episodes, this was, for many years (and for many fans still is) the major way these stories can still be experienced and known. And several of the missing stories have classic and memorable novelizations.

The Smugglers doesn't. But to be fair, that's mostly down to *The Smugglers*, and not to the steadfastly capable Terrance Dicks.

You Were Expecting Someone Else: The Polystyle Strips

The fact that this volume is a second edition poses a problem for this particular essay, in that I already wrote an essay on the Patrick Troughton-era strips for *TV Comic* that appears in the Troughton book. There I suggested that the Polystyle strips provided a sensible look at what Doctor Who would look like filtered through the structure of the 1960s British comics industry. This time, then, I'd like to approach it from the other direction.

First we should discuss the 1960s British comics industry. We've already done that a fair amount back in the *Dan Dare* essay, but there's one point we haven't made quite yet, which is that the British comics industry is largely a working-class phenomenon. This means that a lot of them were cheap and thrown together with a minimum of effort. Polystyle, the company that published *TV Comic*, was par for the course in this regard. And *TV Comic* is, initially, where Doctor Who comics appeared.

Actually, it was technically split between *TV Comic* and the more upmarket *TV Century 21*, a Gerry Anderson-centric comic that acquired the rights to the Daleks and dutifully provided a few pages of kinetic space battles that were an integral part of the Daleks' early popularity. But *TV Comic* got Doctor Who itself. Or, more accurately, it got the Doctor, the TARDIS, and . . . not much else. None of the companions made it, with the Doctor instead getting stuck with two human grandchildren named John and Gillian who wander by the TARDIS, meet their grandfather for the first time, and get swept off on some adventures. And actually, it's not so much that the Doctor gets stuck with them as that Dr. Who does.

Clearly this is not a comic with a huge amount of connection to the television series, although it does feature a lead character who is nominally based on William Hartnell, and every once in a while the artist appears to have ever actually seen a photograph of Hartnell. John and Gillian have thus taken a somewhat odd role in Doctor Who's fandom, serving as a sort of limit point for canon. It's functionally impossible to reconcile the Hartnell-era Polystyle strips with any singular theory of continuity, but because they focus the correct Doctor for the period (unlike, say, the Cushing films) and aren't simply adaptations of something else (i.e. *Doctor Who in an Exciting Adventure with the Daleks*), there's a strange desire to try to integrate them.

(For what it's worth, *The Doctor Who Reference Guide* uses a 2004 short story in which the Doctor wanders around London on his own at the end of *The War Machines* to postulate an entire run of solo First Doctor stories that include the John and Gillian stories. This unlikely sequence of events requires the Doctor to go on several adventures for the World Distributors annuals, then to stop back on present day Earth to pick up John and Gillian, then to travel again, then presumably to return John and Gillian and pick up Ben and Polly for *The Smugglers*. The Polystyle strips featuring John and Gillian with the Second Doctor, on the other hand, are positioned in Season 6B. The *Doctor Who Magazine* comic went with the comparatively simpler explanation that John and Gillian were figments of the Doctor's imagination, while the New Adventures located them in the Land of Fiction.)

As with most British comics of the time, *TV Comic* was an anthology, which spent two pages a week on Doctor Who. This meant that the bulk of any given strip was either given over to resolving the previous installment's cliffhanger or to setting up a new one. The strips are thus overwhelmingly action-based, with extremely episodic plots that just move from threat to threat. They read like cheap versions of *Dan Dare*, basically.

As I said, in the Troughton book we discussed the ways in which the sort of manic energy of the Polystyle strips provided a British comics equivalent of Doctor Who. But what's also interesting, and what we didn't talk much about there, was the degree to which Doctor Who opened up a gap in expectations. One type of sci-fi existed in the *Dan Dare* approach of spectacular action. Another existed in the televisual tradition of "literary" science fiction, which included things like the Quatermass serials, but also things like *Out of This World*, which did TV adaptations of proper literary science fiction stories by Isaac Asimov, Clifford D. Simak, and Philip K. Dick. (Somewhat improbably, the Philip K. Dick episode was adapted by Terry Nation, in what has to be one of the strangest juxtapositions in sci-fi history.)

On the one hand Doctor Who was presented as a serial – extremely so in the Hartnell era, where individual stories weren't identified. And like *Dan Dare* and other comics its focus is on creating new ideas. Sure enough, the Polystyle strips do that, with Doctor Who and company encountering Santa, various evil goblins, and a host of gleaming spaceships. The focus on visual spectacle is certainly an element of both the television and comic adaptations of Doctor Who.

But the television version also has a leisurely pace more associated with the literary. Doctor Who isn't just about bizarre concepts; it's about strange places. Its slow pace compared to a two-page continual cliffhanger format means that instead of going through a big action-packed plot it's able to spend time looking at what Vortis is like as a place.

This example is not accidental, as Polystyle did a sequel to *The Web Planet*. But its sequel amounts to space adventure with insects, whereas *The Web Planet* is an extended exploration of Vortis and its cultures. *The Web Planet* is interested – perhaps more interested than is entirely sensible

– in questions like "what would it be like to be a subterranean woodlice person?" Whereas its Polystyle sequel is interested in flying Zarbi attacks. That both depend on a logic of the spectacular obscures a very, very different focus in what the stories do.

Which is to say that Doctor Who's position as being about both the logic of the spectacular and about exploring conceptual worlds made it unusual in British science fiction, giving it a position in the middle of an immensely populist tradition and a more literary one. This sort of thing was what the BBC did, and for a time they did it better than just about anyone in the world. The third season of Doctor Who in many ways marks a turning away from that tradition, and over the course of the next volume we'll see that tradition all but abandoned in favor of a more formulaic action-adventure approach. Doctor Who's odd status as being unlike anything else in British science fiction couldn't last forever. But here, in its earliest days, this was what was remarkable about Doctor Who: it found a space between two science fiction traditions and made something genuinely and entirely new.

A Chrysalis Case After It Has Spread Its Wings (*The Tenth Planet*)

It's October 8, 1966. Jim Reeves is posthumously at number one with "Distant Drums." The Rolling Stones, the Supremes, the Who, Dusty Springfield, and the Troggs are all charting. "Distant Drums" will hold number one for three weeks before the Four Tops take it. In the news, we have our standard smattering of '60s misfortune with a side of a massive coal disaster that kills 144 people, mostly children, in the Welsh village of Aberfan, and the infamous escape of George Blake, a British spy and double agent for Russia, from prison in London.

But let's be honest, it's hard to approach this one from that direction. Which is a pity. There are stories fandom has done some mean things to over the years, but few we've been as brutal to as this one. Ask a reasonably dedicated fan, and there are two things to know about this story – it's the first regeneration story, and the first Cybermen story. And that basically defines it. The trouble is, it's neither.

It's certainly not the first regeneration story. Wood and Miles make a compelling case for this, including their observation, much ignored by the rest of fandom, that for years *Doctor Who Magazine* didn't even count this story as a regeneration, instead saying it was a "rejuvenation," and thus a completely different thing from what happens in, say, *The Caves of Androzani*. Even if you do take the modern viewpoint that what happens at the end of this story is the same thing that happens at the end of *The End of Time Part II*, the fact of the matter is, treating this as the first regeneration story reads it the wrong way. Calling it a regeneration story treats the ending as a defined, known thing. We get to read the story in the context of the other seven regeneration stories (for a variety of reasons, I don't count *Time and the Rani*), and get to define it via a raft of stuff that came later.

The same problem exists with calling it the first Cybermen story. Never mind that the Cybermen never look or act like this again. The real problem is that this means that when they show up, the audience reaction is "Oh, it's the Cybermen." Which is a fine reaction, but it's manifestly not the reaction the story is going for. The Cybermen in this story are not the classic monsters who are returning for another round. They're the bizarre new villains who are making their first appearance.

It is admittedly a challenge to scrape off the forty-five years of reputation that have been built on this story. The problem is, at this point the reputation is spoiling our view. Read from the future, we see all sorts of cracks. The Cybermen look like men in Lycra. The regeneration is unexplained and doesn't seem a natural extension of what went before, meaning Hartnell gets a kind of feeble sendoff. (Pertwee gets "A tear, Sarah Jane?" Baker gets "It's the end, but the moment has been prepared for." Davison gets "I might regenerate. I don't know. It feels different this time." Hartnell? He gets "Keep warm." He doesn't even get any carrot juice.) And a legion of slicker bases under slicker sieges make this one look a bit cheap. But all of those cracks are only visible because for forty-five years one of the basic mandates of Doctor Who has been "Take *The Tenth Planet* and do it again with more modern sensibilities." Which is (not that *The Tenth Planet* is as good as *Hamlet*) kind of like saying *Hamlet* is rubbish because *The Lion King* has better songs.

No. If we're going to come at this one in a remotely sensible manner, we're going to have to throw the future out and look at this as the 1966 story it is.

Much has been made of the way that the story seems business as usual until the regeneration crops up. Our standard reference books – Wood and Miles and Shearman and Hadoke – insist studiously that it isn't. The truth is somewhere in between. Certainly nothing in the beginning of the story suggests that it is anything other than a continuation of the cod-Quatermass vibe we got from *The War Machines*, which is by far the second most important antecedent to this story. The establishing shots of the story are a rocket launch and some mucking about in a control room – as direct a structural quote of *The Quatermass Experiment* as can be managed.

So when we get a bog-standard sequence of Hartnell and his companions in the TARDIS, we have every reason to expect we're getting *The War Machines* redux. The only reason to suspect anything is amiss is if you've been reading the papers and know that Hartnell is on his way out.

On the other hand, there are at least some things amiss. The base is full of ethnic acting, giving it an international feel, at least when it isn't busy giving it an "oh god make the pain stop" feel. (I will be the first to admit that the ethnic acting is this story's weakest spot. Although the worst offender, Robert Beatty's General Cutler, is probably supposed to sound that way, for better or for worse.) The cutting among monitors and space capsules gives this story a global feel only hinted at in *The War Machines*. And the setting – 1986 – is compelling, in that it is a date that is obtainable within people's lifetimes. (Remember that *The Time Travellers* got much of its impact from the fact that it was set at a time Ian and Barbara would conceivably survive into. Its debt to this story, which it overtly recognizes along with *The War Machines*, and to which it is a de facto sequel, is considerable.) This is not a "five minutes in the future" style, contemporary Earth story like *The War Machines*, but it is still trying

TARDIS Eruditorum Volume 1

something in the same vein – a vision of the future that is of something that the viewers are likely to see.

And then, as the first episode winds on, things get even weirder. One of the basic appeals of Doctor Who is its sheer pluck – the fact that it's the sort of show that, to pick a non-random example, can give you the Doctor teaming up with Richard Nixon to fight UFO-type aliens despite the fact that this premise is completely mad. This sort of spectacle-based storytelling is a fairly modern invention – the Hartnell stories indulged in it occasionally, but usually only when Daleks were involved. But here we get a whopper – more or less out of nowhere, an entire new planet drops into existence near the Earth.

It's tough to say how weird this would have seemed in 1966. You'd need someone who was more of an expert on pop astronomy than I am to know whether anyone seriously believed planets might just drop by unexpectedly and say hi. (Let's be fair, mere months ago Doctor Who was in movie theaters with the Daleks wanting a planet to drive around, so as insane as this seems now, the problem might be us, not them.) But regardless of whether the show blew all credibility with that plot twist, or, perhaps more importantly, when nobody is easily able to recognize that Mondas is very obviously an upside-down Earth (Polly is the first one to get it, because she can identify, of all things, Malaysia, but throughout the story this is treated as a controversial point despite the fact that the audience can see it within seconds), surely the arrival of another planet in orbit is a sign that this is not business as usual.

Especially because, and here's where things really get wacky, the Doctor knows this is going to happen. We've had a lot of "you can't rewrite history" and the importance of historical inevitability before, but this is the first time that attitude has been projected on our future. This is not merely a story about another planet showing up in the sky alongside ours – it's a story about how this is necessarily and absolutely going to happen as an inevitable part of human history.

From there we get the first cliffhanger – a sort that we actually haven't seen since *The Daleks*, at least as an opening cliffhanger. An alien ship lands outside the Snowcap base, and out step strange looking men who butcher the humans. Then we end on a close-up of their expressionless, mummified faces. This is a lot of why I insist on not reading this story as "the first Cybermen story." Because of this cliffhanger, which is very clearly not "Oh crap, it's the Cybermen," but rather "What the hell is THAT?"

Which raises an interesting question. What the hell is that? If we reject reading these things as the lovable robots who faff around in *Silver Nemesis*, what are we left with? Well now, that's a good question. Let's stop here and say that if you haven't read the Pop Between Realities essay about 1966 counter-culture, this might be a good time to do that (specifically the bits about Kenneth Grant).

The key thing to know here is that there exists a model of spiritual enlightenment in which enlightenment is a horrifying and bleak thing. The adjective I'm going to use for this sort of enlightenment – Qlippothic – is important. Basically, it suggests that there is a form of enlightenment that can be found by encountering and contemplating the darkest parts of humanity. The Qlippoth refer to the hollowed out, vacant, and rotted shells of spiritual concepts. And the whole radical idea of Kenneth Grant is that there's not actually a difference between those, which are basically the horrible nightmares within humanity, and actual enlightenment.

I mention this because it's completely necessary to understanding the Cybermen. I'm not saying that Kit Pedler was chillaxing in the Typhonic order with Kenneth Grant (though that would be awesome), but the ideas are clearly similar. Certainly it's worth noting that Pedler's original conception of the Cybermen was as a race of "star monks." Here it is instructive to look at the origin of the Cybermen, as completely and utterly screwed up as it may be. Mondas and Earth are twin planets – the one an inversion of the other. The Cybermen tell us that they and Mondas "drifted away on a journey," making a sweeping arm motion as they do, and that they went to the edge of space, then returned. In the course of that journey, their bodies wore out and they steadily replaced themselves with spare parts, removing human weaknesses in the process.

The Cybermen, in other words, are an alternative version of humanity – the dark mirror of humanity, who went on a quest for spiritual enlightenment and succeeded at terrible cost. This is the heart of their debate with Polly towards the start of the episode – one that is very cleverly staged. The audience, naturally, sympathizes with Polly, who has several built-in advantages when it comes to debating the Cybermen, namely that she is a human, a regular character, fairly attractive, and is arguing for fairly intuitive points like "Letting people die is mean." This is contrasted with the Cybermen, who are cold, inhuman, and all for letting major characters die. But the thing is, the Cybermen get to win the debate with their brilliantly cutting line "There are people dying all over your world, yet you do not care about them."

In other words, the narrative leaves just enough space for us to sympathize with the Cybermen. The Doctor continually treats them with respect and fear. Polly is shot down by them. Their explanations make sense. They offer a world of positive freedom – a world free of pain and misery and fear. And so when they say that they'll just be bringing all of humanity over to Mondas to be converted into Cybermen, well, that's certainly not nice, but it's not a bunch of Daleks shouting "Exterminate" (or a bunch of Cybermen shouting "Delete") either.

Let's pause here also to talk about the look of the Cybermen. These are the most human they'll ever look in the series' history, with still-human hands. It's easy to view this as a mistake, and to decide that their appearance in *The Moonbase* four months later is the show going back and doing them "right." But again, nobody watching this would know that this isn't how the Cybermen are supposed to look. And they do look terrifying – human but not. Much has been said both praising and mocking the voices of the Cybermen in this story. There's a certain tiresome nature to this debate. Those who mock the voices correctly point out that they sound absurd, and that they are nothing like the harsh robotic conquerors of later Cybermen. True enough, of course, but when the Cybermen of *Attack of the Cybermen* or *Revenge of the Cybermen* are your benchmark, you're not exactly setting your goals very high.

Those who praise the voices appreciate the harsh, shocking nature of them, and are largely on target. Certainly Nicholas Briggs does some amazing stuff with them in the Big Finish audio *Spare Parts*, but then, Briggs has at this point become a bewildering yet amazing voice artist specializing in recreating old Doctor Who monster voices and making them capable of acting. As Toby Hadoke points out in *Running Through Corridors*, it's easy for him and Shearman to praise them because they're the sort of people who look for the existential body horror in things.

I am, predictably, more on the side of Shearman and Hadoke, but the thing I think they sell short in their praise of the voices is that the entire story interprets very well from an existential body horror angle, as opposed to just the Cybermen. The entire point of the voices is to be a grotesque parody of human speech – the Cybermen's mouths open and the synthesized speech seems to pour horrifically out of their mouths. Given that the show makes the extremely brave decision to let the Cybermen win the ethics debate in this episode, the voices are an important move to make sure we realize just how horrific these people are. Not evil, mind you, but horrific.

Which is a crucial thing about the Cybermen. Wood and Miles have about three solid pages in *About Time Volume 2* about this, but the basic point is that Pedler is extrapolating from a sort of harmful medicine here, combining fears of artificial hearts with anxiety over the use of mood-altering drugs (both prescription and recreational) and a general ambivalence about artificial goods in general. But he's not quite choosing to seal the deal, and that's significant. He could make the Cybermen into the Autons – plastic monsters who are just evil. He doesn't. Instead, through plasticity and inhumanity, the Cybermen reach a sort of terrible apotheosis. They are at once the best that humans can be and terrifying monsters – a set of anxieties and hopes blended together chaotically.

In the face of these, the Doctor runs into a problem that he's been having for a while. He starts to drop out of the narrative. He looks out of place in this base. With nobody but a loud American to talk to (and we've already talked about how ill-suited the Doctor is to Americans), the Doctor is forced to the perimeter of the plot, with the center being consumed by the Cybermen.

Then comes the third episode, and we get what is frankly a happy accident – William Hartnell falls ill, and is abruptly written out of the episode. Not that I don't like Hartnell. Hartnell is absolutely fantastic. But given that he's already being pushed to the margins of this story (as he has been for several stories in a row), having him actually drop out entirely is, ironically, the best thing that could happen to his character. When the Doctor is present but sidelined, he appears to be a weak character, but as soon as he is actually removed from the narrative we realize something we haven't been able to see clearly in some time – we do actually need him.

I said that *The War Machines* is the second biggest antecedent to this story, and left what the biggest one is deliberately vague. But since this is the last Hartnell story, there's never going to be a better time to dust off the Hartnell's Greatest Hits reel, so let's go ahead talk about *The Chase*. You may recall that I created an elaborate interpretation there based on the idea of narrative collapse – i.e. that the Daleks are not merely threatening the lives of the TARDIS crew, they're threatening the entire ability to tell Doctor Who stories. It's a very interesting mode of storytelling, and one that Doctor Who is very good at, because it is basically the only mode of fictional storytelling where the stakes in the story are actually stakes that directly impact the audience. If the audience is watching, presumably it is because they like the show they are watching. So if you threaten to destroy the very means of storytelling in the show, not some alien colony or a single character on the show, that's a real threat.

The problem is, with *The Chase*, it's never quite possible to tell whether the narrative collapse reading is a fun deconstruction or what's actually going on (and I largely suspect it is the former, though it's a very fun deconstruction and I don't rule out the latter). But here, that's absolutely what is going on. The Cybermen represent a completely different form of humanity, and they have a real ability to impose that new vision upon us. It is not merely that they are going to destroy all humans. That would be a scheme that is clearly not going to happen. Rather, it is that they are going to destroy the basic idea of humanity and replace it with something else.

So when the Doctor and his companions are increasingly pushed to the fringes of the story, and then when the Doctor drops out of the story entirely, it's scary because suddenly it seems like there are no rules. The tension stops being "how will this Doctor Who story turn out" and instead becomes "wait, what sort of story is this?" Again, to a modern viewer, it's easy to miss this, because we're so convinced we know what kind of story it is – a Cybermen story and a regeneration story. But 1960s viewers wouldn't have known this, and as a result, couldn't possibly have seen it that way.

And suddenly, amongst all this ratcheting of tension, the Doctor's collapse highlights just how much the show has quietly thrown overboard. Our characters are in the hands of a psychotic American, humanity is confronting its dark mirror and the dark mirror looks better than us, and, for good measure, something called a Z-Bomb is about to be launched and possibly destroy the entire planet. And then the Cybermen land again, and this time they seem to be a force of nature, marching with calm relentlessness. (Plus there are so many of them! Seven usable costumes! We never have seven of a Doctor Who monster! There might as well be seventy!)

Again, the present screws us over in trying to watch this. We know that the Doctor is absent because an increasingly frail Hartnell fell ill. We know that Hartnell was bullied/eased out of the role over the summer, and that he came back to this as a guest star. We know the entire script was already written to minimize the strain on him. So we view this as an irritation – especially because it means that our last glimpse of Hartnell is a fairly thin scene in the second episode, and thus his illness combined with the missing fourth episode means that we lose out on the end of his tenure. And this becomes part of the overall fan tendency to pretend that Hartnell's regeneration was being built towards over the course of multiple stories.

As we'll see shortly, it wasn't. Yes, there were some murmurings in internal memos that regeneration is simply something that happens every 500 years or so, but that's markedly not how it's written. In fact, let's go ahead and formally bust this myth that the Hartnell to Troughton transition is arbitrary. Not that it's the same process as we'll see in later regenerations – it's not, largely because it's not presented as routine. But it is something that happens for a plot-related reason, and that follows specifically from the previous episodes of *The Tenth Planet*.

So, we're up to the fourth episode now. And as it opens, crucially, Hartnell rumbles back into the story full of fury and passion. The strong sense is that he stopped the Z-Bomb (as he was originally scripted to do before Ben had to take over) and saved the day. He gets, in other words, the hero's entrance, full of terrible rage. This is absolutely the same man we see at the end of, for instance, *The Family of Blood* – a man who, when put with his back against the wall, roars back even stronger.

But there's a sense that something isn't quite right as well. The Doctor complains of an outside influence affecting him, and murmurs that his body is wearing a bit thin. Still, that is quickly set aside as the Doctor manages to finally completely unhinge General Cutler (who is quickly gunned down) and take over the situation. It's a fantastic sequence, and it's tough to remember when we last saw Hartnell this in control and decisive.

Here's where things get interesting. I mentioned way up at the start of the entry that this story has a global scope. One aspect of that was a set that was used as an office in Geneva, allowing people on the opposite side of the world to comment on and weigh in over the action at the Snowcap base. So we have the Snowcap base – the base under siege by Cybermen – and Geneva, the place far away that is commenting on what goes on at Snowcap. And then, suddenly, a Cyberman shows up in Geneva and kills the characters there. It's a fantastic violation of the rules of the story – because we treated Geneva for so long as a distant location, it seemed safe from the invasion, which was mostly threatening the Snowcap base. So when the Cybermen show up there, it's a decisive sign that things have gotten very bad.

From there, the Doctor says and does something truly strange – he, out of nowhere, deduces that the Cybermen are planning on destroying the Earth. There's little setup for this, and it does not really seem like a rational deduction at all. But it makes sense. Many commentators take this as the point when the Cybermen's interesting motivations go away and they become generic monsters. It's not. Quite the contrary, it's the logical extension of everything we've seen. We've already been told Mondas is draining the Earth's power. In other words, Mondas is effectively a vampiric planet. It and Earth are not peacefully coexistent twins, but parasitic twins, and one of them has to consume the other. So when the Cybermen are accused of being bent on destroying the Earth, it's simply a confirmation that they are the dark mirrors we initially took them for.

Crucially, however, they don't actually change their behavior much. They still offer a peaceful resolution in which humanity just gets converted, and we see people who want to

TARDIS Eruditorum Volume 1

take them up on it. It's only when that's shot down that Plan B – murder everyone so they survive – comes to the fore. But at the end of the day, this is not a straightforward alien invasion at all. If we read the Cybermen as the Qlippothic parodies of humanity, this is simply its natural endpoint. They have ascended, and now it is our turn to follow them.

But what's really odd is that the Doctor's re-emergence in the narrative suddenly crumbles. He's taken off to the Cybermen ship, where he immediately starts to feel the effects of Mondas's energy drain, fading by the second as his own energy is sapped by the Cybermen. The Cybermen sweep to center stage again, and the plot becomes about Ben's attempts to hold them off and ensure a stalemate. Which he does . . . for a while. And then . . .

Mondas explodes. Pretty much out of nowhere. And the Cybermen explode with it, suddenly becoming withered plastic shells of people (much like they always were). Humanity is safe, not because it saved itself, but because it lasted long enough that Mondas destroyed itself. The essential conflict between Mondas and Earth, where they are both dark reflections of one another, resolved itself. One world lived, the other died, and that was that. Game over, back to the TARDIS, on to another adventure.

And again, now we complain. The Cybermen just disintegrated. There's no satisfying resolution. We've been cheated. All the good ideas of this story have turned rubbish and disappointing.

Nope. Not at all. Remember, in *The Chase*, that the Doctor ultimately defeats the Daleks by luck. Eventually the Mechanoids happen by and kill all the Daleks, and he escapes, but at a terrible cost – Ian and Barbara leave him. That's the same resolution we get here. The Doctor manages to hold on long enough that Mondas takes care of itself. But what's the cost?

The answer is chilling. When next we see the Doctor, he is, quite simply, dying. Frail, unable to follow what's going on, and stumbling around, he gathers himself up and says he needs to return to the TARDIS, telling his companions to keep warm. It's scary. Something is clearly wrong here. The Qlippothic energy of Mondas has spared the world, but . . .

It hasn't spared the Doctor. He's been drained too far. Perhaps because he's old and his body is wearing thin, but this adventure was simply too much for him. Being drained of life energy by a hideous parody of humanity was fatal.

And so when we return to the TARDIS with Ben and Polly, we see something terrifying.

Back in *The Chase*, we formulated the basic rules of the narrative collapse story. The entire storytelling apparatus of Doctor Who is threatened, then it spontaneously reforms itself, but at some cost. And the cost is this: Doctor Who gets cancelled.

What that means changes from time to time. Certainly the Doctor Who we knew from the first two seasons – the one that did weird, inventive experimental theater, pseudo-Shakespearean comedies, and existentialist drama in rapid succession – went away with Ian and Barbara. But that's a subtle change to what we get here. We've been talking about how the format is changing out from under William Hartnell, and here that becomes inexorable.

And this is part of being a Doctor Who fan. You are absolutely guaranteed to see the show die in front of you, and then get replaced with a strange, different show using the same name. Eventually, everything that Doctor Who is comes to a crashing halt and something new happens instead. Sometimes it's wonderful. Sometimes it's heartbreaking. But it's inevitable. It's why one of the few sections of fandom that I get actively angry at is the "bring back David Tennant" crowd. Frankly, you only got David Tennant because nine previous versions of the show got cancelled. You knew your turn would come. You don't get to pull a version of the show other people enjoy away from them and replace it with your own. If you did, we'd bring Ian, Barbara, and the Doctor back.

Yes. The Doctor. What is about to happen is not the end of the First Doctor's tenure. No. It's the end of the Doctor. William Hartnell only played the First Doctor once, in 1973. Otherwise, he was always simply the Doctor – playing the part for an audience that had no idea anybody else could be the Doctor. And what is about to happen is not the replacement of the first version with the second. It's the replacement of the only version with something completely new.

And we know that the moment Ben and Polly return to the TARDIS, as the Doctor, silently, desperately, flings switches around while other switches flick on and off themselves. And the TARDIS screams. That's the only way to describe it – harsh, metallic noises unlike anything we've seen the ship make. It's scary. It's scary in a way not even *An Unearthly Child* tried to make it.

And we know why it's happened. It's happened because the Doctor came into contact with horrible, Qlippothic forces. It happened because the Doctor encountered these horrible, dark parodies of humanity. And the question we have to ask is, what has happened to him? Because suddenly, he collapses. He collapses, and we can see it. In the past, we've seen some man in a silly wig fall over from behind. It's a bit of a joke, spotting the lame Hartnell duplicates. But this is unmistakably William Hartnell crumpled on the ground. The Doctor. Our Doctor – the silly old wizard with a terrible fire within.

And he is dying on the ground of his magic box, which screams around him.

He doesn't get last words. He just dies. And we know why. We know full well it is Mondas that destroyed him and that his energy was drained by that monstrous other world. And it's stark and horrific. It's the sort of cosmic, psychological horror we associate with Lovecraft – that this dark, Qlippothic energy stalks the universe like a cosmological vampire and has now taken our hero away from us.

And as the TARDIS dematerialization sounds, now harsh, mechanical, and scary like it hasn't been for three years, the Doctor fades away, and some new face sits where he used to be.

And here is where our second error happens. Just as we misread the Cybermen, who in fact never reappear after *The Tenth Planet* (although their name and home planet are recycled for some very silly looking robots) we misread regeneration. We know what happens at the end of this episode, and it's almost comforting to us – here comes Troughton! He's fun!

That's not what we're watching. Not even a little bit. This is not the rise of the Second Doctor. It is nothing whatsoever except the death of the Doctor – the death of the only Doctor. And we forget that. We forget that the Hartnell era goes out on an astonishingly bleak cliffhanger, that *The Tenth Planet* feeds directly into *The Power of the Daleks* a week later, and that all of this is terrifying, not a triumphant moment of the show's history. We treat this scene as something that ends the book on an era. And it is that, but it is so much more.

Yeah, this entry marks the end of a major period of Doctor Who. But for all of that, the Troughton era also dovetails right off the end of this, and it's going to be important when reading about the start of his era to forget everything you think you know about this show. Doctor Who is over. The Doctor is dead. The horrible plastic monsters offering a grotesque parody of spiritual enlightenment have destroyed him, and replaced him with something else, just as they wanted to replace us with them. The operating assumption, given that the Cybermen wanted to help us ascend to be like them, and given that the Cybermen did in fact kill the Doctor, is that he is now going to "ascend." And whatever this terrible, awful man who replaced the Doctor is, the odds are very, very poor that it's going to be a good thing.

Now My Doctor: William Hartnell

Actually, I can't write this essay. Not honestly. I don't have "my Doctor," although Matt Smith comes amazingly close. I have no favorite. I may well have a least favorite, but it's not Hartnell. So when I write the essay about why Hartnell is "my Doctor," well, remember that there are ten more of these waiting to be written.

Beyond that, there's a certain impossibility to the task. Eras of the show divide more usefully on production staff than they do on the lead actor. The fact of the matter is, the jump from *Mission to the Unknown* to *The Myth Makers* is a much larger jump than the one from *The Tenth Planet* to *The Power of the Daleks*, because *The Tenth Planet* is at least written to feed into *The Power of the Daleks*.

But this is a case where reason doesn't get as much say as one might hope. Even if it makes a lot more sense to talk about the Verity Lambert years and the Wiles/Lloyd/Bryant/Sherwin years (yes, that's four producers lumped into one era, but they played musical chairs so much that it seems silly to separate them out) than it does to talk about the Hartnell years and the Troughton years, the default division is by Doctor.

All of this is made trickier, in this case, by the fact that William Hartnell never played the First Doctor. As I've said, he played the Doctor – the only Doctor. So talking about

Hartnell's take on the character is misleading. Every actor after Hartnell came to the job having to find a take on the character as defined by past actors. Hartnell alone simply got to create a character. He didn't have a take on that character. He had that character.

So what character did he create, and how should we evaluate it? And here is where we run into a tricky bit. It's easy to see a massive difference between the Doctor as he appears in *An Unearthly Child* and the Doctor as he appears in, say, *The Gunfighters* (to pick a late story with an unusually cuddly Hartnell). Often this is taken as evidence of how the character changed midway through the run. Some people, seemingly without the use of actual evidence, claim this happens as a result of Hartnell's episode unconscious in *Marco Polo*, which is bewildering on several levels. If one is hell-bent on picking a particular scene where the Doctor mellows out, it is surely his reconciliation with Barbara at the end of *The Edge of Destruction*, but even there one runs into the problem that he's deeply cruel to Susan in *The Sensorites*, and a total jerk again in *The Reign of Terror*.

And it's important to note that this inconsistency has little to do with Hartnell, who does a solid job of trying to sell everything he's given. It's that what he's given is bizarrely inconsistent. Over the first season, the show lurches back and forth awkwardly on what the Doctor is supposed to be like. A large part of this is something you'll see in several of the essays in the early part of this book – it takes a bizarrely long time for the writers to figure out that their lives will go a lot better if the Doctor actually wants to have adventures and if they don't need to find elaborate ways to break the TARDIS every story. And until they figure that out, they consistently run into the problem of writing the Doctor in a way that actively inhibits him from being effective in the stories.

This was not all bad – the best of the Doctor/Barbara scenes – scenes that are, for me, solidly among the highlights of the Hartnell era – all depend on the cantankerous nature of the Doctor. But on balance, it is, even more than the pacing, a lot of why the first season of Doctor Who is so hard to watch. (Though to be fair, some of the unfriendly Doctor might be a factor of pacing. An easy way to pad a story out to six episodes is to have the Doctor do less stuff and have characters spend more time being stuck. When the standard story length contracts to four episodes in the second and third seasons, the Doctor gets more proactive.)

Whereas if you start from the end on Hartnell, you run in to a different problem – by then, Hartnell was, whether by necessity or by dint of the producers, being marginalized in his own program. It's in the end impossible to, using only the evidence on the screen, quite judge exactly how necessary forcing Hartnell out of the role was. Clearly by 1973 he was physically incapable of playing the part. But where exactly that line was crossed is tough to tell, especially since reports of Hartnell's growing difficulty on set are difficult to fully sort out – are they due more to Hartnell's deteriorating health, or the fact that John Wiles and Innes Lloyd were openly hostile to Hartnell in a way Verity Lambert never was?

The result is that once Verity Lambert leaves after *Mission to the Unknown*, the series stumbles around. It still has some real highlights – both of the Donald Cotton stories and *The Massacre* are glorious. But it's all too obvious watching the program that no matter how well Hartnell acts, the production staff doesn't want him and that their zeal to get rid of him or sideline him is, at times, a higher priority than effective storytelling.

But sandwiched in between these two extremes is Season Two. And for me, it is in Season Two that you can see most clearly what Doctor Who in the Hartnell style can aspire towards. Here the writers have begun to find a level of confidence in what they're doing, and Susan has been discarded in favor of Vicki, a companion who is basically just Susan except that it's plausible for the Doctor to leave her to fend for herself. This small change goes a huge way towards making the character work, and Maureen O'Brien's ability to infuse the character with an energy and enthusiasm that, at least according to interviews with her, she herself did not have at all.

And so from *The Rescue* through to *The Chase* you have a half-dozen stories where every element of the series as originally conceived is there and working right. The bugs in plotting from the first season have mostly been worked out, but the basic dynamic of the Doctor, the starchild, and the two ordinary humans with very different ways of making sense of the impossible things they witness is still there. And when all the companions and plot are basically working right, you can really see what Hartnell is doing with his character and how that character is supposed to work.

The thing about Hartnell's Doctor is that the central paradox of the character is shared by the actor. On the one hand, it is impossible to overstate how much Hartnell loved the show and how committed to it he was. He has been described (by Miles and Wood at least, and I am pretty sure by others) as the show's first fan, and that's not entirely inaccurate. Many of his spats with the production staff came from his insistence on consistency. Hartnell believed it was important, for instance, that the TARDIS controls be in the same places week to week, and repeatedly pointed out things that he didn't think made sense. On top of that, he genuinely loved the character and loved entertaining children.

On the other hand, there are more than enough historical records to confirm that Hartnell was difficult to work with, racist, cranky, and erratic. It's also clear that by the end of his time on the program, his health was negatively impacting his performance. That said, many of the stories of Hartnell circulated on the convention circuit are simply untrue, and trivially proven as such. Many people have claimed he had his lines written around the set so he could check them, and that was why his character kept looking around all the time. Which is rubbish. The claim that his objection to Max Adrian in *The Myth Makers* was down to Adrian's homosexuality? He'd worked with Adrian before – by all appearances, he just didn't like the script that month. (See also the essay "Was William Hartnell a Bigot" in this volume.)

But this contradiction between Hartnell's friendly grandfather tendencies and his cranky tendencies does more than just define the actor. It also defines his character, and in those Season Two episodes, you can see the character working properly. And, notably, what you see is miles from the usual brief on Hartnell – that he's the ultimate "mysterious" Doctor. In fact, although the Doctor's origins are basically utterly unknown in the Hartnell period, they're also basically utterly irrelevant to any of the stories. Not a single story in the entire Hartnell era actually hinges in any way, shape, or form on the Doctor's past. The closest you get is *The Massacre*, where it vaguely sort of plays into one character decision, or at least, it might except that Dodo blunders through the doors a second later and ruins the whole thing (and by thing I mean series).

No, the thing about Hartnell's Doctor that you can really see in those stories is that he was never meant to be the sole leading man. Which you can tell just by watching the first story, where Ian is obviously the lead character and the Doctor is a supporting character played by a character actor instead of a leading man actor. The Doctor, as designed originally, was always meant to function as part of an ensemble cast. Other than the slight problem of Susan not quite working and needing to be replaced with Vicki, this was how he did work, and quite well, for two seasons. Even when Ian and Barbara were replaced with Steven, it still worked, because Steven was basically able to fulfill Ian's functions, and Barbara's functions could be split.

But once Vicki left, Hartnell stopped working because his character was never meant to work in those circumstances. He was never a leading man character, but rather a background character who served as the backdrop for everyone else. And if you look at a Hartnell story from Season Two, that's mostly what you'll see: a story where Ian, Barbara, and Vicki actually provide most of the story while the Doctor quietly and often in the background solves the plot. In other words, under Hartnell, Doctor Who isn't quite an adventure story. Rather, it's a story about a bunch of ordinary people who are stuck in an adventure story, traveling with an old man who inexorably drags them towards adventure stories, but who also seems almost magically capable of getting them out again. But the stories aren't about the magical old man who solves the problems – they're about being stuck along for the ride with the magical old man. The magical old man, in this view of the series, has to be somewhat detached from both the other characters and the audience.

Unsurprising, when you take a very unusual character part and try to force it into being the straightforward leading man – as John Wiles and Innes Lloyd did – it doesn't quite work. And once Patrick Troughton shows up and makes the Doctor into a successful, charismatic leading man, the opportunity for the sidelined character part is gone, and what Hartnell did can never quite be recaptured.

Which is the strange and remarkable thing about Hartnell; his is the only era of Doctor Who that it is almost impossible to pay homage to. Comb through the new series and you can find homages to Troughton, UNIT-style romps, Hinchcliffian scarefests, banter à la Williams, Saward-esque runarounds with pseudo-space marines, and seething political analogies to do Cartmel proud.

The one thing you won't find – and never will find again – is a William Hartnell story. This is because none of them can be him. Not my Doctor.

Now my Doctor, I've seen him cower in fear and then, made a companion at last, learn to be a man. I've seen him stare down monsters and make them blink. I've seen him quietly die as he does his duty, with no one to understand. I've seen him stand by and make a man of a boy, and a hero of a man. I've seen him make a woman of a girl, and a goddess of a woman. I've seen him grow from less than a man to more than a man, and then just swagger off to his

TARDIS and open it with a tap of his ring – The Doctor in the TARDIS.

My Doctor.

Elizabeth Sandifer

Coda: Before the Beginning

(Essays on what happened before *An Unearthly Child*)

Elizabeth Sandifer

What Happened Before Totters Lane?

As I'll argue in the essay on Kim Newman's *Time and Relative,* the answer to what happened before the first episode of Doctor Who should be "not much." But equally clearly, the answer isn't "nothing." More to the point, the appeal of it is difficult to resist. Writers, understandably, like going back to the primordial space before November 23, 1963. Whether it be the teased revelations of *The Name of the Doctor* and *Listen* or the bevy of stories explicitly set before it, this is an aspect of Doctor Who that has to be dealt with.

The appeal of this primordial era is, of course, clear. The questions of who the Doctor was on Gallifrey, how and why he stole the TARDIS, and, at least until *The War Games,* where he's from and why he's running are huge ones, and Doctor Who fandom hangs on every clue towards their answers. (This is, of course, why answering them is mostly a terrible idea.) And, of course, it also gives an opportunity to rehabilitate the character of Susan, whose problems as a character will form the bulk of several essays to come.

But equally, as the essays for the first few televised stories show, it doesn't quite make sense to treat the space before *An Unearthly Child* with much detail, because so much of the television show's first season is about the Doctor becoming the character we know from the subsequent forty-nine years. Which raises a very basic continuity question: just how much stuff could we fit prior to the start of the series if we really wanted to?

We'll start with what we know for certain. In the Hartnell era, the Doctor namedrops historical figures with considerable frequency. However, as I argue in the essay for *The Romans*, most of these seem likely to fall under the header of "The Doctor lies." But there are some confirmable adventures – we know for a fact he must have visited Quinnus in the Fifth Universe, for instance, because both the TARDIS and Susan corroborate the incident in *The Edge of Destruction*. Past that, the Doctor often has knowledge of places and events, but that's very distinct from experience. Certainly he does not regularly show up places where people recognize him – a marked change from, say, *Victory of the Daleks*, where he has a long-standing and multi-regeneration relationship with Winston Churchill.

Plus it's very hard to square a significant number of adventures with the events on screen in a sensible, organic way. The Doctor is terrified of being tied up in the Cave of Skulls. Given how normal kidnapping is from there on out, and how well he takes all of it, the obvious conclusion is that he's not used to situations where he's kidnapped. Which is to say, he's not used to adventures. The first three stories have a clear plot line of the TARDIS crew learning to trust each other, and the impetus for this is the adventures they're having. If the adventures were normal to the Doctor, it would shatter the entire emotional foundation of the early episodes. Furthermore, Susan is stated to be sixteen, and no effort is made to contradict that. (Nor would it be – Hartnell is clearly intending the Doctor to be in his sixties or seventies, and the show, even though it establishes him and Susan as aliens, rarely commits to this fact and treats them as human with some regularity. It's not until *The Power of the Daleks* that the idea of the Doctor being centuries old really becomes set.)

On the other hand, there are some unavoidable retcons from later in the series. The most obvious is *Remembrance of the Daleks*, where we discover that the Doctor stashed a Time

Lord superweapon in London while he was staying at Totters Lane. But this isn't that big a problem. We've always known there's a reason the Doctor is on the run from his people. Presumably the Hand of Omega is part of it.

The larger problem is the Doctor's age. Though this is a massive problem that we'll square away in a later volume, the big three signposts people pay attention to are usually Troughton's claim to be 450 in *The Tomb of the Cybermen*, Baker's various claims in the 700s, and the Tennant-era claim of 907 (and, conveniently, not any of the various claims that contradict these). If we assume those three to be correct, we're fine. Or at least, we were right up until Neil Gaiman slipped in the figure "700 years" in The Doctor's Wife to refer to how long the Doctor had been traveling in the TARDIS.

There are two problems here. First is that the Hartnell era clearly isn't written with any of this in mind. Second, it means he started traveling at around age 200. Which means he has 250 years of travel under his belt by *Tomb of the Cybermen*. The problem is that there's nowhere in his on-screen time prior to *Tomb of the Cybermen* to put in 250 years of travel. He's had humans on board the entire time that haven't aged significantly. This leaves us with three options.

1) Take seriously the claim from *The Sarah Jane Adventures* that Ian and Barbara haven't aged since the 1960s and decide that their adventures with Susan or without her could have lasted centuries. This is, however, even more stupid than assuming massive pre-Totters Lane adventures – it does grave violence to Ian and Barbara's character arcs, completely trivializing the ending of *The Chase*.

2) Dismiss all claims about the Doctor's age, and just go with the TARDIS's claim. Reasonable, since they're necessarily contradictory, the Doctor lies, and the current timekeeping means the Doctor's regenerations up to Matt Smith are only a couple of years each, which is unsatisfying for a number of reasons. But there's something still irritating

about solving the problem by just ignoring swaths of episodes because they don't fit. Especially when we can just say:

3) Assume that the Doctor has traveled substantially but not in the manner we're used to. If we assume that the Doctor stole the TARDIS at around 200 and assume (generously) that he's about 425 or so in *An Unearthly Child*, we're left with 225 years of travel. But, notably, those years presumably didn't include Susan (who is also not mentioned at all in *The Doctor's Wife* in the descriptions of the Doctor stealing the TARDIS, suggesting she wasn't there). We can thus, if we like, assume that the Doctor ran off with the TARDIS, journeyed passively for 225 years, then went back and picked up Susan. This is consistent with Simon Guerrier's *The Time Travellers*, also discussed in this volume, which has a lovely retcon for why the TARDIS has a chameleon circuit – because the Time Lords just park them and observe. It also goes a long way towards explaining the Doctor's startling levels of knowledge.

The only problem is that Idris says that the Doctor has been walking past the "PULL TO OPEN" sign for 700 years, not that he's been traveling for 700 years. And the TARDIS clearly becomes a police box for Totters Lane.

Or does it? Susan expresses surprise when it doesn't change upon arriving in *100,000 BC*. But the Doctor, in that story, explains that he can't steer the TARDIS without knowing where it was exactly. Perhaps the chameleon circuit works similarly, and the Doctor was assuming that if he could get the TARDIS to a place where it might disguise itself as a police box then the chameleon circuit would start working again, and this is why Susan is surprised that it doesn't. This also helps explain some of the details about stashing away the Hand of Omega – he did that on his first visit to '60s Britain, then later picked up Susan and eventually returned to 1960s Britain where he began working to repair the chameleon circuit, only to have his work interrupted by Ian and Barbara and to have to take off with it unrepaired, hence Susan's surprise when it doesn't change – she thought the Doctor had fixed it.

This does mean he was somewhat less sensible than the standard Time Lord according to Guerrier, but then again, he was the only Time Lord mad enough to let the TARDIS steal him. Perhaps he even ventured outside, poked around a bit, had a few larks, but stayed out of doing anything too big. These are, one might assume, what the Doctor defaults to when he is without a companion, which is why we see so few adventures in which he's alone – without someone in the Ian and Barbara mould, he doesn't actually quite have it in him to be the hero. So he has lengthy stretches traveling alone in most of his incarnations – the third, fourth, sixth, seventh, and eighth clearly, and the fifth, ninth, and tenth implicitly – for centuries, perhaps, where he goes and does nothing important and wastes his life staying out of trouble and flirting with famous people. And it's because he's still a scared little child, even as an adult sometimes. (There's no point in being grown up if you can't be childish sometimes.) So he chickens out of doing things that are quite as impressive. (The "less canonical" stories, by which we mean the more niche ones, are almost always set in these gaps, oddly reflecting their half-real status.)

Because he's still profoundly childish.

As he is in these stories – a scared little child who puffs up and plays a cranky old man because that's the part he's learned to play to inflate himself these days. (He does this a lot – finds ways of puffing himself up. This includes, but certainly is not limited to: exaggerating his historical exploits, strutting about, mugging for his fans, and lying about his age.) Towards the end of his first life and still, thus, in his teenage years with all the anxieties thereof, he's an old man who's a child. Which is what we see in Hartnell throughout his stories. So yes, he's gone and hung out with historical figures across multiple planets and galaxies, including many on Earth, his dirty little secret of a planet. (It's why he doesn't mind that it's looked like a police box for centuries – only Susan, who's really new to all of this, does.)

Then whatever incident that leads to him running off with Susan and being "cut off" from his own people occurs. Although this incident is clearly not the theft of the TARDIS (if that were a big deal there wouldn't be so many renegades running around, seemingly without getting into massive trouble). It is something done towards the end of his first incarnation. So he grabs his granddaughter, whisks her away to his favorite place, 1960s London (where he also sentimentally hid the Hand of Omega), and hangs out there until she screws up and blunders Ian and Barbara into his TARDIS. He then panics, flees, and is stuck having terrifying adventures that finally make him grow up. And in growing up, he becomes a hero.

This solution, of course, worked marvelously until *The Name of the Doctor*, where we see the Doctor stealing the TARDIS accompanied by Susan. Still, we can patch the theory up only slightly if we want to – *The Name of the Doctor* visibly does not include anything that looks like the Hand of Omega, after all. So all we have to do is assume that Susan was, in fact, with him for the running around and passively adventuring, and that they then went back to Gallifrey to get the Hand of Omega, with 1960s London being their first stop after that.

I mention this solution not because it's the best solution – there is no best solution to a problem that, if we're being honest, exists because multiple writers working over forty-eight years paid minimal attention to each other's work and did what they felt like. But assuming that the Doctor had a lengthy period of passively running around before picking up the Hand of Omega and arriving in London does allow for a reasonably tidy explanation of the various pieces of data. And, perhaps most importantly for a theory that primarily explains things that happened in the William Hartnell era, unlike most of the other theories, it doesn't screw up the events visible on the screen. What more can one ask for out of a silly romp through continuity?

Auld Mortality

It is, of course, debatable whether this even belongs here. It is not, strictly speaking, a story featuring Hartnell's Doctor. Instead it's a part of Big Finish's *Unbound* line, which offers "what if" takes on Doctor Who featuring various distinguished actors playing alternate Doctors. Marc Platt's *Auld Mortality* was the first of the line, featuring Geoffrey Bayldon as a Doctor who never left Gallifrey. But this is a narrow distinction. Platt has clearly written for what is basically Hartnell's Doctor, and Bayldon, who was offered the part of the Doctor and declined, plays him that way.

So what we have is, in effect, a story about Hartnell's Doctor set on Gallifrey, and telling the story of his departure. It is, in many ways, a rewriting of Platt's novel *Lungbarrow*, the last of the Virgin Books' New Adventures series to feature Sylvester McCoy's Doctor. That book offered a variety of revelations about the true nature of Gallifrey and the Doctor's role in it, revealing details of his family and, ultimately, telling the entire story of how and why he came to leave.

Auld Mortality is not quite compatible – *Lungbarrow* has a very different explanation of Susan's origins grounded primarily in the New Adventures continuity, which has a whole elaborate mythos involving why Time Lords reproduce asexually, and has Susan not as the Doctor's literal granddaughter but as the granddaughter of the ancient

Gallifreyan known as the Other, who the Doctor is a reincarnation of, and as the last natural-born child of Gallifrey. *Auld Mortality* doesn't engage with this, instead telling a narrower story about the Doctor and, subsequently, Susan and their desire to do something other than engage in the stultifying politics of Gallifrey.

Even still, there's something odd within the story. Its central premise is the play of possibilities – instead of fleeing Gallifrey the Doctor has become a novelist, writing adventure stories and endlessly exploring the various possibilities of the world. And yet as a pre-origin for the Doctor there's something profoundly limiting here. *Auld Mortality* celebrates the multiplicity of Doctor Who, with allusions to John and Gillian, *Doctor Who in an Exciting Adventure with the Daleks*, and various other alternate versions of Doctor Who, as well as several alternatives of its own invention such as the Thaleks. And yet it offers all of these possibilities out of a fixed origin – a view of who the Doctor was on Gallifrey.

It's certainly true that there is a vast multiplicity of takes on Doctor Who. But equally, Doctor Who, though not singular, has a clear, primary take in the form of the television show. Whereas the question of what happened before *An Unearthly Child* is a matter of continuous speculation. Exactly why the Doctor left Gallifrey and who he was on Gallifrey before his departure is, in the end, one of the untellable mysteries of the series. And so *Auld Mortality*, in a strange way, switches around the certainties of Doctor Who, treating the series itself as a source of infinite possibility, but having it all stem out of a singular vision of Gallifrey and who the Doctor was there.

Within the story the fixed nature of Gallifrey is treated as a problem. To be fair, it always is. There may be no consensus on exactly why the Doctor left Gallifrey, but the answer generally comes down to the facts that it was boring and that he opposed its non-interventionist standpoint. Both of these are acknowledged within *Auld Mortality*, and both gesture towards the idea that the Doctor is a creature of possibility and change in overt contrast to Gallifreyan fixity.

Within *Auld Mortality* this is further stressed by the presence of Ordinal-General Quences, an elder of the Doctor's family with political ambitions. In a rather poorly set up, late twist, it turns out that Quences is in fact the embodiment of death and represents the inevitability of endings and decay. Quences seeks to elevate one of his own family members to the presidency, linking the Time Lord's stodgy systems of power to the idea of death in a fairly tight and straightforward symbolic knot.

And yet the role of Gallifrey itself in this narrative confounds that. The Hartnell era, after all, could have been anything. Or, at least, it could have been many things other than Gallifrey. Had Sydney Newman liked the pilot episode more, the Doctor's origin would have been fixed from the start. Had the ratings held up six years later, Malcolm Hulke and Terrance Dicks would never have needed to come up with the ending of *The War Games*. Had any number of things gone slightly differently the series would be different. Gallifrey is a historical accident with nothing whatsoever to do with the Hartnell era.

And yet here it is, infesting it, turning Susan, a character who was never conceived as a Time Lord, into the president of Gallifrey. Many of the earlier essays in this book discuss the Problem of Susan – her role in the series' premise (i.e. what the people making *An Unearthly Child* thought they were making) and her implications for the long-term future of the series (which nobody trying to get it off the ground was thinking seriously about). Here it is discarded almost entirely, with Susan becoming subsumed into the later premises of the show.

It is, of course, unfair to treat this as a criticism. The *Unbound* line celebrated the series' fortieth anniversary, long after the Hartnell era had passed. And this is explicitly an alternate take on Doctor Who. It's not quite the Hartnell era, and doesn't actually overwrite it so much as play what-if. The moving of uncertainty away from the question of "who is the Doctor" and towards "what is the series" is a conscious reversal and commentary on the show.

And yet underneath this the Hartnell era drops out quietly. Some of this is necessary – new stories featuring William Hartnell are, after all, sadly impossible. But it's still the Hartnell era being evoked here; the presence of Susan makes that unavoidable. But the result has little to do with the early days of Doctor Who the television series, and everything to do with its future.

Which is, in the end, an important thing to note about these pre-*Unearthly Child* stories. For the most part, they are not about fitting in before *An Unearthly Child*, but rather about making some commentary on the future of the series. Which is fine, and a perfectly worthwhile game for what it is, but there is a real sense in which it does textual violence to the Hartnell era, which is, as the rest of this book is concerned with demonstrating, an interesting and fascinating beast in its own right. There's much to like about *Auld Mortality* – it's an interesting statement of the show's moral premises and a commentary on the vast number of ways in which it could have gone. But it's not a commentary on the way it did go in those first few years.

This is, of course, something of a theme for the essays in this section of the book, all of which are, to some extent, about the way in which attempts to delve into the pre-Hartnell era lose sight of major parts of the Hartnell era itself, thus failing to actually connect to the series' beginnings. *Auld Mortality*, at least, admits that, while suggesting that perhaps this isn't the point. After all, the prospect of a fixed and steady world is antithetical to it. *An Unearthly Child* may be the beginning of Doctor Who. But beginnings aren't everything.

The Beginning

One might reasonably ask "why?" This is Marc Platt's sixth time pulling back the curtain and looking before *An Unearthly Child* in some form or another. (We'll look at another one of them in a few essays.) It's clearly a point of fascination for him, but equally, it's a point where one can only do so much.

Much of this comes from the fact that there's a veil drawn in the prehistory of the character. By near-universal consensus, you're not allowed to tell the story of why the Doctor left Gallifrey. Of course, Platt did that on his first go-round at this, the 1997 novel *Lungbarrow*, published as part of Virgin's New Adventures line, but we were all young and foolish once. These days nobody tells the story of why the Doctor left – Carole Ann Ford, in fact, bemoans the fact that it's still mysterious in the interviews at the end of the disc.

But that means that *The Beginning* pointedly isn't quite. It starts with the Doctor and Susan on the run, having already taken some nebulously defined action that forces them to leave their planet. They duck into a TARDIS (complete with a scene of the Doctor pulling Susan out of the first one she enters, presumably on the advice of an unseen and unmentioned Clara) and run away. What we get, in other words, is their first adventure, not their departure itself.

But the first adventure is not that big of a prize. If there's one thing that fifty years of Doctor Who have demonstrated, after all, it's that the format of a Doctor Who adventure is very extensible. The truth of the matter is that the first adventure isn't all that much different from any of the others. There's nothing particularly special about it. You could tell the basic story – the Doctor thwarts aliens who want to dictate the progress of evolution on Earth – just about anywhere in the series' history.

Yes, there's something touchingly sweet about the Doctor's first adventure taking him to Earth, in that it provides some sense of why it would be his favorite planet. Except even this doesn't quite come out here. He visits it and saves it from having its evolution diverted by a bunch of order-obsessed aliens, but there's no opportunity for him to fall in love with it as such. Again, it feels like just another adventure.

Which is not to say that the audio is without magic. Its first quarter, consisting purely of Susan and the Doctor on the run and first trying to get the TARDIS working, is marvelous. Unlike why they fled from Gallifrey, these scenes seem necessary, extending as they do not from creating new bits of mythology for the show but from thinking through the nature of the characters. Simply put, the Doctor and Susan would act like that in those circumstances. There's no other way those scenes could go, and Platt writes them well, full of mourning for the past and the giddy thrill of the future.

The problem is that that's about a fifteen-minute scene that could be done well by any decent fanfiction writer. Marc Platt, to be sure, is a better than decent fanfiction writer, and he recognizes that there's only fifteen minutes worth of scene there. The problem is that he then has to do forty-five minutes of other stuff.

To this end, he creates an interesting character: Quadrigger Stoyn. The conceit of Stoyn is at once a charmingly bleak joke and very clever – he's a technician in charge of dismantling the TARDIS who happened to be working in it when the Doctor and Susan stole it. On the one hand, this is perfectly sensible. If you take the bit of lore that says that the TARDIS was in the repair shop, then it's almost obvious that when it was stolen there was probably somebody working in it. Likewise, the moment where Susan finds a room with dusty shelves and stains from beverage containers on the desk is lovely, hinting at something we never really get, which is that the TARDIS had a history before the Doctor. The idea of thinking about that, and about what the TARDIS was before it was stolen comes close to justifying the entire exercise.

Beyond that, there's a wonderful tragedy to Stoyn. He's the invisible, ordinary worker who gets trapped in the Doctor's life. There's nothing odd or special about him. He doesn't want to go on a grand adventure. He wants to finish his job, get paid, and go home. And instead this sneaky lunatic has stolen the TARDIS he was working on, badly injured him in the process, and dumped him on a foreign planet from which he can never return.

There's a sharp commentary here about the nature of the people who get caught in the Doctor's wake. It's rare that the Doctor gets confronted with the possibility that his actions might kind of suck for the ordinary people. I mean, there's always a couple of people who approvingly thank the Doctor for liberating them at the end, but we never really see the random janitor who was perfectly happy without the entire social order of his world being overthrown. And Quadrigger Stoyn is a perfect representative of that problem. Lodging him in the series' origins is sharp and incisive.

The problem is that he becomes a pantomime villain. When you have the aliens being a bunch of genocidal jerks who want to wipe out humanity because they prefer a tidier, more ordered course of evolution and then you have Quadrigger Stoyn joining them because he's appalled at the Doctor's rulebreaking, you're going well beyond just stacking the deck. Within Doctor Who, Quadrigger Stoyn is so flagrantly coded as a villain that it's not even funny.

And there's a real missed opportunity here. Stoyn deserves better, instead of becoming a paper tiger for the show's embrace of disorder and rejection of the rules. There's an insidious logic here that quietly suggests that Stoyn deserves his fate because he's just a working-class bloke following the rules. Stoyn is clearly not responsible for why the Doctor and Susan have to flee. He's miles from the levers of power. And yet his position, which should be entirely sympathetic – he has his face burnt off because the Doctor steals a TARDIS while he's repairing it – becomes a source of villainy. The result leaves an unpleasant taste around the entire story.

And yet in spite of the shockingly dissonant note, the story retains a bit of magic. It's not necessary – indeed it's hard to fit in with *An Unearthly Child*, to say nothing of *Remembrance of the Daleks*, to which it makes a quiet nod in the form of the Doctor's luggage. The Doctor is far too virtuous here, and far too eager to fight for the downtrodden. This isn't the paranoid and cowardly man who nearly smashes in a man's skull to make his escape. It's manifestly not the beginning. It's a story that exists fifty years in, and that is about almost any story but *An Unearthly Child*. But it's a wonderful and joyful celebration. And that, at least, is what it's intended to be, and why it's worth doing in the first place.

Hunters of Earth

It is in some ways surprising that the fiftieth anniversary of Doctor Who only brought two stories set prior to *An Unearthly Child* – one would have thought, honestly, that there would be more of a flood of them. It is even more surprising that one of the two should be set on Earth, in London. Much of the appeal of going before *An Unearthly Child*, after all, is the filling in of mythology. This, more than anything, is what's so jarring about material set in this gap; it attempts to add stories involving the mythos of Gallifrey to a period that had nothing to do with Gallifrey.

Nigel Robinson, however, who was the editor of the Target novels in the latter days of the line when it involved a lot of novelizing of old '60s stories, is a different sort of writer. He wrote the novelizations for *The Sensorites*, *The Time Meddler*, and *The Edge of Destruction*, and filled in to finish off *The Rescue* after Ian Marter passed away. He is, in other words, familiar with the era, whereas he's not ever really written continuity porn about Gallifrey.

And so with *Hunters of Earth* he turns in an unusual story – one that feels as though it starts from *An Unearthly Child* and works backwards, as opposed to starting with Gallifrey's mythology and trying to fill in the gap between it and *An Unearthly Child*. The usual problem with working backwards from *An Unearthly Child* is, as we've seen, that the Doctor learns to be a hero over the course of the first few stories.

But in *Hunters of Earth* this problem becomes the point. We have a story in which the Doctor doesn't really know what he's doing. Things that would make the Doctor suspicious even midway through Season One are completely overlooked, as he wanders blithely into trap after trap.

Indeed, it's not until the end, when the Doctor provides vital scientific knowledge, that he actually becomes active in the story at all. Prior to that he wanders around as a trap steadily closes in. Instead of following the Doctor the plot follows the surprising realization that there are two completely independent traps – the suspicious people hunting for the Doctor and the strange mind control signal that causes people to attack aliens are, in fact, wholly separate plots. The former are a bunch of proto-UNIT military types looking to recruit the Doctor, while the latter is an unfortunate side effect of an unexploded Nazi secret weapon.

The result is a neat double trick. On one level, the listener is constantly left feeling like they're ahead of the Doctor. As standard issue tropes of Doctor Who stories unfold around him, he remains oblivious while the reader connects the dots. On another level, though, the story has a surprise in store. The Doctor doesn't connect the dots, it's true, but crucially, the reader is led to connect them wrongly and to assume that the people searching for the Doctor and the people trying to kill Susan are the same thing, and probably some sort of alien threat.

Instead, though, everything in this story save for the Doctor is human. This is a terribly effective way of filling in the space before *An Unearthly Child – Hunters of Earth* is, in the end, a story entirely about the Doctor and Susan on Earth, and adds no new concepts to the mythology. It's just an exploration of what them being on Earth for several months would be like.

Adding to this is the story's intense focus on the material reality of 1963. This is a story in which the music, politics, and social attitudes of the time are intensely relevant. It's not just a story about the Doctor and Susan on Earth, but about the Doctor and Susan on Earth in 1963, in the material conditions that led to Doctor Who existing.

All of this serves to make it a particularly effective anniversary story simply because it manages to celebrate the show as it existed fifty years prior instead of projecting some future aspect of it onto the past. And yet despite this there are parts of the story that clearly set up the larger *Destiny of the Doctor* series that it's designed to fit into. Susan receives a mysterious message from a future Doctor – later revealed to be Matt Smith's Doctor – and the story ends with ominous portents of some future disaster.

But, of course, there is a causal line from *An Unearthly Child* to the fiftieth anniversary. What's interesting about *Hunters of Earth* is that it fits along that line. Even the future Doctor's intrusion feels like the present of the series stopping back to visit the past, as opposed to rewriting it. But this also reveals why this sort of story has limited return value. Neither the Doctor nor Susan are particularly good protagonists here. This is as it should be in terms of their characters, but equally, means that it's difficult to do that many stories like this.

This is not a problem as such – the story of Doctor Who really does begin with *An Unearthly Child*. Even this, set before *An Unearthly Child*, stems from it, not the other way around. But equally, this celebrates the fiftieth anniversary in many ways better than any other story, in that it really is a story that stems from *An Unearthly Child*. Nothing about it requires a whit of continuity from anywhere else, save the detail of Susan's psychic abilities, which is only a few stories later. This is not just a story set in the earliest days of the series, but a story set in how the series was originally conceived, out of its original premises.

Notably, there's a moment where the dialogue seems to veer towards mentioning the Time Lords, then self-consciously stops, leaving them unmentioned. This is not uncommon in stories set before *The War Games* – there's an odd convention of avoiding mentioning the Time Lords before the series itself did. But it's touching in the context of this story, preserving as it does the purity of its reference.

There are loads of Doctor Who stories set in the Hartnell era that try to relate it to future eras, and loads of discussions of the many different ways Doctor Who could have gone besides the way that it did. What-ifs and retcons abound. And in that sea, *Hunters of Earth* stands out precisely because it's something very different: a Hartnell story, featuring Hartnell's Doctor, and set among the very first days of the program. It seems in many ways a small achievement, but it is no less extraordinary for it.

Time and Relative

The Telos Novella line was a short-lived series of premium Doctor Who fiction that alternated between established Doctor Who writers and established SF writers new to Doctor Who. The line kicked off with Kim Newman's *Time and Relative*, a pre-*Unearthly Child* story featuring the adventures of Susan Foreman, and one of the better regarded entries into this peculiar subgenre of Doctor Who.

The thing that's most striking about Newman's book is that it is manifestly a prequel to *An Unearthly Child*. It takes place in the early days of 1963, in the midst of a brutally harsh winter (which really happened in England in 1963 – the snow was on the ground until April. It also happens to describe Connecticut in early 2011 while most of these essays were being written). We've spoken several times in this volume about stories that are written as though they are part of an earlier era in the show. This is an important concept for the show, in no small part because the idea of revisiting the past to tell new stories about it is kind of the entire point of the show. And more to the point, it tells us useful things about how the past of the show is understood at various times in its future. What a William Hartnell story is taken to be in 1995 is different from one in 2005 and different again from what we'll get when we get neo-Hartnell stuff in 2015.

I say all of this because, somewhat astonishingly, the central concept of Newman's book is to write Doctor Who as it was in March of 1963. Which may seem like a challenge, given that the most obvious answer to the question of what Doctor Who was like in March of 1963 was "it wasn't."

Which is basically the point of the book. Right on the second page, it stakes out its position, as the Doctor proclaims that continuity "doesn't exist, child. Except in the minds of the cretinously literal . . . without contradictions, we'd be entirely too easy to track down." Instead we get a far stranger story – one that winds its way through the various antecedents and dead ends that Doctor Who could have taken and did take. References to *Dan Dare* and the Mekon, or to John and Gillian (companions of the Doctor in the TV Comic strips of the 1960s) are sprinkled throughout, as are vague allusions to the program's future. Ian and Barbara make cameos, there's a vague reference to the Daleks (and a skeptical one – the Doctor mocks someone mentioning a flying saucer by saying "You'll be seeing flying teacups and creeping pepperpots next") and Susan repeatedly returns to her fear of a man who is obviously the Master.

But this is mere window dressing. Let's be honest. Just as the lurking terror of the ice monsters throughout the book is window-dressing, this too is an excuse to have a plot. The real story here is about Susan Foreman, an alien in London in March of 1963. By far the book's most interesting segments are those that deal with her personality. Take for instance the lengthy section in which she speculates on what kind of boys might like her, and what celebrities she likes. ("I don't like Albert Finney, except I don't like him in a special way that might mean I like him more than any others I mention.")

One of the things you'll notice over the rest of the book is a recurring fascination with Susan as a character. Most of this centers around the Problem of Susan – namely that as a character, she destabilizes the narrative in some significant ways. As we've discussed, when she's present she prevents the Doctor from quite acting Doctorly because he has to treat her as his primary concern. Once she leaves, her absence and the Doctor's failure to ever go back for her becomes a gaping hole that is at the root of the Doctor's steadfast refusal to go back for companions. (A problem that, admittedly, stems mostly from a later point in the series where the Doctor can at least occasionally make the TARDIS go where he wants.) And, though I don't really talk about it at all in this book, the problem is exacerbated further when the question of the Time War comes in.

The nature of the Problem of Susan is that there is no such thing as "the" solution to it. But Newman offers one solution that is compelling, as Newman has Susan write: "I think this is why Grandfather took me with him. There are things I can do that he can't." And the reason for this is simple – while the Doctor still obeys some of the rules, specifically the so-called primary rule, that his people do not meddle, Susan says "I don't think I believe in rules at all . . . I think meddling is an obligation."

(The use of the word meddling, and it's being stressed, echoes with *The Time Meddler* interestingly, it should be noted.)

As with Simon Guerrier's *The Time Travellers*, Newman's book is interesting in that it is the rare retcon that seems wholly consistent with the spirit of what we see on television. Newman's account – that Susan was somehow necessary for the Doctor's flight – is impressive because it's so obvious in hindsight. Of course that's why a sixteen-year-old girl ran off with her grandfather – because more accurately, he ran off with her. This is not to say that he wasn't the sort to do that – he's clearly a rebel as well.

One of my favorite plays ever written is Michael Frayn's *Copenhagen*, which offers various hypothetical accounts of the final meeting between Werner Heisenberg and Niels Bohr. At one point, the play has Bohr's wife, Margrethe, speculate on the nature of their final meeting, saying "that was the last and greatest demand that Heisenberg made on his friendship with you. To be understood when he couldn't understand himself. And that was the last and greatest act of friendship for

Heisenberg that you performed in return. To leave him misunderstood."

Newman, it seems to me, offers a very similar solution to the Problem of Susan – one that finally makes sense of the troubling end of *The Dalek Invasion of Earth* (even more sense than Guerrier's, in many ways). In the end, Susan and the Doctor were equal partners in their rebellion, running off together. The Doctor's last, great act of love for Susan was to force her to rebel one final time, and to run away even from him.

But that, in the end, is just one of the many future echoes left by *Time and Relative*. More interesting, in many ways, is what happens when the Doctor finally confronts the Cold Knights. The book is structured to defer this scene for as long as possible – much of its length is spent with Susan and her friends trying to get across London to the Doctor. This deferral relies on the reader's knowledge that this book is ultimately a Doctor Who story. Because it is a Doctor Who story, we know that the Doctor is the one to save the day from alien threats. So Susan's struggle to get to the Doctor is naturally assumed by the audience to double as the struggle to get to the part of the story where the villains are defeated.

Except that when they reach the Doctor, he is not the Doctor we know from the series. This is unsurprising – as we'll see over the next few entries, it's very clear that the story being told over the first thirteen or so episodes of the series is the story of how this cranky old man called the Doctor becomes a hero by virtue of meeting Ian and Barbara. Great lines like "fear makes companions of us all" or scenes like the Doctor giving in to despair in the Cave of Skulls, or even the Doctor and Barbara's reconciliation at the end of *The Edge of Destruction* have power precisely because the Doctor is, with those lines, becoming the Doctor.

This is, in many ways, the fundamental problem with pre-*Unearthly Child* adventures. If you put the Doctor in an adventure prior to the start of the series you do violence to the actual episodes at the start of the series, replacing them with a fannish reconstruction. This is a problem we'll see throughout Doctor Who, in which fanlore about what past eras were like overwrites the actual episodes in a deeply unsatisfying way.

And so when Susan and company finally get to the Doctor, he calmly refuses to help. He stands by the fundamental rule of his people – not to meddle. And when Susan implores him to help, he points out that her stated consequences – that they would be "a part of things, not apart from them" – are a "dreadful state of affairs." It is only when he is presented with a child's toy – "a feat of the imagination" – that the Doctor agrees to become a part of things, and in the process to lose the freedom from fixed reference or involvement in continuity that he praises at the start of the novel.

In other words, *Time and Relative* functions as a pre-*Unearthly Child* story by positing a Doctor who is even less of a hero than the one we see in *An Unearthly Child*, and then giving the Doctor one of the missing traits over the course of the novel. It fits into the non-existent slot before the first story, curiously, by making it clear why stories cannot fit into this slot and remain Doctor Who stories.

The result is a rarity among neo-Hartnell stories – one that actually seems to pay tribute to the episodes that aired on television instead of fictionalizing memories of them, and one that is an admirable and oddly satisfying start to the era, albeit thirty-eight years late.

Elizabeth Sandifer

Deadline

Stretching the concept of the *Unbound* line to its limit, Rob Shearman's *Deadline* posits a world where Doctor Who never existed as a program. But this suggests that it is like the other *Unbound* releases – effectively alternate histories – Doctor Who equivalents of Marvel's old *What If?* comics that explore the consequences of taking other narrative routes at various points in the series' history. *Deadline* is something altogether stranger – not so much a Doctor Who story as a story about Doctor Who.

It is, certainly, about the Hartnell era in particular, weaving together a patchwork of Doctor Who that takes bits of *An Unearthly Child*, *100,000 BC*, *The Daleks*, *The Masters of Luxor*, and *Auld Mortality* (*Deadline* was originally envisioned as the last *Unbound*, and so adopts *Auld Mortality*'s Doctor/Hannibal meeting for some nice parallelism). But it weaves them together into something that feels like a half-remembered dream of Doctor Who.

This, however, provides a backdrop to a story that is, to say the least, clearly rather more personal – the story of Martin Bannister, a writer who has abandoned essentially everything in his life in the name of a dogmatic pursuit of his artistic vision, and who manages to fail at that as well. There are several moments in which this feels consciously like a character who is meant to parallel Shearman himself: a respected playwright whose work focused on the theme of "the horror of isolation" and whose later work involves writing for trashy mass media properties. This gives the story an awkward but potent energy, particularly when it descends into self-critique, such as when Bannister admits to being rather better and more focused on theme than characterization.

This sets up the story's central tension: the idea that writing has to be grounded in the real world and in human experience instead of just in intellectual constructs and fantasy. Bannister, we are told, is a bad writer because of his screw-ups in his life and his decision to focus on the obsessions of his career instead of on his life. Doctor Who becomes understandable, within this, as a sort of white whale – a dangerous obsession parodied, with some savagery, by Shearman's imagined *Juliet Bravo* fandom.

The knowledge that this was Shearman's last real contribution to the Big Finish line, and expected to be his last contribution to Doctor Who until Davies offered him a slot on the new series (which he, obviously, accepted) makes all of this more uncomfortable. The story ends in such a way as to make Bannister's obsession with Doctor Who most easily explained as mental illness, and while the story leaves one tentative toehold on Todorov's concept of the fantastic as a genre based on the ambiguity between the supernatural and mental illness, it's a slender reed at best.

So what we appear to have is a story that treats Doctor Who as a dangerous waste of time best left behind by its sad obsessives, who really need to get in touch with the real world again. And yet this reading is clearly not right. Shearman is obviously consciously playing with that idea. But though Shearman may be on the brink of departing Doctor Who, the idea that he's decided the program is fatally flawed and unhealthy is, to say the least, a bit of a stretch.

It's worth looking again at the ending. The possibility that Bannister has actually successfully retreated into the TARDIS and taken off into a more romantic and idealistic life than the life of disappointment and regret that he's lived is real. This is, after all, a Doctor Who story. It says so on the front, and it has the right theme music, and that means it's a world where redemption is possible. For all that *Deadline* is structured as a crushingly bleak, existential comedy, it's carefully positioned in an altogether more hopeful milieu.

At the center of it, of course, is Shearman's own anxiety – but this is moved to stand in for a larger category of anxiety over writing as a career. And this, perhaps, becomes the real point of *Deadline* – a point that is epitomized in its title, which focuses on the material practice of writing – the fact that it involves the imposition of deadlines and is a job. *Deadline*, in the end, is about the fact that Doctor Who is not some transcendent and perfect ideal, but a thing that exists because of the material contributions of individual people who were, for the most part, just working a job as well and professionally as they could. Or, in some cases, as well and professionally as they had to in order to get paid.

It's easy to romanticize the legend of Doctor Who, and to write a postmodernist collage of its central pillars by recycling famous dialogue and abandoned concepts into a clever, mythic collage. But in reality, Doctor Who is the product of writers imagining things and crafting them into scripts for money. It fits into lives and careers that contain other things, and, more to the point, where the other things outweigh the time spent crafting daft little sci-fi stories for Saturday teatime audiences.

And this is, in the end, is the point. Bannister's only hope at redemption comes from the possibility that he really is in a Doctor Who story, but Doctor Who can only exist as something that is the product of the very material labor that has ruined his life in the first place. The transcendent, mythic structures of Doctor Who and its basic ability to provide a hopeful, idealistic world are inexorably linked to an often corrupt and abusive system of production.

Future volumes will come to conclude that this dualism is, in a real sense, at the heart of what Doctor Who is. That the tension between the material society in which stories are produced and their seemingly magical power is, ultimately, what the combination of the TARDIS (a machine to take people into new stories) and the Doctor (a character defined by a pathological need to foment social revolution) provides.

With *Deadline*, Shearman moves that metaphoric focus to the very development and history of the show itself. There is a sense of perfectly closing the circle here. On the one hand, this is where all discussion of what Doctor Who is begins. On another, it's the natural conclusion of the entire enterprise.

Perhaps there's even a difference.

Elizabeth Sandifer

The Pilot

A commissioned essay for Huw Buchtmann.

There is at least some ambiguity as to what, exactly, we mean here. The pilot of Doctor Who is not an entirely coherent document; it never aired, and, perhaps more to the point, is not actually a single episode edited for airing. So first, let's establish that when we talk about the pilot, we mean the block of recording conducted on September 19, 1963. This consists of a recording of an earlier draft script of the first episode, "An Unearthly Child" in four takes. The first is a successful take of everything up to the point where Barbara pushes into the TARDIS. The second through fourth are takes on what comes subsequently. In the first of these the shot of everybody entering the TARDIS is spoiled by a malfunctioning door, although the take is allowed to run to the end of the episode. The second take is abandoned after only a minute or so. The third is, again, allowed to run to the end of the episode.

There are various changes between the pilot and the transmitted version of *An Unearthly Child*. For one thing, there's the effect that required three takes – a shot of Barbara pushing open the TARDIS doors and entering into the impossibly large space. But the bulk of the changes regarded the characterization of the Doctor.

• 450 •

This requires that we talk at least a little bit about the pre-history of the program. Doctor Who was the brainchild of Sydney Newman, installed as Head of Drama at the BBC in December of 1962. Newman wanted a family-friendly program for the Saturday night lineup, and both he and the BBC had been itching to do something with science fiction. And so, after a lengthy development process that has been well documented in other sources, came Doctor Who.

It was Newman who rejected the pilot, and he did so for two basic reasons. The first was a number of technical goofs, many, though not all, related to the abandoned Barbara-entering-the-TARDIS scene. The second was displeasure at how the Doctor was characterized. This led to a substantial rewrite of virtually every scene after Ian and Barbara arrive at Totter's Lane.

Let's start with what wasn't changed, despite lots of people claiming otherwise. There is a line of discussion about the pilot that it contains an alternate explanation for the Doctor and Susan's origins, and that they are not aliens in it. This is nonsense – the Doctor explicitly says that he and Susan are "not of this Earth," and the line about being "cut off from our own planet" remains, with the added note that they are cut off by "eons and universes." That Susan later clarifies that she is from the forty-seventh century might be interesting in terms of later debates over the exact temporal placement of Gallifrey, but since Gallifrey is still over a decade away from being named, this can't really be taken as a substantial alteration to the initial mythos. Indeed, there's nothing televised that it contradicts, and far bigger contradictions to be had between televised episodes.

No, the changes to the Doctor have more to do with whether he's The Doctor. In the pilot, he is much more angrily suspicious of Ian and Barbara, where in the transmitted version he appears to get distracted. In the pilot, after Ian asks the Doctor to let him look inside what turns out to be the TARDIS, the Doctor snaps, "you have no right to be here! You're hiding and trespassing!" Whereas in the transmitted version the idea of the Doctor as a sort of absent-minded professor is introduced – he responds to the same line of dialogue from Ian by going and staring at a picture frame.

Similar changes abound – in the pilot the Doctor explicitly upbraids Susan and blames her for Ian and Barbara's intrusion into the TARDIS. And, of course, there's the biggest change – the Doctor's reason for kidnapping Ian and Barbara. In the transmitted episode his motivation is a desire not to lose Susan, who insists that she'll stay in London of 1963 if the Doctor insists on leaving. This is a reasonably complex motivation that manages to be at once sympathetic and callous. The pilot, on the other hand, gives an altogether more abstracted motivation, having the Doctor kidnap Ian and Barbara because even seeing the TARDIS risks too major a change to history. ("Think what would have happened if the ancient Romans had been given the power of gunpowder . . . if Napoleon had been given the secret of the aeroplane!") This is on the one hand a motivation that is purer – his kidnapping of Ian and Barbara becomes a matter of pure principle. But it's also a more alien motivation that puts the Doctor at a greater remove from the audience. For all that his revised motivation is selfish, it's also much more human than an abstract point about the sanctity of linear technological progress.

One of the things we will see over the next few stories is a steady transformation of the Doctor's character. In the first few stories he is unpredictable and as likely to cause problems as solve them. Steadily, over the course of the first season, he becomes a more straightforward hero. This transition is generally treated as running from *100,000 BC*, in which the Doctor is shown to be tremendously morally dodgy, up through the start of *Marco Polo*, during which the Doctor basically withdraws into a tent for the bulk of an episode and effectively emerges as a retooled character. But in truth, as the pilot reveals, this was a process that was underway from before the series began, and what we see over the course of the first four stories is just the lingering end of that development.

Which is, perhaps, the thing to take away from the pilot. It is easy to treat Doctor Who's success as in some way inevitable from the start. Sure, nobody realized it at the time, but there's a mythology that suggests that something about Doctor Who's premise made it inevitable that it would run forever. The truth, however, is both more prosaic and more fascinating: the form Doctor Who took on transmission was down to the input of a large number of people, and there were a profound number of changes made as it went on. What aired on November 23, 1963 was not even the end of the process of development. And there was nothing inevitable about its success. It is not that there is no reason for Doctor Who's extended success – rather it is that there are many reasons. There are crucial decisions that enabled its success and bits of blind, dumb luck. And the question that inevitably comes up when looking at something like the pilot – "would the series have worked if this had been the first episode?" – is ultimately meaningless. All we can do is look at the often idiosyncratic reasoning of what did happen, and be glad that it did.

An Adventure in Space and Time

Depending on how one opts to read this book, this is either the first essay before it transitions into the Hartnell era proper, or the last one period. So it's either a setup for the book or something of an apologia for its existence. Which is fitting, as ultimately this is an essay about another take on the same material – an attempt to tell the story of what Doctor Who was in the Hartnell era.

There are, of course, many stories about the creation of Doctor Who. There are so many that in this book I've mostly kept a slight distance from the production history. I mean, it's not ignored, but it's not the point of the book either. But even within the production history the narrative is complex and confused. Doctor Who is, in truth, a profoundly collaborative show, including, in its first season alone, dozens of actors, seven writers, eight directors, on top of a bunch of behind the scenes personnel and, for that matter, Sydney Newman, who created the whole shebang in the first place.

So any attempt to tell that story, especially in a relatively small narrative container like a ninety-minute TV movie, is going to say as much about the people telling the story as it does about the story itself. Which is to say that *An Adventure in Space and Time* is about the Hartnell era as it existed in 2013, as a foundational document for the enormously popular television series Doctor Who, and not really about the business of getting a television series off the ground in the first place. And, more specifically, it's about Mark Gatiss's take on all of this.

All of which is a subject worthy of an entire book. Gatiss, in particular, is a complex figure. If you told anyone around at the time that in 2013 the BBC would do a big docudrama about the creation of Doctor Who, absolutely everyone would assume that Mark Gatiss was writing it. This is the man who wrote *The Idiot's Lantern*, a love letter to the early days of television. And, perhaps more to the point, this is a man whose aesthetic is profoundly one of nostalgia.

But Gatiss's nostalgia is idiosyncratic. He has always been interested in a nostalgia of mood and imagery as opposed to a nostalgia of substance. The result is a story that collapses to a singular vision of what Doctor Who was in its early days. Gatiss's nostalgia requires a clear aesthetic to celebrate. And so the era in which Doctor Who was the furthest from actually having one is forced into a coherent shape.

This manifests in the figures that *An Adventure in Space and Time* opts to focus on. Its central character is William Hartnell. Few people would argue against the idea that Hartnell is a fundamental figure in the history of Doctor Who (fewer still, one imagines, reading a book about his era). But the traditional practice of slicing eras of Doctor Who up according to the lead actor obscures other shifts that are often more fundamental, if less immediately obvious. I indulge in it because it's the easiest way to organize books for sale, but there are numerous points where the transition between Doctors is barely a change. Tom Baker's first and last stories are far more similar to the eras before and after than they are to much of anything else within his seven-year run. As fundamental a shift as *Power of the Daleks* was, it's still better understood in terms of *The War Machines* than it is in terms of *Tomb of the Cybermen*. Lawrence Miles and Tat Wood's sublimely good *About Time* series organizes based on season instead of Doctor, and is stronger for it. I wish I were as brave, really.

More broadly, Hartnell is the star of Doctor Who. But that means that he's the part of it the eye focuses on first, not that he's the most fundamental. A focus on Hartnell obscures most questions of how the series came to be the way it is, instead becoming a piece about a difficult but fundamentally decent man who's forced out of a job he loves when his faculties desert him in the face of advancing age and illness. David Bradley plays Hartnell well, doing an uncanny imitation of his performance as the Doctor, but the focus is still on Hartnell's tragic story.

Oddly, the result is, if anything, unfair to Hartnell. His speech at the end of *The Massacre* is shown to be a shambles, used to indicate just how difficult he'd become to work with. A core of competence remains – he's the only one who knows how to get the central rotor on the TARDIS to operate – but he trips over his lines and the overall point of the scene is to show his decline. In reality, however, Hartnell nailed what was a difficult monologue, and the result is widely suspected of being one of the high moments of his performance in the part, despite the fact that it was only a few months before his forced retirement. It is, in other words, a supremely inappropriate scene to contort into being about Hartnell's declining faculties.

Elsewhere, Hartnell's status as the star becomes a strange occasion to reduce his standing. Bradley does supremely well with the scene where Hartnell breaks down to his wife, sobbing, "I don't want to go." But any dedicated fan watching will realize that this moment is not merely a (entirely hypothesized) moment of emotional drama, but a reference to David Tennant's final words as the Doctor. So Hartnell's life and decline become little more than fodder to position him as one of many stars of the series. Similarly, although Matt Smith's cameo as Hartnell prepares for his final scene as the Doctor is wonderfully touching, it seems to function entirely in terms of 2013. Smith had barely a month remaining as the Doctor when *Adventure in Space and Time* aired, and much of the power came from the fact that it was a genuine surprise upon transmission. Stripped of that context the scene is touching, but serves as much to diminish the role that Hartnell himself played in the show's creation, turning him into merely one of many focal points.

The choice of which behind the scenes staff to focus on is similarly revealing. Sydney Newman, who originated the idea of Doctor Who, becomes a stereotype of an American (actually Canadian) producer, all catch phrases and bluster. Verity Lambert and Waris Hussein are occasions to look at minorities breaking through in the television industry, but are little more. The fact that Hussein was a phenomenally talented director is sidelined in favor of the fact that he's a young, gay, Indian director making a name for himself. Similarly, Verity Lambert becomes a woman learning to stand up for herself and not the hard-as-nails visionary she was. In every case the creative contributions of people are replaced by their personal stories, so that the creation of Doctor Who becomes less about the ideas involved and more about the stars.

Particularly poorly served by Gatiss's narrative are the writers, who are entirely absent. Every single actor to play a major part in the Hartnell era is represented, with a point made of showing all the press photos, even though the bulk of them never get a line. Not a single writer, however, shows up on screen – not Dennis Spooner, not Terry Nation, not even David Whitaker. This last is, of course, particularly galling, though I'm obviously a fairly fierce Whitaker partisan.

To Gatiss's credit, it appears that Whitaker was cut from the script for timing reasons, not out of any active decision to marginalize him. And the opening shot, a police box in the fog at Barnes Common, is a straightforward reference to *Doctor Who in an Exciting Adventure with the Daleks*, and thus to Whitaker. Still, in a story that goes out of its way to awkwardly include Delia Derbyshire there should have been a way to include the writer whose vision most shaped Doctor Who.

His absence, in other words, is symptomatic of the larger decision to have *An Adventure in Space and Time* be about the personalities involved in creating Doctor Who and the iconography of the early series than it is about capturing how Doctor Who was made. Doctor Who is, in effect, treated as a fully formed concept. It goes through very little development – the only real shift in it is the decision to abandon the initial first .episode and reshoot it with Hartnell giving a less cantankerous performance. Other than that, however, Doctor Who remains constant through the entire story, which, as a review of what actually happened within the Hartnell era will show, is the polar opposite of actually true.

So what we get is various magnetic personalities responding to the timeless concept of Doctor Who, a concept that is already framed in terms of a half-century of future development. It's not a celebration of the Hartnell era, but of what the Hartnell era became, told from a perspective that finds putting a couple of Menoptra costumes on screen in the background during an unrelated conversation entertaining. Which, to be fair, it is.

But equally, there's a spark that's lost in this. The idea of Doctor Who as a magical and radical concept is absent. The result isn't a story of how Doctor Who came to be, but a celebration of the fact that it did. None of this is quite a problem – indeed, *An Adventure in Space and Time* is a terribly sweet love letter that's quite easy to enjoy on its own merits. But its relationship to the Hartnell era is odd. It's not about the era itself, but about the fifty-year cultural shadow it cast.

But this only increases the obligation to look at the real Hartnell era, in all its weirdness, contradictions, and stumbling steps towards what became Doctor Who. To treat the Hartnell era as equivalent to the forty-seven years of history that followed it is to miss the real truth of its genius: that it came up with a way to cause that history. That's a story worth telling too.

Elizabeth Sandifer

About the Author

Elizabeth Sandifer lives in Ithaca, New York and writes about
Doctor Who, British comics, and whatever else happens to
be obsessing her at any given moment.

She blogs at eruditorumpress.com.

12/20

Made in the USA
Columbia, SC
28 July 2020

14914095R00259